W9-AHX-903

THE HYPO

Noah Van Sciver

The Hypo
By Noah Van Sciver

Editor and Associate Publisher: Eric Reynolds
Designed by Noah Van Sciver
Production by Paul Baresh and Preston White
Cover colors by Raighne Hogan 2dcloud.com
Published by Gary Groth and Kim Thompson

Fantagraphics Books, Inc.
7563 Lake City Way NE
Seattle WA 98115 USA
fantagraphics.com

The Hypo is copyright © 2012 Noah Van Sciver. This edition © 2012 Fantagraphics Books, Inc.
All rights reserved. Permission to reproduce material from this book, except for purposes of
review and/or notice, must be obtained by the publisher or author.

Distributed in the U.S. by W.W. Norton and Company, Inc. (800-233-4830)
Distributed in Canada by Canadian Manda Group (800-452-6642 x862)
Distributed in the U.K. by Turnaround Distribution (44 020 8829-3002)
Distributed to comic book specialty stores by Diamond Comics Distributors
(800-452-6642 x215)

First printing: July 2012

ISBN 978-1-60699-619-5

Printed in China

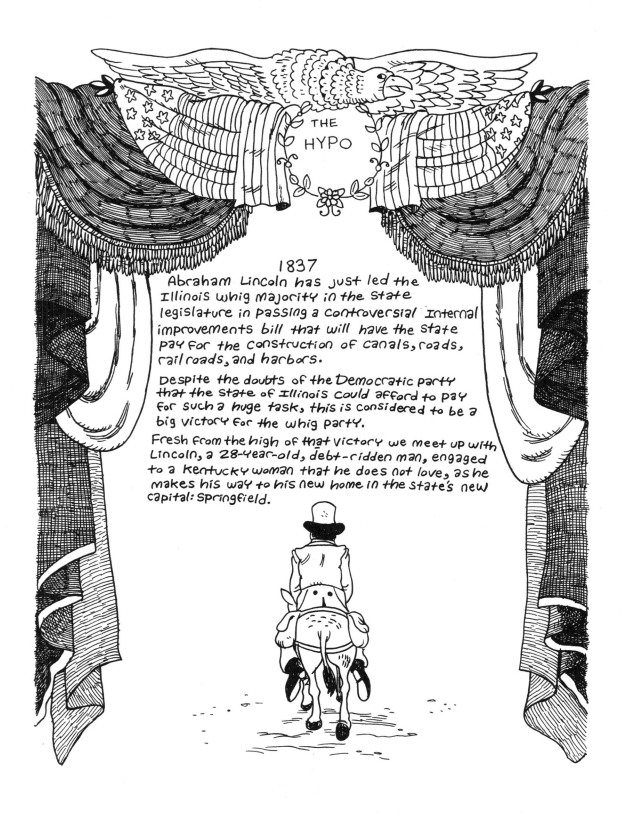

THE
HYPO

1837
Abraham Lincoln has just led the
Illinois Whig majority in the state
legislature in passing a controversial internal
improvements bill that will have the state
pay for the construction of canals, roads,
rail roads, and harbors.

Despite the doubts of the Democratic party
that the state of Illinois could afford to pay
for such a huge task, this is considered to be a
big victory for the Whig party.

Fresh from the high of that victory we meet up with
Lincoln, a 28-year-old, debt-ridden man, engaged
to a Kentucky woman that he does not love, as he
makes his way to his new home in the state's new
capital: Springfield.

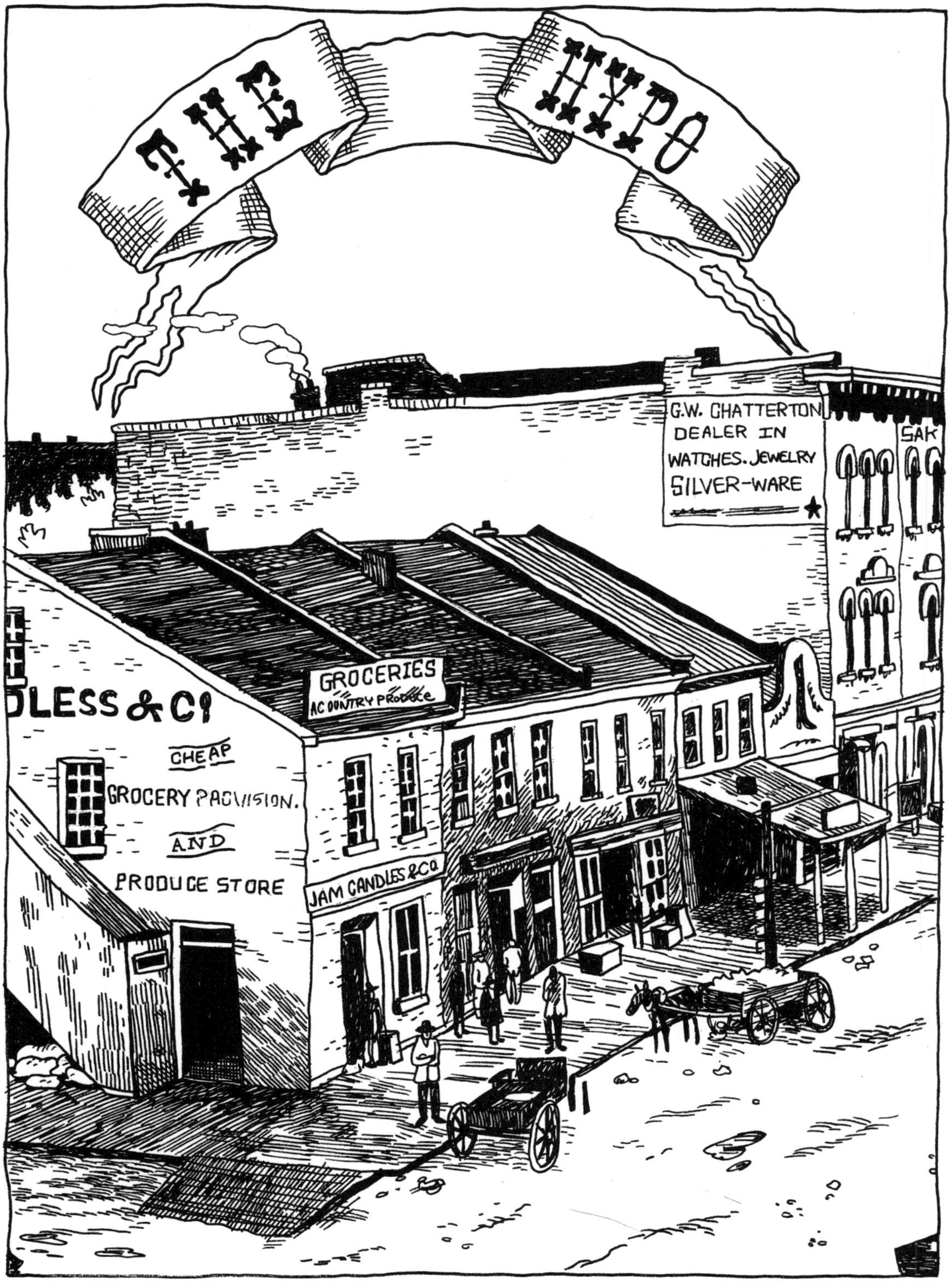
THE HYPO
G.W. CHATTERTON
DEALER IN
WATCHES. JEWELRY
SILVER-WARE
SAK
GROCERIES
AC OUNTRY PRODUCE
OLESS & Cº
CHEAP
GROCERY PROVISION.
AND
PRODUCE STORE
JAM CANDLES & Cº

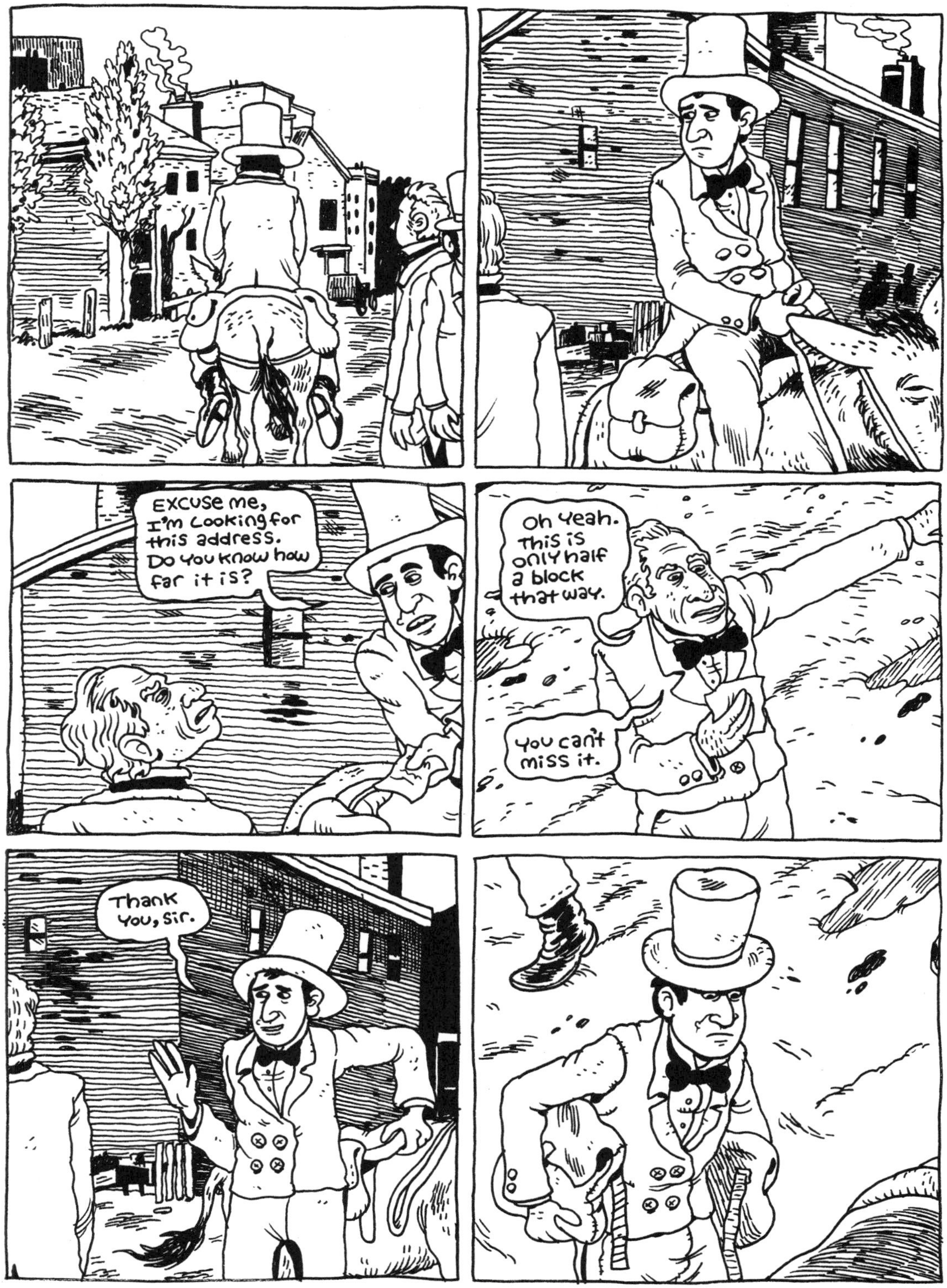
Excuse me, I'm looking for this address. Do you know how far it is?
Oh yeah. This is only half a block that way.
You can't miss it.
Thank you, sir.

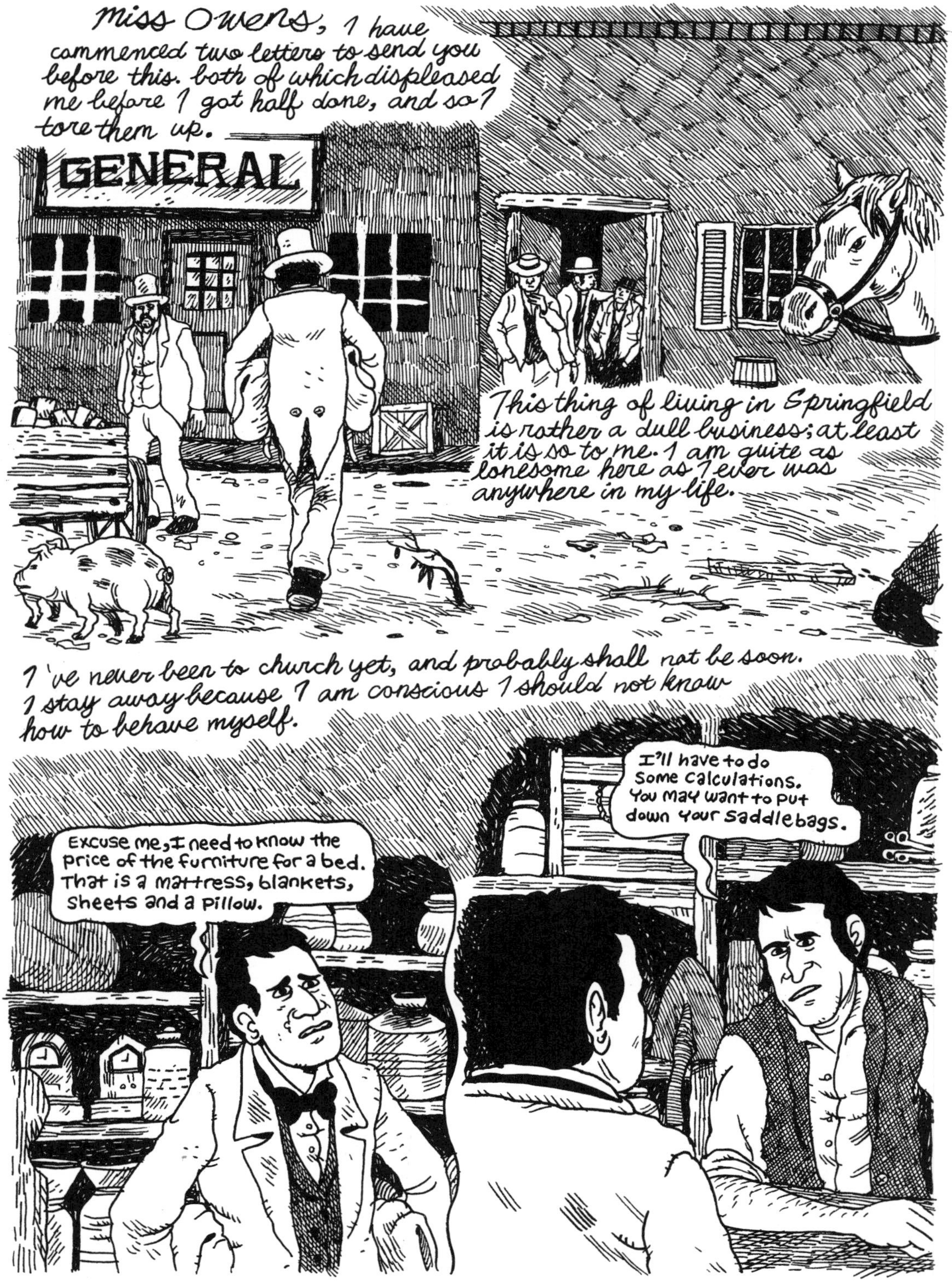
Miss Owens, I have commenced two letters to send you before this. both of which displeased me before I got half done, and so I tore them up.
GENERAL
This thing of living in Springfield is rather a dull business; at least it is so to me. I am quite as lonesome here as I ever was anywhere in my life.
I've never been to church yet, and probably shall not be soon. I stay away because I am conscious I should not know how to behave myself.
Excuse me, I need to know the price of the furniture for a bed. That is a mattress, blankets, sheets and a pillow.
I'll have to do some calculations. You may want to put down your saddlebags.

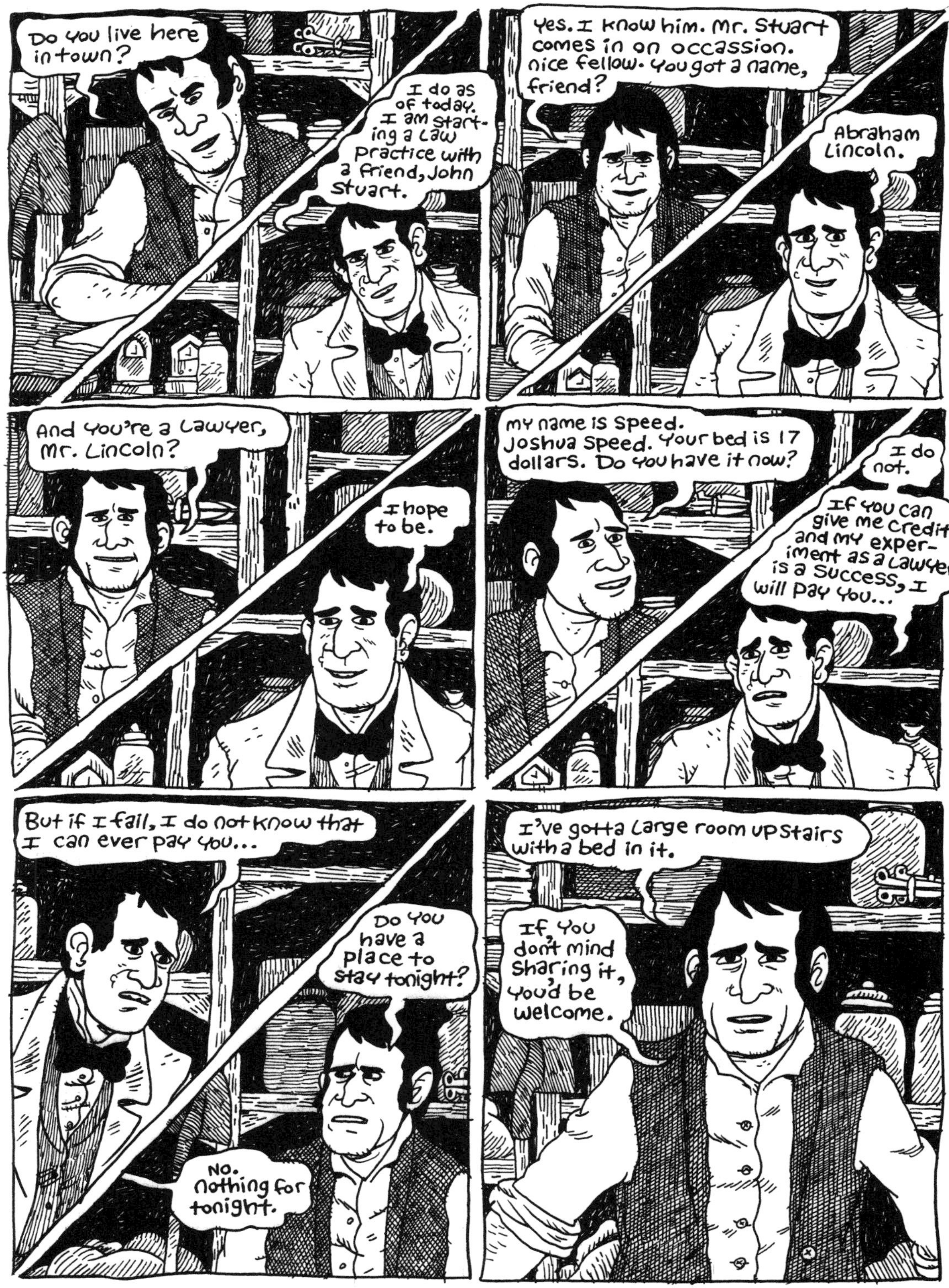
Do you live here in town?
I do as of today. I am starting a law practice with a friend, John Stuart.
Yes. I know him. Mr. Stuart comes in on occassion. nice fellow. You got a name, friend?
Abraham Lincoln.
And you're a lawyer, Mr. Lincoln?
I hope to be.
My name is Speed. Joshua Speed. Your bed is 17 dollars. Do you have it now?
I do not.
If you can give me credit and my experiment as a lawyer is a success, I will pay you...
But if I fail, I do not know that I can ever pay you...
Do you have a place to stay tonight?
No. Nothing for tonight.
I've gotta large room upstairs with a bed in it.
If, you don't mind sharing it, you'd be welcome.

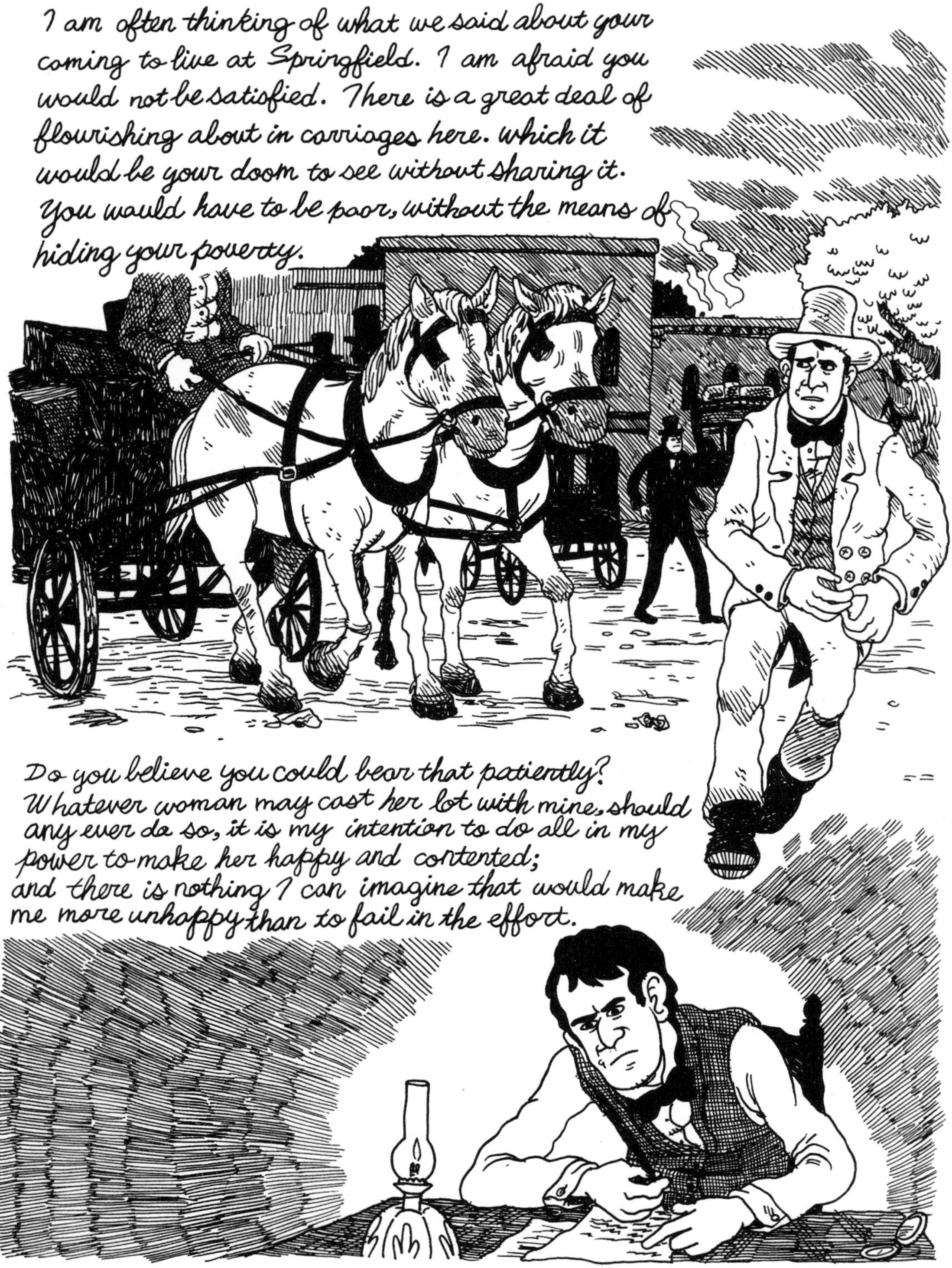
I am often thinking of what we said about your coming to live at Springfield. I am afraid you would not be satisfied. There is a great deal of flourishing about in carriages here. which it would be your doom to see without sharing it. You would have to be poor, without the means of hiding your poverty.
Do you believe you could bear that patiently? Whatever woman may cast her lot with mine, should any ever do so, it is my intention to do all in my power to make her happy and contented; and there is nothing I can imagine that would make me more unhappy than to fail in the effort.

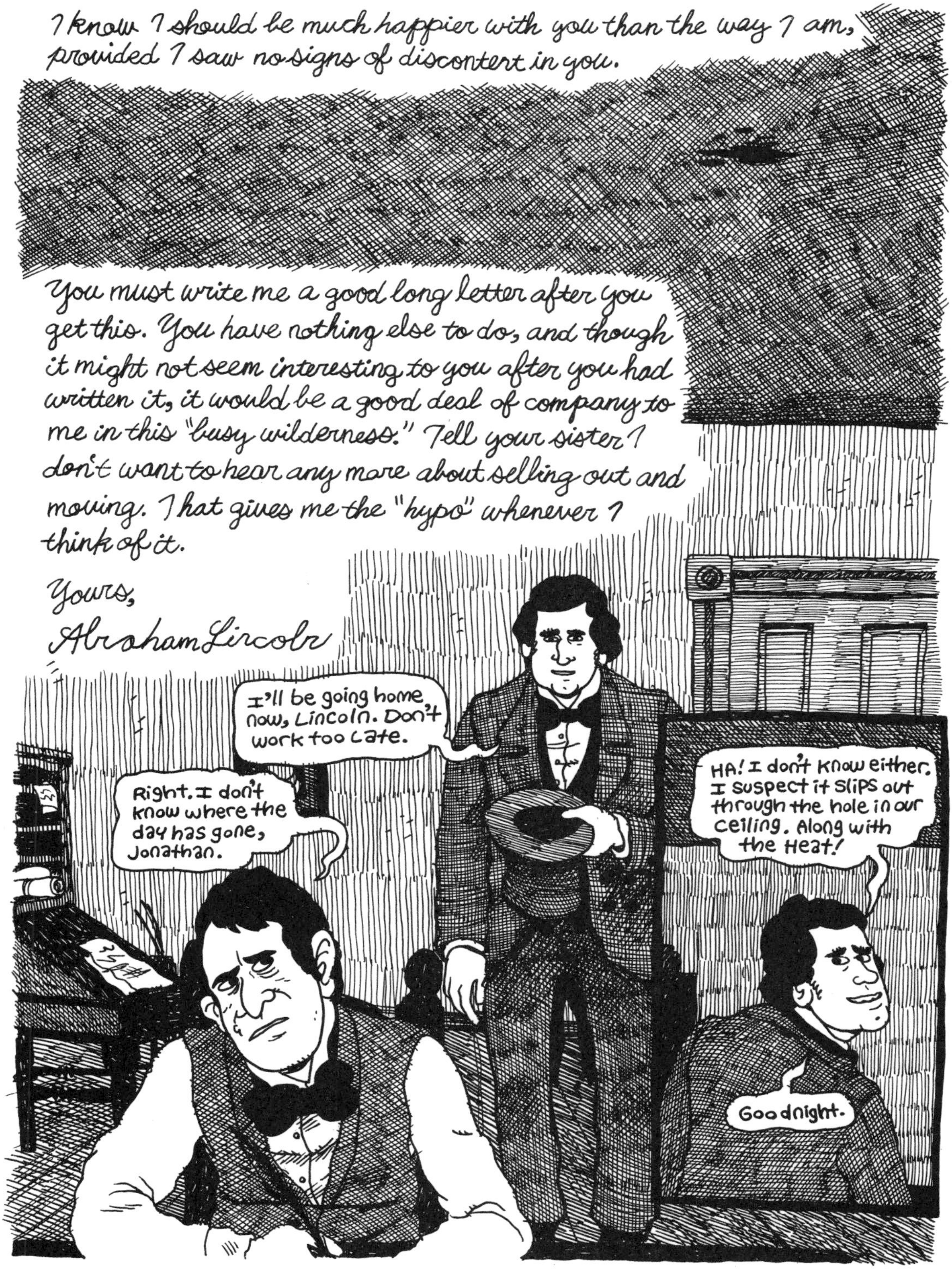
I know I should be much happier with you than the way I am, provided I saw no signs of discontent in you.
You must write me a good long letter after you get this. You have nothing else to do, and though it might not seem interesting to you after you had written it, it would be a good deal of company to me in this "busy wilderness." Tell your sister I don't want to hear any more about selling out and moving. That gives me the "hypo" whenever I think of it.
Yours,
Abraham Lincoln
I'll be going home, now, Lincoln. Don't work too Late.
Right. I don't know where the day has gone, Jonathan.
HA! I don't know either. I suspect it slips out through the hole in our ceiling. Along with the Heat!
Goodnight.

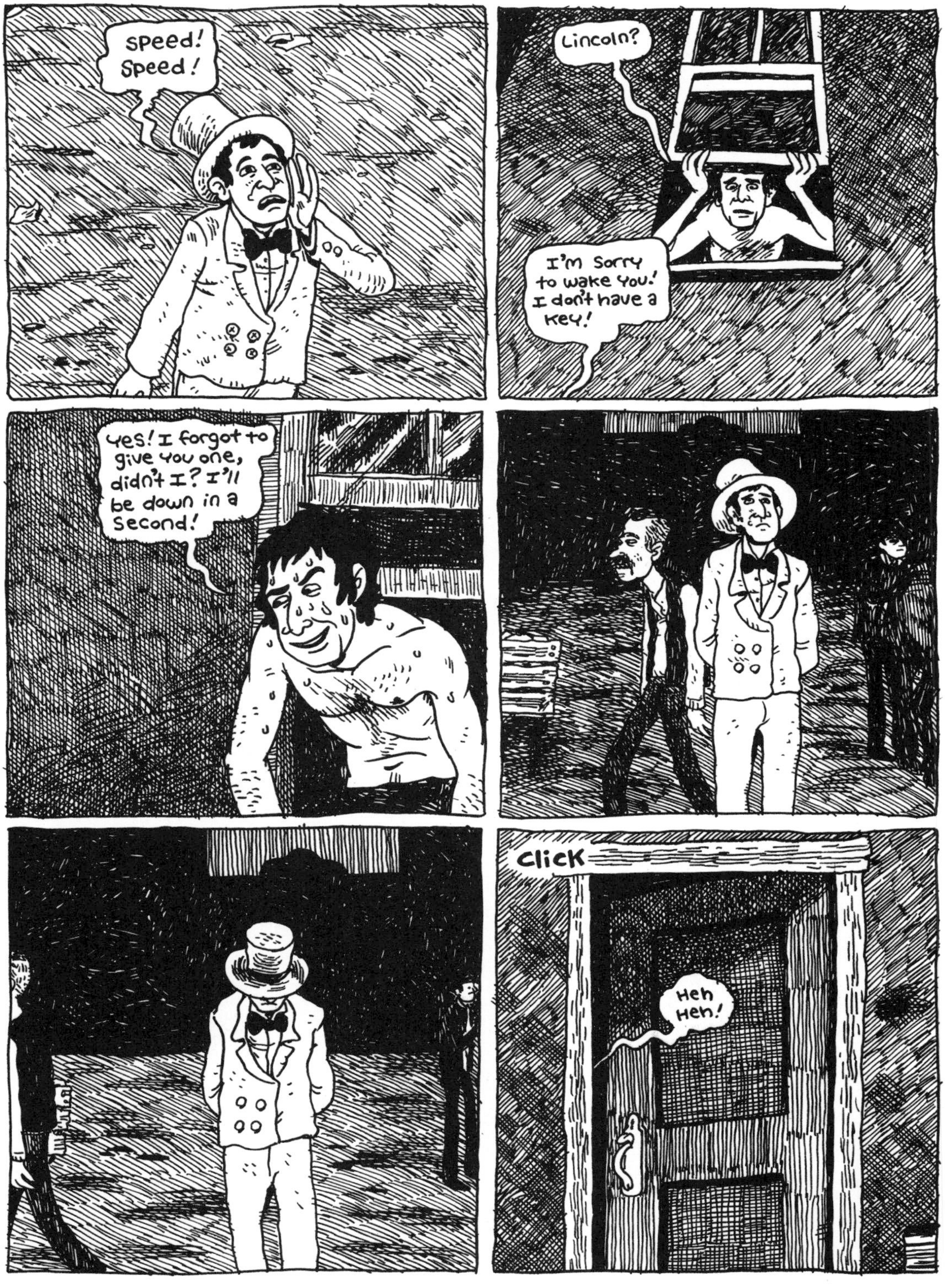
Speed! Speed!
Lincoln?
I'm sorry to wake you! I don't have a key!
Yes! I forgot to give you one, didn't I? I'll be down in a second!
Click
Heh Heh!

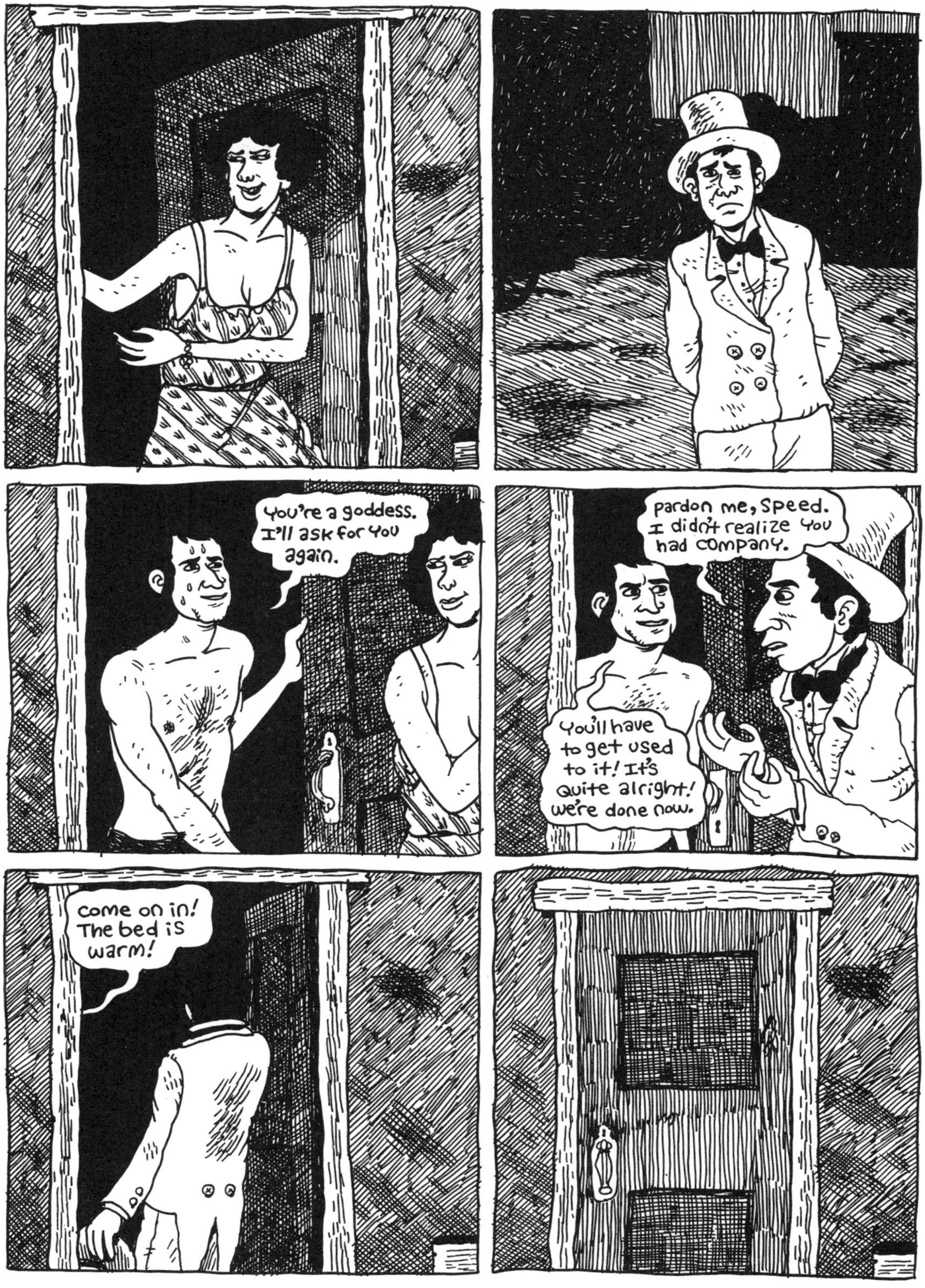
You're a goddess. I'll ask for You again.
pardon me, Speed. I didn't realize You had company.
You'll have to get used to it! It's quite alright! we're done now.
come on in! The bed is warm!

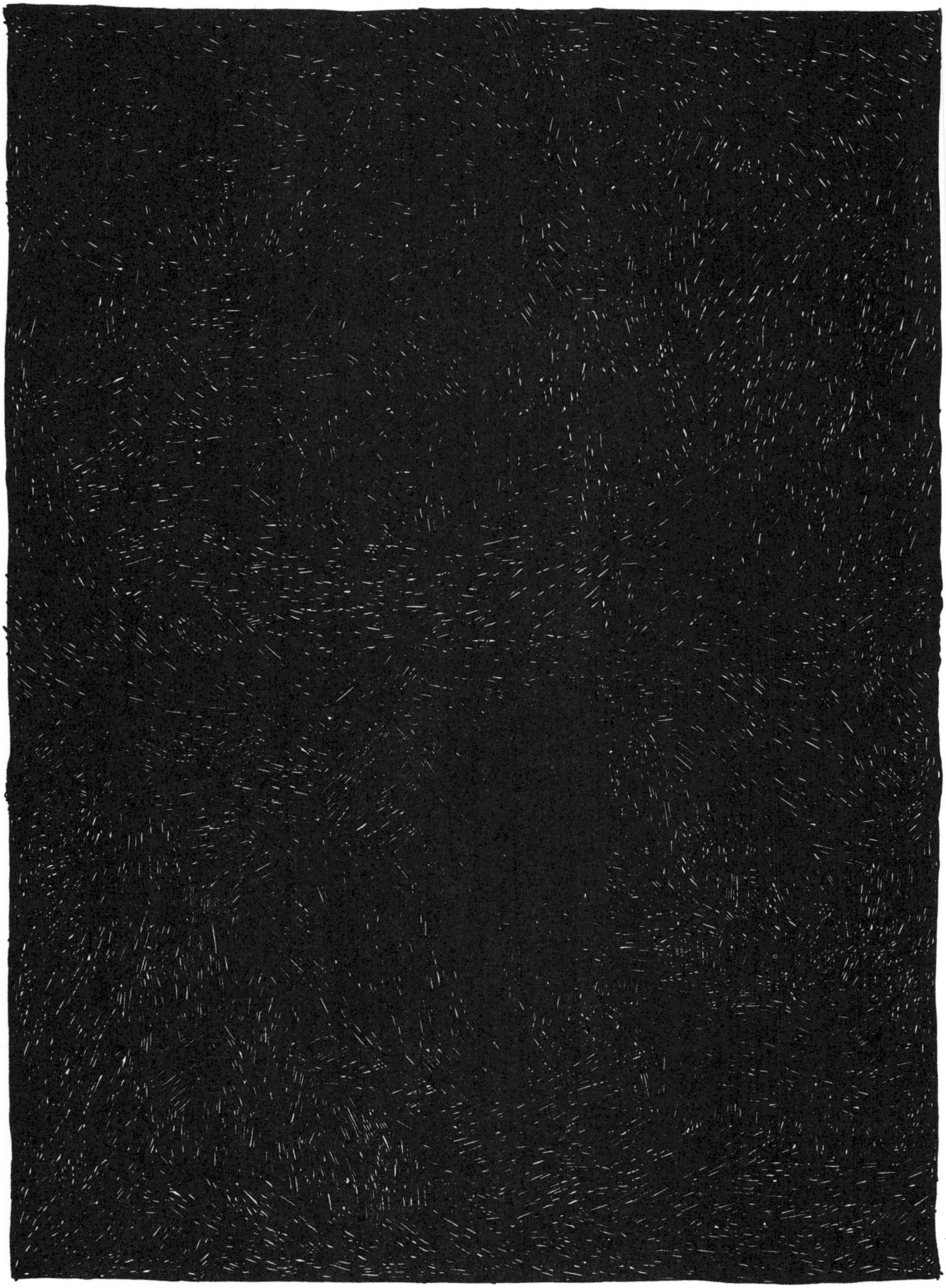

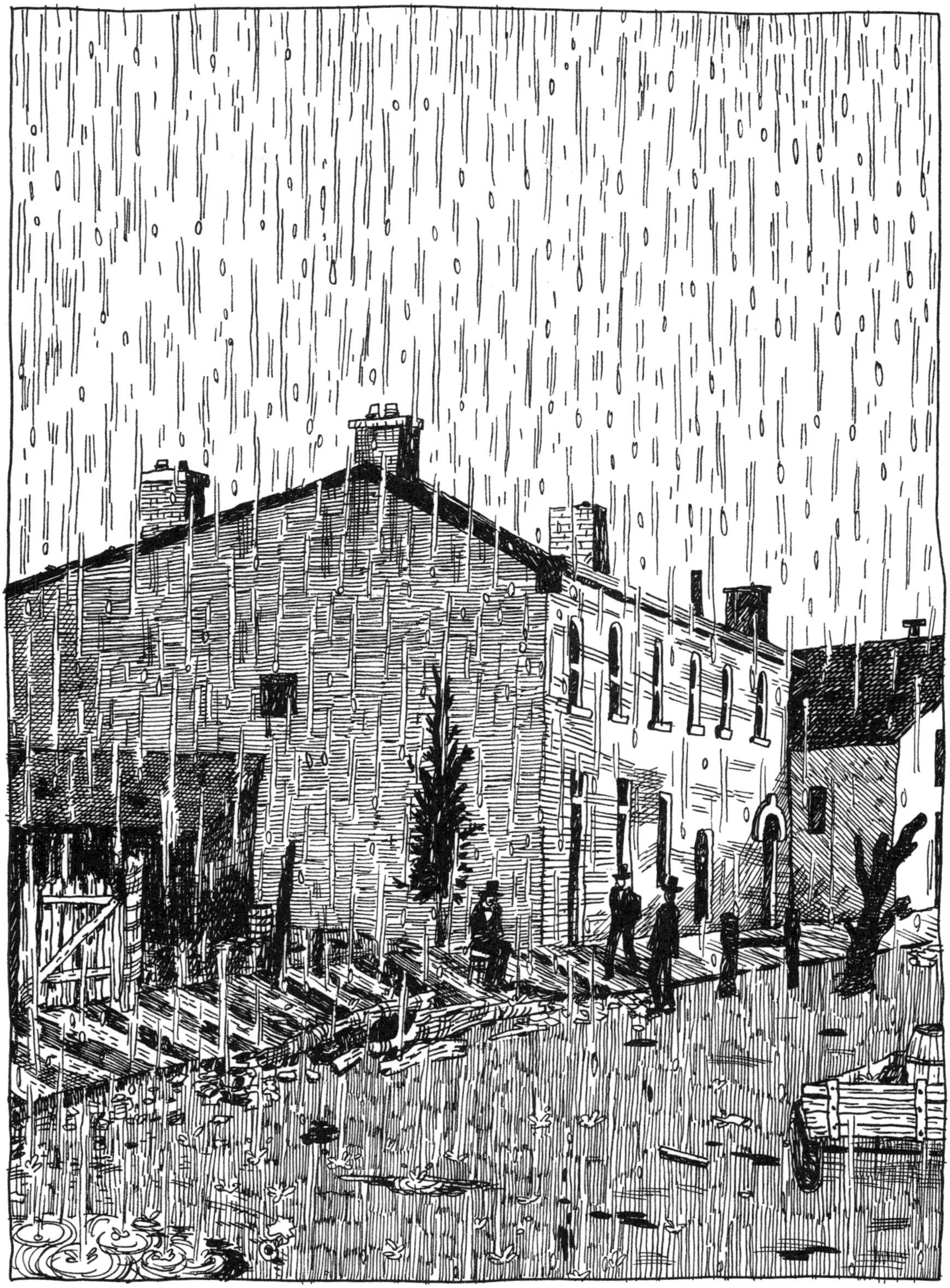

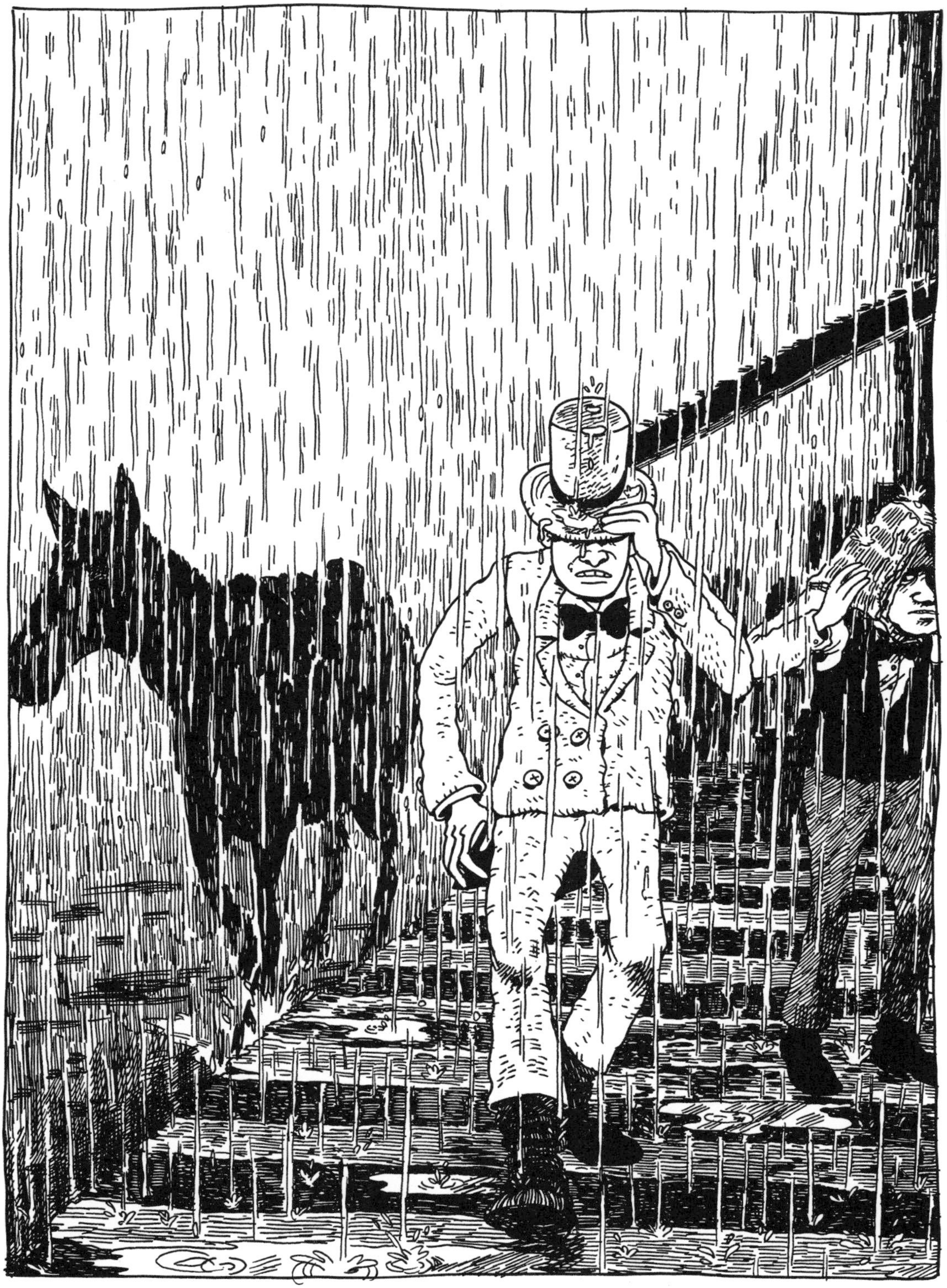

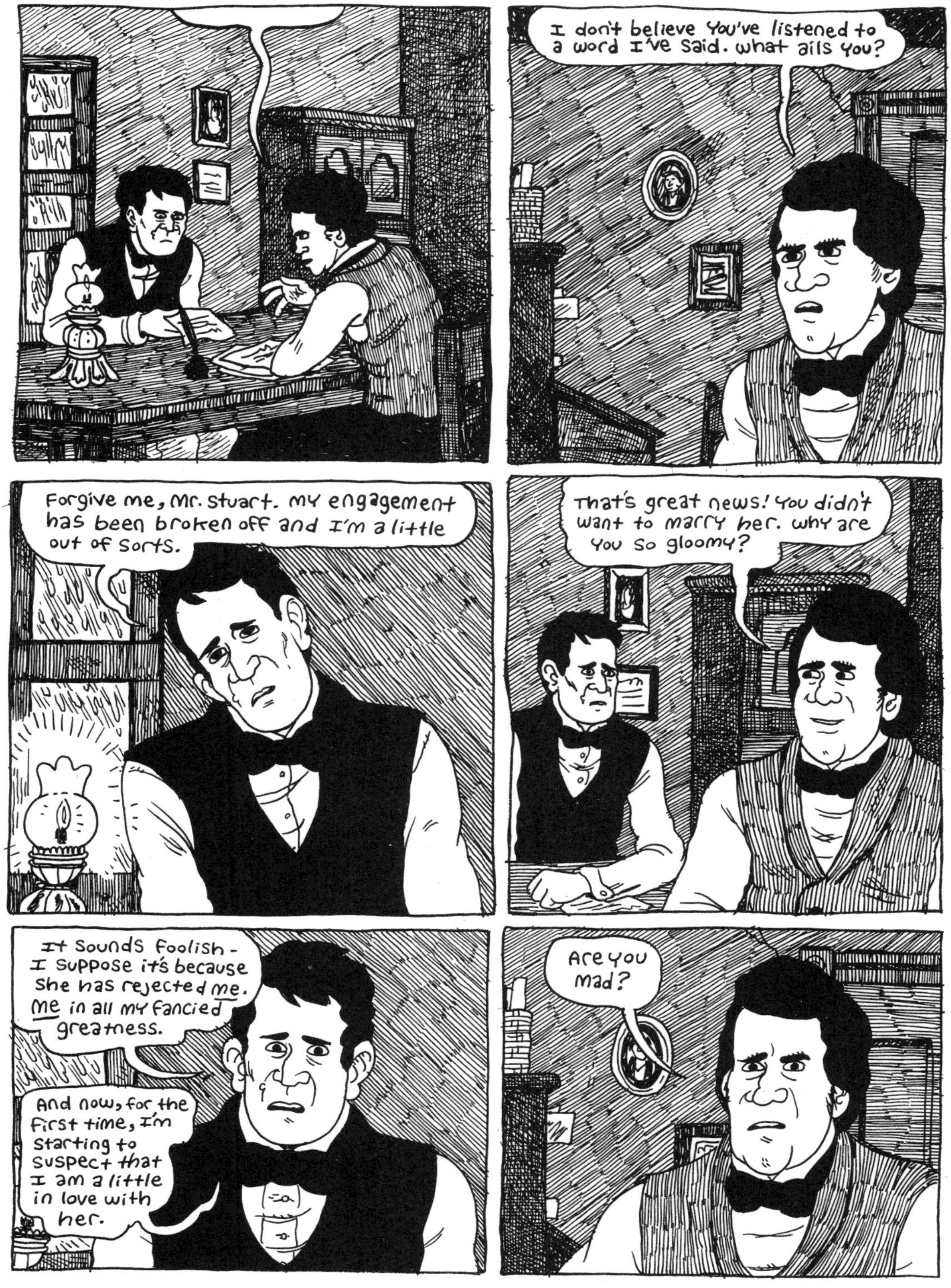
I don't believe you've listened to a word I've said. what ails you?
Forgive me, Mr. Stuart. My engagement has been broken off and I'm a little out of sorts.
That's great news! You didn't want to marry her. why are you so gloomy?
It sounds foolish - I suppose it's because she has rejected me. me in all my fancied greatness.
And now, for the first time, I'm starting to suspect that I am a little in love with her.
Are you mad?

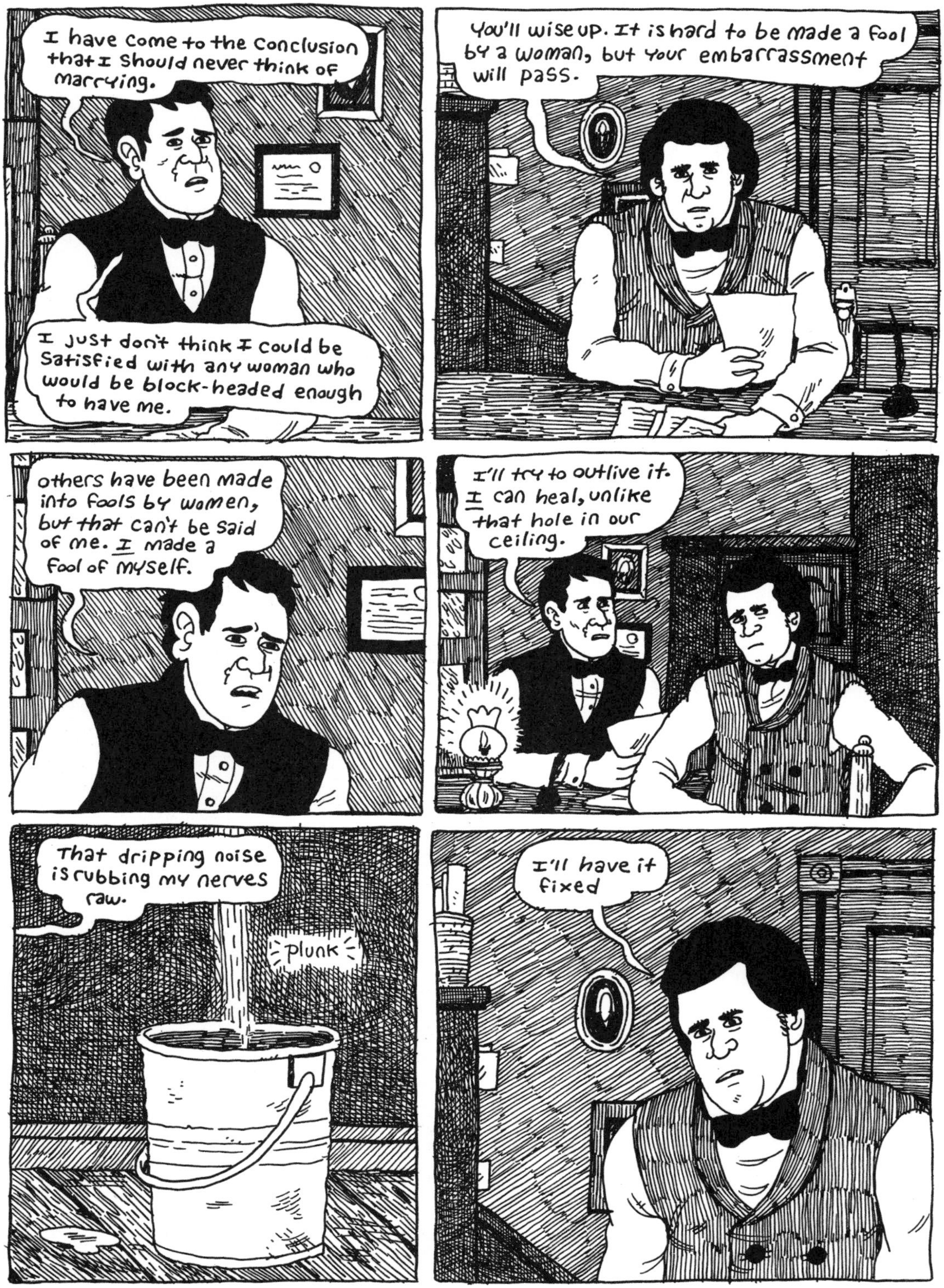
I have come to the conclusion that I should never think of marrying.
I just don't think I could be satisfied with any woman who would be block-headed enough to have me.
You'll wise up. It is hard to be made a fool by a woman, but your embarrassment will pass.
others have been made into fools by women, but that can't be said of me. I made a fool of myself.
I'll try to outlive it. I can heal, unlike that hole in our ceiling.
That dripping noise is rubbing my nerves raw.
plunk
I'll have it fixed

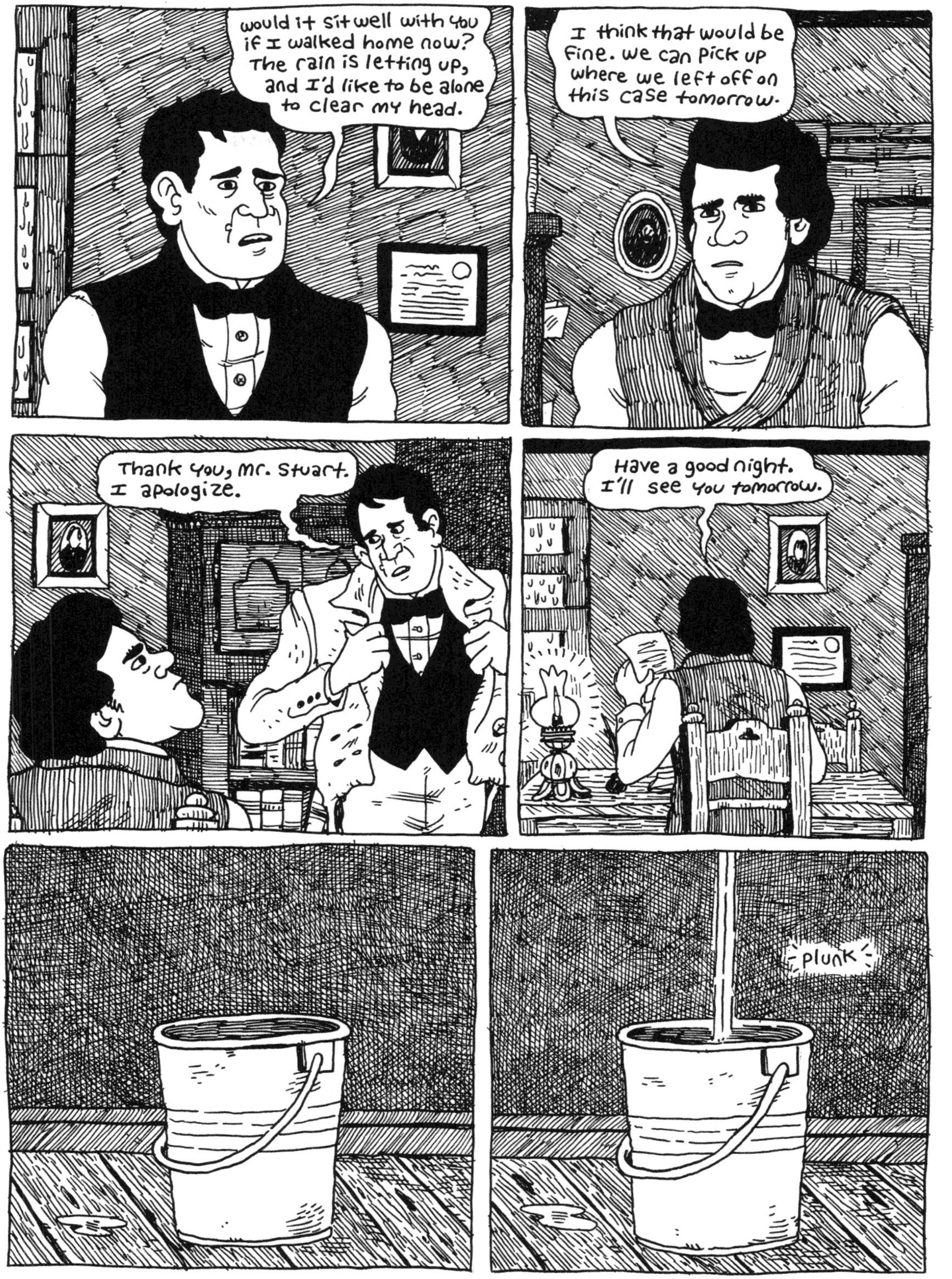
would it sit well with you if I walked home now? The rain is letting up, and I'd like to be alone to clear my head.
I think that would be fine. we can pick up where we left off on this case tomorrow.
Thank you, mr. Stuart. I apologize.
Have a good night. I'll see you tomorrow.
plunk

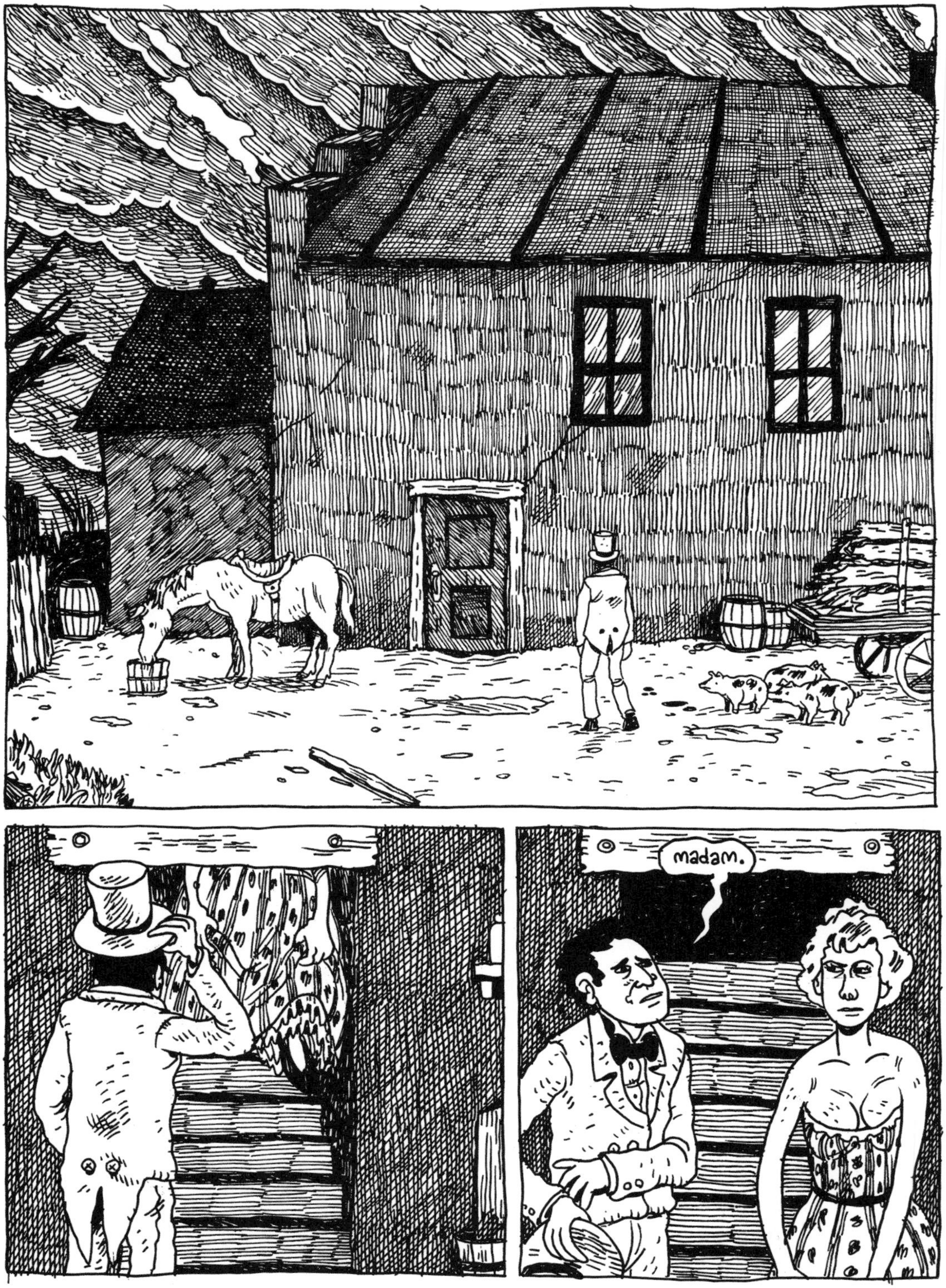
madam.

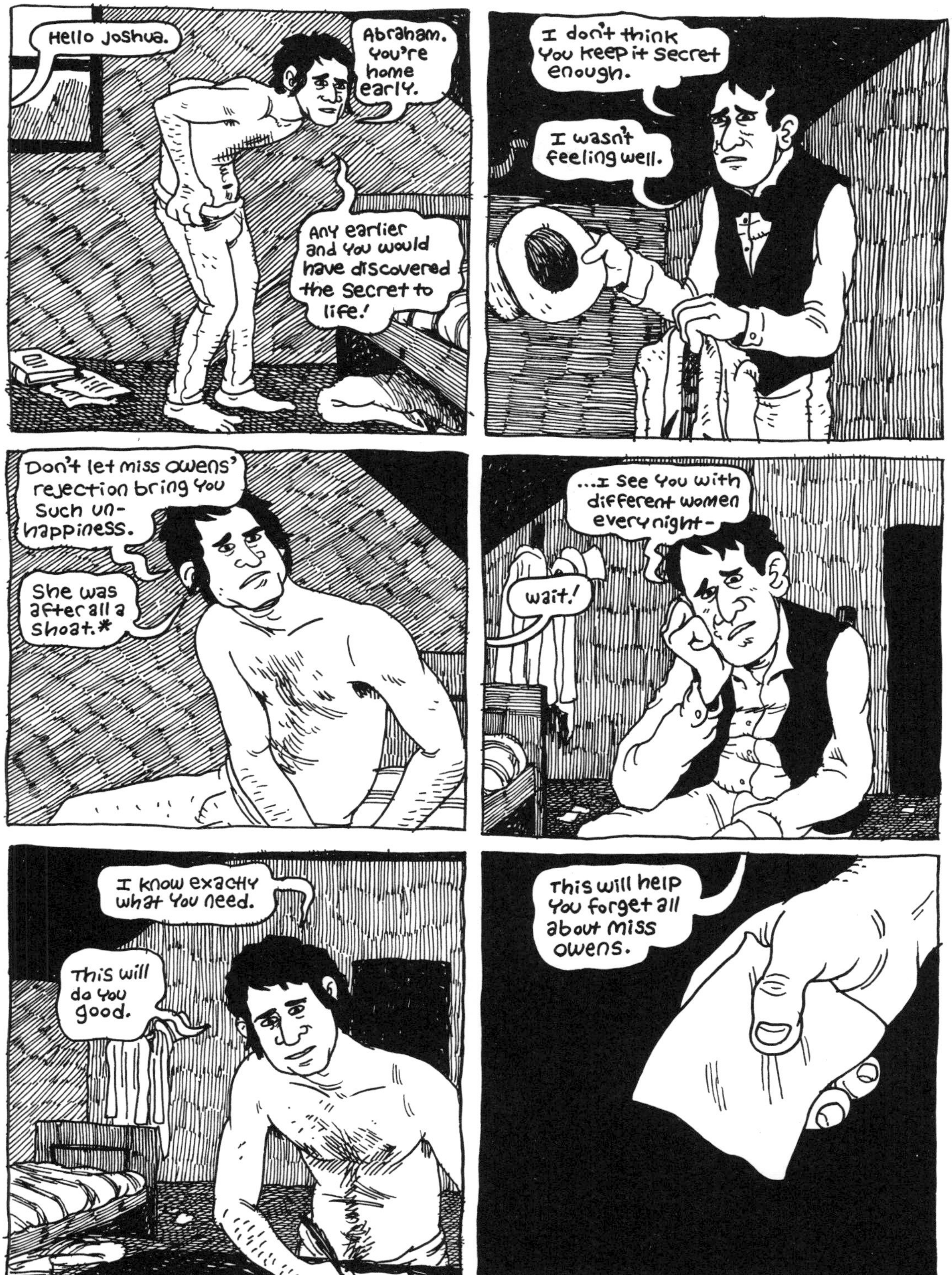
Hello Joshua.
Abraham. You're home early.
Any earlier and you would have discovered the secret to life!
I don't think you keep it secret enough.
I wasn't feeling well.
Don't let miss owens' rejection bring you such un-happiness.
She was after all a shoat.*
...I see you with different women every night-
wait!
I know exactly what you need.
This will do you good.
This will help you forget all about miss owens.

* Young Pig

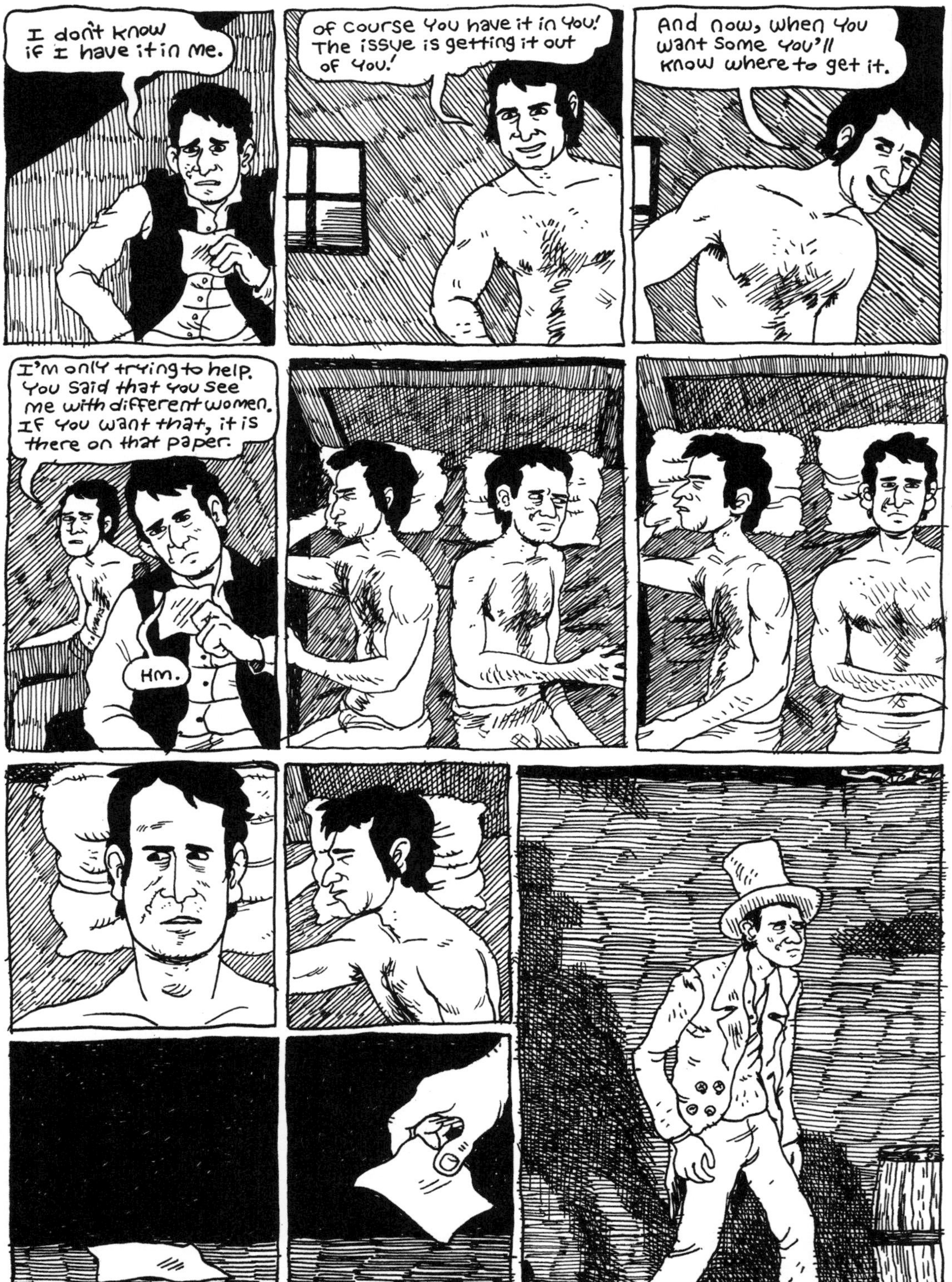
I don't know if I have it in me.
Of course you have it in you! The issue is getting it out of you!
And now, when you want some you'll know where to get it.
I'm only trying to help. You said that you see me with different women. If you want that, it is there on that paper.
Hm.

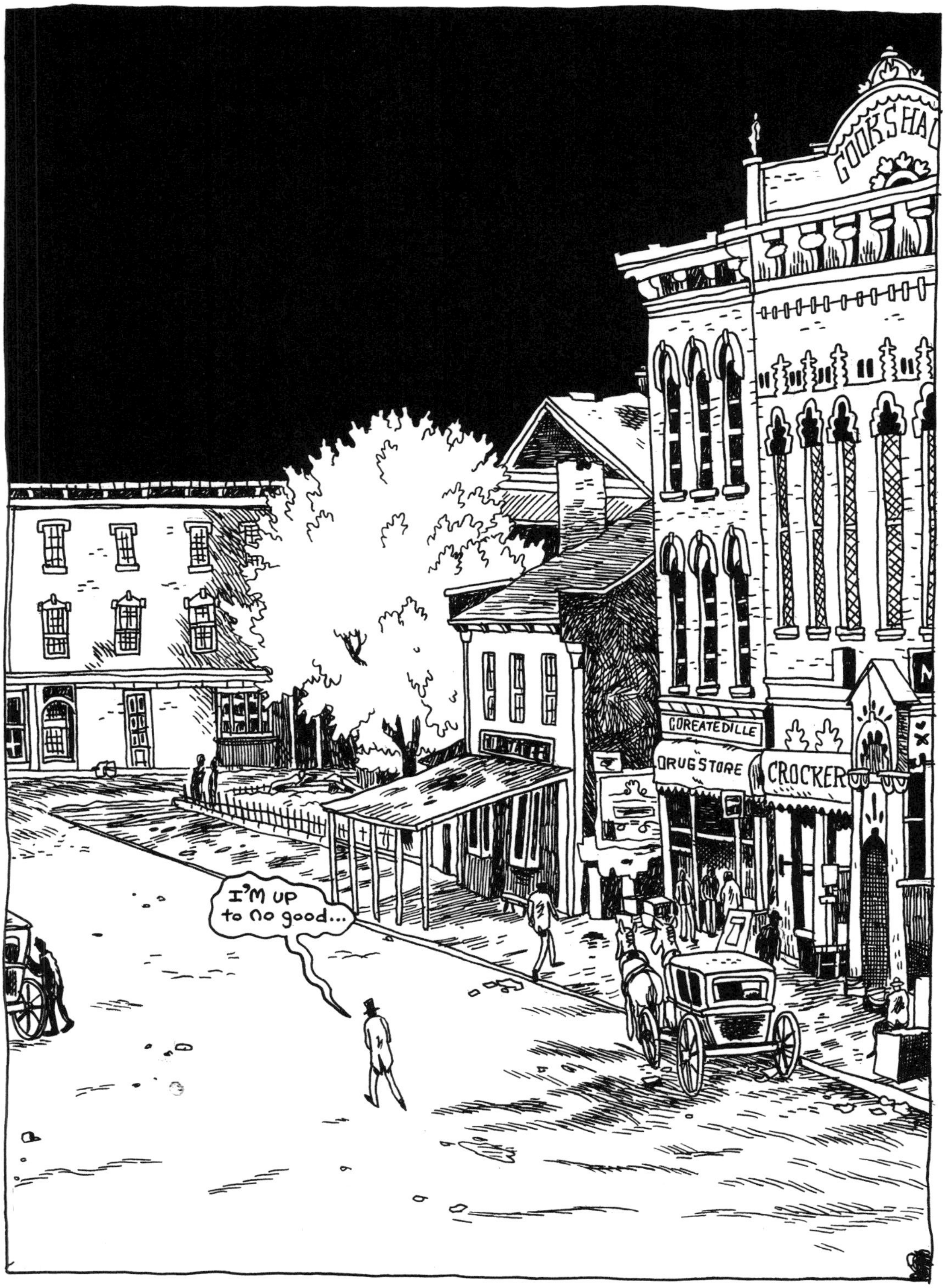
I'M UP to no good...
DRUGSTORE
CROCKER

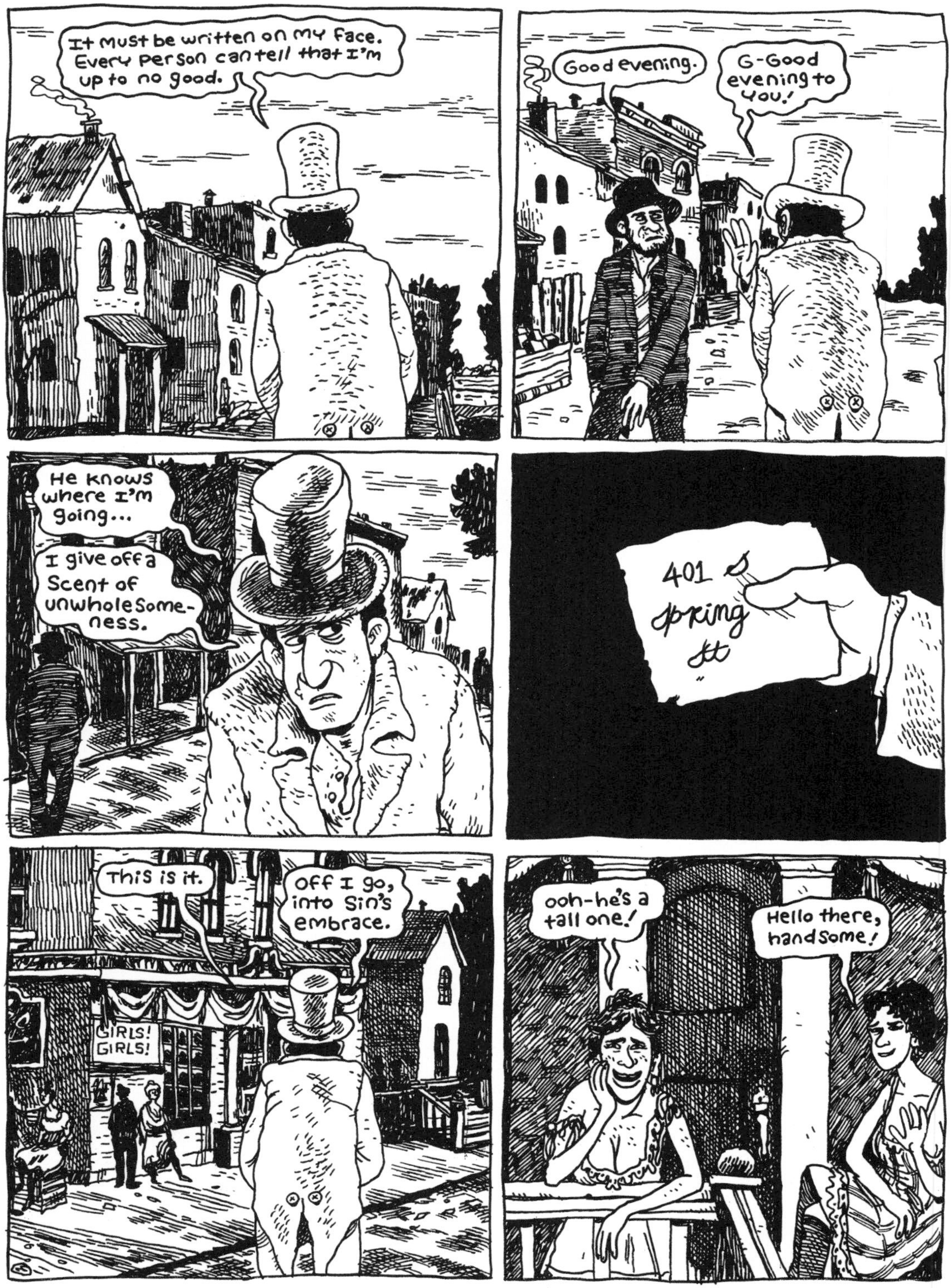
It must be written on my face. Every person can tell that I'm up to no good.
Good evening.
G-Good evening to you!
He knows where I'm going...
I give off a scent of unwholesome-ness.
401 Spring St
This is it.
Off I go, into Sin's embrace.
GIRLS! GIRLS!
ooh-he's a tall one!
Hello there, handsome!

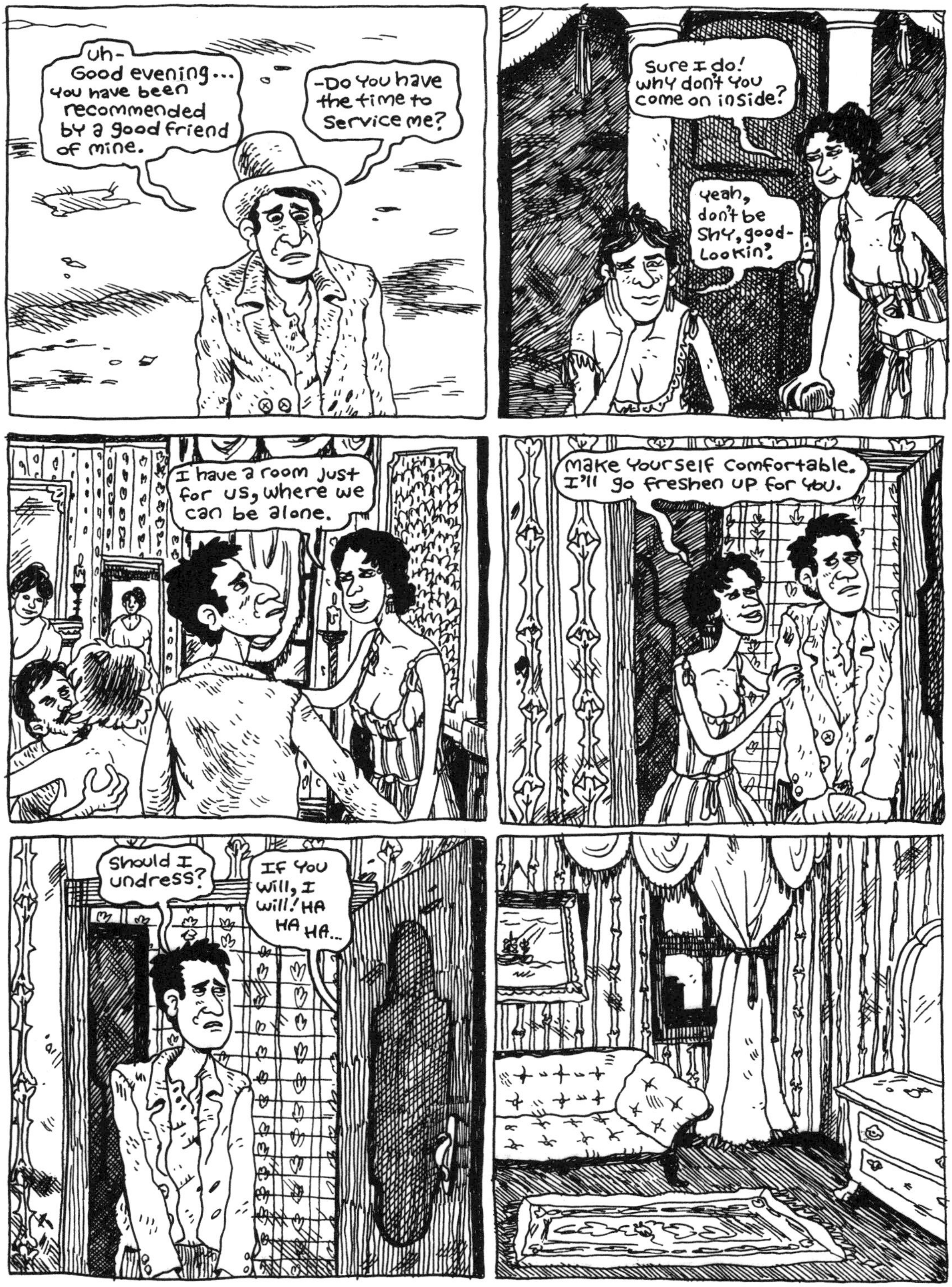
uh-
Good evening... you have been recommended by a good friend of mine.
-Do you have the time to service me?
Sure I do! why don't you come on inside?
yeah, don't be shy, good-lookin'.
I have a room just for us, where we can be alone.
Make yourself comfortable. I'll go freshen up for you.
Should I undress?
If you will, I will! HA HA HA...

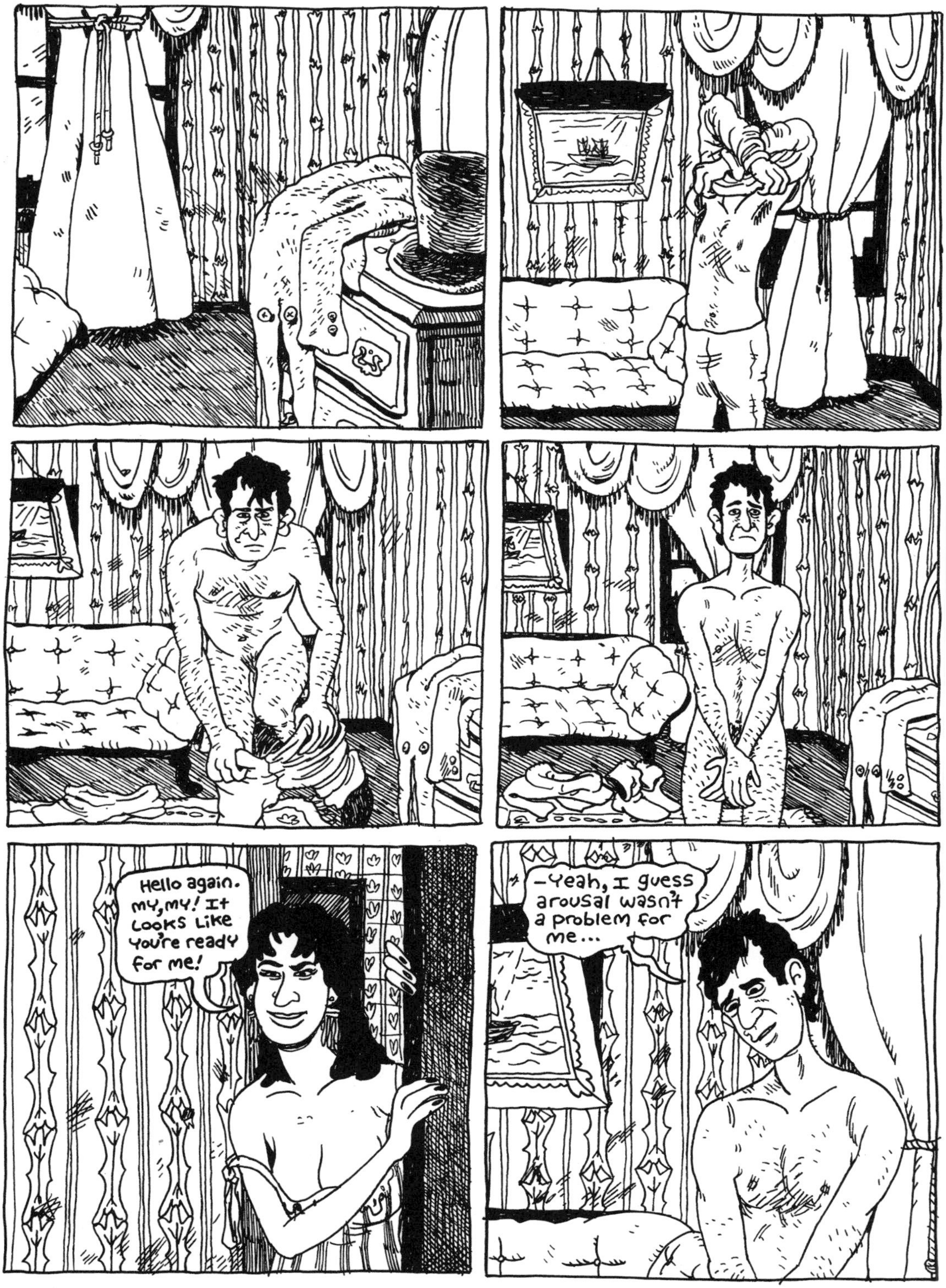
Hello again. My, My! It Looks Like You're ready for me!
—Yeah, I guess arousal wasn't a problem for me...

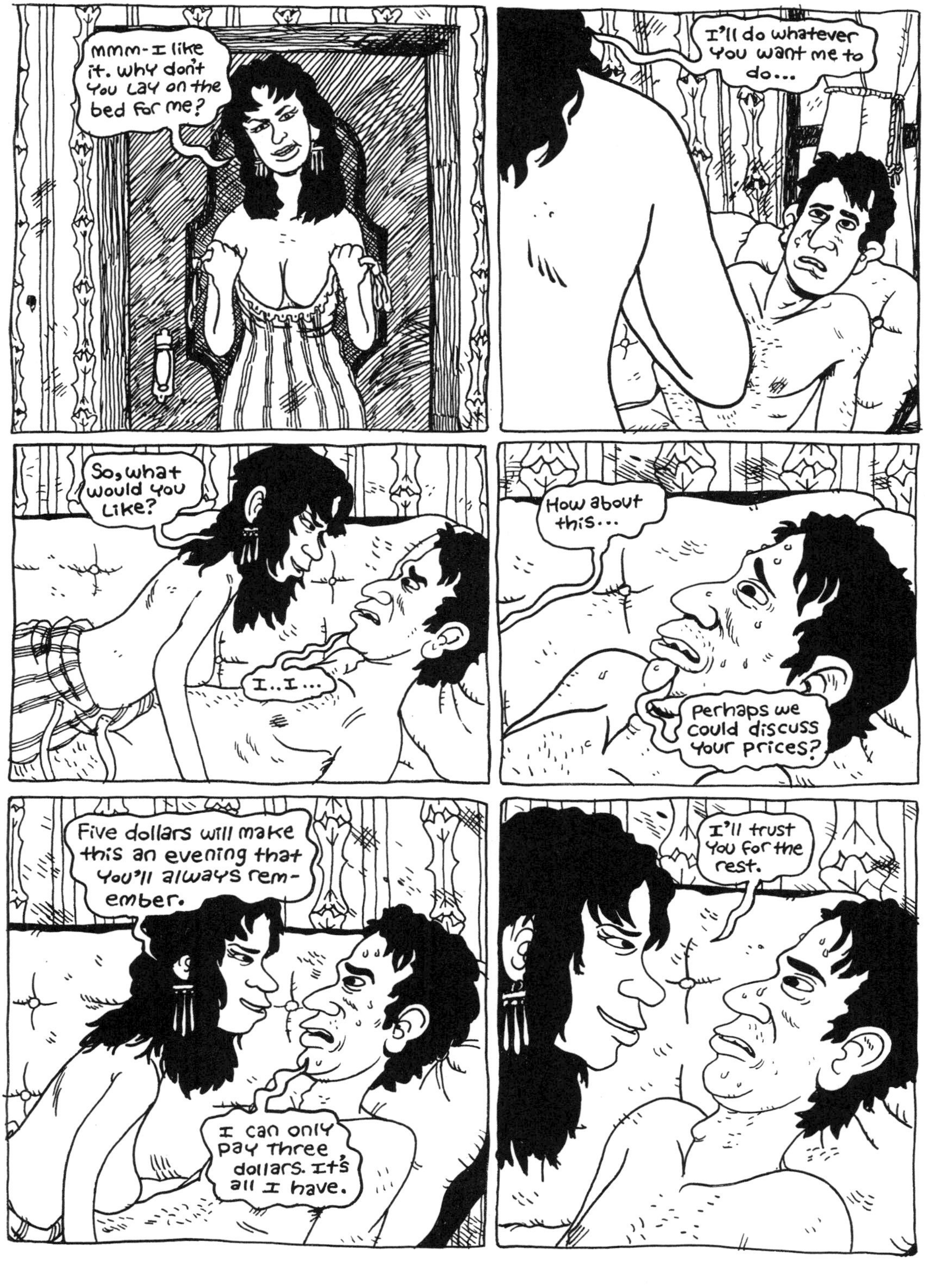
mmm- I like it. why don't you lay on the bed for me?
I'll do whatever you want me to do...
So, what would you like?
I..I...
How about this...
Perhaps we could discuss your prices?
Five dollars will make this an evening that you'll always rem-ember.
I can only pay three dollars. It's all I have.
I'll trust you for the rest.

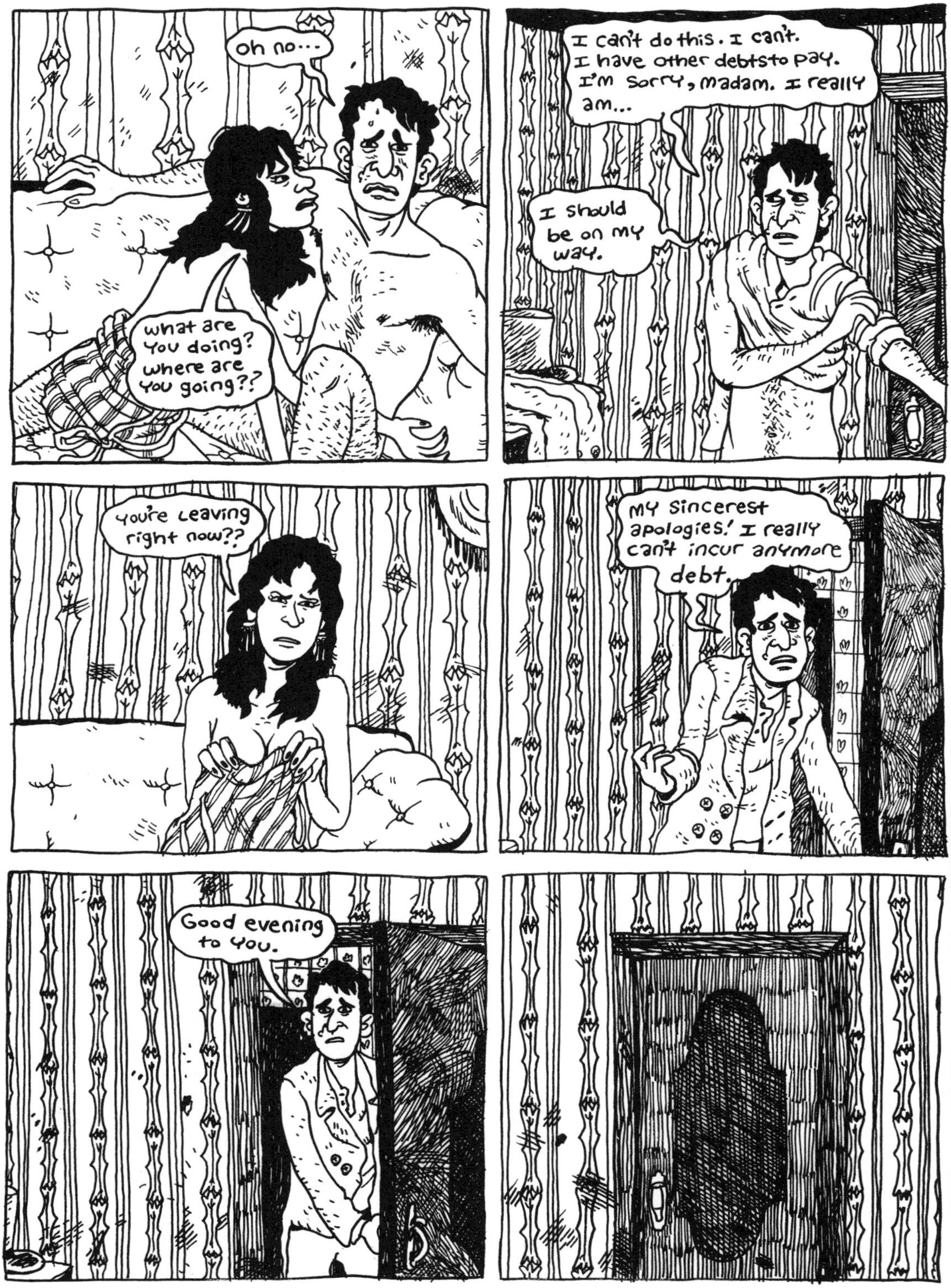
oh no...
what are you doing? where are you going??
I can't do this. I can't. I have other debts to pay. I'm sorry, madam. I really am...
I should be on my way.
you're leaving right now??
My sincerest apologies! I really can't incur anymore debt.
Good evening to you.

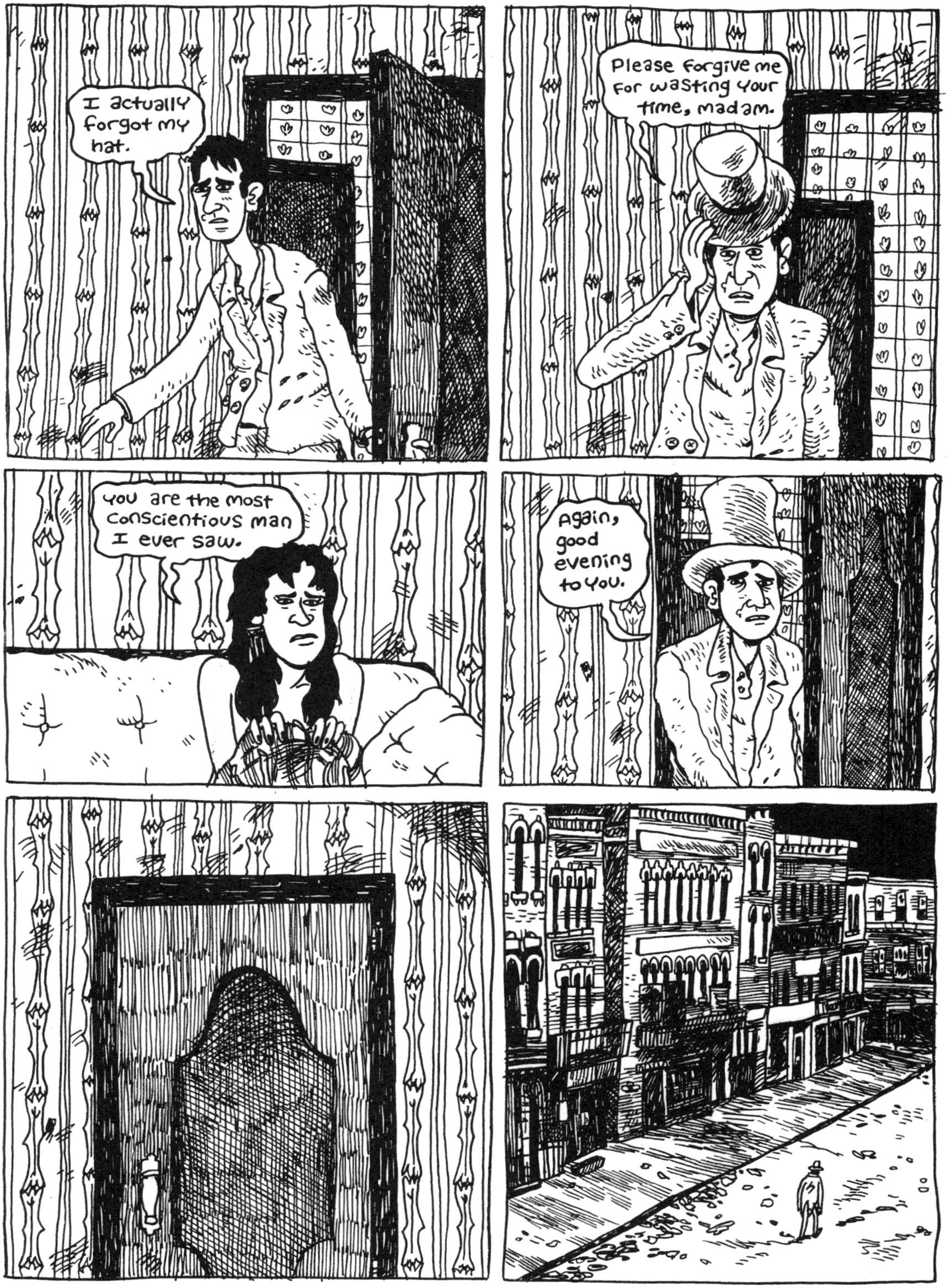
I actually forgot my hat.
Please forgive me for wasting your time, madam.
You are the most conscientious man I ever saw.
Again, good evening to you.

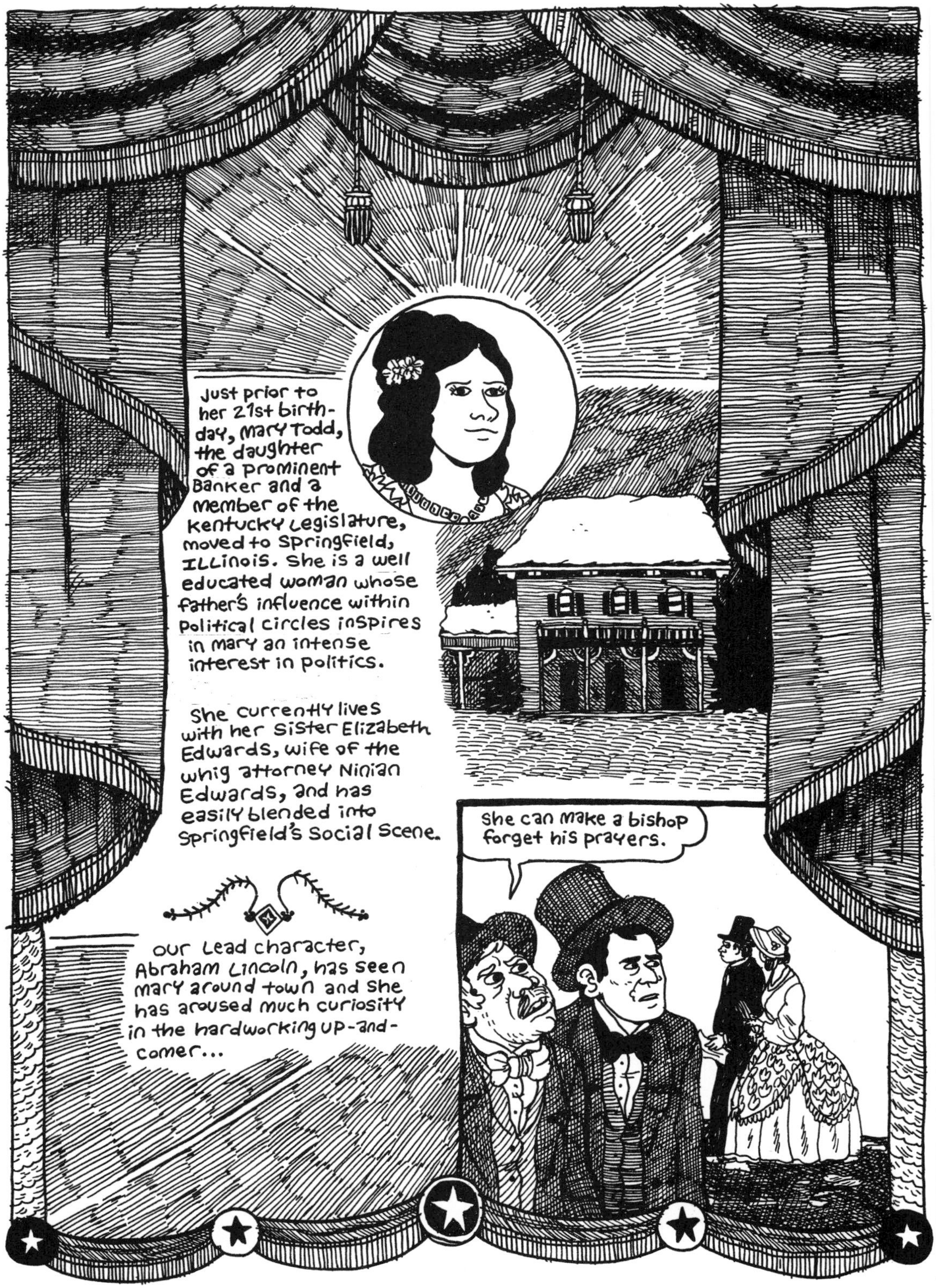
Just prior to her 21st birthday, Mary Todd, the daughter of a prominent Banker and a member of the Kentucky Legislature, moved to Springfield, ILLinois. She is a well educated woman whose father's influence within political circles inspires in Mary an intense interest in politics.
She currently lives with her sister Elizabeth Edwards, wife of the whig attorney Ninian Edwards, and has easily blended into Springfield's social scene.
Our lead character, Abraham Lincoln, has seen Mary around town and she has aroused much curiosity in the hardworking up-and-comer...
She can make a bishop forget his prayers.

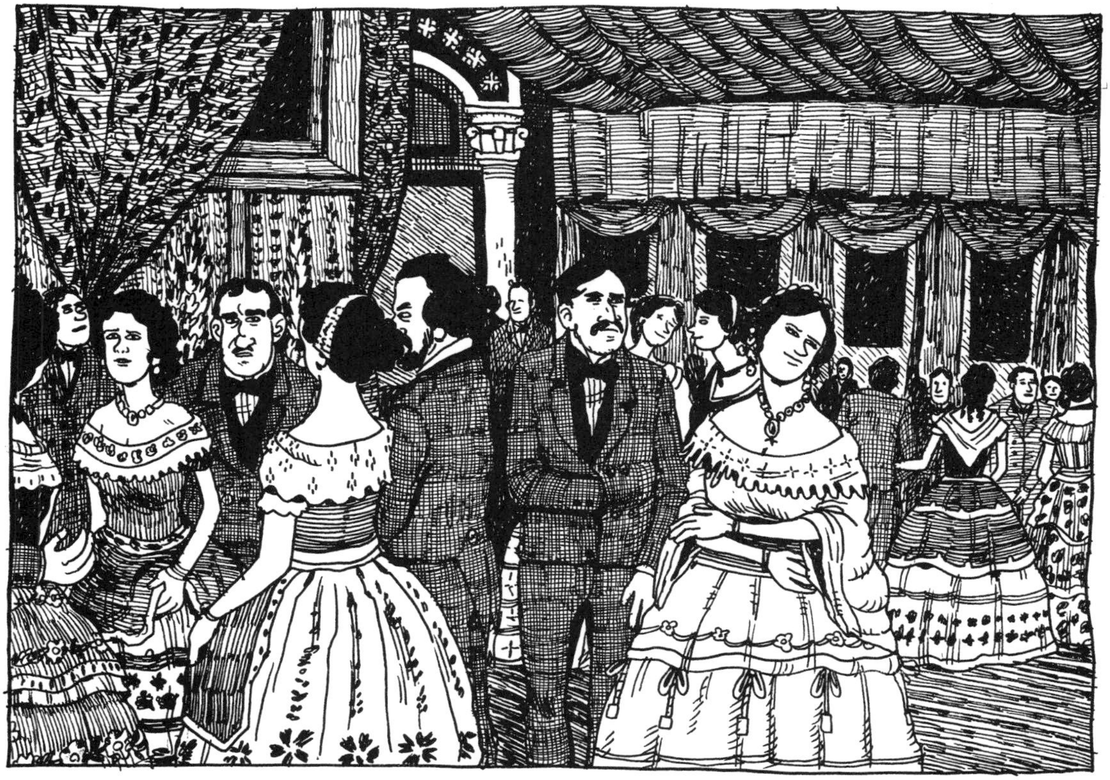

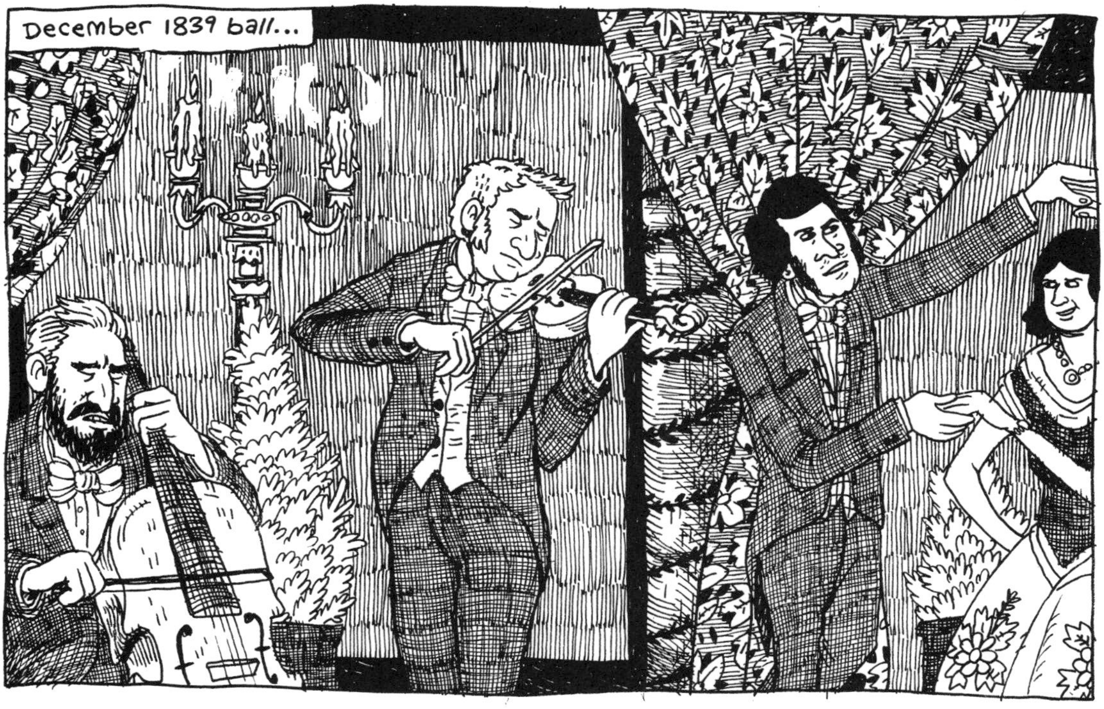
December 1839 ball...

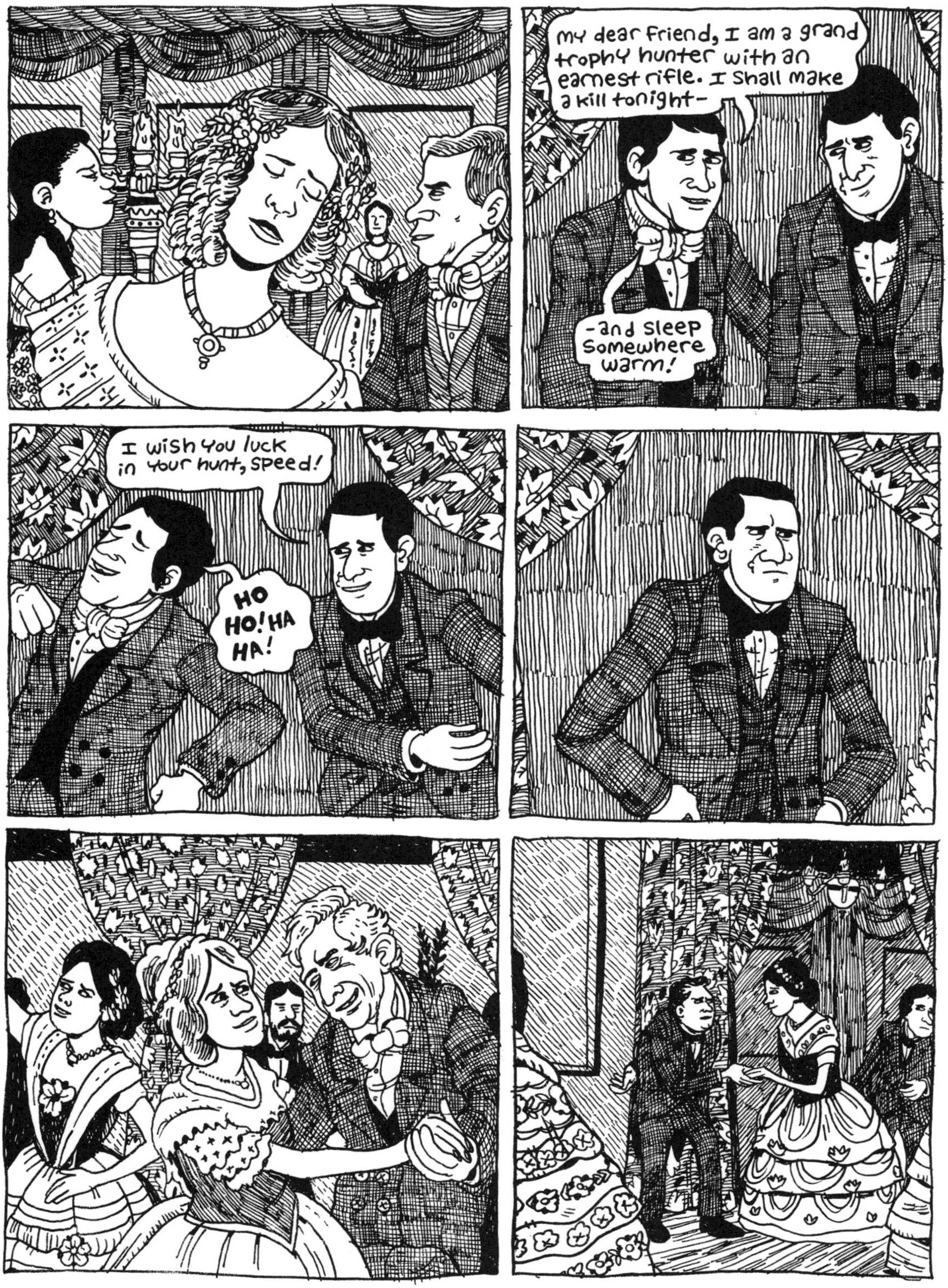
my dear friend, I am a grand trophy hunter with an earnest rifle. I shall make a kill tonight-
-and sleep somewhere warm!
I wish you luck in your hunt, speed!
HO HO! HA HA!

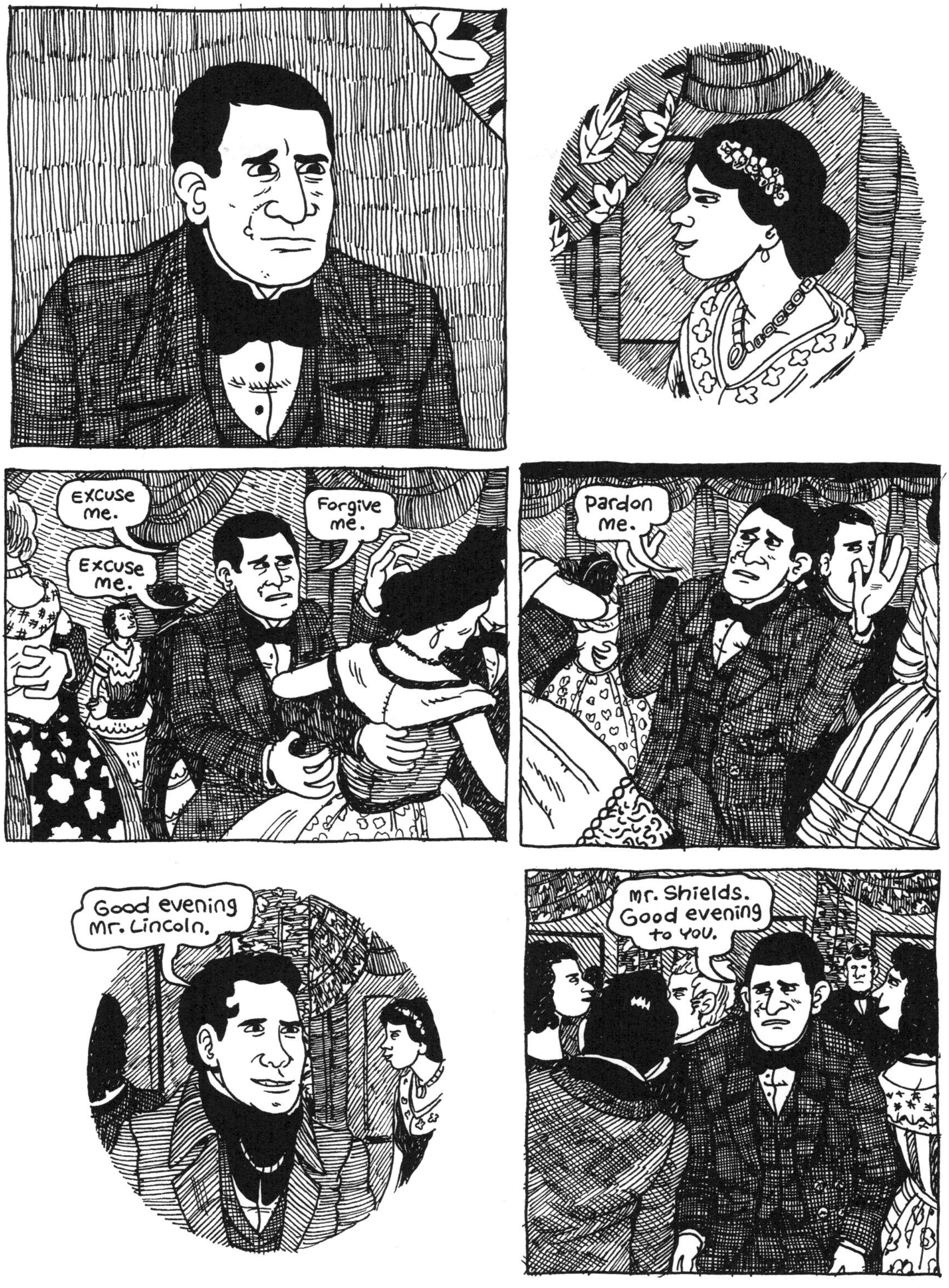
Excuse me.
Excuse me.
Forgive me.
Pardon me.
Good evening Mr. Lincoln.
Mr. Shields. Good evening to you.

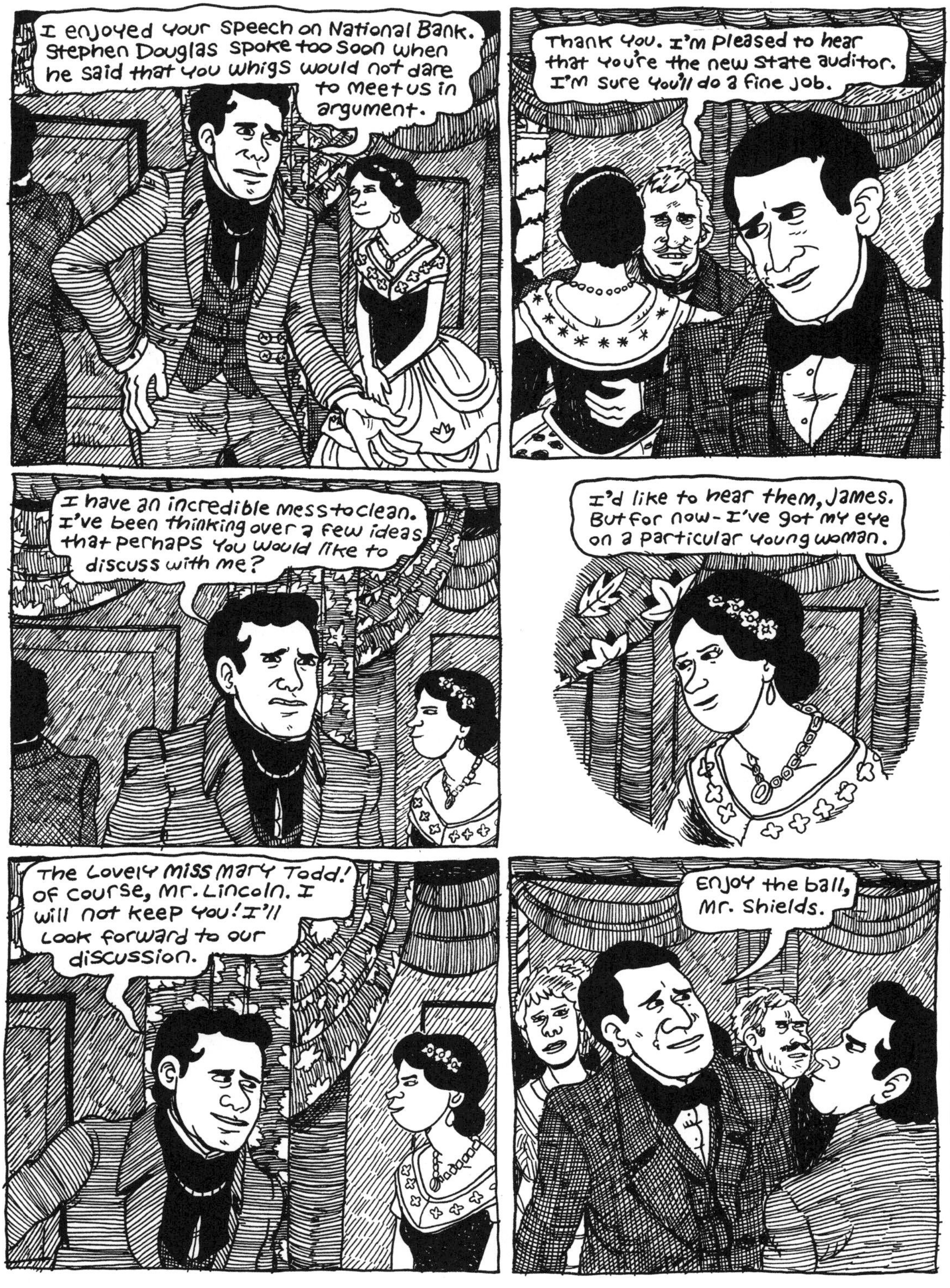
I enjoyed your speech on National Bank. Stephen Douglas spoke too soon when he said that you whigs would not dare to meet us in argument.
Thank you. I'm pleased to hear that you're the new state auditor. I'm sure you'll do a fine job.
I have an incredible mess to clean. I've been thinking over a few ideas that perhaps you would like to discuss with me?
I'd like to hear them, James. But for now - I've got my eye on a particular young woman.
The lovely Miss Mary Todd! Of course, Mr. Lincoln. I will not keep you! I'll look forward to our discussion.
Enjoy the ball, Mr. Shields.

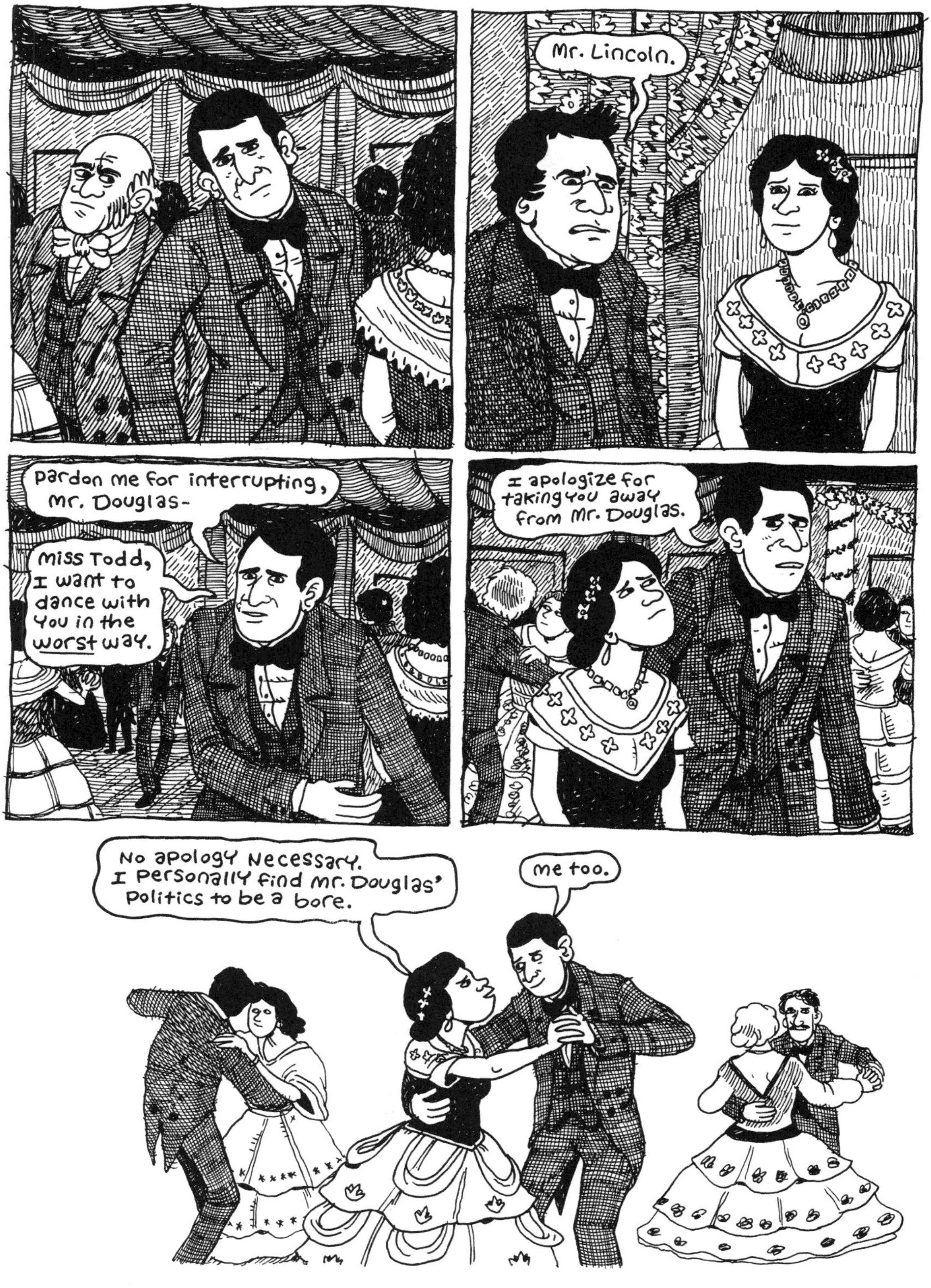
Mr. Lincoln.
pardon me for interrupting, Mr. Douglas-
Miss Todd, I want to dance with you in the worst way.
I apologize for taking you away from Mr. Douglas.
No apology Necessary. I personally find Mr. Douglas' politics to be a bore.
me too.

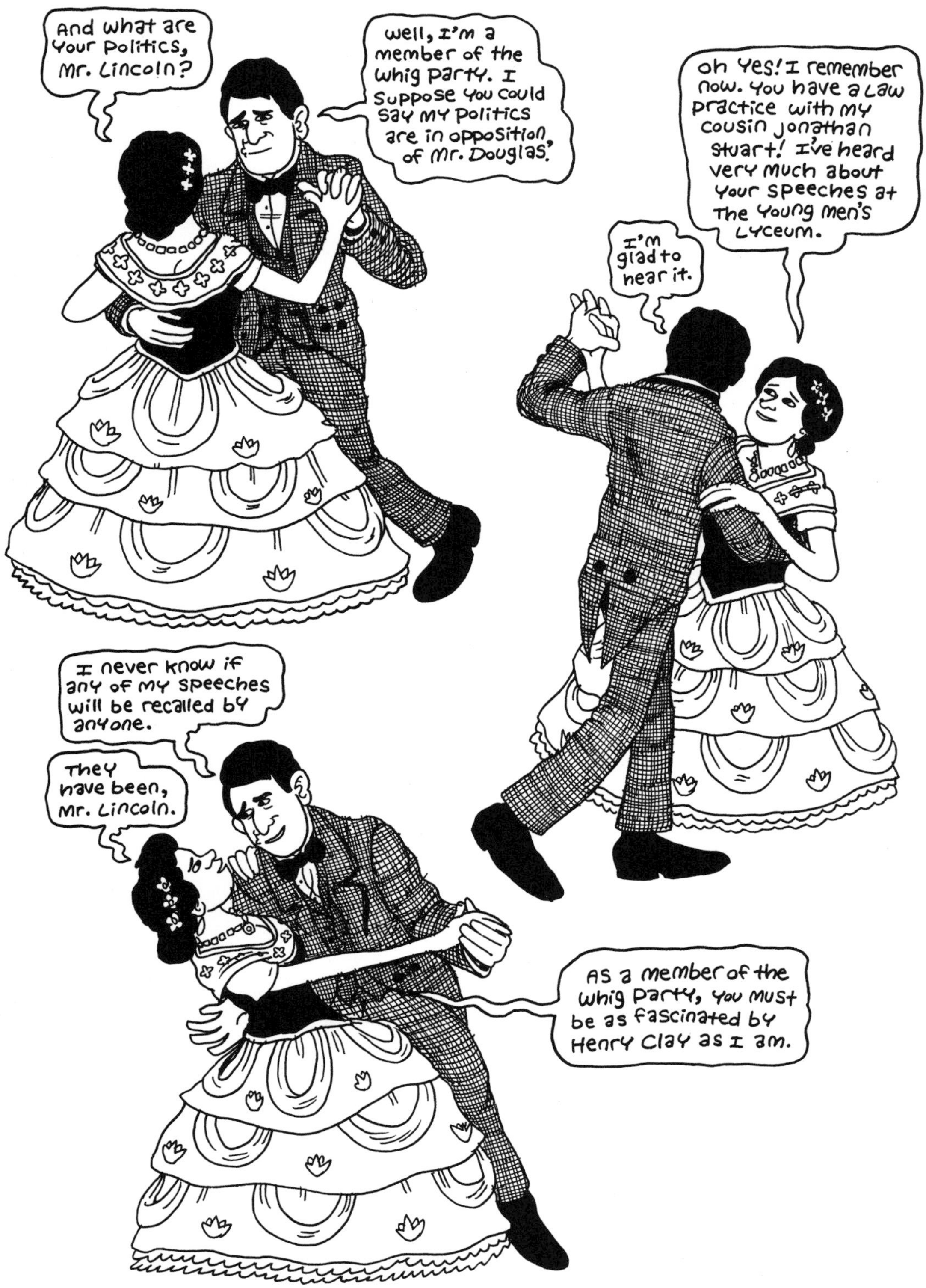
And what are your politics, Mr. Lincoln?
Well, I'm a member of the Whig party. I suppose you could say my politics are in opposition, of Mr. Douglas.
Oh yes! I remember now. You have a law practice with my cousin Jonathan Stuart! I've heard very much about your speeches at the Young Men's Lyceum.
I'm glad to hear it.
I never know if any of my speeches will be recalled by anyone.
They have been, Mr. Lincoln.
As a member of the Whig party, you must be as fascinated by Henry Clay as I am.

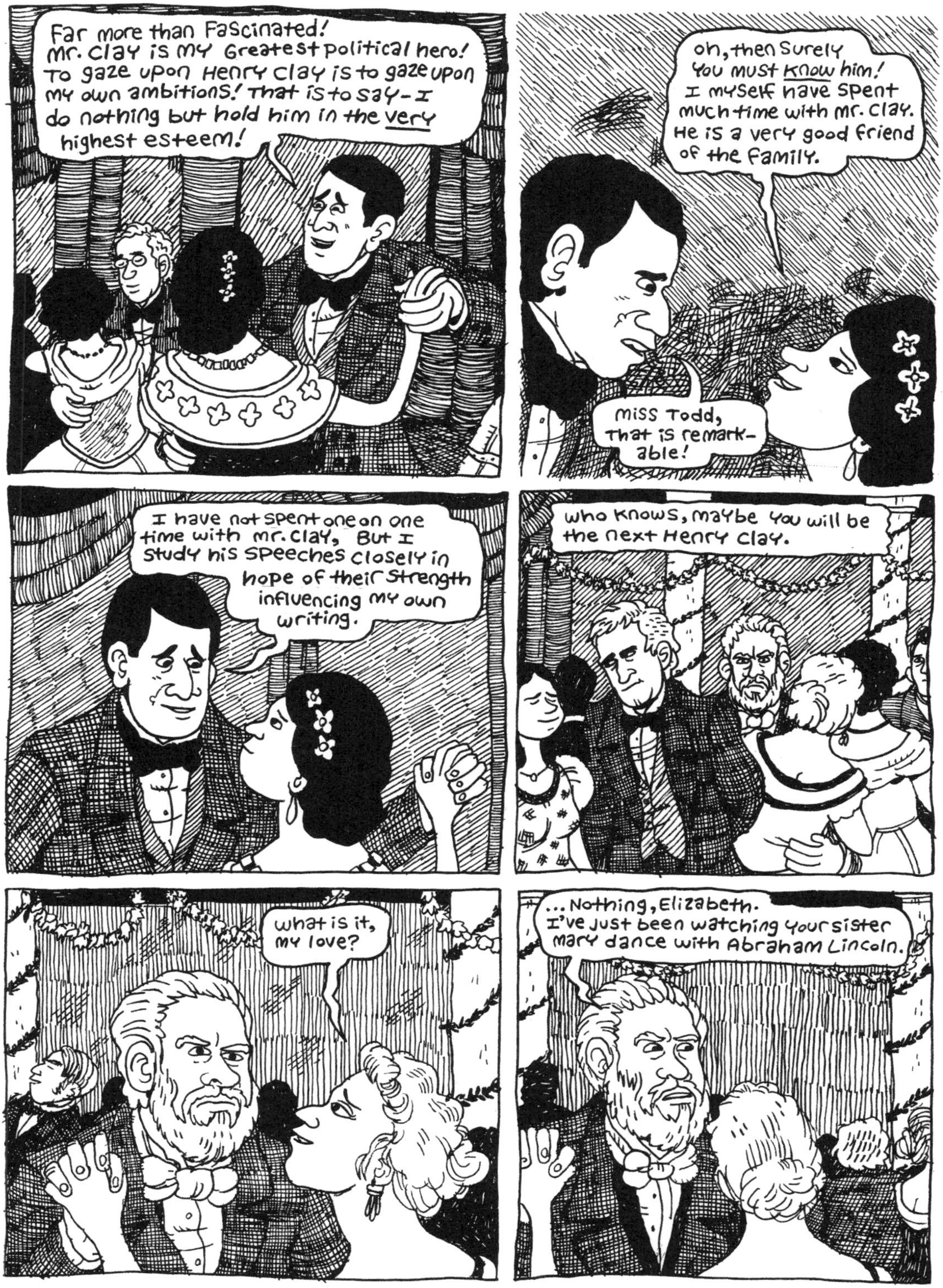
Far more than Fascinated! Mr. Clay is my Greatest political hero! To gaze upon Henry Clay is to gaze upon my own ambitions! That is to say- I do nothing but hold him in the very highest esteem!
oh, then Surely you must know him! I myself have spent much time with mr. Clay. He is a very good friend of the family.
Miss Todd, that is remarkable!
I have not spent one on one time with mr. Clay, But I study his speeches closely in hope of their Strength influencing my own writing.
who knows, maybe you will be the next Henry Clay.
what is it, my love?
...Nothing, Elizabeth. I've just been watching your sister Mary dance with Abraham Lincoln.

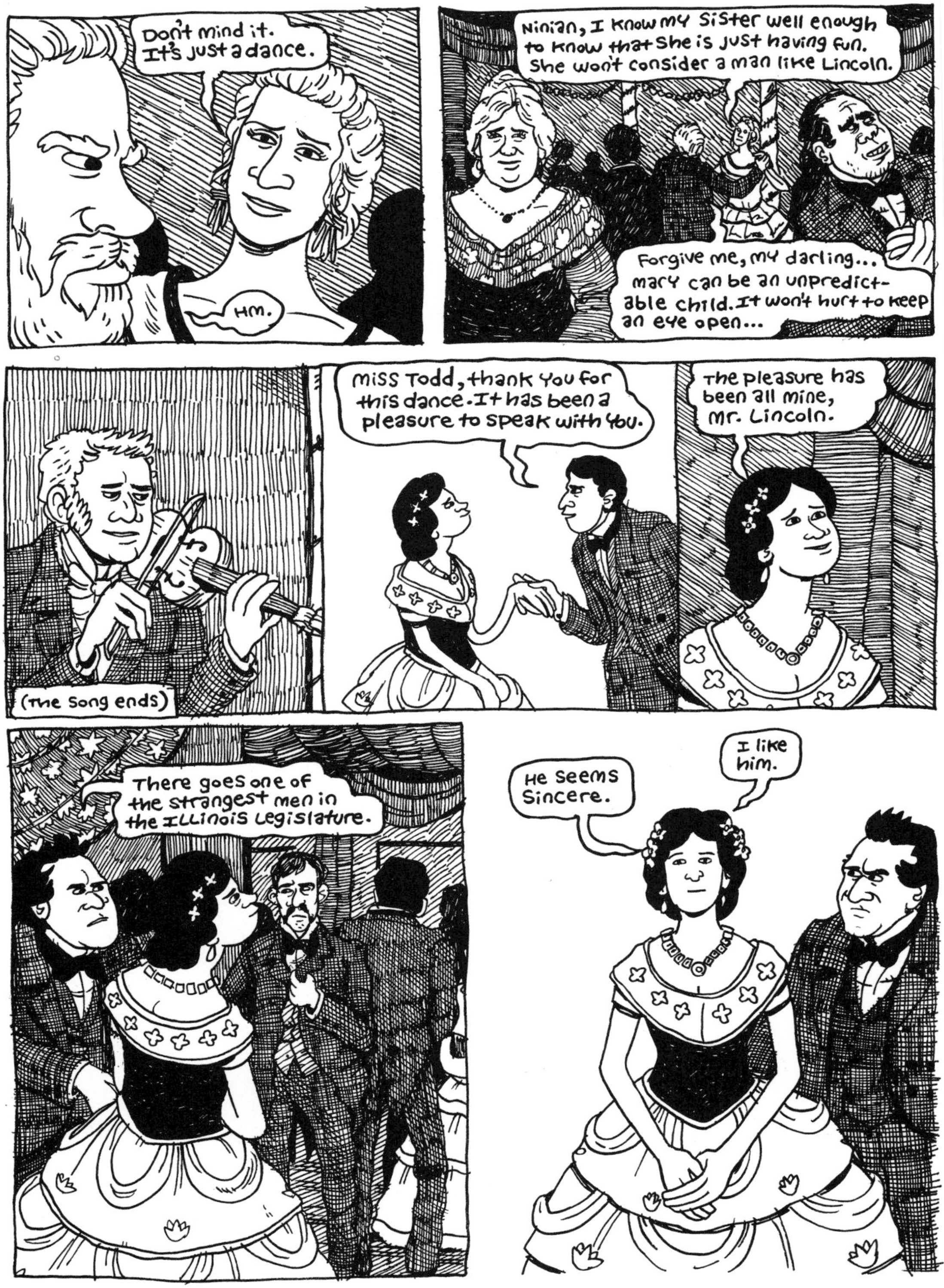
Don't mind it.
It's just a dance.
Hm.
Ninian, I know my sister well enough to know that she is just having fun. She won't consider a man like Lincoln.
Forgive me, my darling... Mary can be an unpredict-able child. It won't hurt to keep an eye open...
(The song ends)
Miss Todd, thank you for this dance. It has been a pleasure to speak with you.
The pleasure has been all mine, Mr. Lincoln.
There goes one of the strangest men in the Illinois Legislature.
He seems sincere.
I like him.

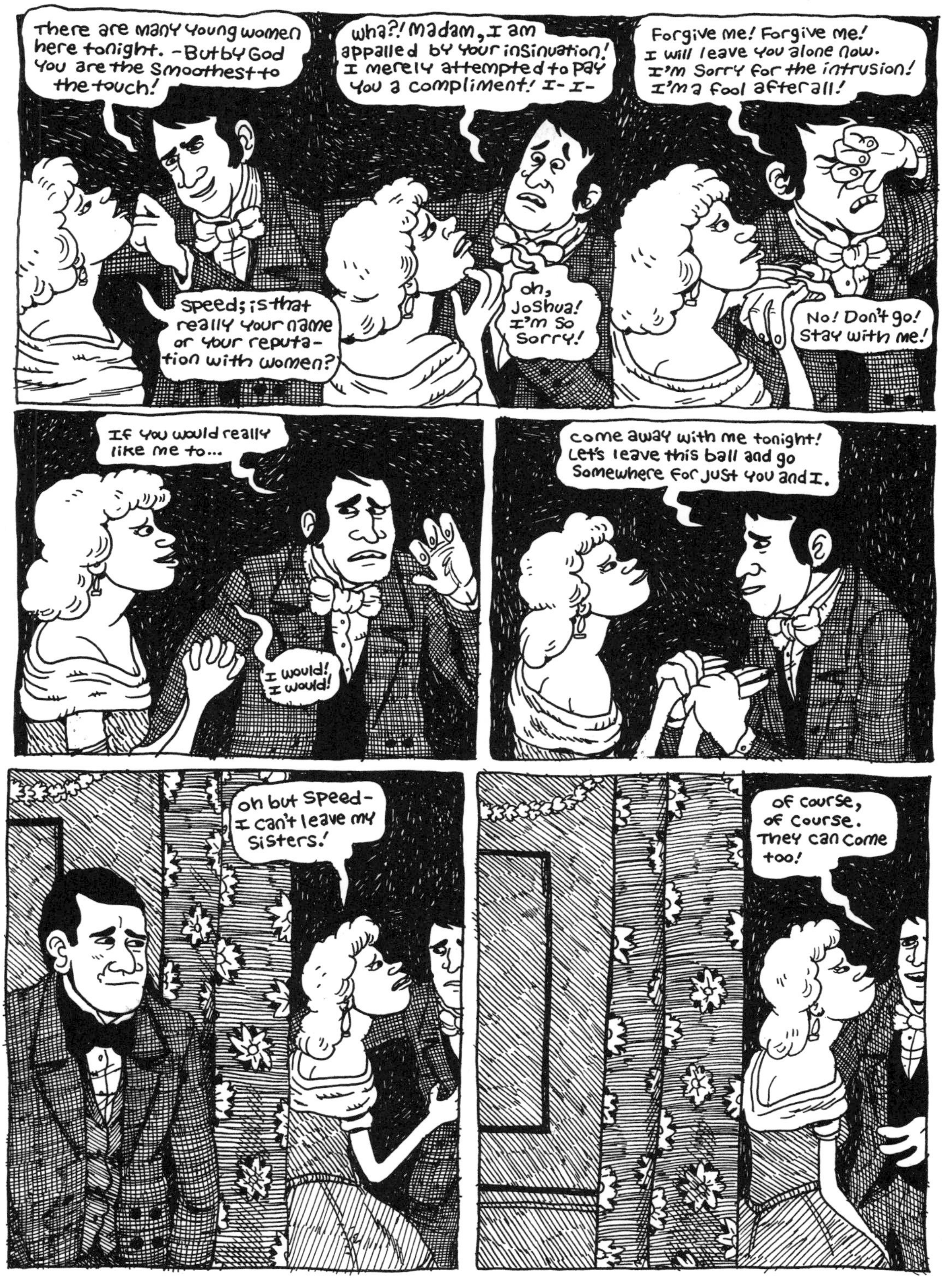
There are many young women here tonight. -But by God you are the smoothest to the touch!
Speed; is that really your name or your reputation with women?
wha?! Madam, I am appalled by your insinuation! I merely attempted to pay you a compliment! I- I-
Oh, Joshua! I'm so sorry!
Forgive me! Forgive me! I will leave you alone now. I'm sorry for the intrusion! I'm a fool after all!
No! Don't go! Stay with me!
If you would really like me to...
I would! I would!
Come away with me tonight! Let's leave this ball and go somewhere for just you and I.
Oh but Speed- I can't leave my sisters!
Of course, of course. They can come too!

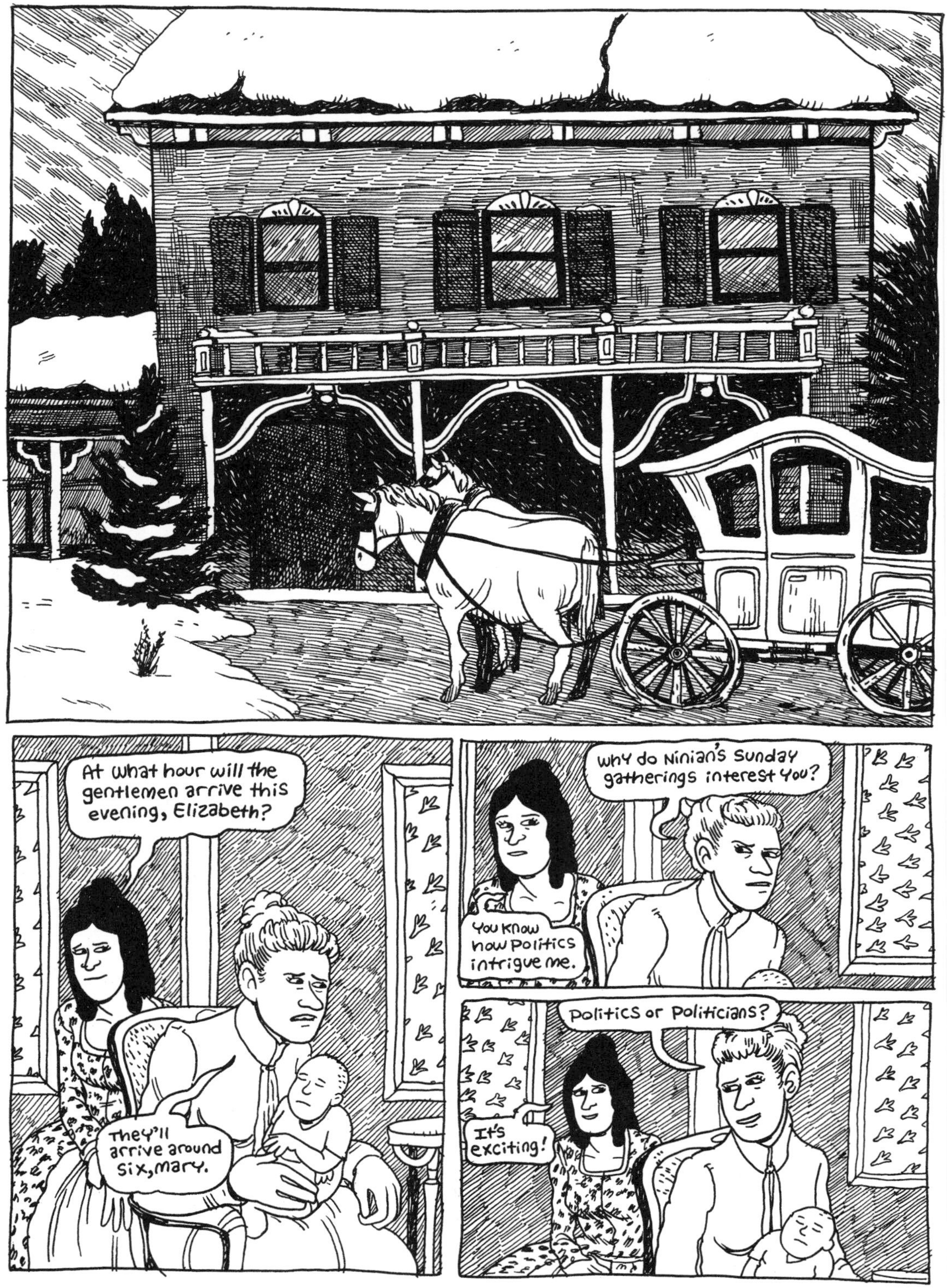
At what hour will the gentlemen arrive this evening, Elizabeth?
They'll arrive around six, Mary.
Why do Ninian's Sunday gatherings interest you?
You know how politics intrigue me.
Politics or politicians?
It's exciting!

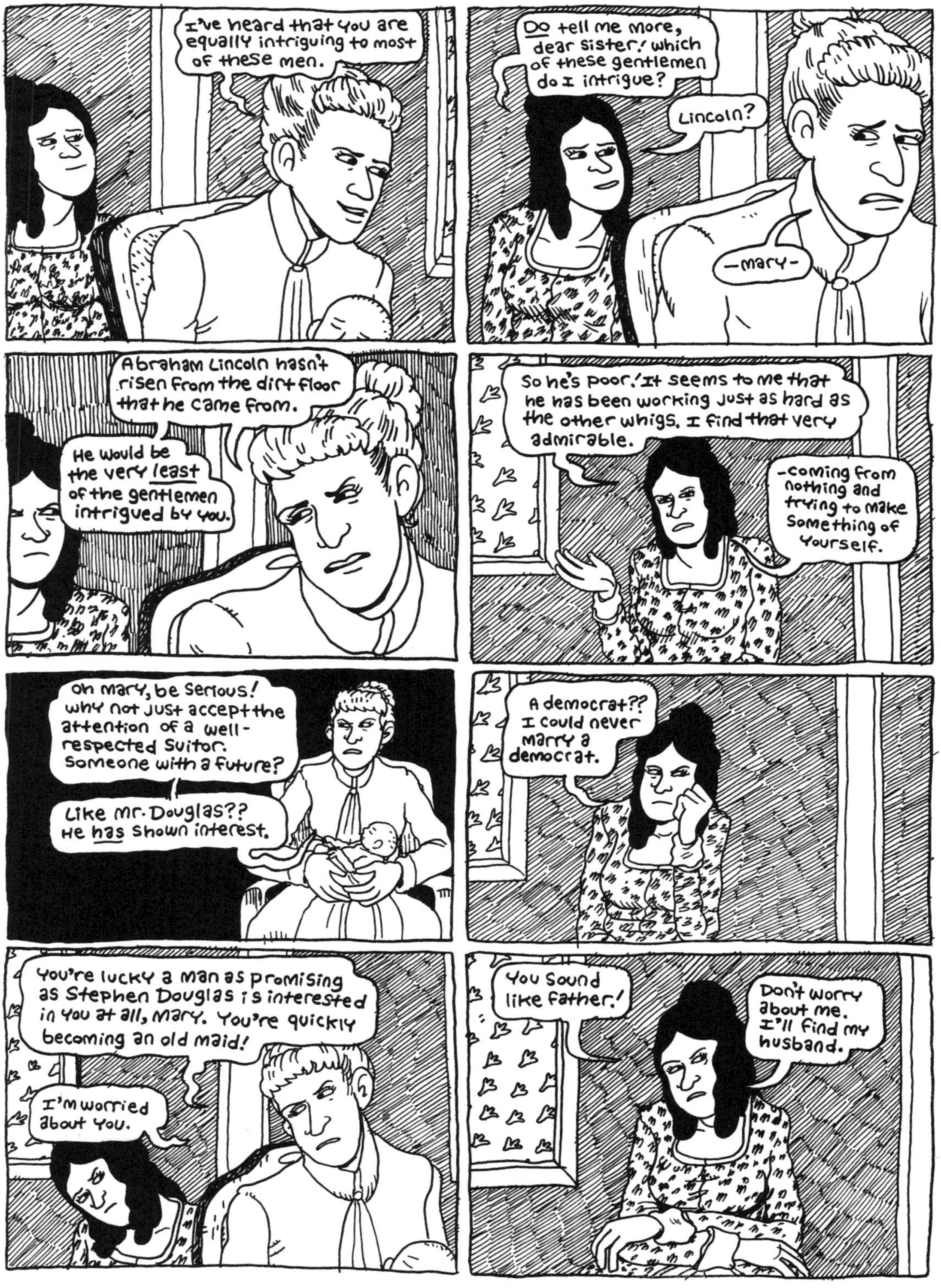
I've heard that you are equally intriguing to most of these men.
Do tell me more, dear sister! which of these gentlemen do I intrigue?
Lincoln?
—mary—
Abraham Lincoln hasn't risen from the dirt floor that he came from.
He would be the very least of the gentlemen intrigued by you.
So he's poor! It seems to me that he has been working just as hard as the other whigs. I find that very admirable.
-coming from nothing and trying to make something of yourself.
oh mary, be serious! why not just accept the attention of a well-respected suitor. Someone with a future?
Like Mr. Douglas?? He has shown interest.
A democrat?? I could never marry a democrat.
You're lucky a man as promising as Stephen Douglas is interested in you at all, mary. You're quickly becoming an old maid!
I'm worried about you.
You sound like father!
Don't worry about me. I'll find my husband.

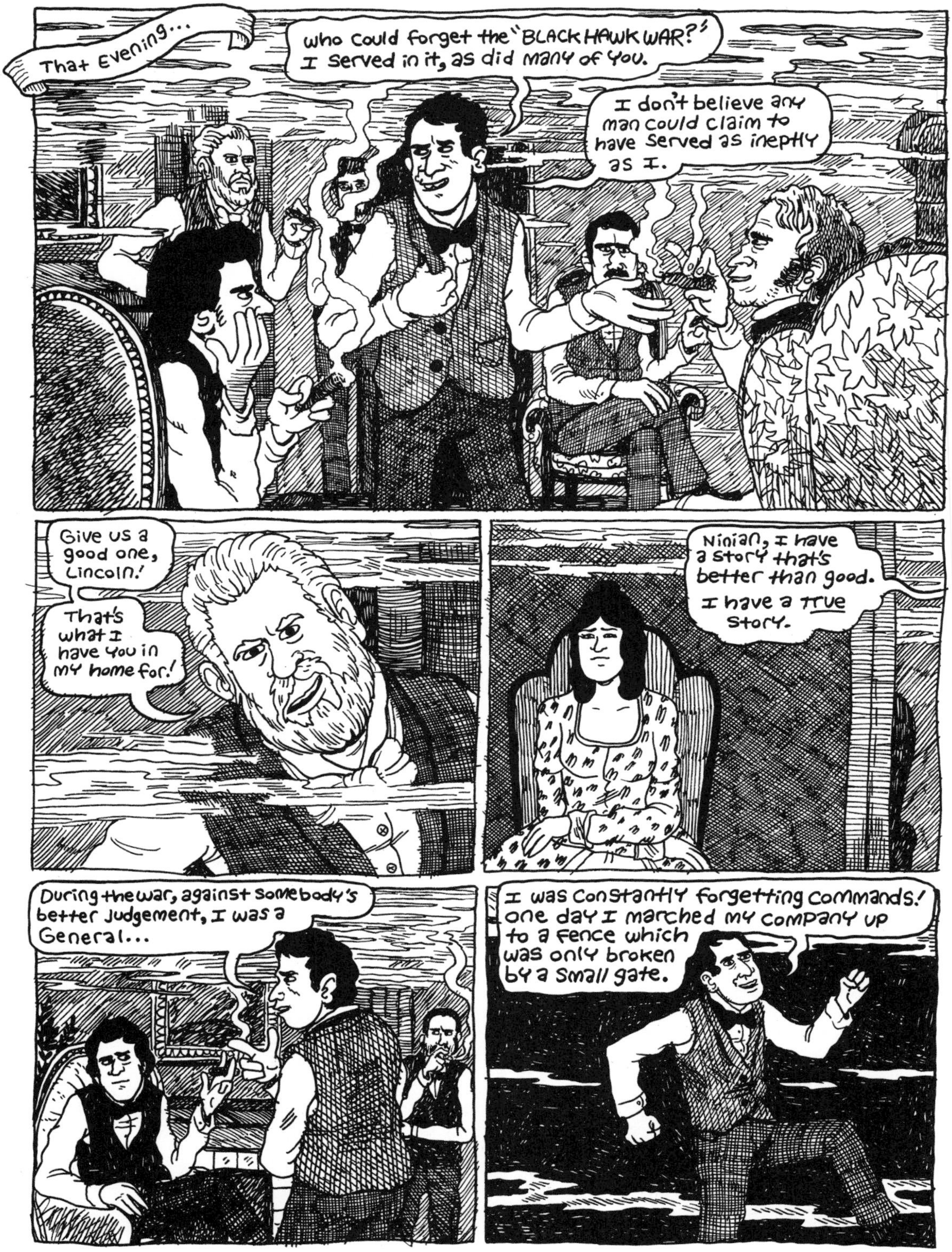
That Evening...
Who could forget the "BLACK HAWK WAR?"
I served in it, as did many of you.
I don't believe any man could claim to have served as ineptly as I.
Give us a good one, Lincoln!
That's what I have you in my home for!
Ninian, I have a story that's better than good.
I have a true story.
During the war, against somebody's better judgement, I was a General...
I was constantly forgetting commands!
One day I marched my company up to a fence which was only broken by a small gate.

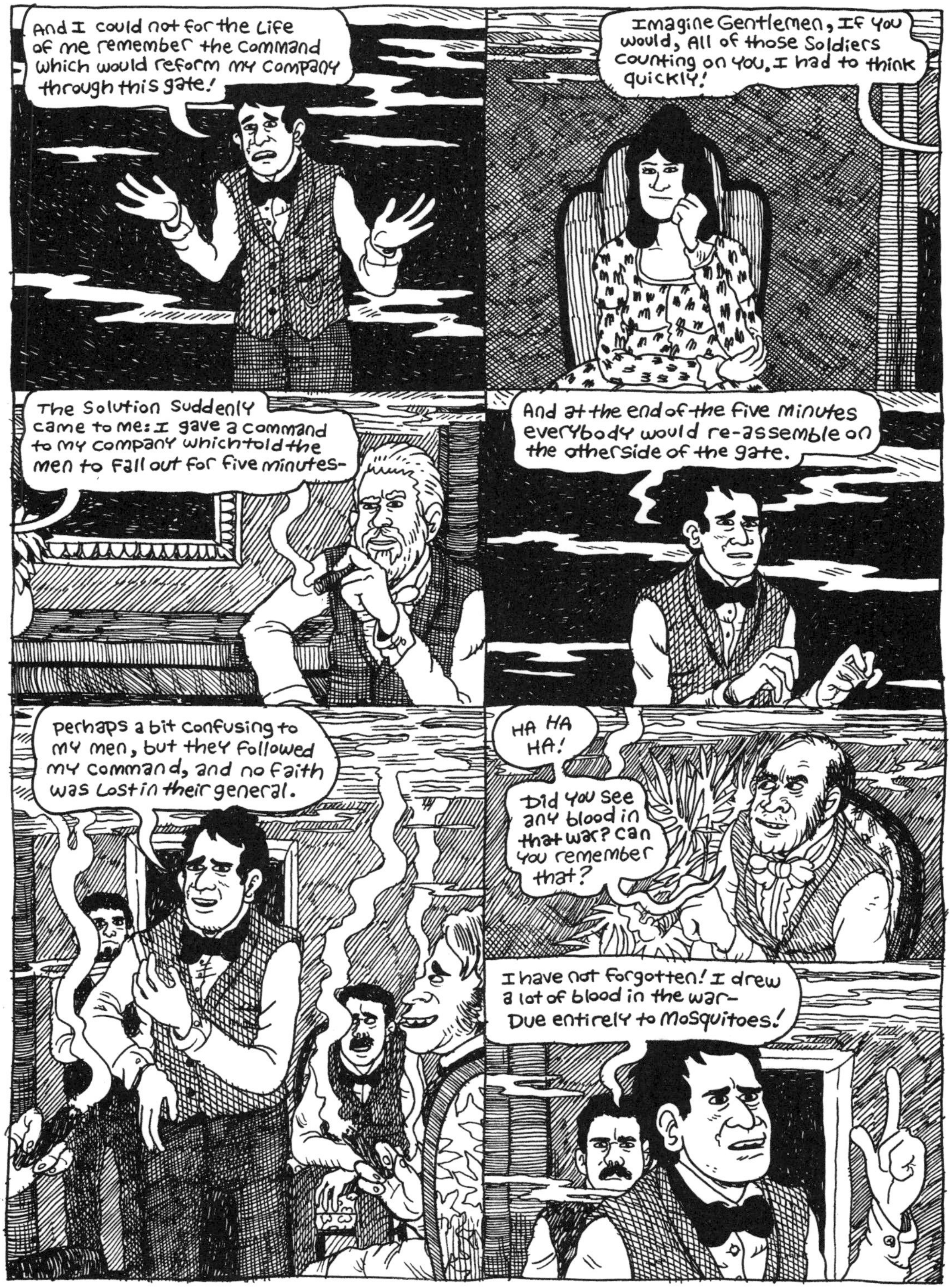
And I could not for the life of me remember the command which would reform my company through this gate!
Imagine Gentlemen, if you would, all of those soldiers counting on you. I had to think quickly!
The solution suddenly came to me: I gave a command to my company which told the men to fall out for five minutes-
And at the end of the five minutes everybody would re-assemble on the otherside of the gate.
Perhaps a bit confusing to my men, but they followed my command, and no faith was lost in their general.
HA HA HA!
Did you see any blood in that war? Can you remember that?
I have not forgotten! I drew a lot of blood in the war- Due entirely to mosquitoes!

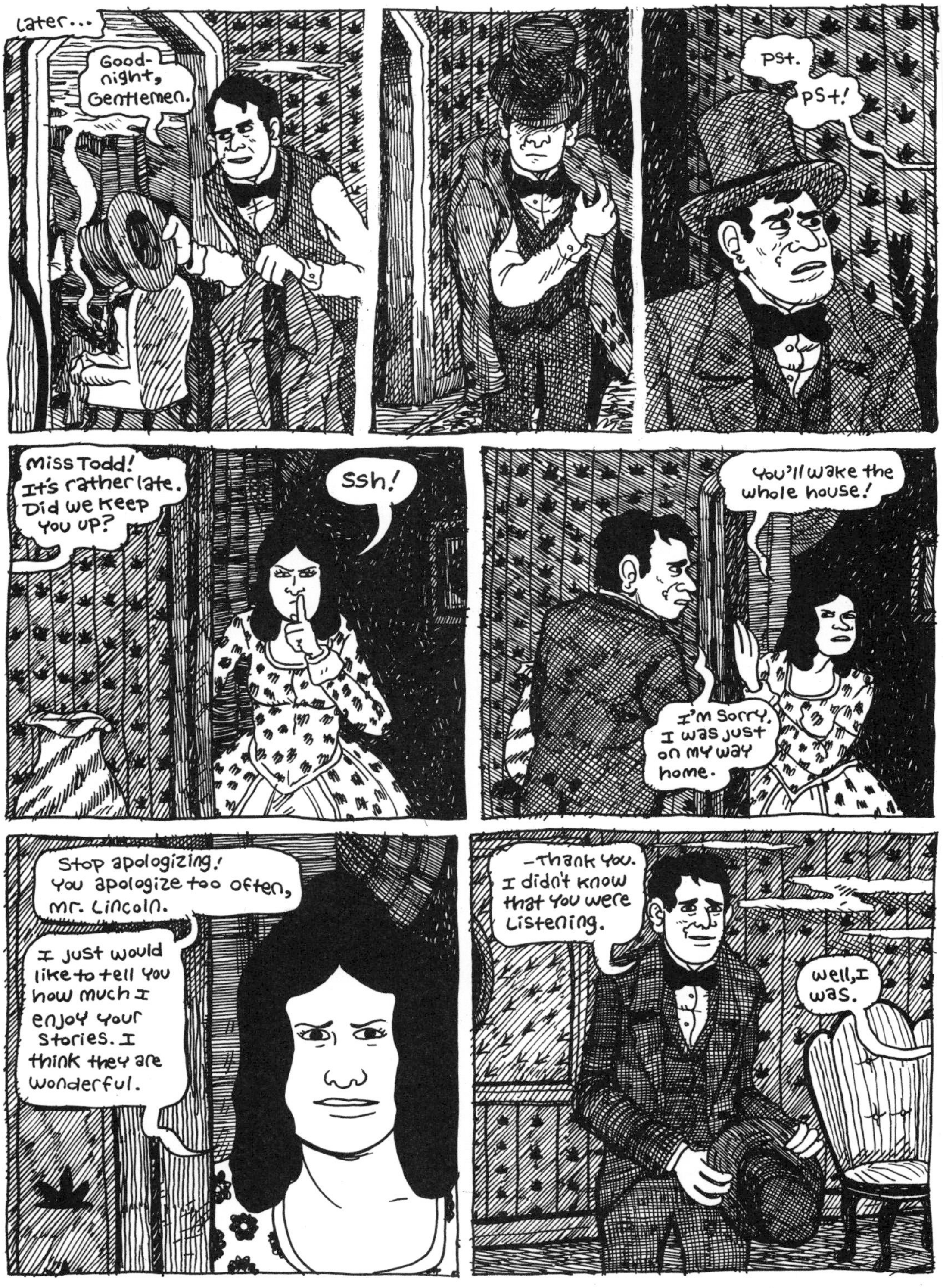
Later...
Good-night, Gentlemen.
Pst.
Pst!
Miss Todd! It's rather late. Did we keep you up?
Ssh!
You'll wake the whole house!
I'm sorry. I was just on my way home.
Stop apologizing! You apologize too often, Mr. Lincoln.
I just would like to tell you how much I enjoy your stories. I think they are wonderful.
—Thank you. I didn't know that you were listening.
Well, I was.

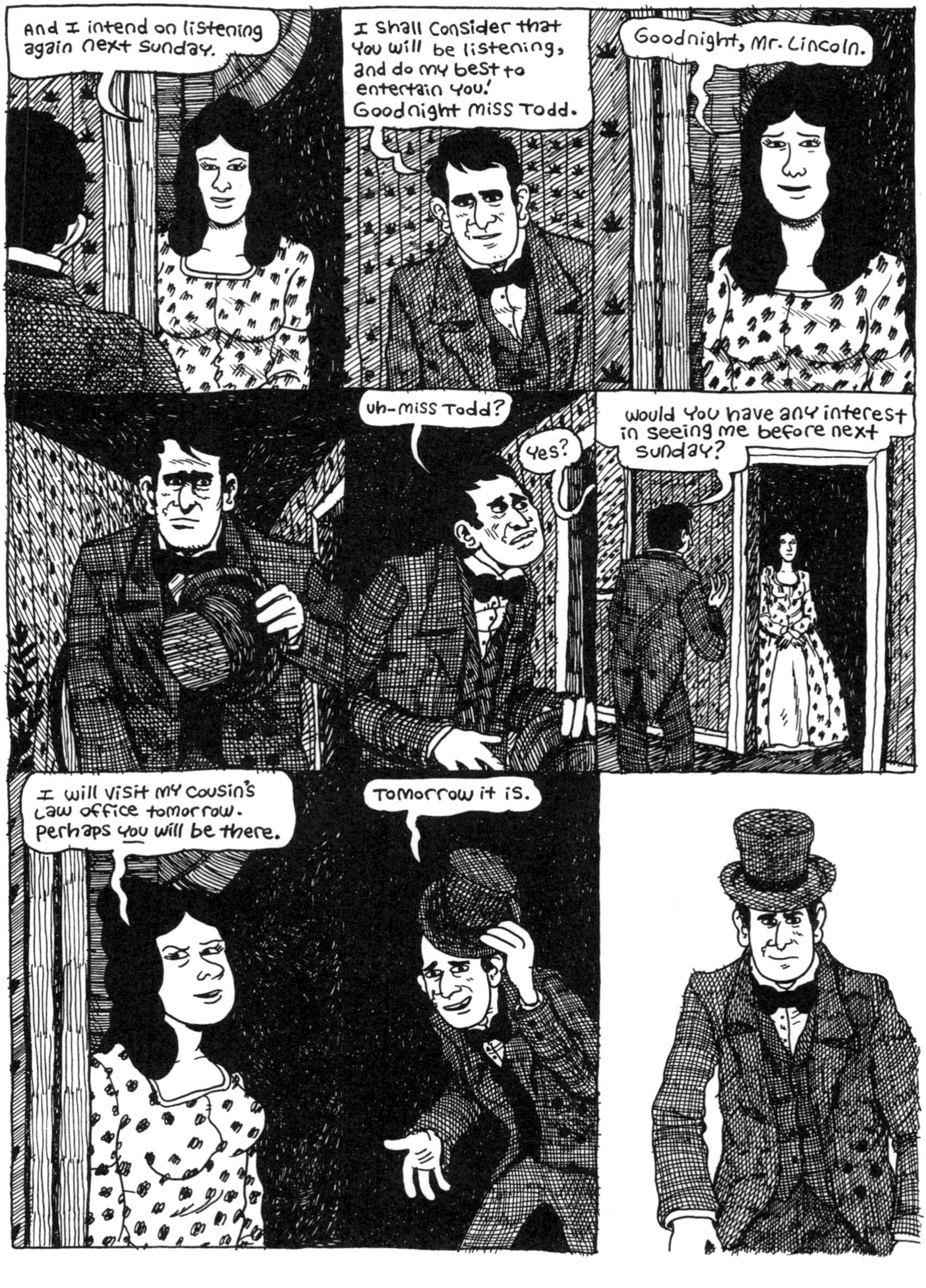
And I intend on listening again next Sunday.
I shall consider that you will be listening, and do my best to entertain you! Goodnight Miss Todd.
Goodnight, Mr. Lincoln.
uh-Miss Todd?
Yes?
Would you have any interest in seeing me before next Sunday?
I will visit my cousin's law office tomorrow. Perhaps you will be there.
Tomorrow it is.

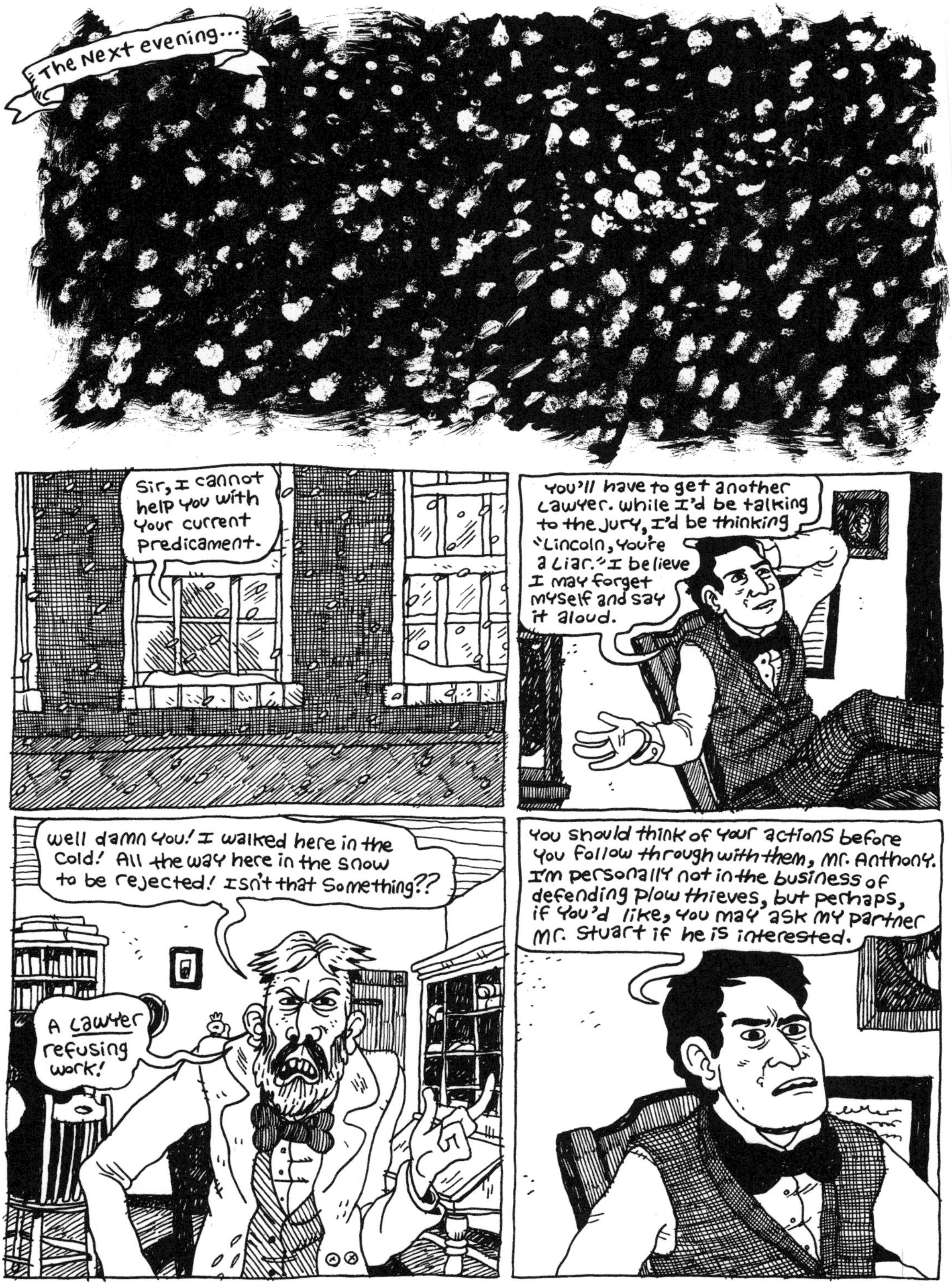
The Next evening...
Sir, I cannot help you with your current predicament.
You'll have to get another Lawyer. While I'd be talking to the Jury, I'd be thinking "Lincoln, You're a Liar." I believe I may forget myself and say it aloud.
Well damn You! I walked here in the Cold! All the way here in the snow to be rejected! Isn't that Something??
A Lawyer refusing work!
You should think of your actions before you follow through with them, Mr. Anthony. I'm personally not in the business of defending plow thieves, but perhaps, if you'd like, you may ask my partner Mr. Stuart if he is interested.

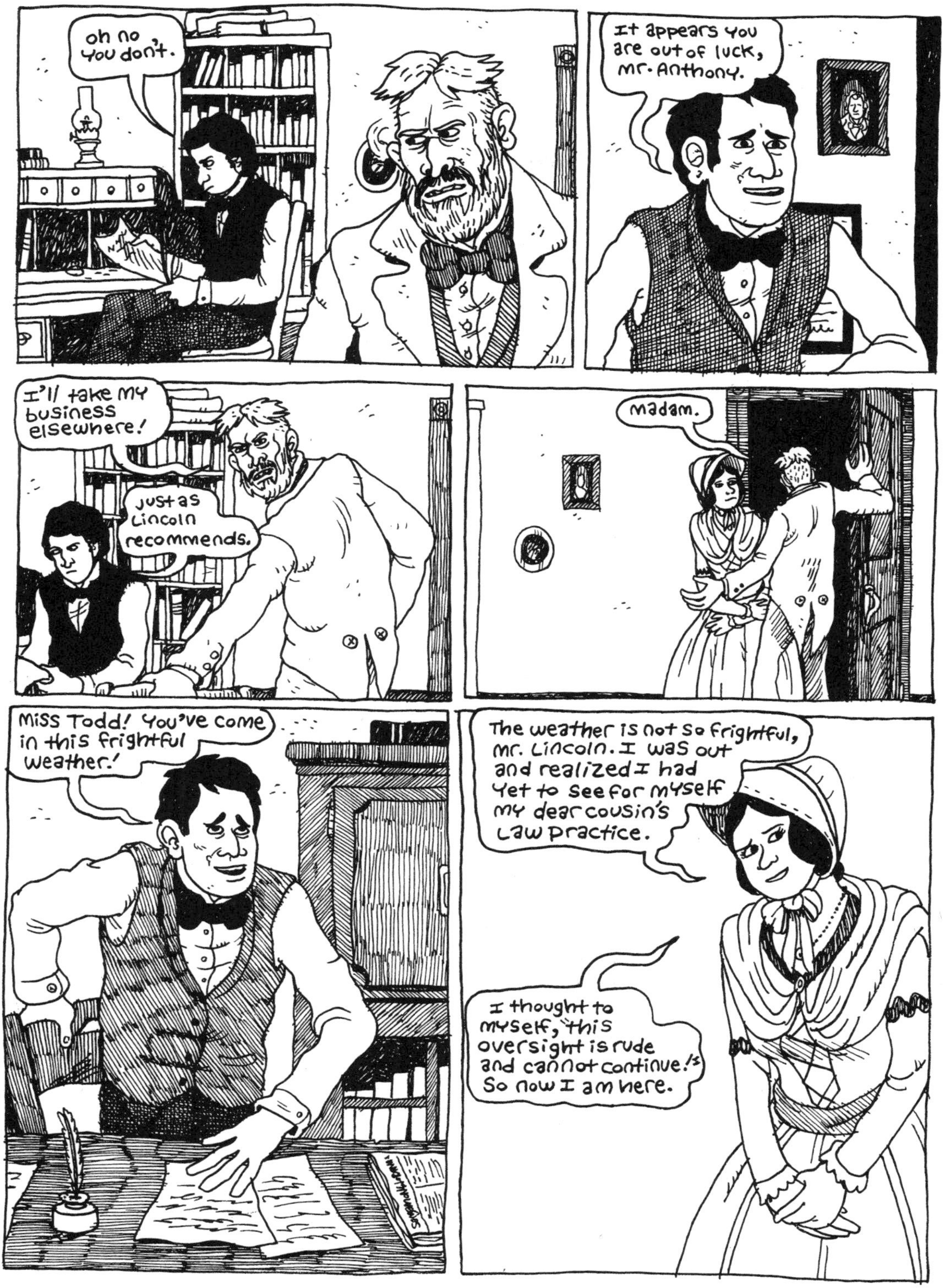
oh no, you don't.
It appears you are out of luck, Mr. Anthony.
I'll take my business elsewhere!
Just as Lincoln recommends.
Madam.
Miss Todd! You've come in this frightful weather!
The weather is not so frightful, Mr. Lincoln. I was out and realized I had yet to see for myself my dear cousin's law practice.
I thought to myself, "this oversight is rude and cannot continue!" So now I am here.

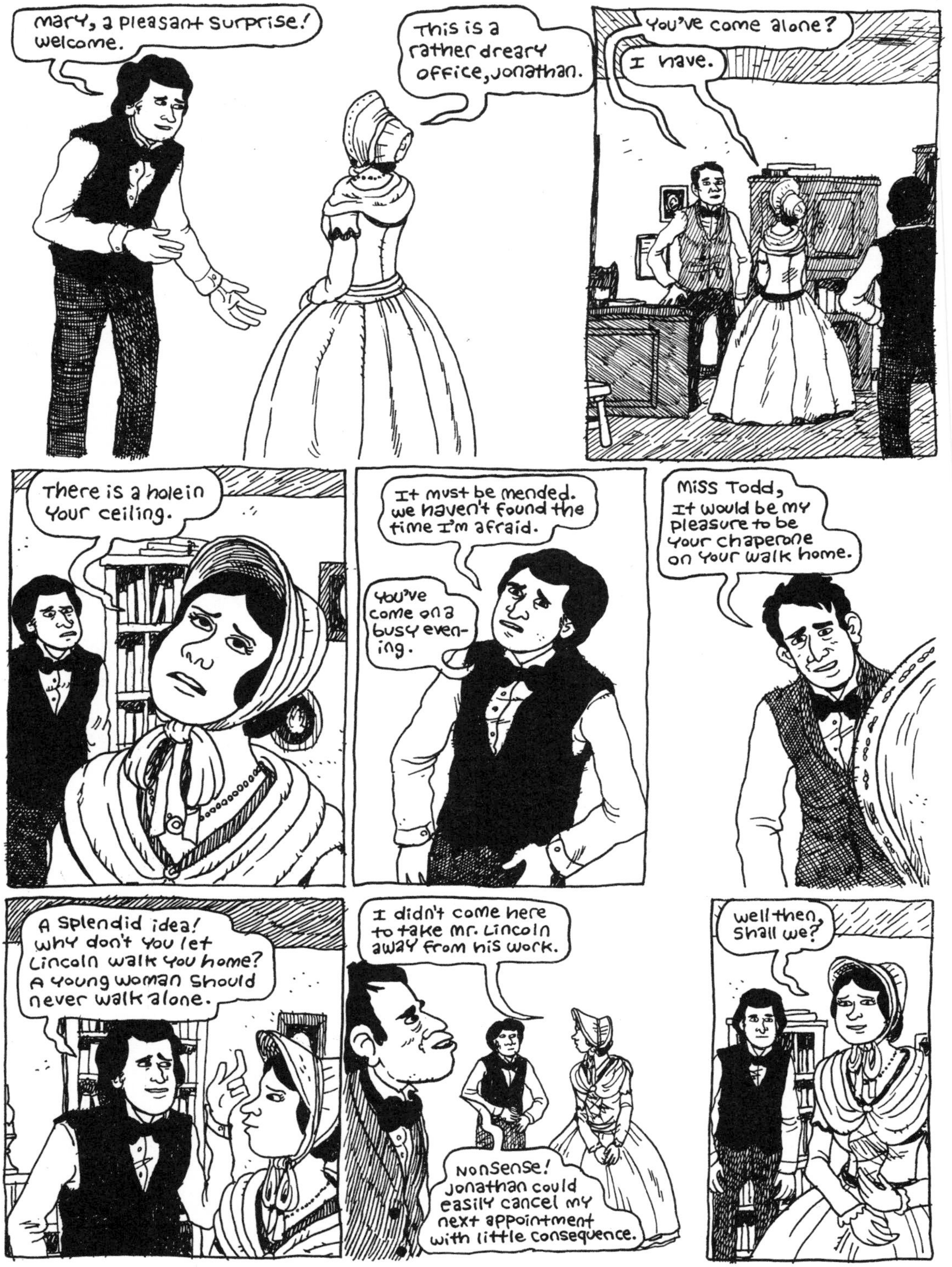
Mary, a pleasant surprise! welcome.
This is a rather dreary office, Jonathan.
You've come alone?
I have.
There is a hole in your ceiling.
It must be mended. we haven't found the time I'm afraid.
You've come on a busy evening.
Miss Todd, It would be my pleasure to be your chaperone on your walk home.
A splendid idea! why don't you let Lincoln walk you home? A young woman should never walk alone.
I didn't come here to take Mr. Lincoln away from his work.
Nonsense! Jonathan could easily cancel my next appointment with little consequence.
well then, Shall we?

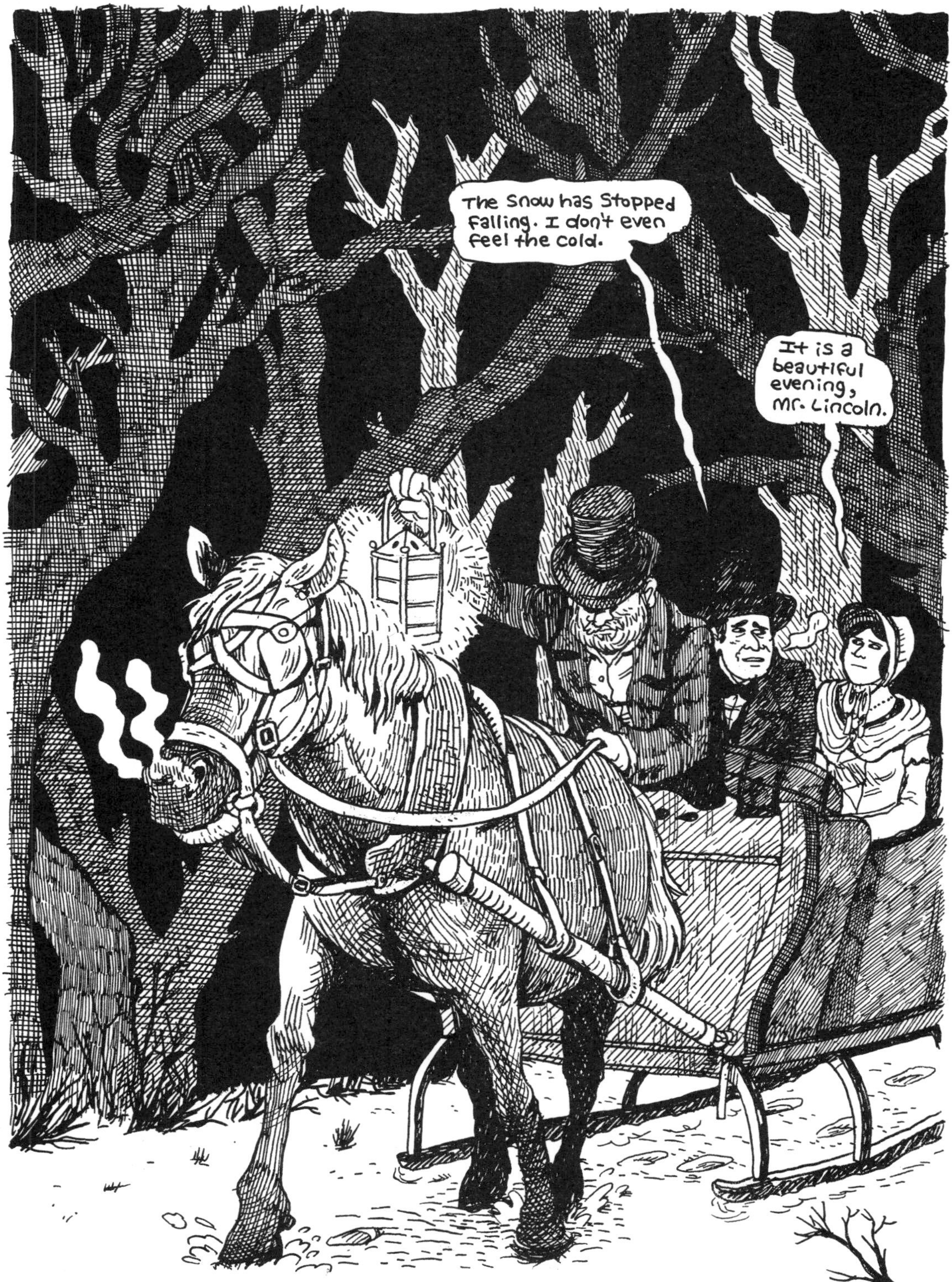
The snow has stopped falling. I don't even feel the cold.
It is a beautiful evening, Mr. Lincoln.

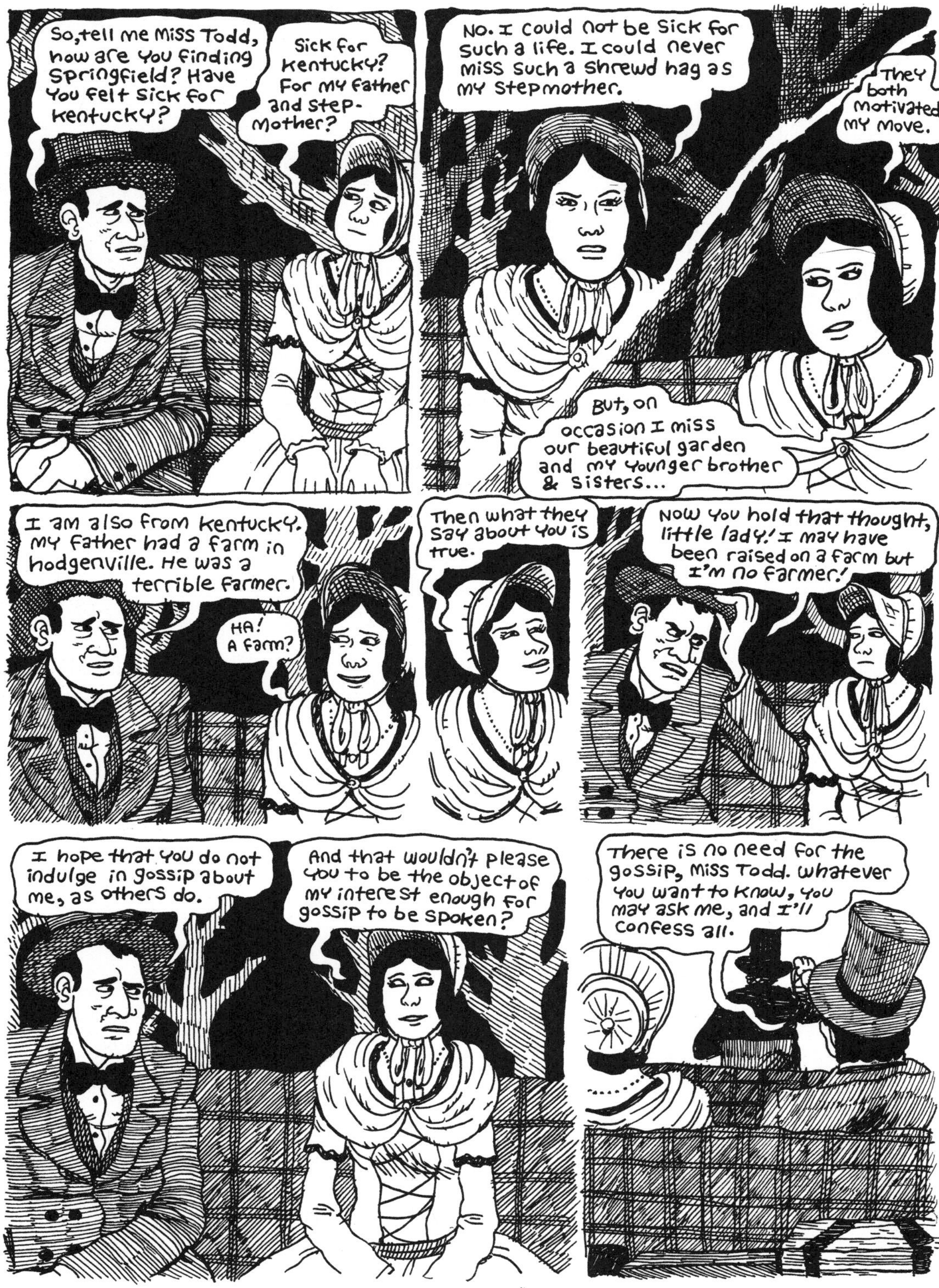
So, tell me Miss Todd, how are you finding Springfield? Have you felt sick for Kentucky?
Sick for Kentucky? For my father and step-mother?
No. I could not be sick for such a life. I could never miss such a shrewd hag as my stepmother.
They both motivated my move.
But, on occasion I miss our beautiful garden and my younger brother & sisters...
I am also from Kentucky. My father had a farm in Hodgenville. He was a terrible farmer.
HA! A farm?
Then what they say about you is true.
Now you hold that thought, little lady! I may have been raised on a farm but I'm no farmer!
I hope that you do not indulge in gossip about me, as others do.
And that wouldn't please you to be the object of my interest enough for gossip to be spoken?
There is no need for the gossip, Miss Todd. Whatever you want to know, you may ask me, and I'll confess all.

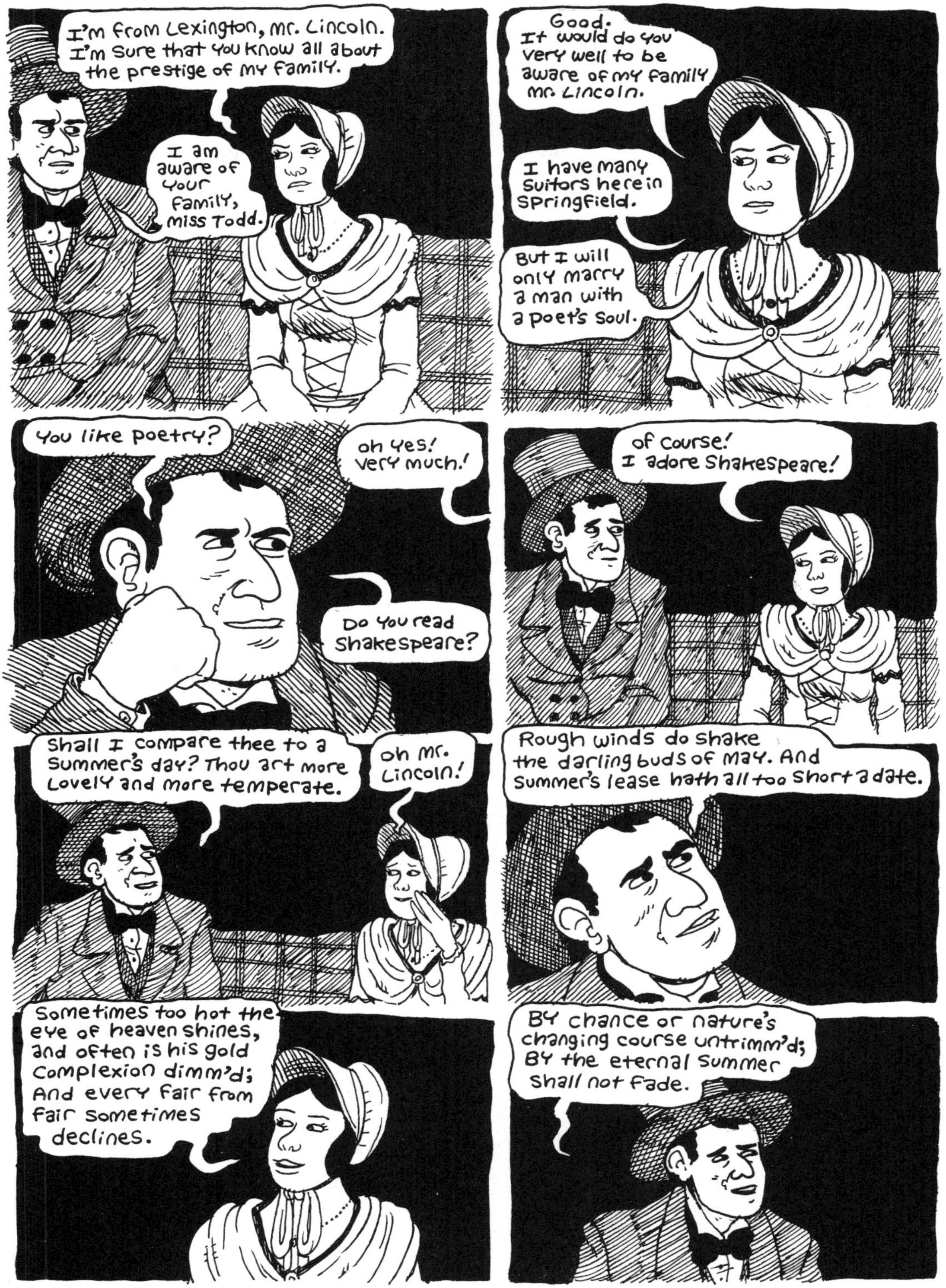
I'm from Lexington, Mr. Lincoln. I'm sure that you know all about the prestige of my family.
I am aware of your family, Miss Todd.
Good. It would do you very well to be aware of my family Mr. Lincoln.
I have many suitors here in Springfield.
But I will only marry a man with a poet's soul.
You like poetry?
Oh yes! Very much!
Do you read Shakespeare?
Of course! I adore Shakespeare!
Shall I compare thee to a summer's day? Thou art more lovely and more temperate.
Oh Mr. Lincoln!
Rough winds do shake the darling buds of May. And summer's lease hath all too short a date.
Sometimes too hot the eye of heaven shines, and often is his gold complexion dimm'd; And every fair from fair sometimes declines.
By chance or nature's changing course untrimm'd; By the eternal summer shall not fade.

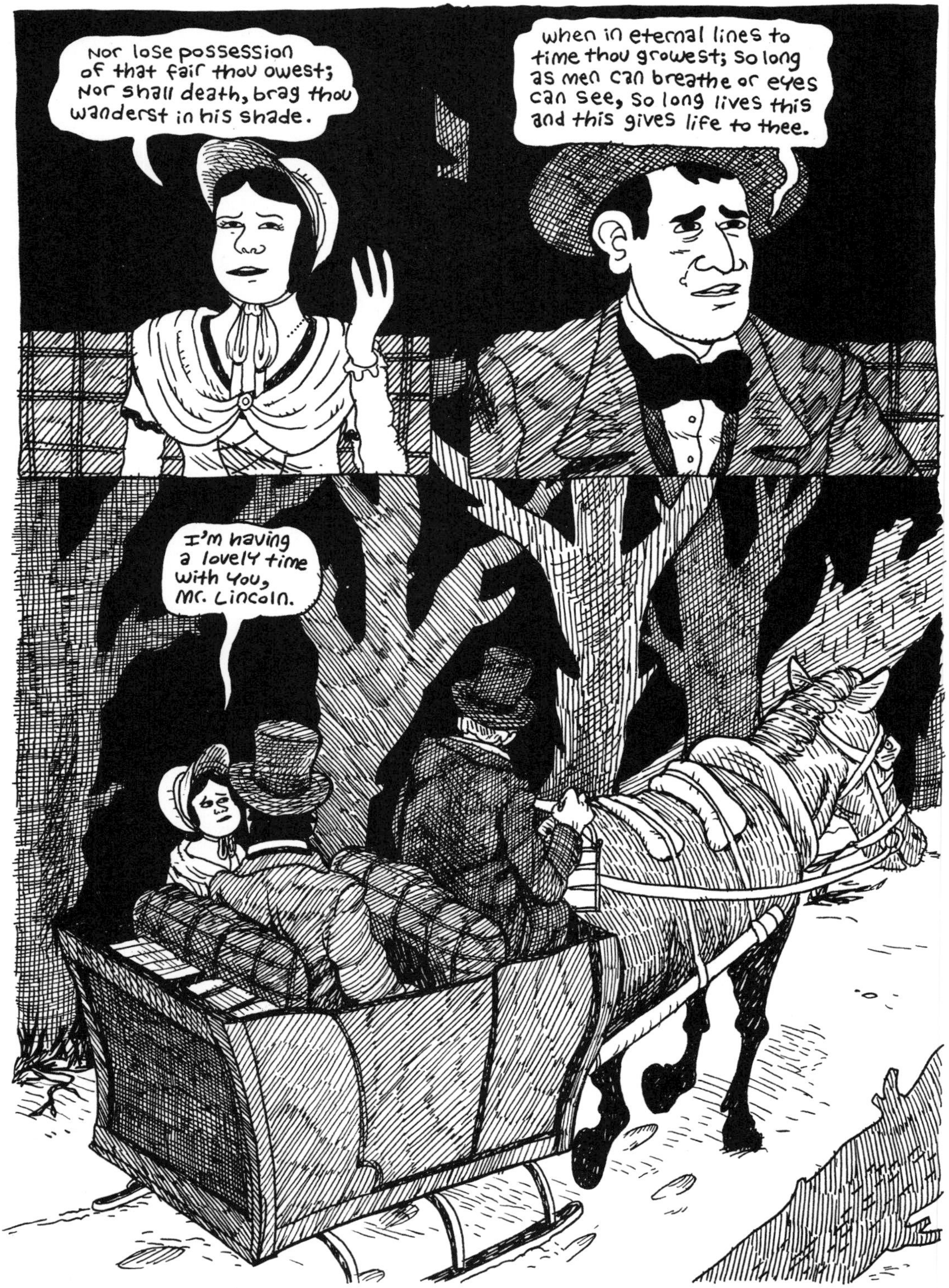
Nor lose possession of that fair thou owest; Nor shall death, brag thou wanderst in his shade.
when in eternal lines to time thou growest; so long as men can breathe or eyes can see, so long lives this and this gives life to thee.
I'm having a lovely time with you, Mr. Lincoln.

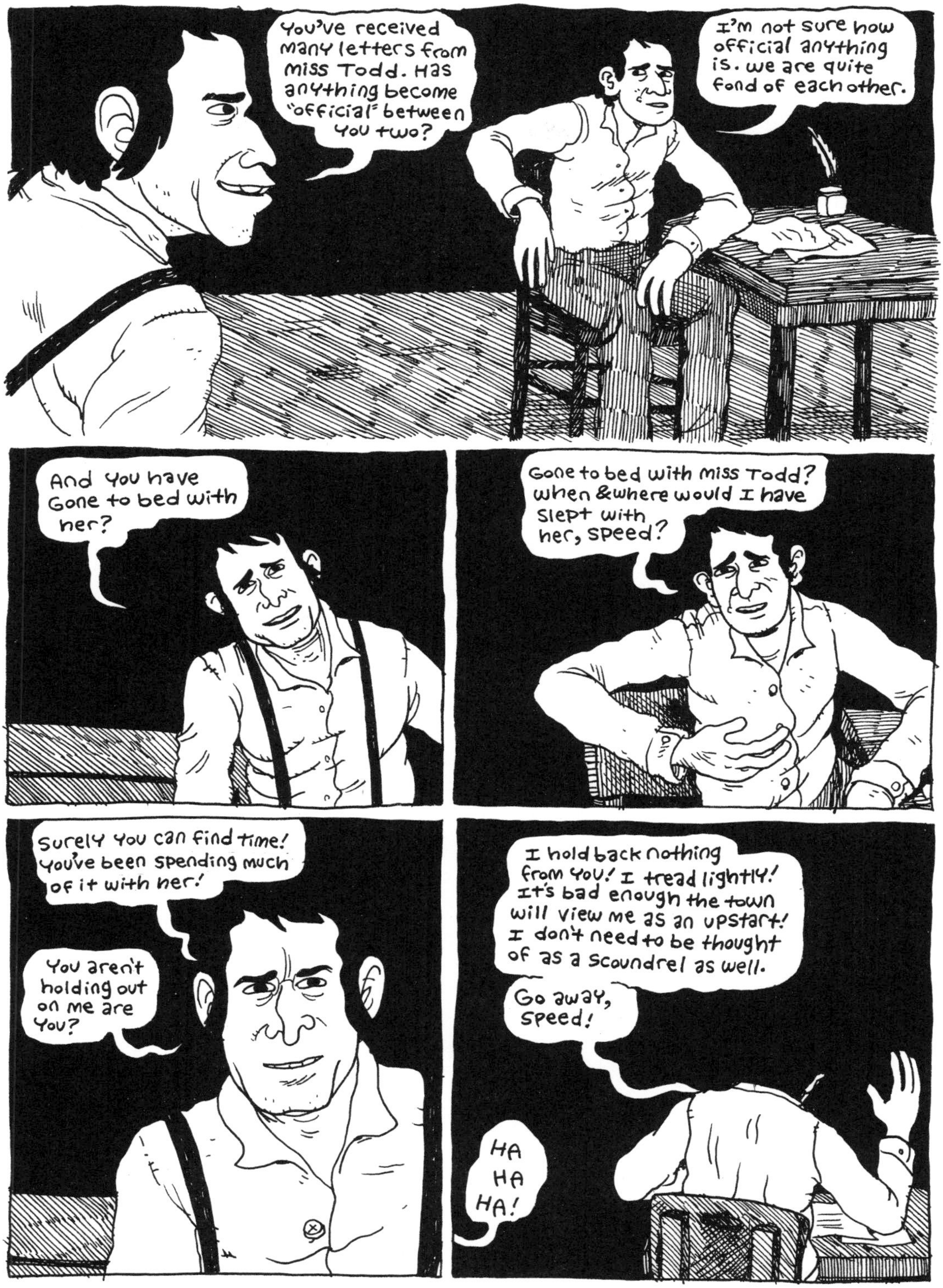
You've received many letters from miss Todd. Has anything become "official" between you two?
I'm not sure how official anything is. we are quite fond of each other.
And you have Gone to bed with her?
Gone to bed with miss Todd? when & where would I have slept with her, speed?
Surely you can find time! you've been spending much of it with her!
You aren't holding out on me are you?
I hold back nothing from you! I tread lightly! It's bad enough the town will view me as an upstart! I don't need to be thought of as a scoundrel as well.
Go away, speed!
HA HA HA!

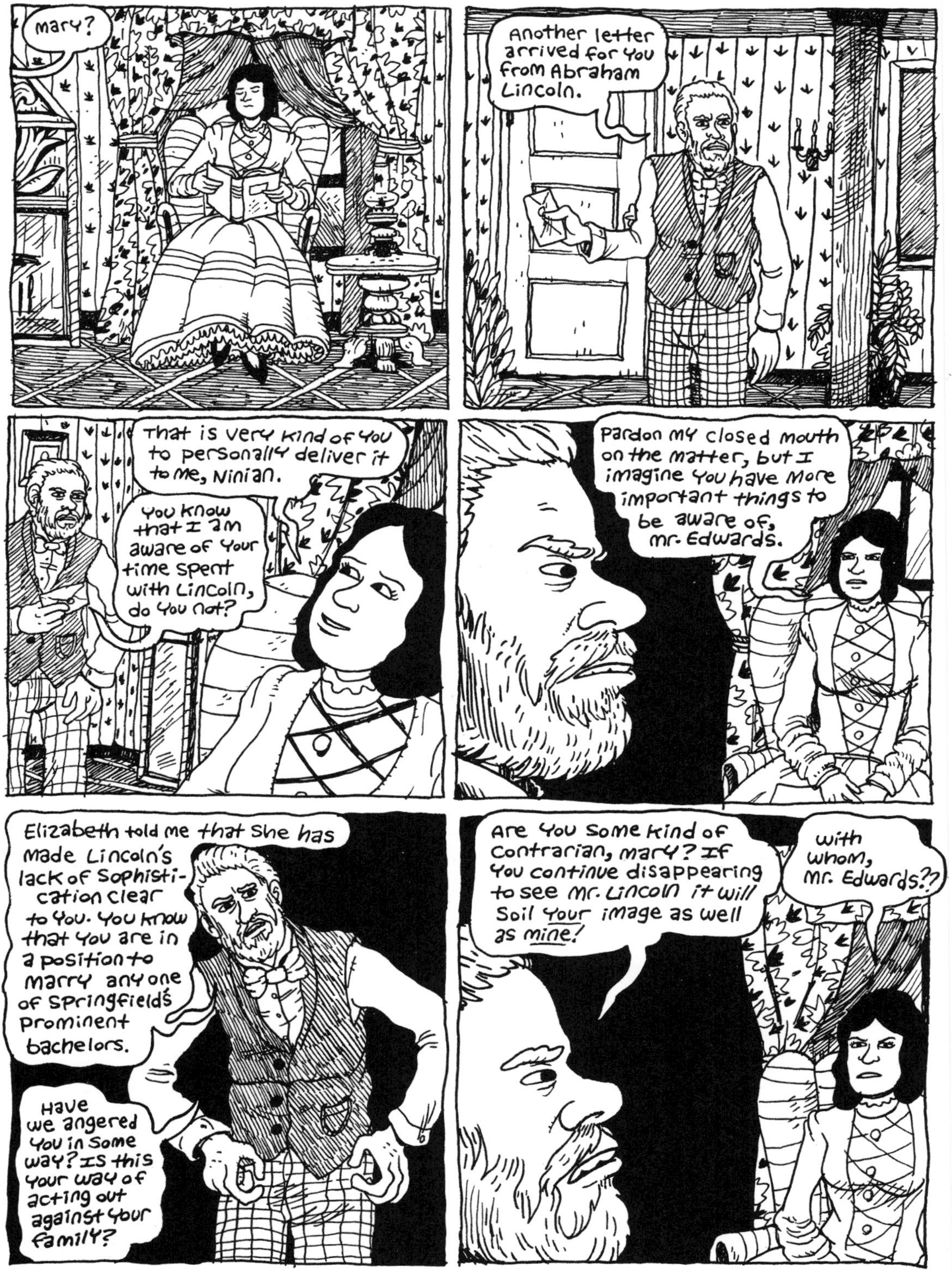
Mary?
Another letter arrived for you from Abraham Lincoln.
That is very kind of you to personally deliver it to me, Ninian.
You know that I am aware of your time spent with Lincoln, do you not?
Pardon my closed mouth on the matter, but I imagine you have more important things to be aware of, Mr. Edwards.
Elizabeth told me that she has made Lincoln's lack of sophistication clear to you. You know that you are in a position to marry any one of Springfield's prominent bachelors.
Have we angered you in some way? Is this your way of acting out against your family?
Are you some kind of contrarian, Mary? If you continue disappearing to see Mr. Lincoln it will soil your image as well as mine!
With whom, Mr. Edwards??

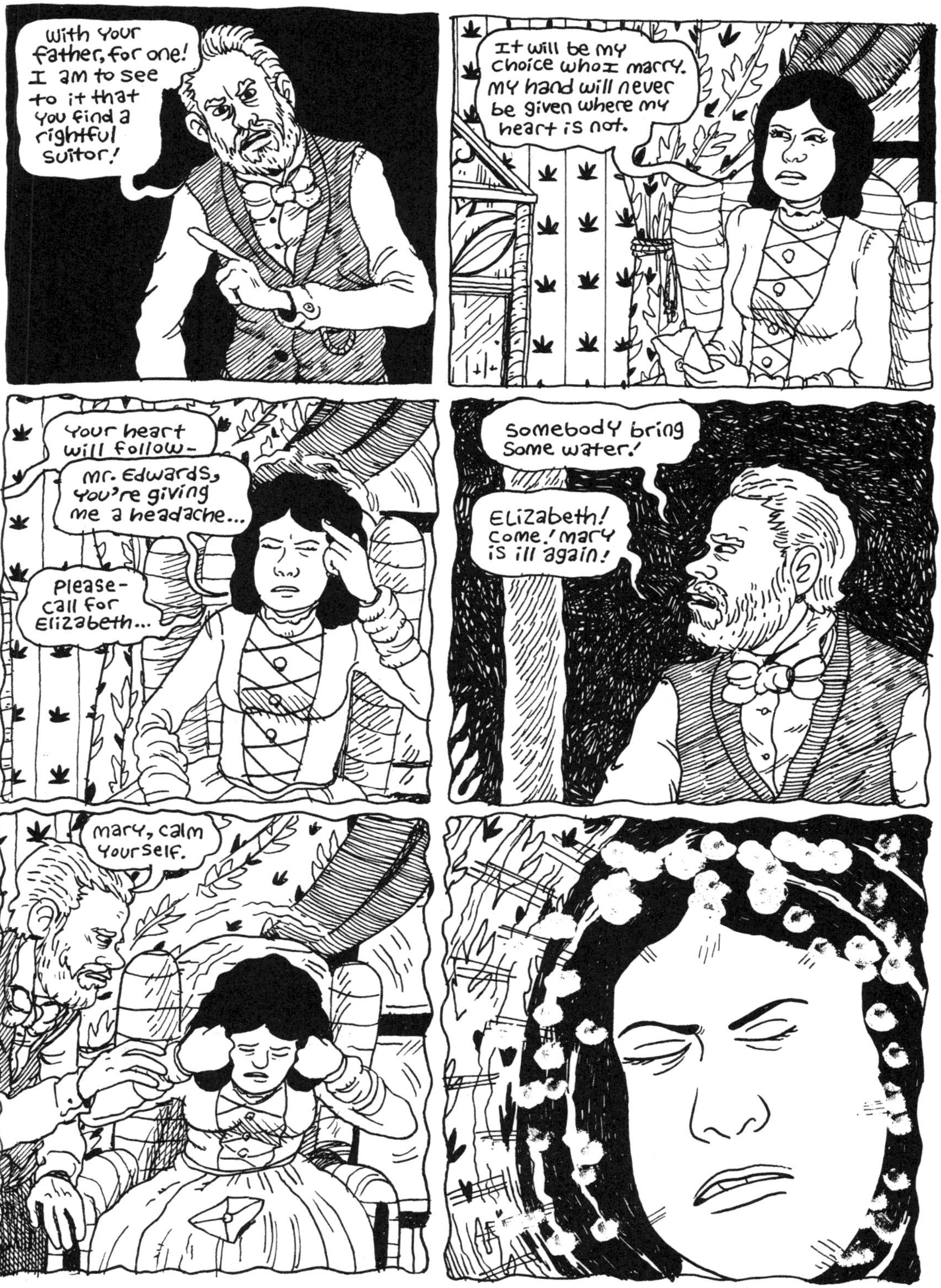
With your father, for one! I am to see to it that you find a rightful suitor!
It will be my choice who I marry. My hand will never be given where my heart is not.
Your heart will follow-
Mr. Edwards, you're giving me a headache...
Please- call for Elizabeth...
Somebody bring some water!
Elizabeth! Come! Mary is ill again!
Mary, calm yourself.

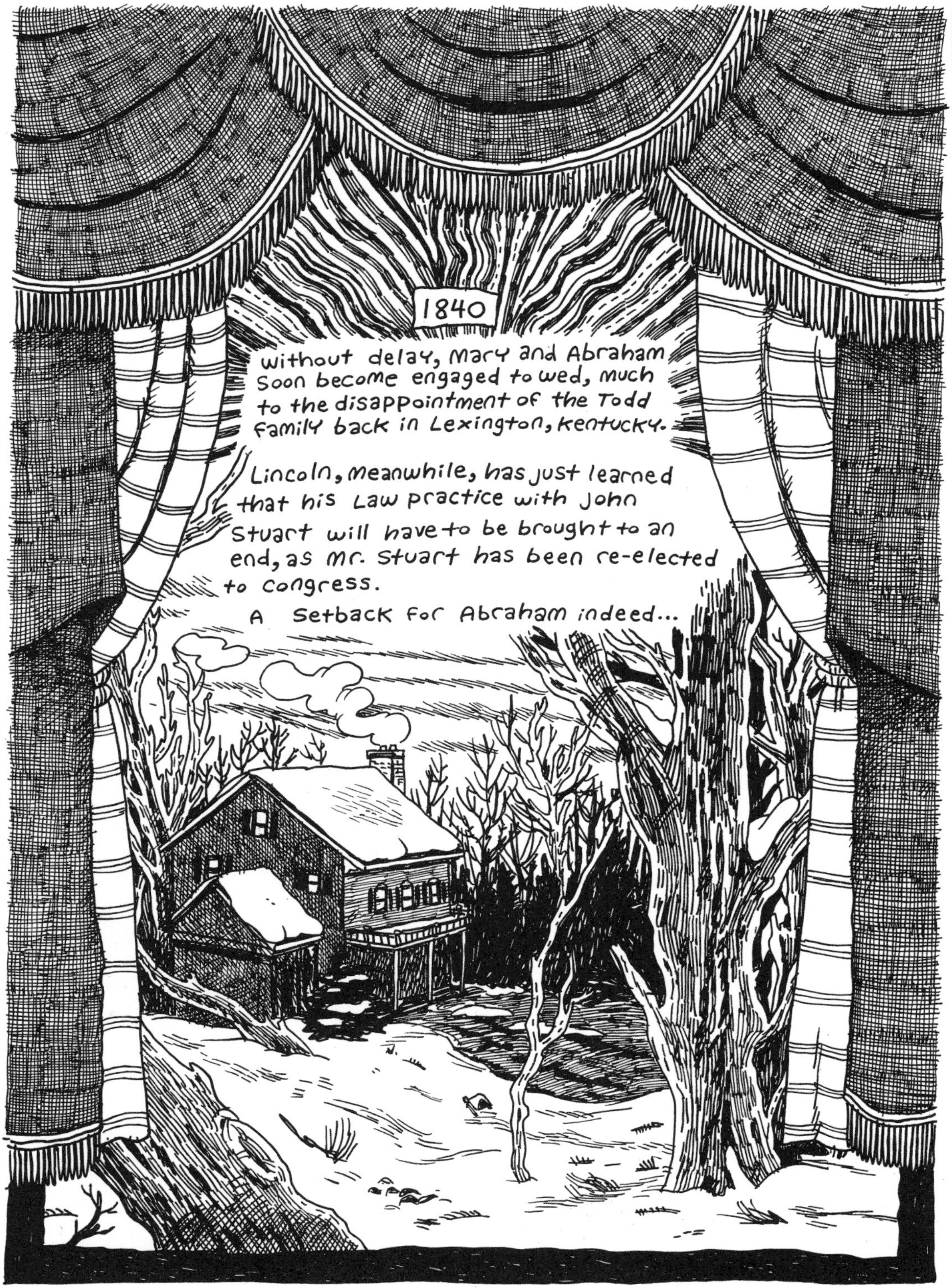
1840
Without delay, Mary and Abraham soon become engaged to wed, much to the disappointment of the Todd family back in Lexington, Kentucky.
Lincoln, meanwhile, has just learned that his law practice with John Stuart will have to be brought to an end, as Mr. Stuart has been re-elected to Congress.
A setback for Abraham indeed...

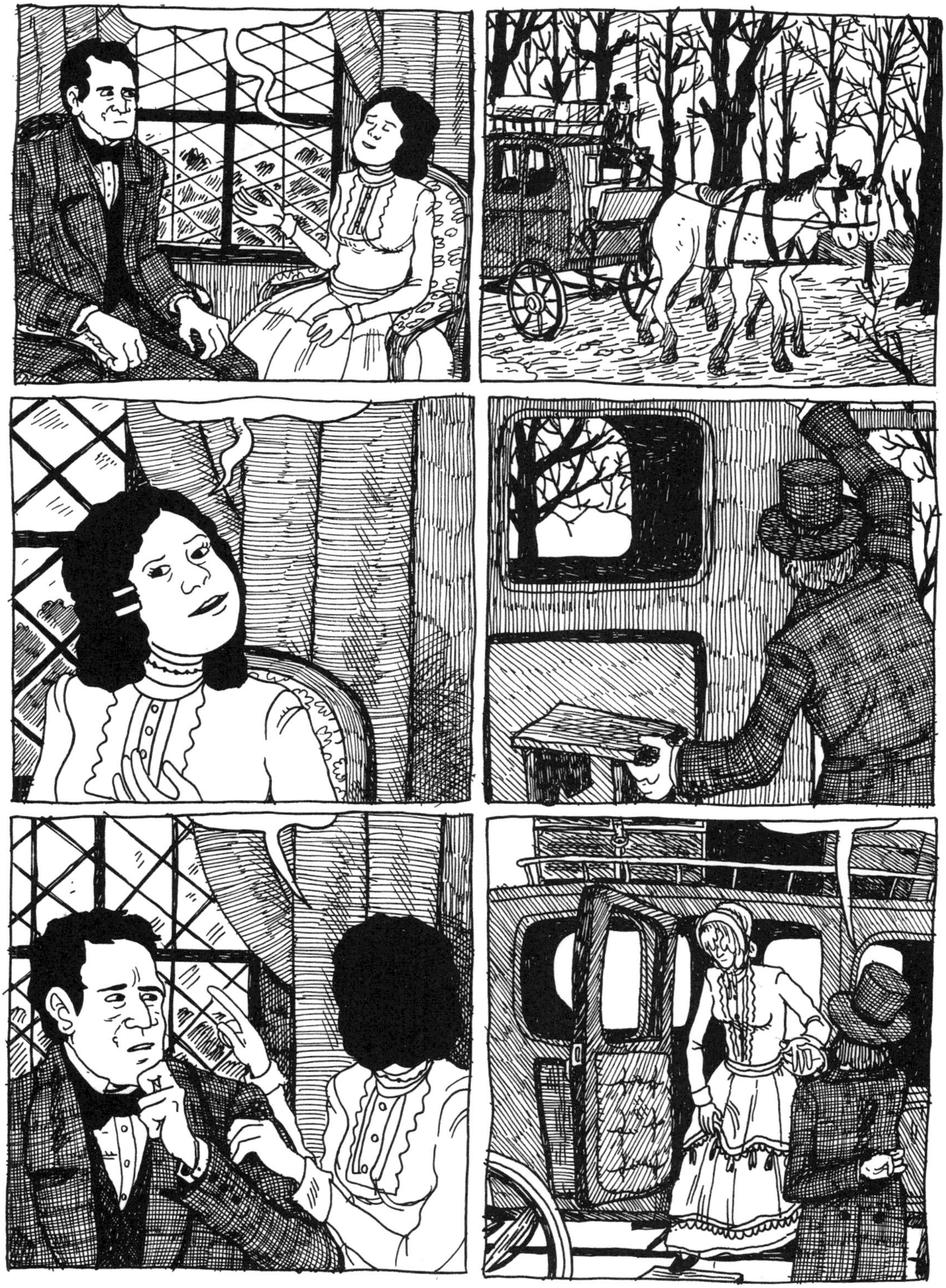

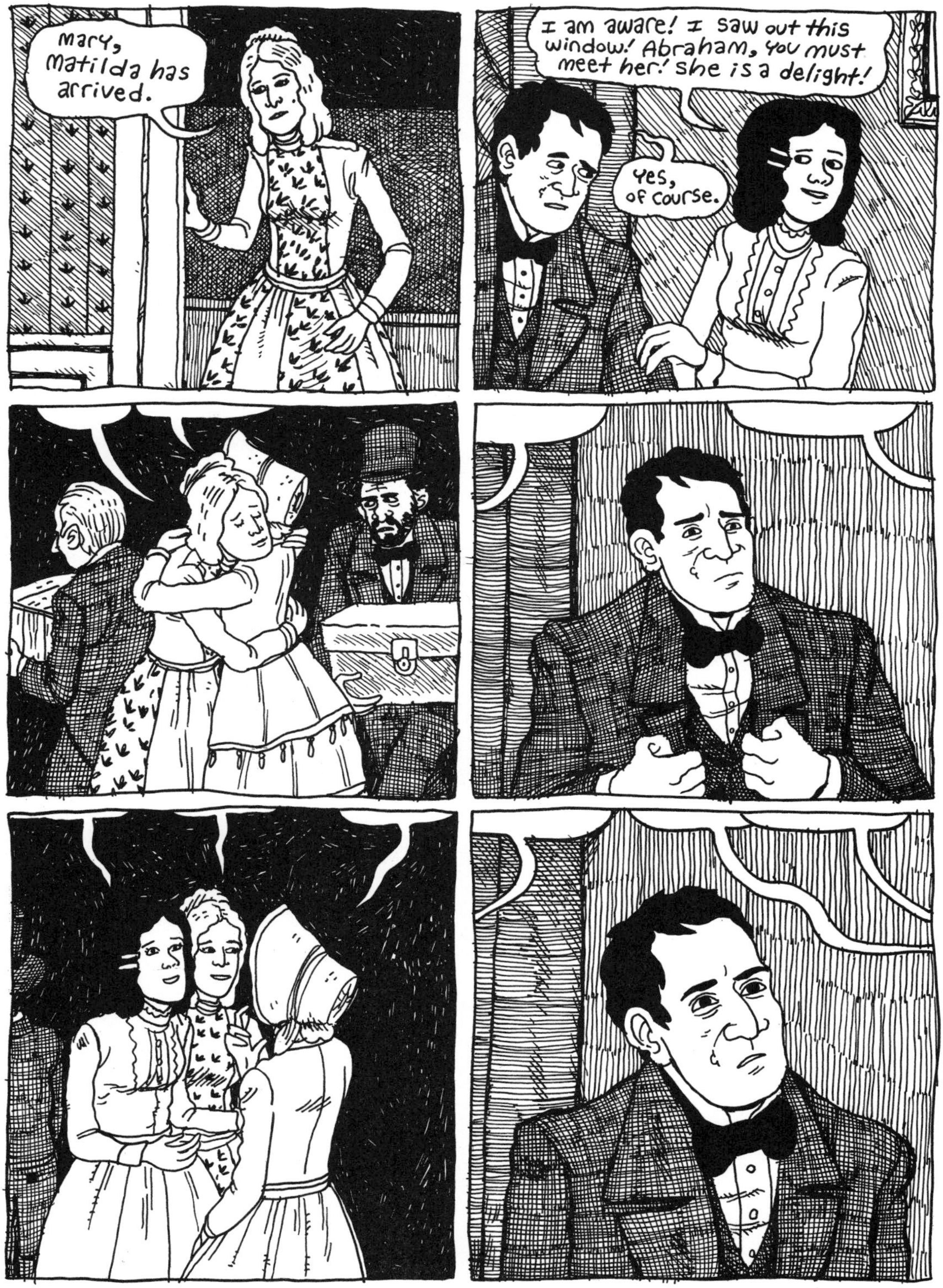
Mary, Matilda has arrived.
I am aware! I saw out this window! Abraham, you must meet her! She is a delight!
Yes, of course.

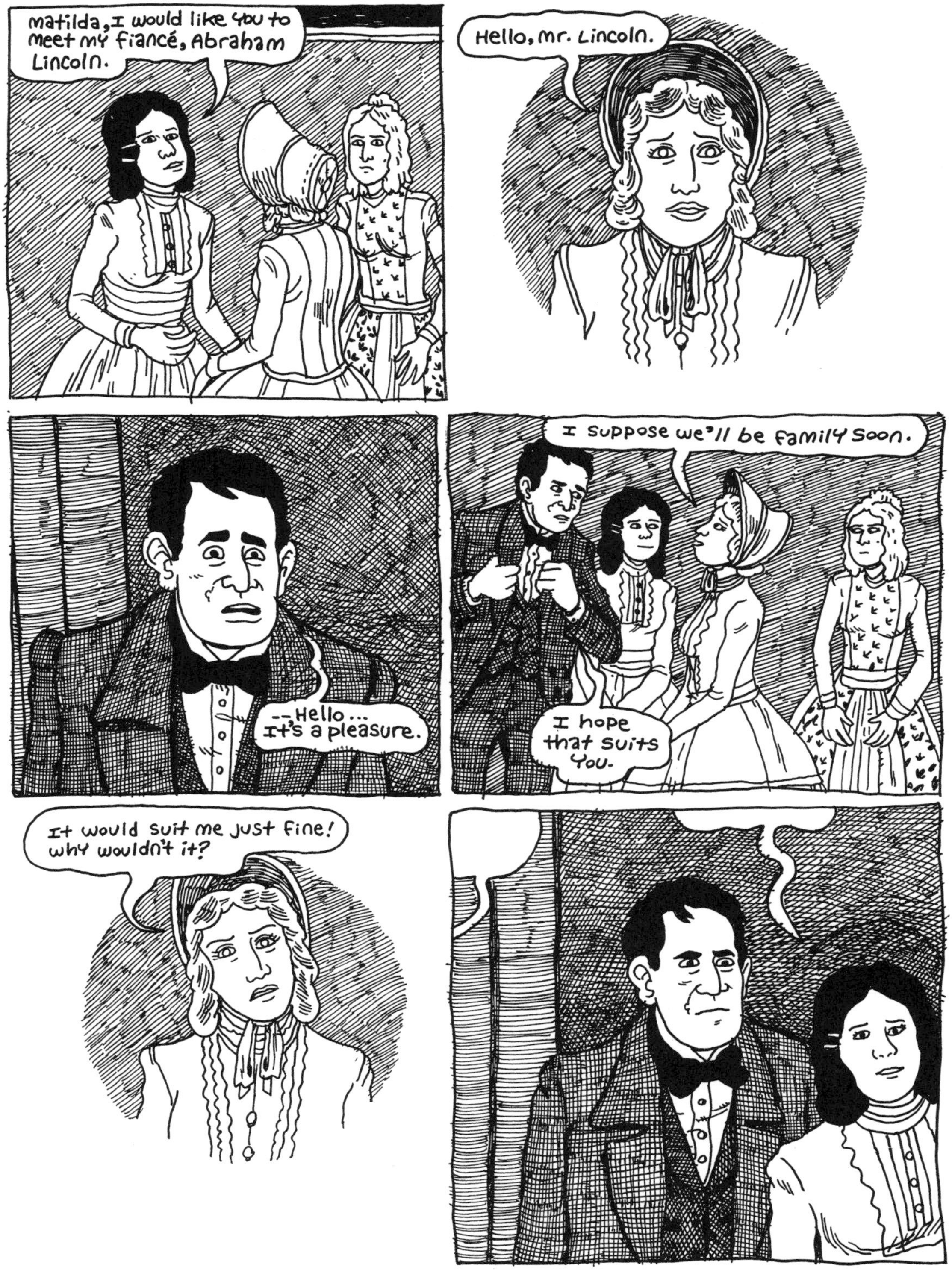
Matilda, I would like you to meet my fiancé, Abraham Lincoln.
Hello, Mr. Lincoln.
--Hello... It's a pleasure.
I suppose we'll be family soon.
I hope that suits you.
It would suit me just fine! Why wouldn't it?

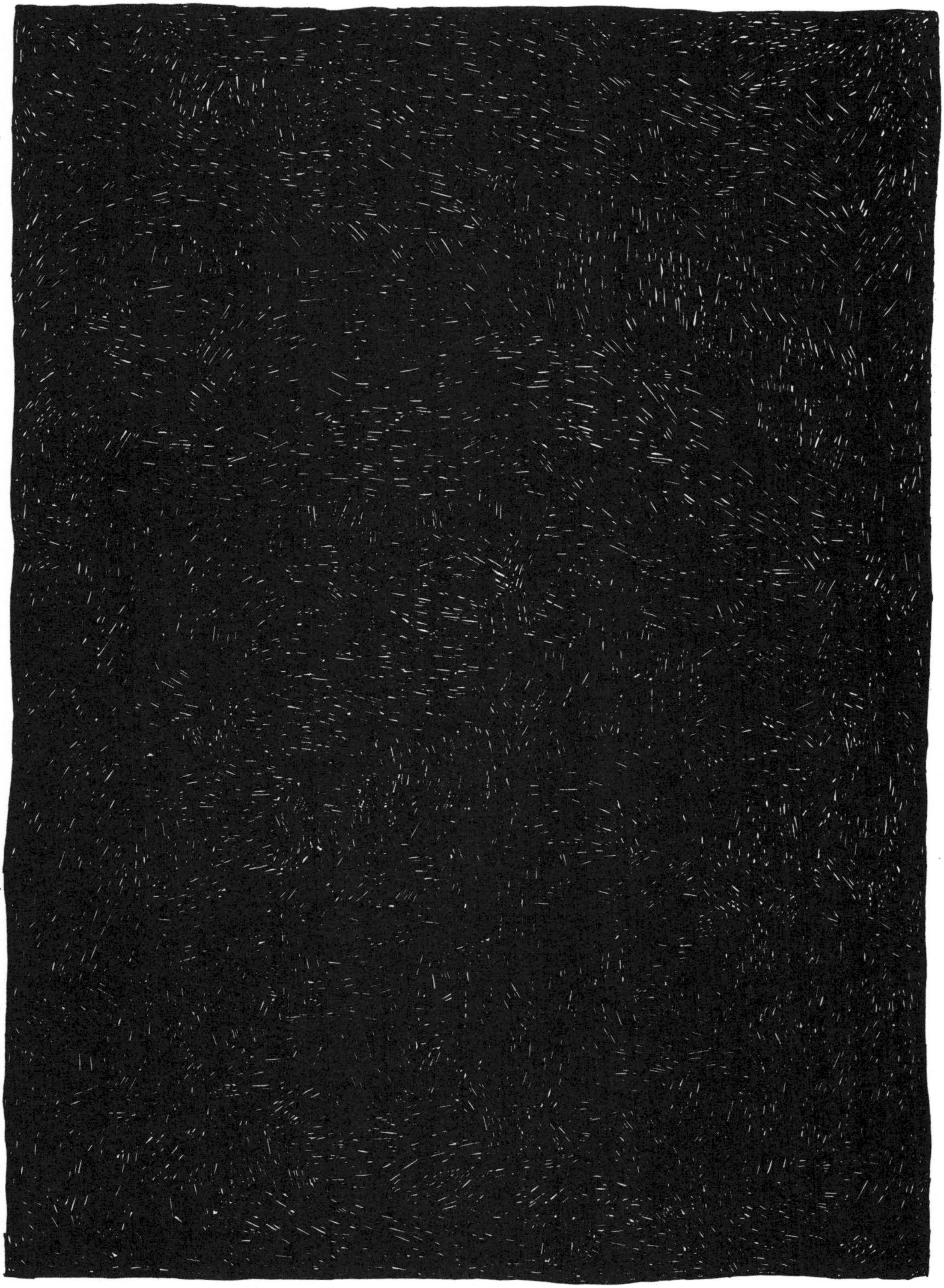

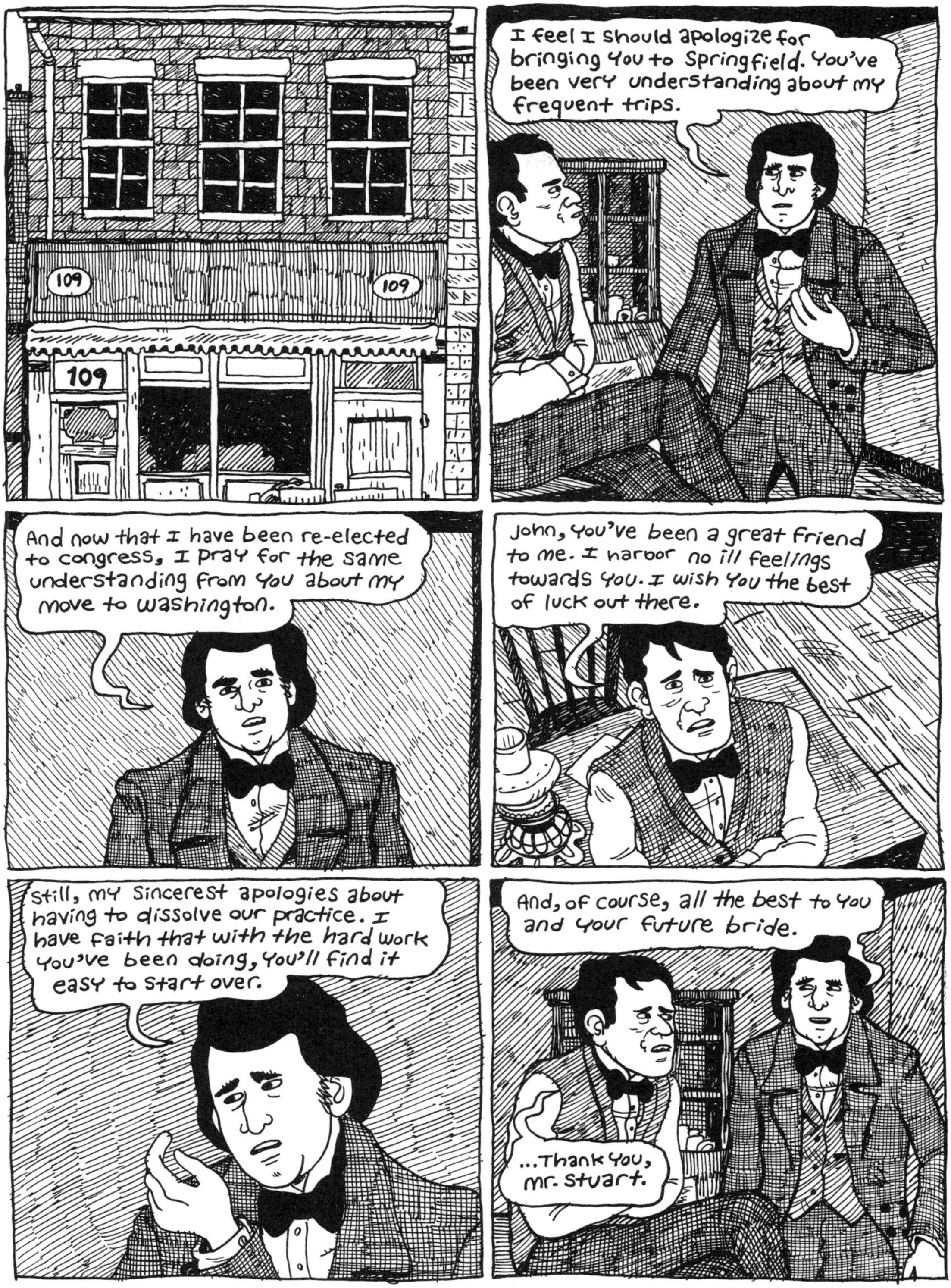
109
109
109
I feel I should apologize for bringing you to Springfield. You've been very understanding about my frequent trips.
And now that I have been re-elected to congress, I pray for the same understanding from you about my move to washington.
John, you've been a great friend to me. I harbor no ill feelings towards you. I wish you the best of luck out there.
Still, my sincerest apologies about having to dissolve our practice. I have faith that with the hard work you've been doing, you'll find it easy to start over.
And, of course, all the best to you and your future bride.
...Thank you, mr. Stuart.

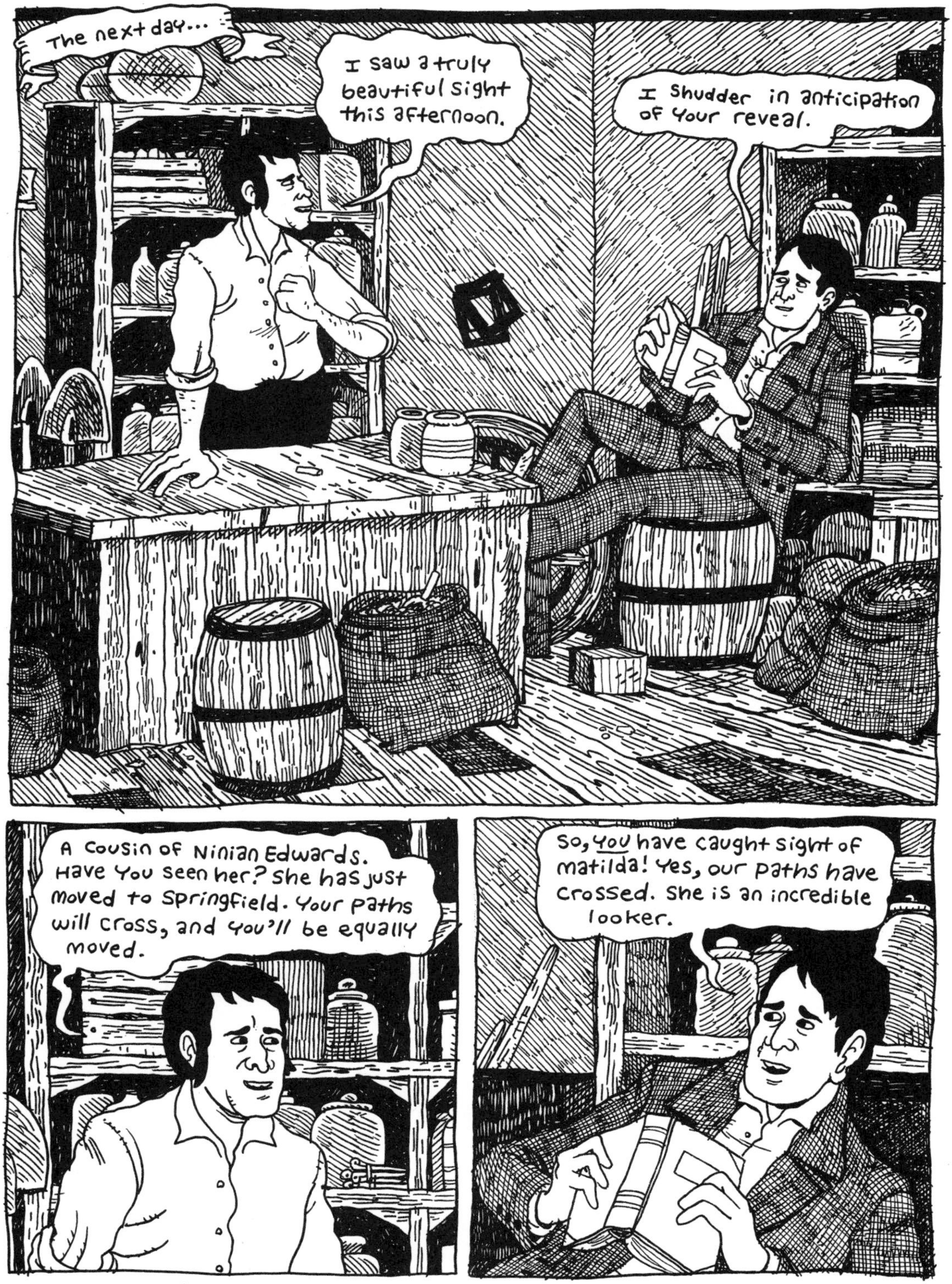
The next day...
I saw a truly beautiful sight this afternoon.
I shudder in anticipation of your reveal.
A cousin of Ninian Edwards. Have you seen her? She has just moved to Springfield. Your paths will cross, and you'll be equally moved.
So, you have caught sight of Matilda! Yes, our paths have crossed. She is an incredible looker.

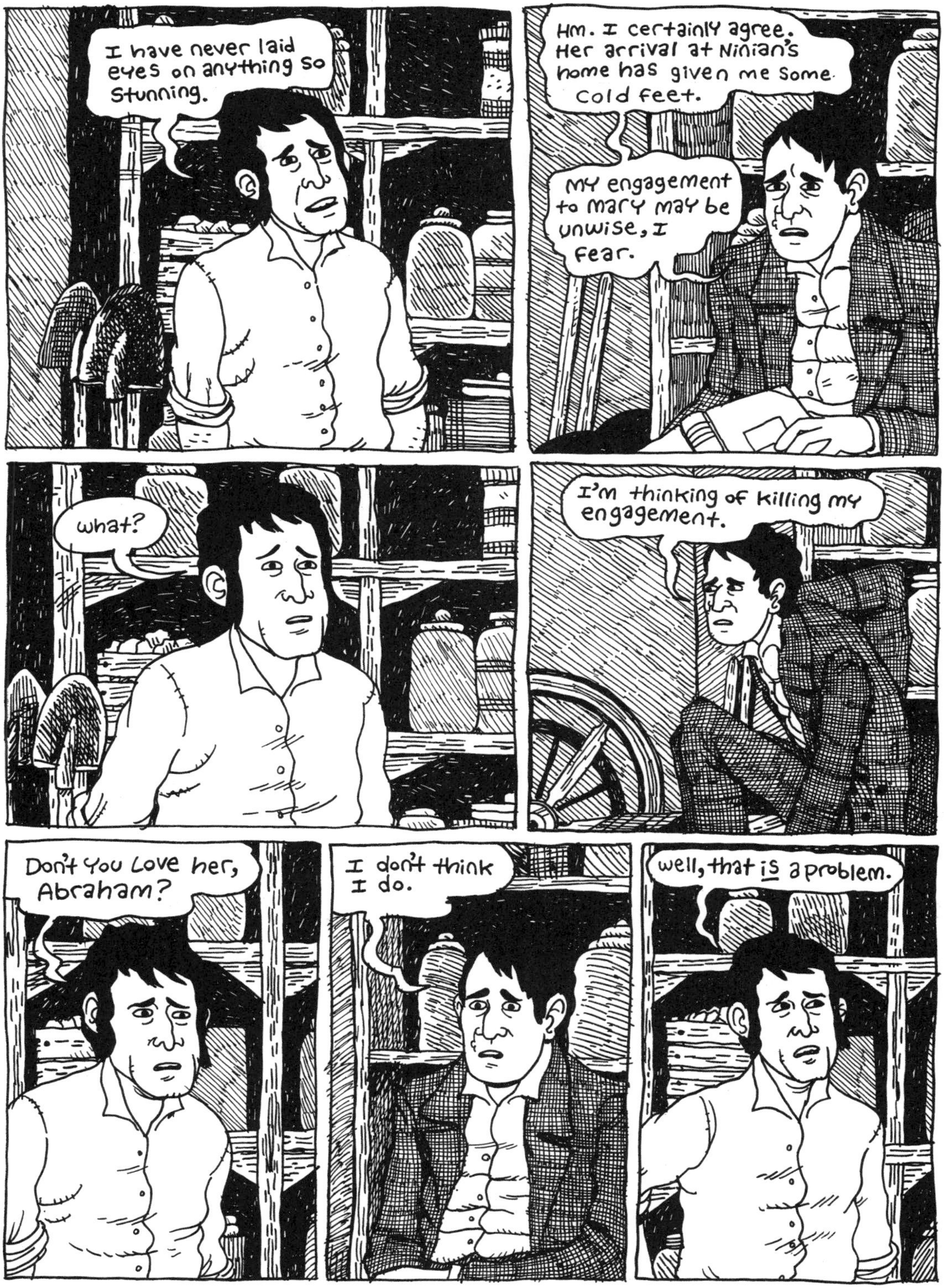
I have never laid eyes on anything so stunning.
Hm. I certainly agree. Her arrival at Ninian's home has given me some cold feet.
My engagement to Mary may be unwise, I fear.
What?
I'm thinking of killing my engagement.
Don't you love her, Abraham?
I don't think I do.
Well, that is a problem.

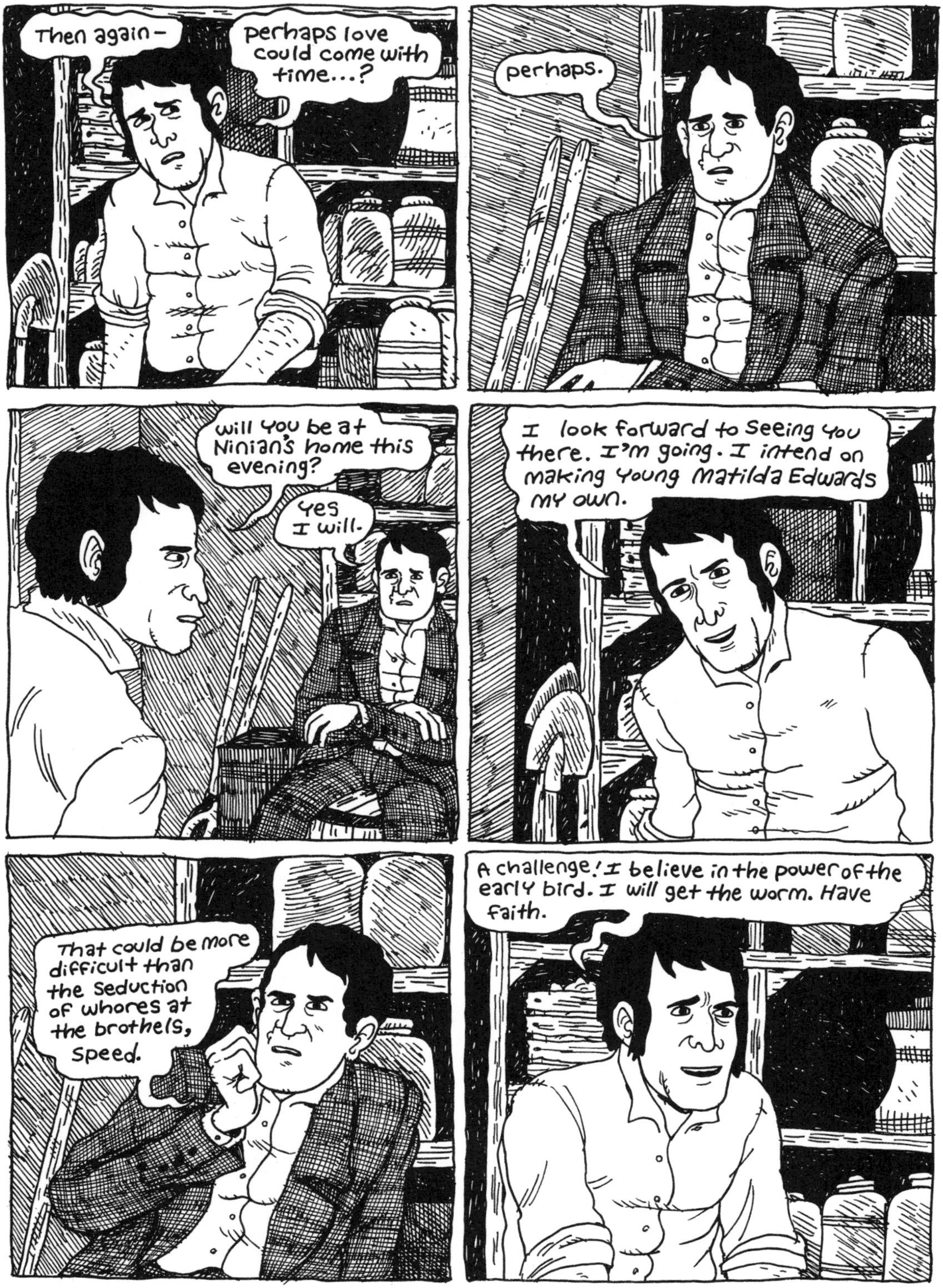
Then again-
perhaps love could come with time...?
perhaps.
will you be at Ninian's home this evening?
Yes I will.
I look forward to seeing you there. I'm going. I intend on making young Matilda Edwards my own.
That could be more difficult than the seduction of whores at the brothels, speed.
A challenge! I believe in the power of the early bird. I will get the worm. Have faith.

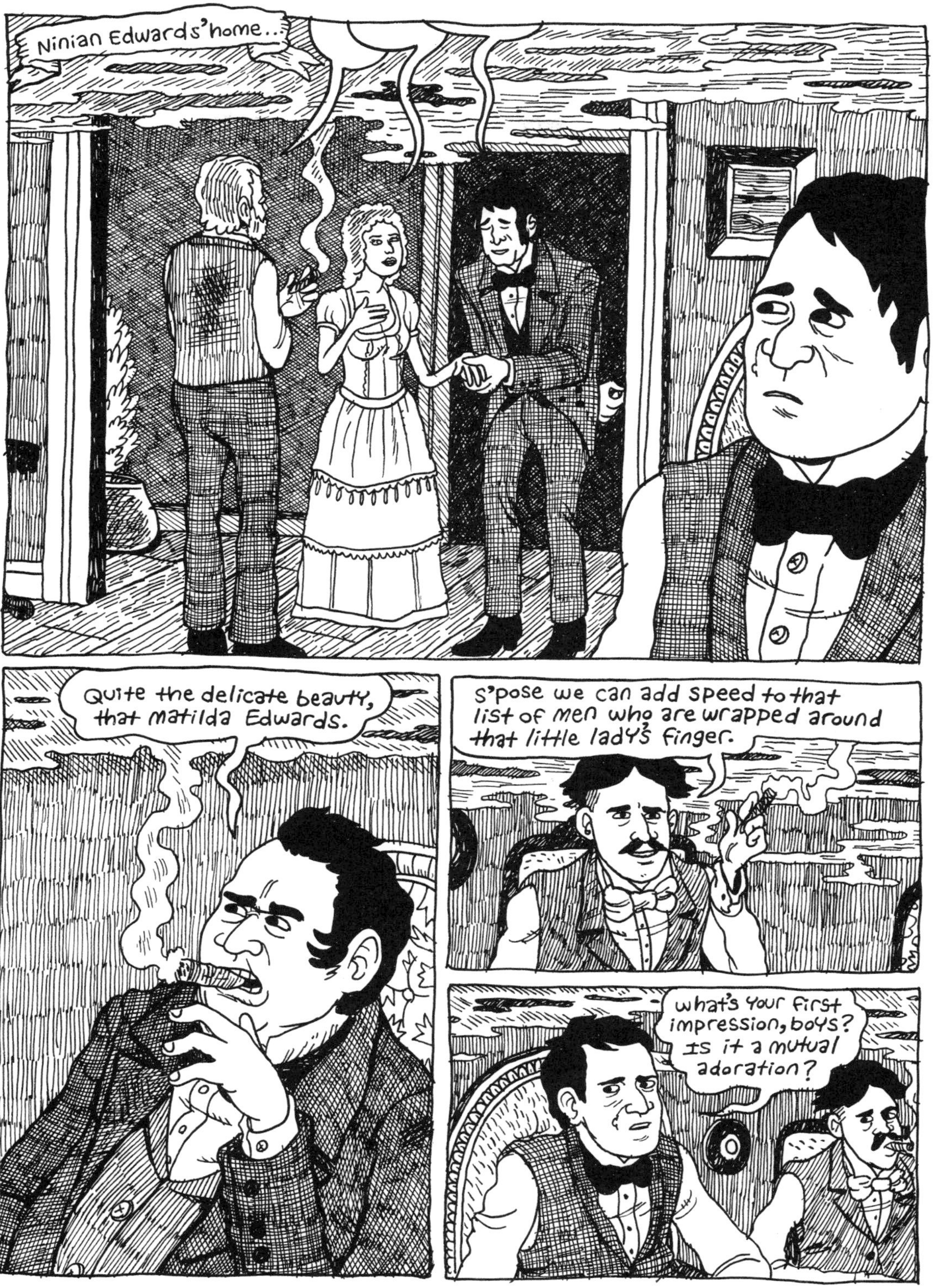

Ninian Edwards' home...
Quite the delicate beauty, that Matilda Edwards.
S'pose we can add Speed to that list of men who are wrapped around that little lady's finger.
What's your first impression, boys? Is it a mutual adoration?

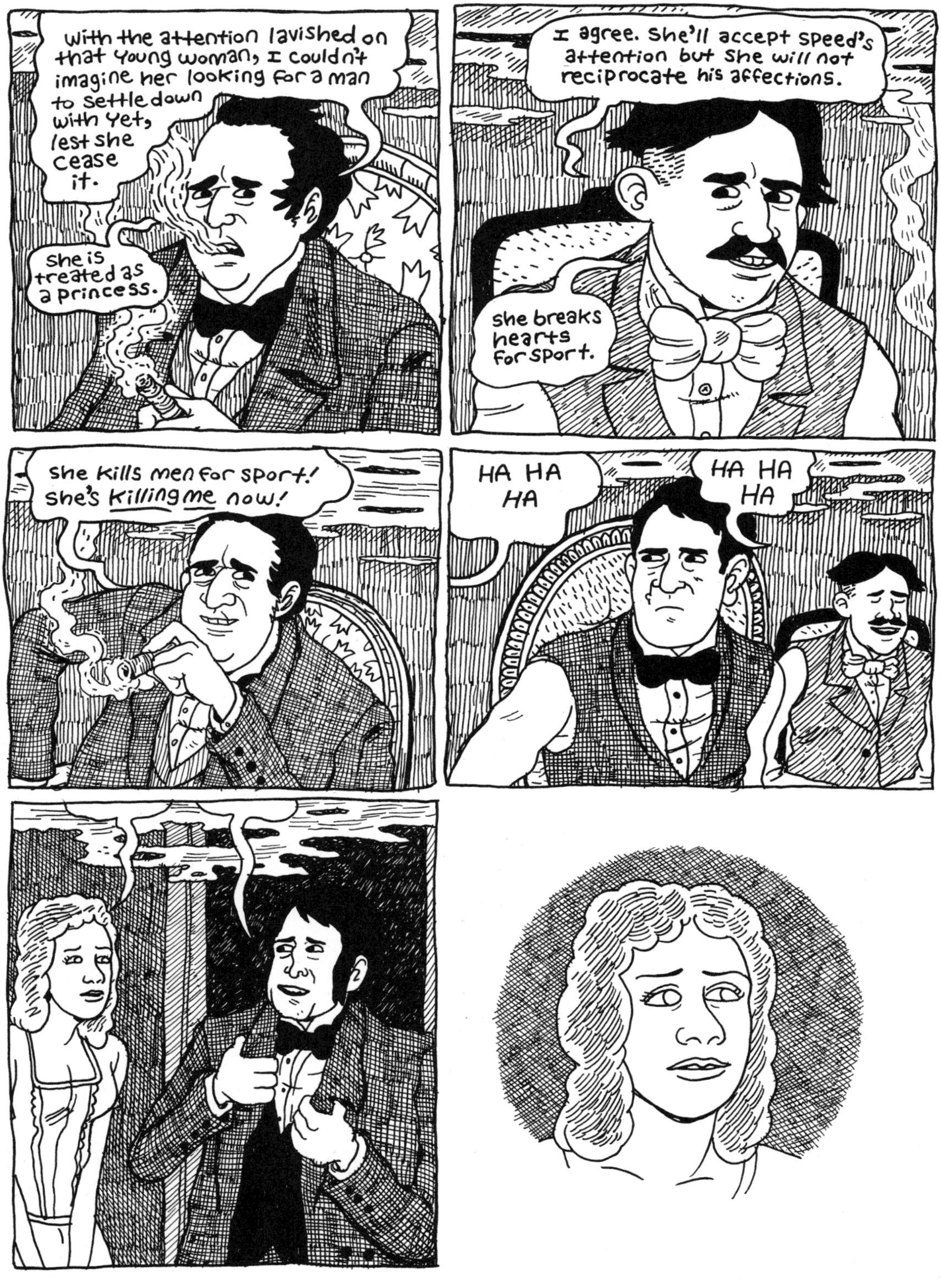
With the attention lavished on that young woman, I couldn't imagine her looking for a man to settle down with yet, lest she cease it.
She is treated as a princess.
I agree. She'll accept Speed's attention but she will not reciprocate his affections.
She breaks hearts for sport.
She kills men for sport! She's killing me now!
HA HA HA
HA HA HA

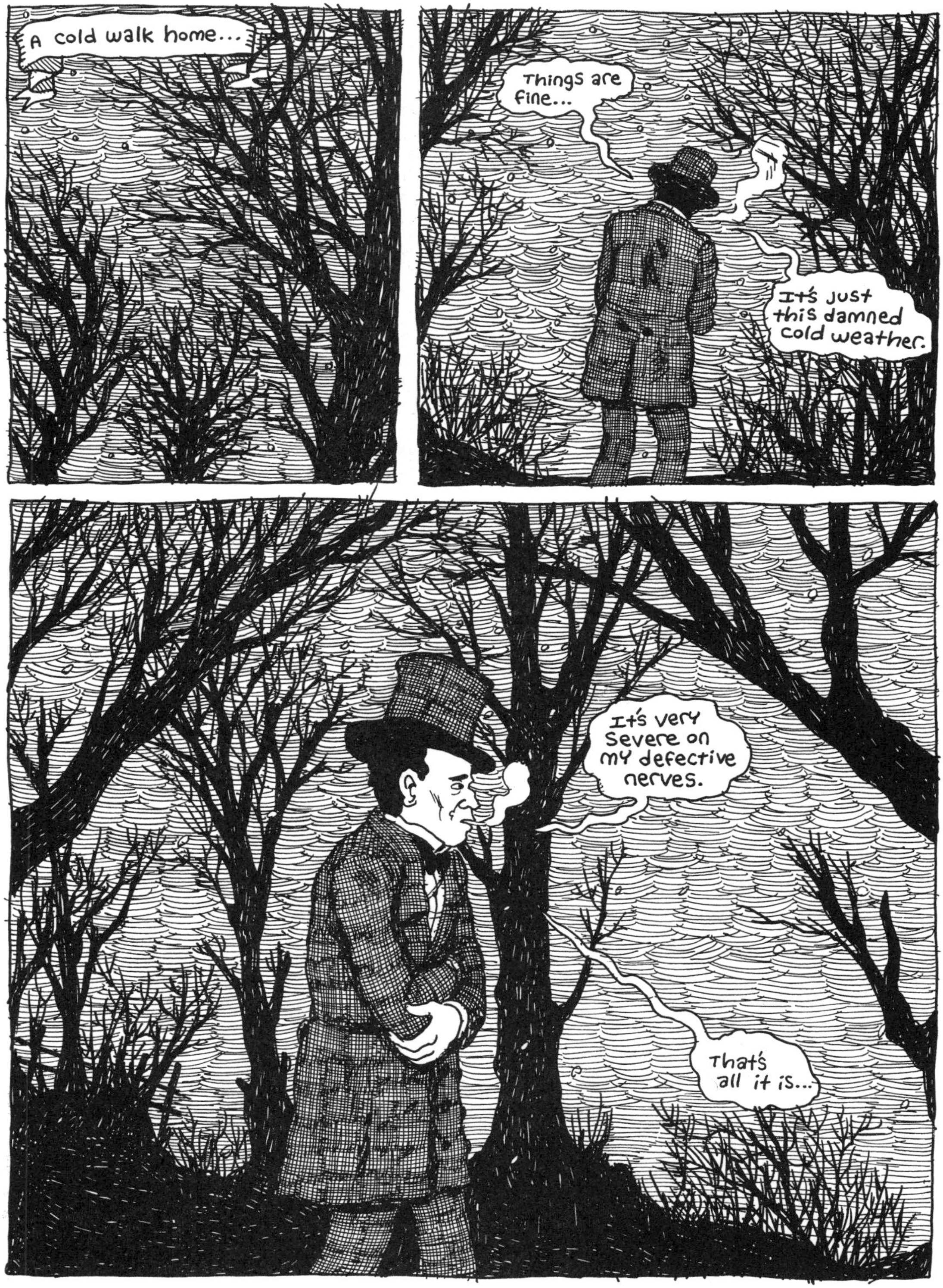
A cold walk home...
Things are fine...
It's just this damned cold weather.
It's very severe on my defective nerves.
That's all it is...

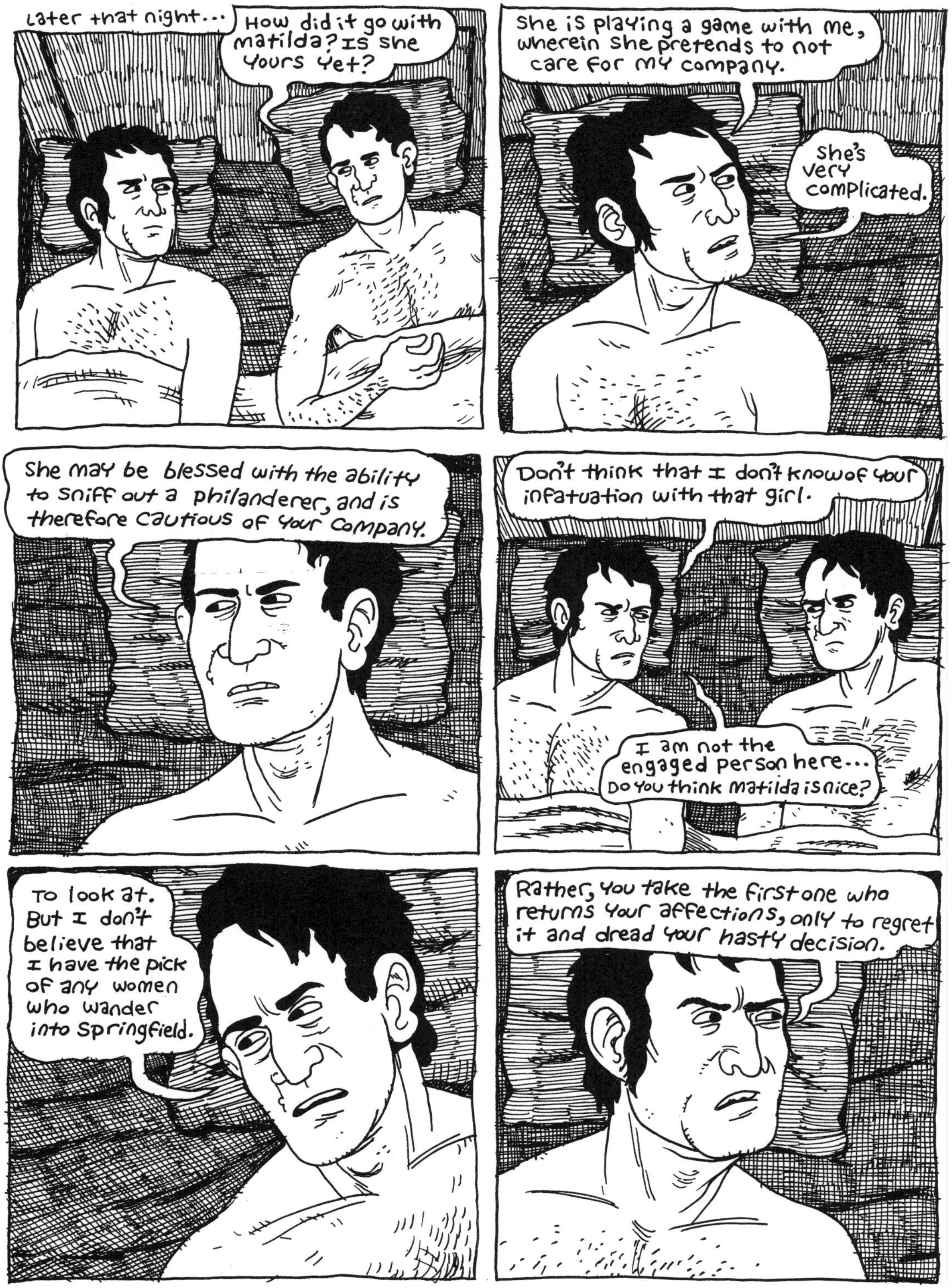
Later that night...
How did it go with Matilda? Is she yours yet?
She is playing a game with me, wherein she pretends to not care for my company.
She's very complicated.
She may be blessed with the ability to sniff out a philanderer, and is therefore cautious of your company.
Don't think that I don't know of your infatuation with that girl.
I am not the engaged person here... Do you think Matilda is nice?
To look at. But I don't believe that I have the pick of any women who wander into Springfield.
Rather, you take the first one who returns your affections, only to regret it and dread your hasty decision.

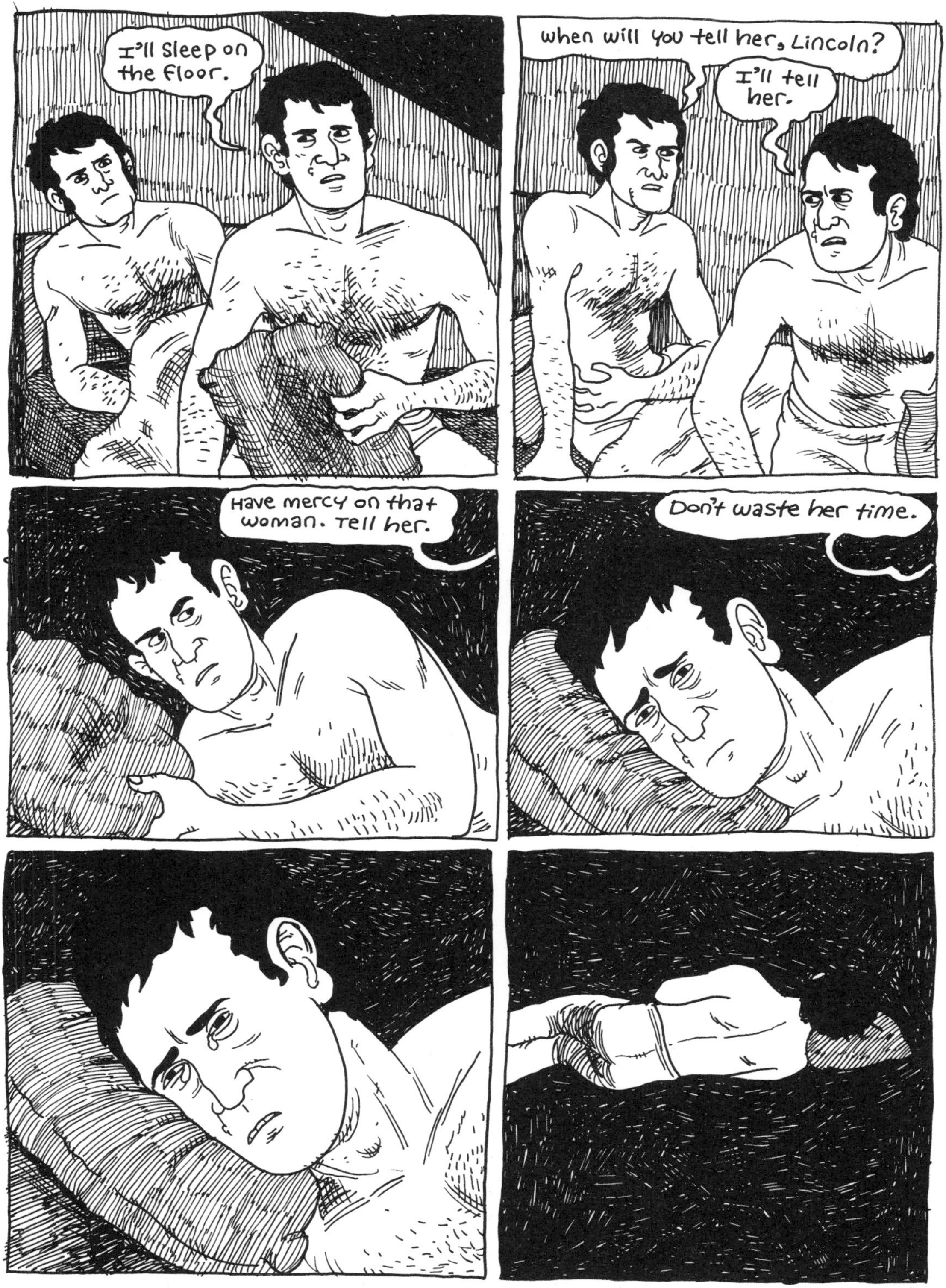
I'll sleep on the floor.
When will you tell her, Lincoln?
I'll tell her.
Have mercy on that woman. Tell her.
Don't waste her time.

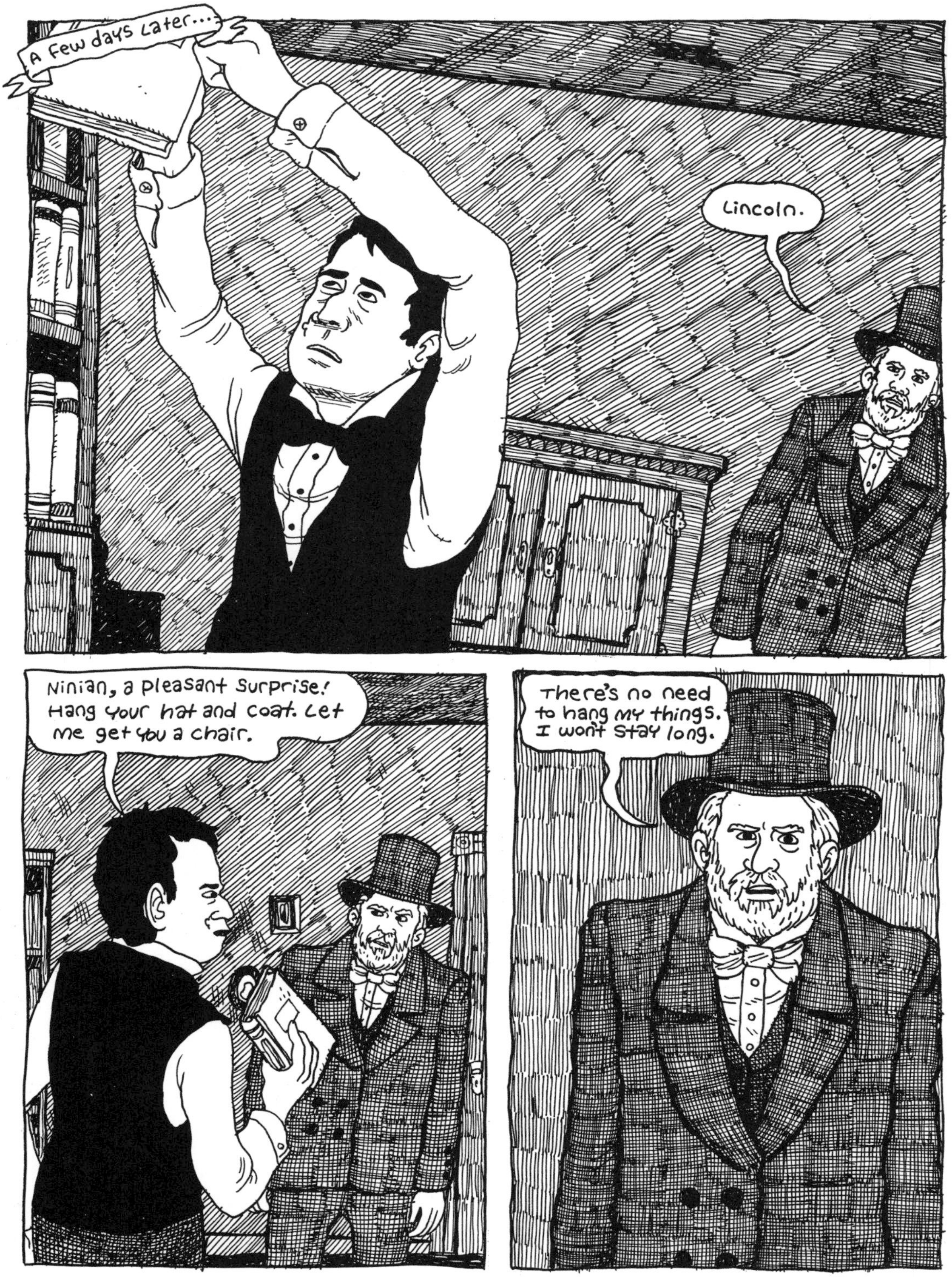
A few days later...
Lincoln.
Ninian, a pleasant surprise! Hang your hat and coat. Let me get you a chair.
There's no need to hang my things. I won't stay long.

I see. Well, what can I do for you, mr. Edwards?

I've been asked to speak with you by the Todd family, concerning Mary.

I don't understand. Has something happened?

Your engagement has happened, Lincoln.

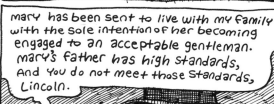

Mary has been sent to live with my family with the sole intention of her becoming engaged to an acceptable gentleman. Mary's father has high standards, And you do not meet those standards, Lincoln.

I feel offended.

My kernel is being Judged by its Shell.

I'm merely a messenger. Truthfully, the stress of this situation has caused Mary Violent migraines. I assure you, your engagement gives her great pain.

For that reason alone, you should consider breaking off your relationship.

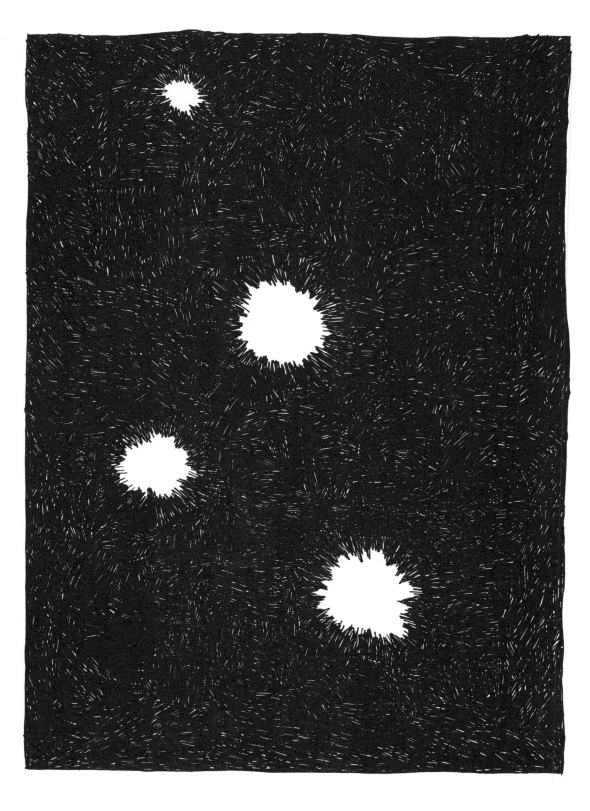

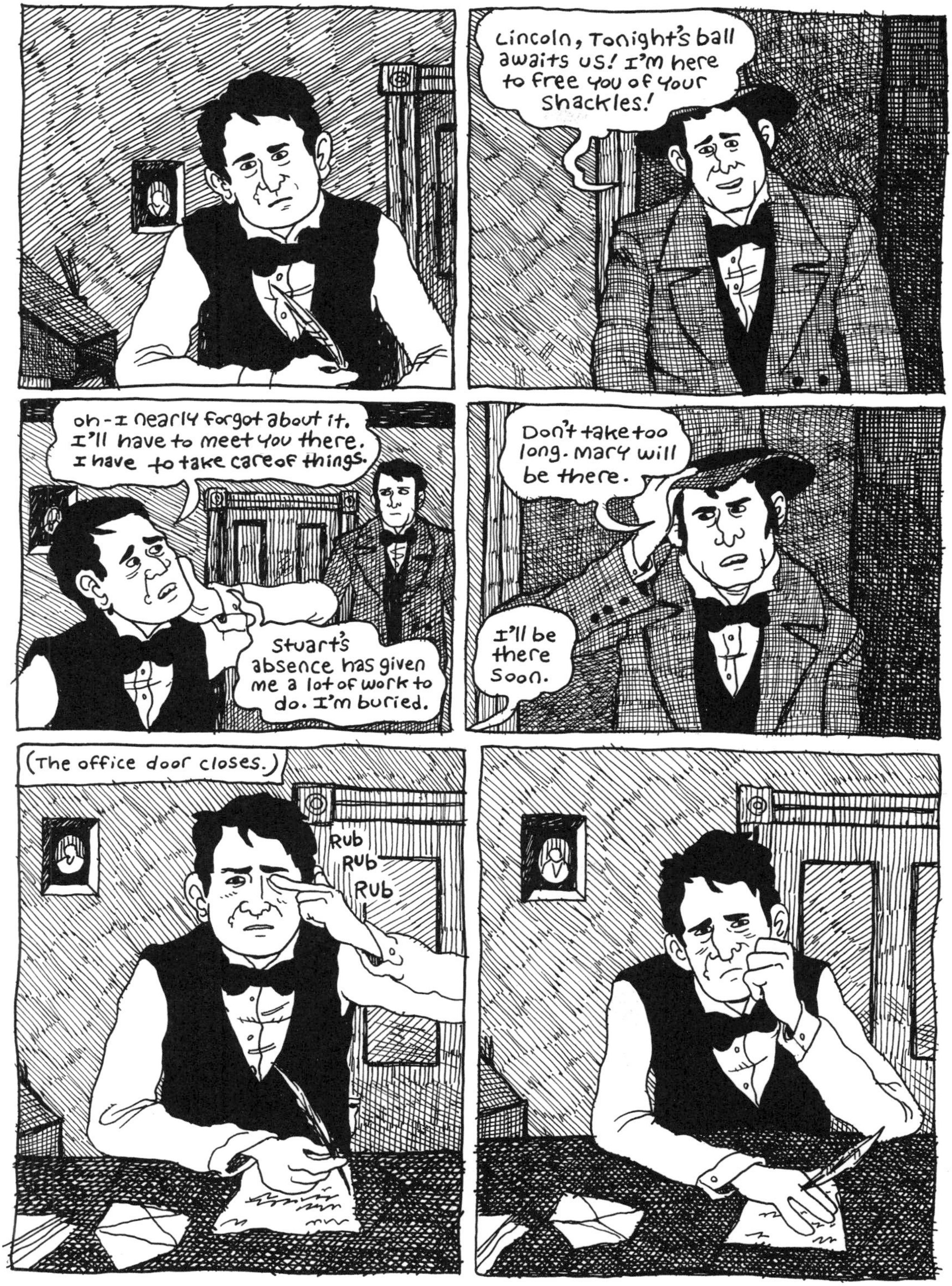
Lincoln, Tonight's ball awaits us! I'm here to free you of your shackles!
oh - I nearly forgot about it. I'll have to meet you there. I have to take care of things.
Stuart's absence has given me a lot of work to do. I'm buried.
Don't take too long. Mary will be there.
I'll be there soon.
(The office door closes.)
Rub
Rub
Rub

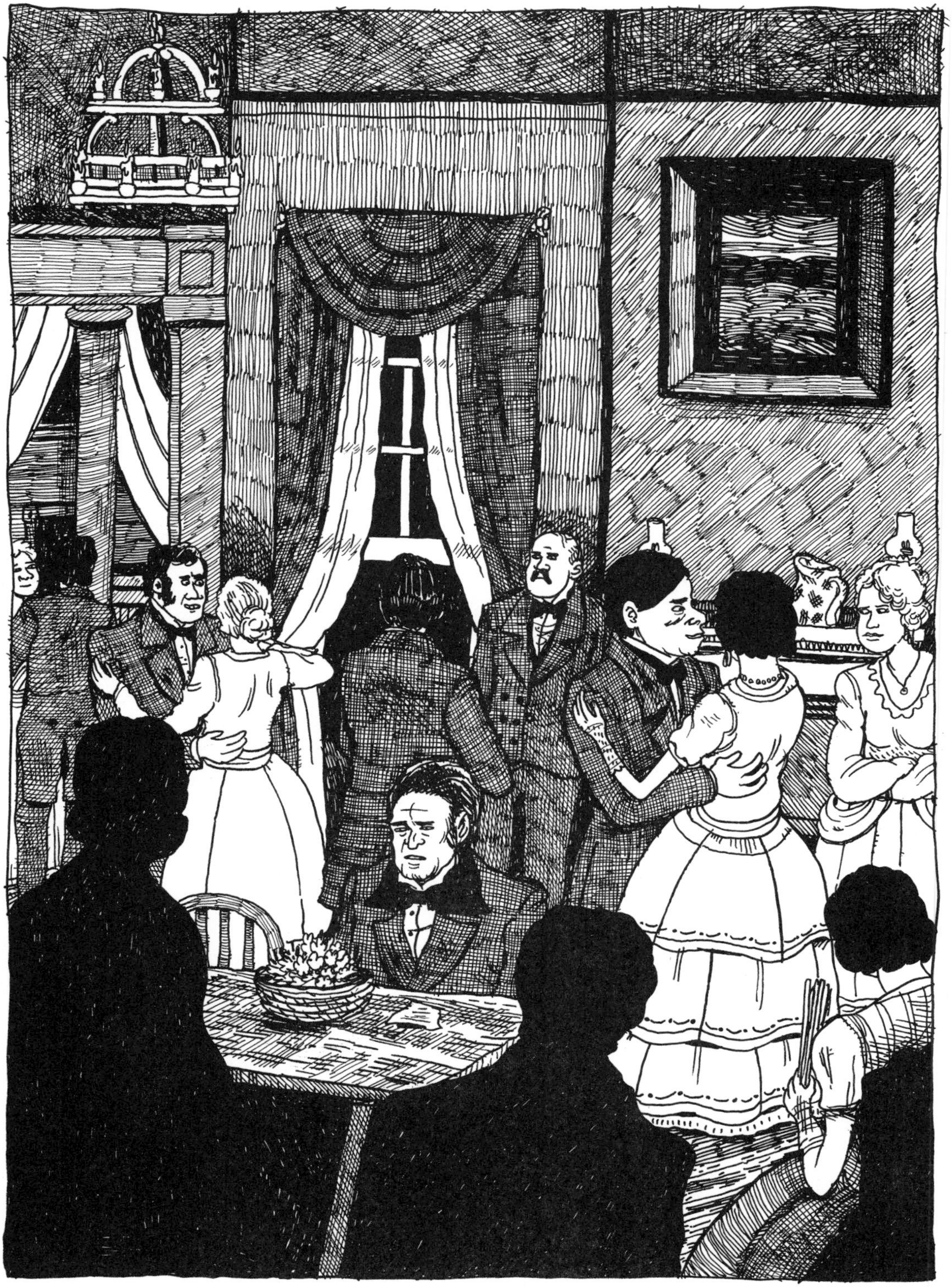

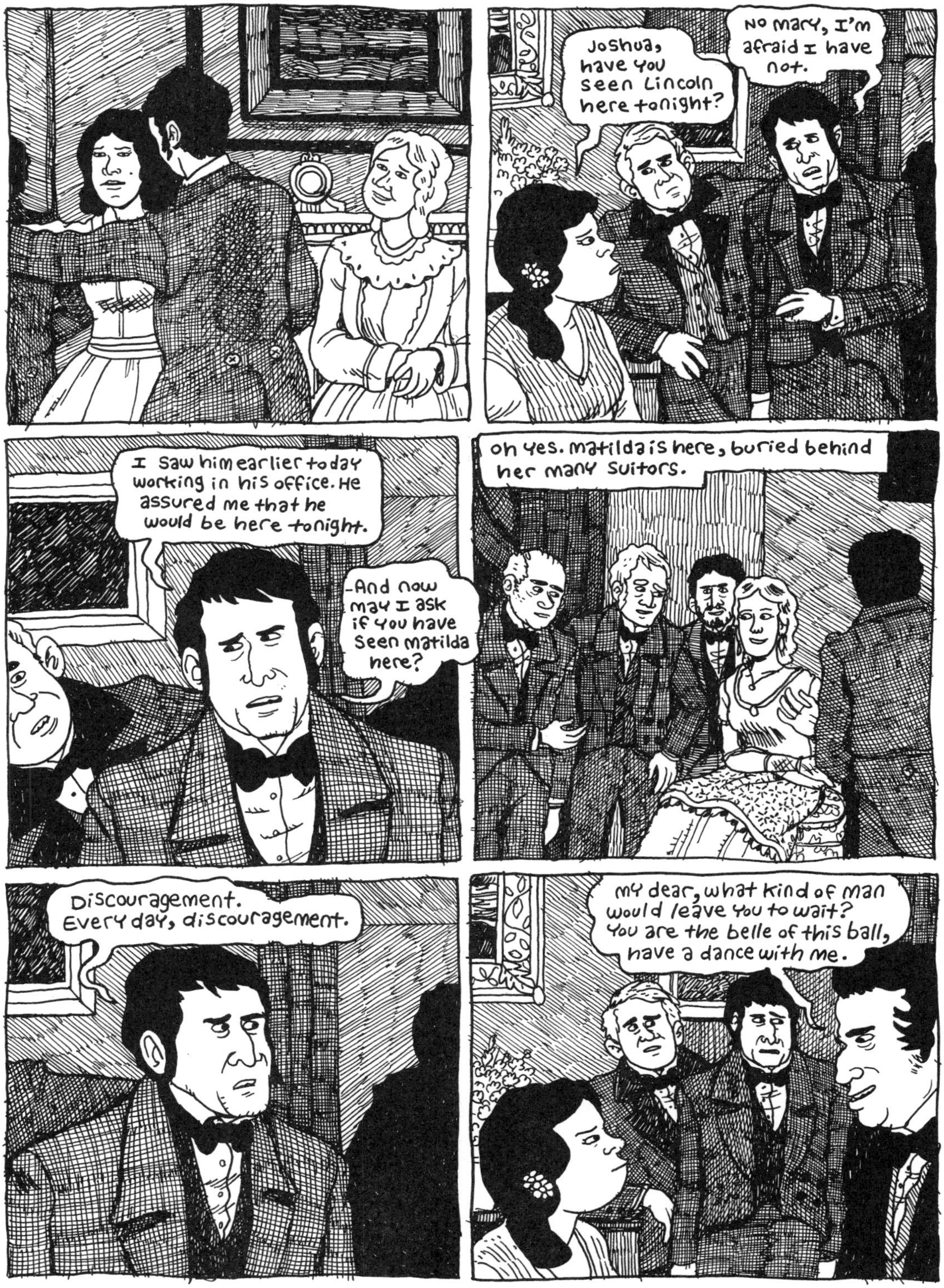
Joshua, have you seen Lincoln here tonight?
No Mary, I'm afraid I have not.
I saw him earlier today working in his office. He assured me that he would be here tonight.
-And now may I ask if you have seen Matilda here?
Oh yes. Matilda is here, buried behind her many suitors.
Discouragement. Every day, discouragement.
My dear, what kind of man would leave you to wait? You are the belle of this ball, have a dance with me.

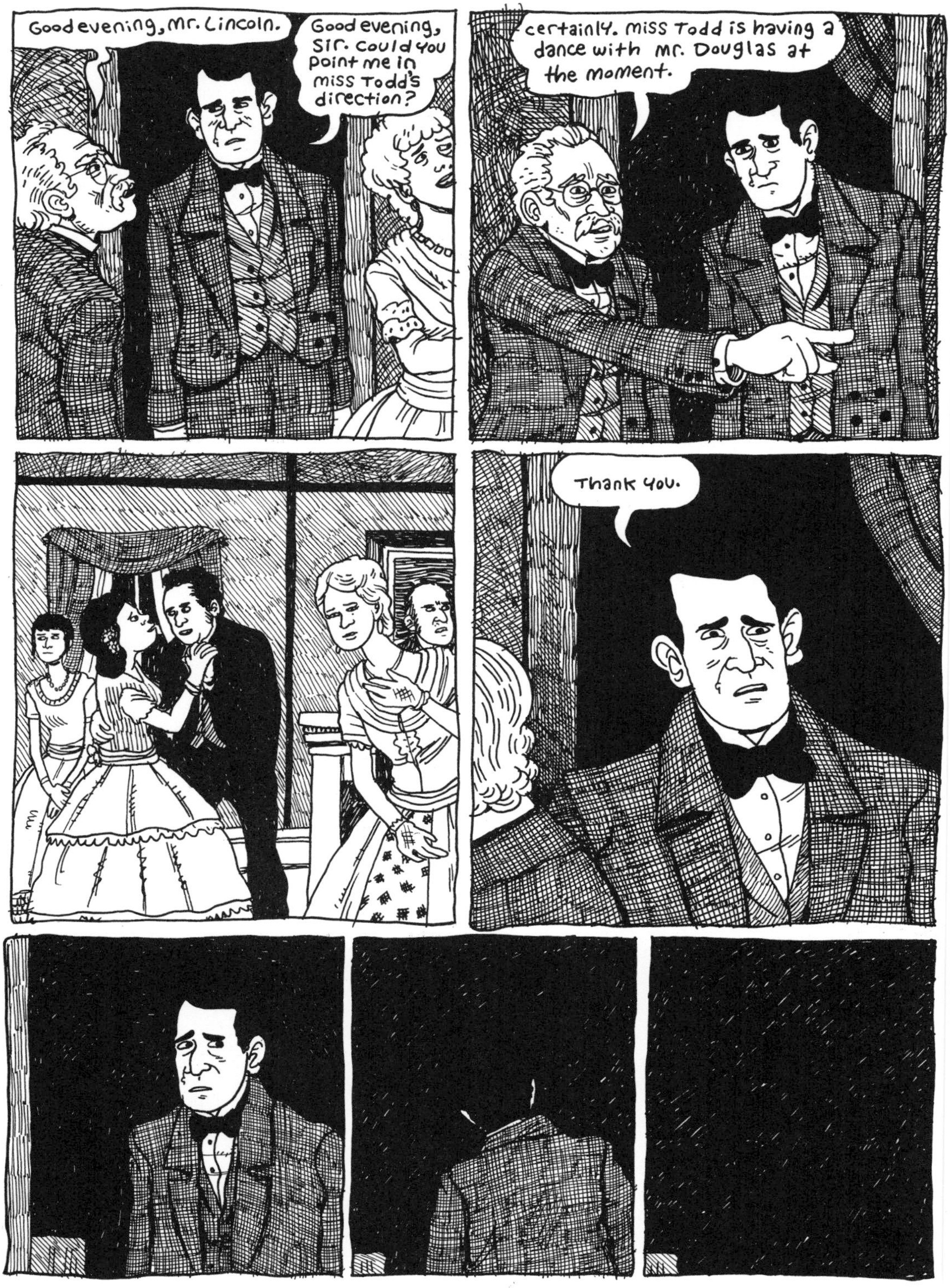
Good evening, Mr. Lincoln.
Good evening, sir. Could you point me in Miss Todd's direction?
Certainly. Miss Todd is having a dance with Mr. Douglas at the moment.
Thank you.

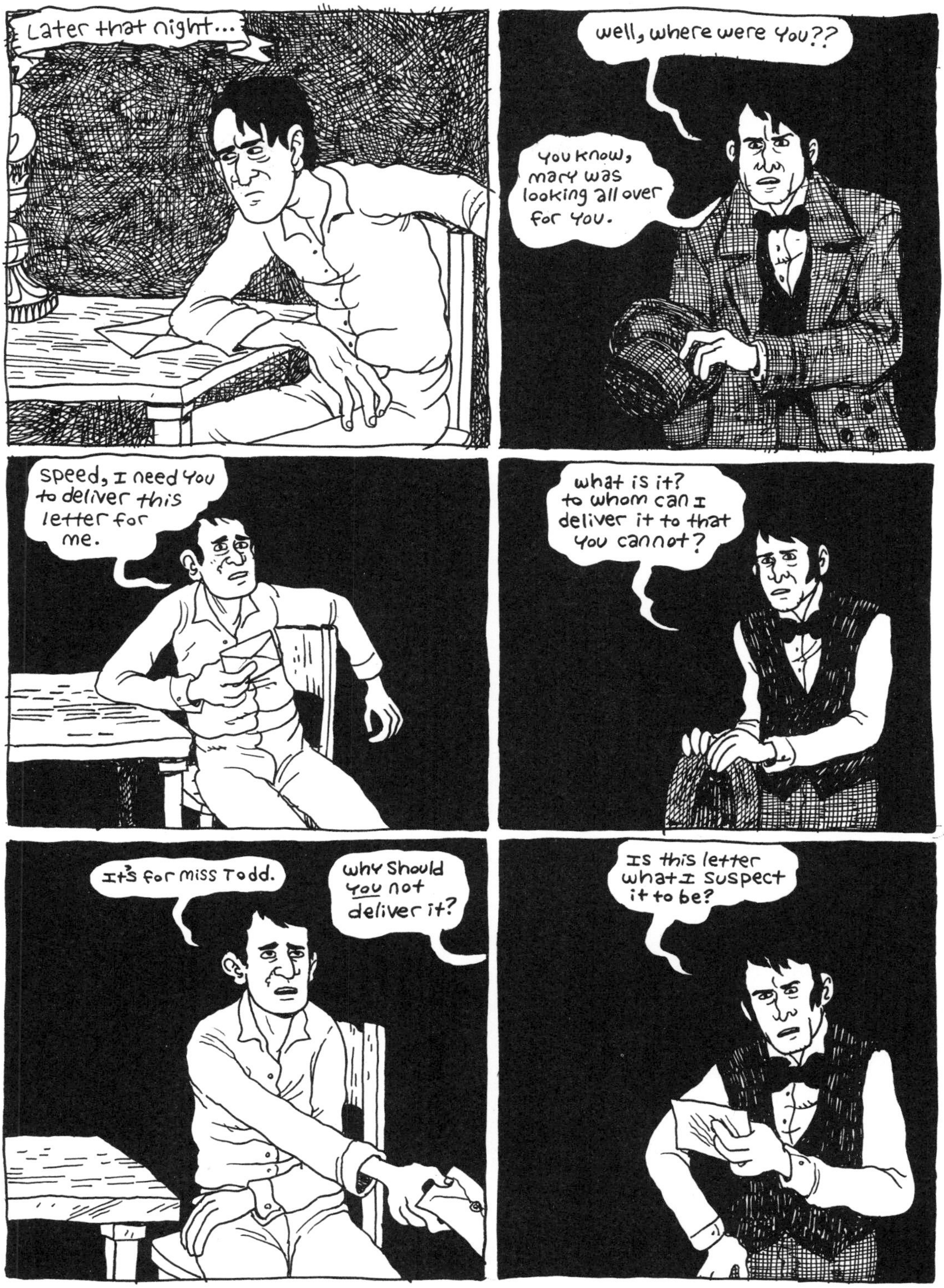
Later that night...
well, where were you??
you know, mary was looking all over for you.
speed, I need you to deliver this letter for me.
what is it? to whom can I deliver it to that you cannot?
It's for miss Todd.
why should you not deliver it?
Is this letter what I suspect it to be?

I'm pained by my nuptial obligation to that woman.

what could I offer a wife?

I will not allow this letter to be delivered to Mary.

You're an obstinate man.

I can find some one else to deliver that letter, Speed.

But you should not! This letter is not the way out.

words are forgotten, misunderstood, passed by! Not noticed in private conversation!

once you put your words in writing they stand as a living and eternal monument against you!

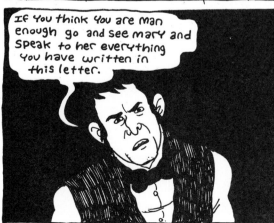

If you think you are man enough go and see Mary and speak to her everything you have written in this letter.

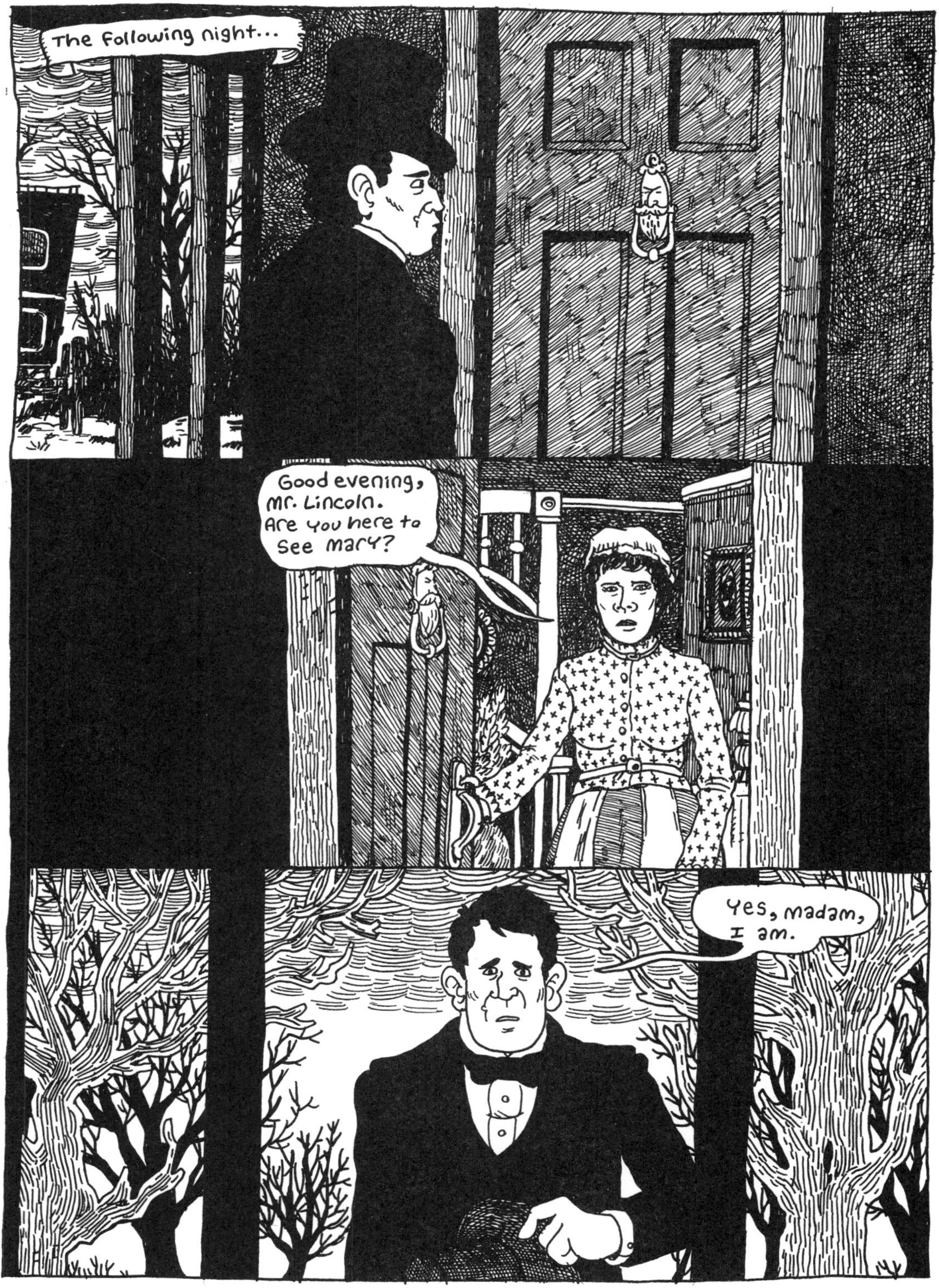
The following night...
Good evening, Mr. Lincoln. Are you here to see Mary?
Yes, madam, I am.

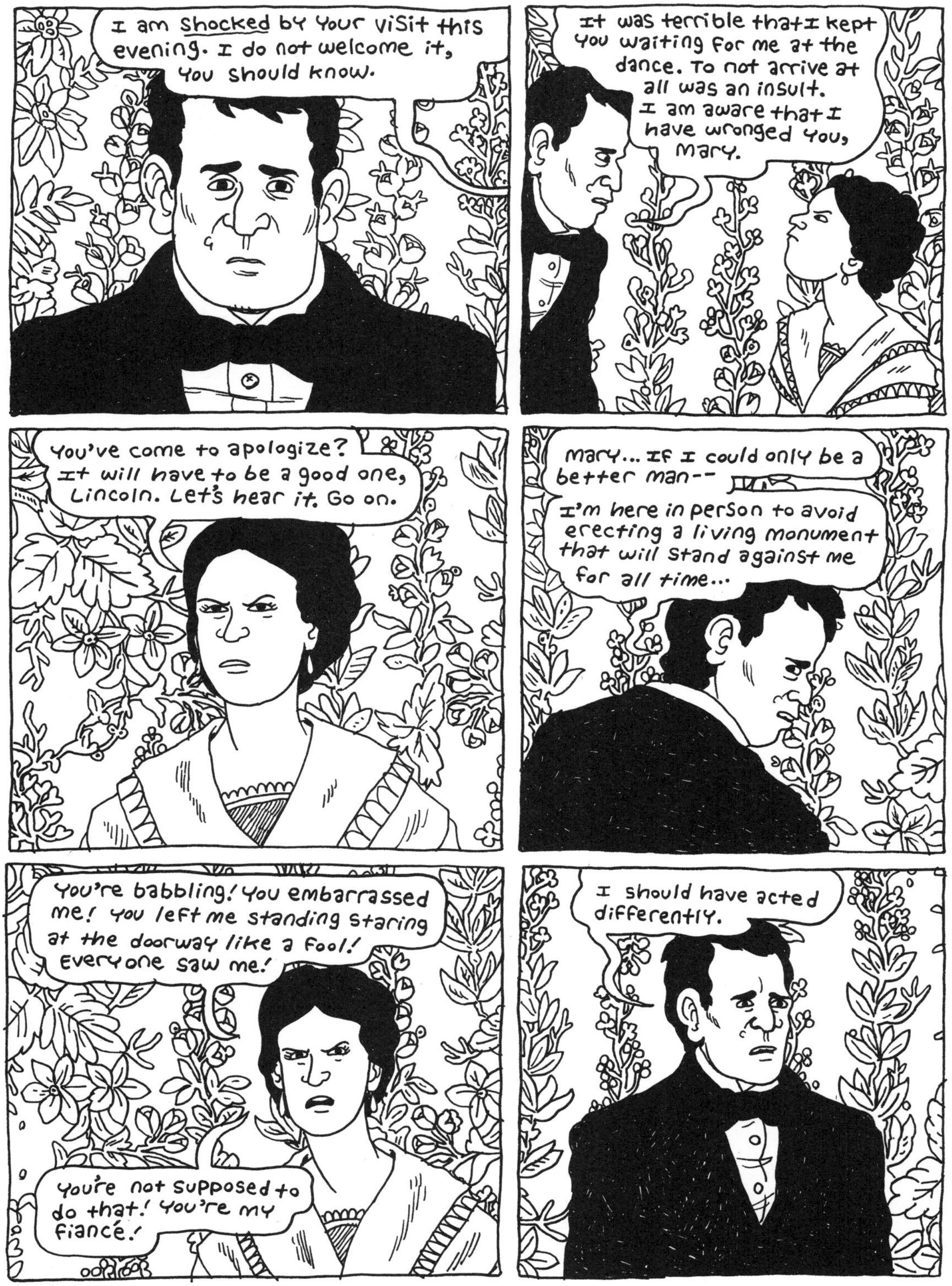
I am Shocked by your visit this evening. I do not welcome it, you should know.
It was terrible that I kept you waiting for me at the dance. To not arrive at all was an insult. I am aware that I have wronged you, Mary.
You've come to apologize? It will have to be a good one, Lincoln. Let's hear it. Go on.
Mary... If I could only be a better man--
I'm here in person to avoid erecting a living monument that will stand against me for all time...
You're babbling! You embarrassed me! You left me standing staring at the doorway like a fool! Everyone saw me!
You're not supposed to do that! You're my fiancé!
I should have acted differently.

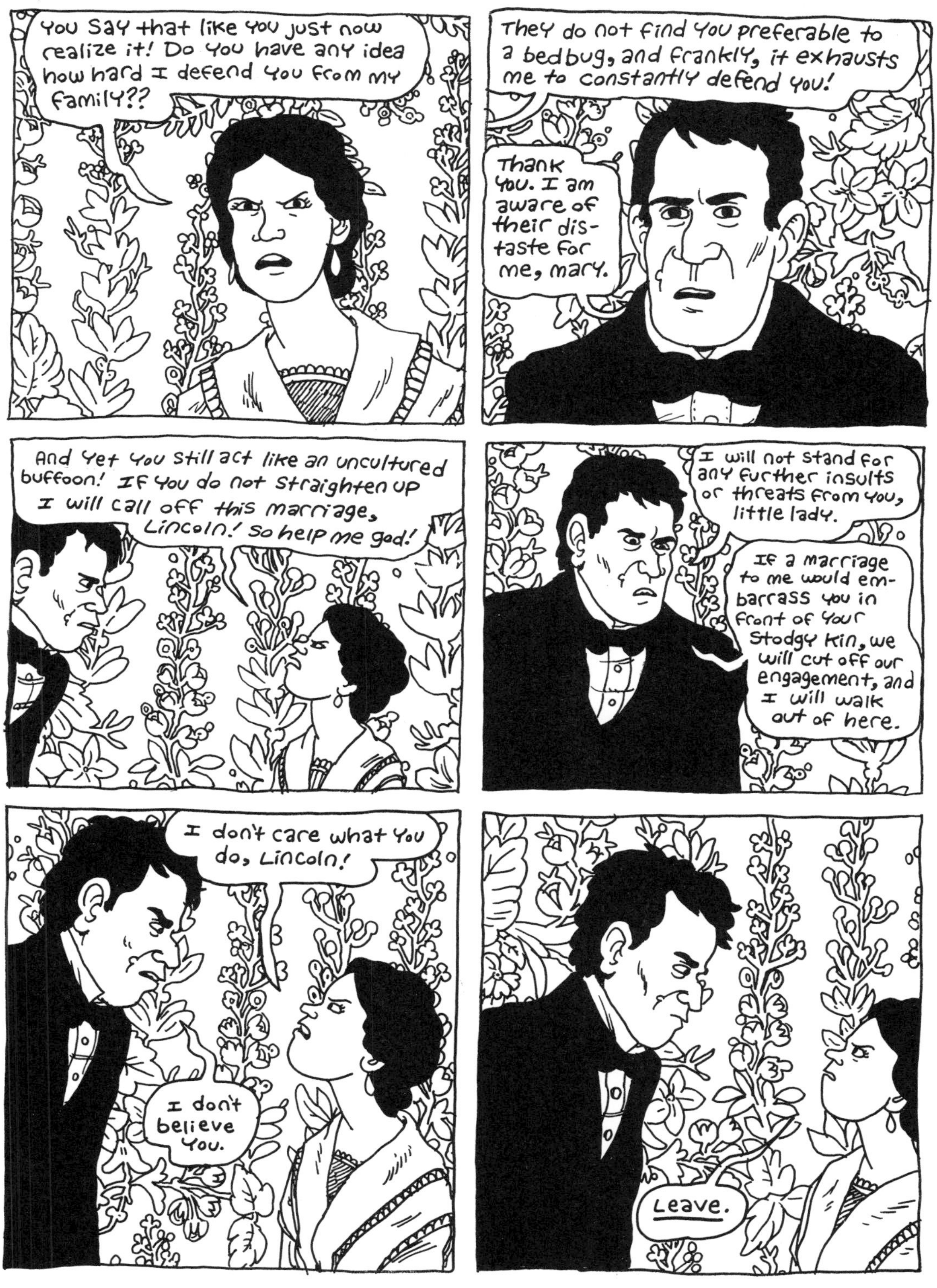
You say that like you just now realize it! Do you have any idea how hard I defend you from my family??
They do not find you preferable to a bedbug, and frankly, it exhausts me to constantly defend you!
Thank you. I am aware of their distaste for me, mary.
And yet you still act like an uncultured buffoon! If you do not straighten up I will call off this marriage, Lincoln! so help me god!
I will not stand for any further insults or threats from you, little lady.
If a marriage to me would embarrass you in front of your stodgy kin, we will cut off our engagement, and I will walk out of here.
I don't care what you do, Lincoln!
I don't believe you.
Leave.

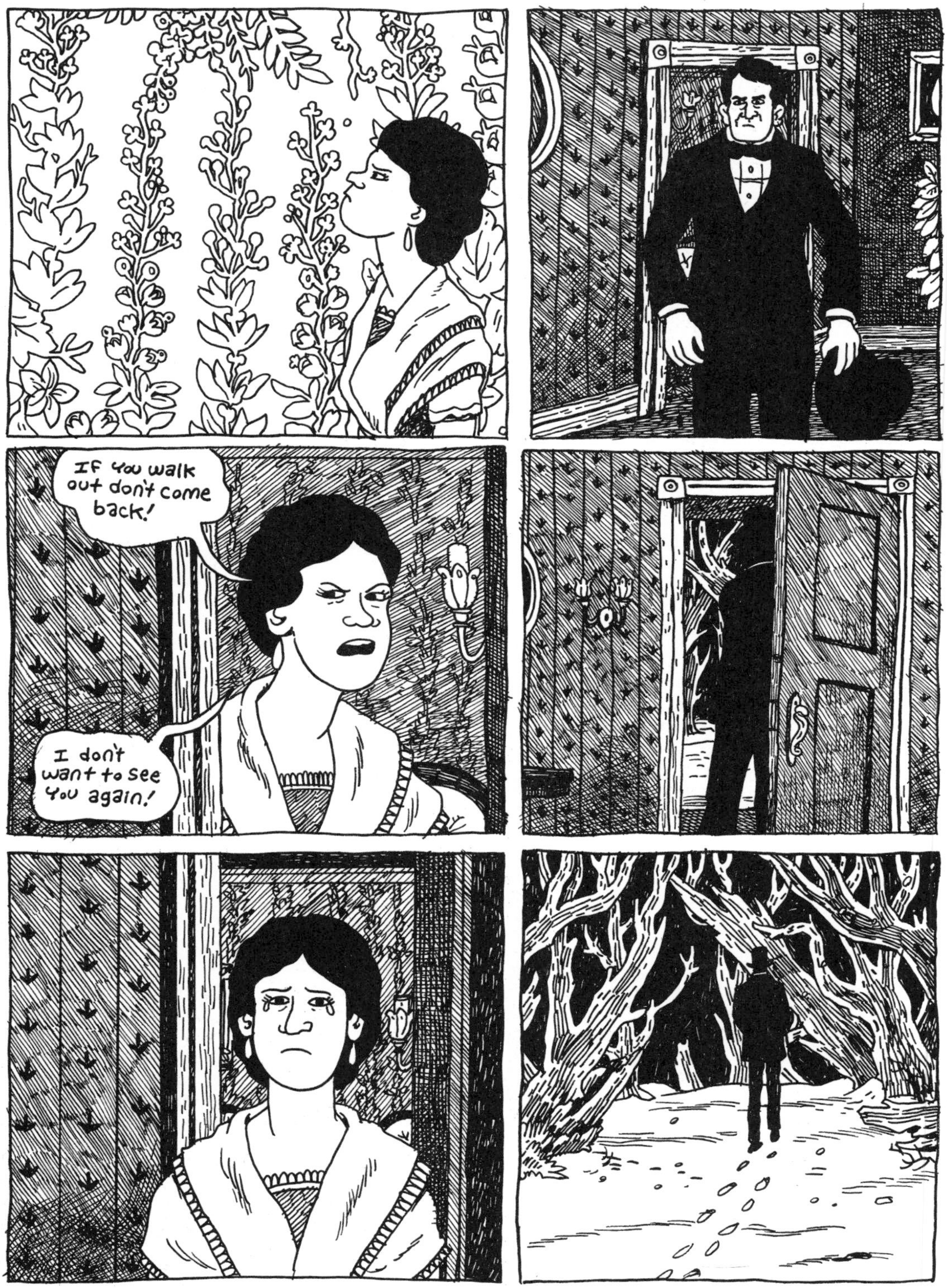
If you walk out don't come back!
I don't want to see you again!

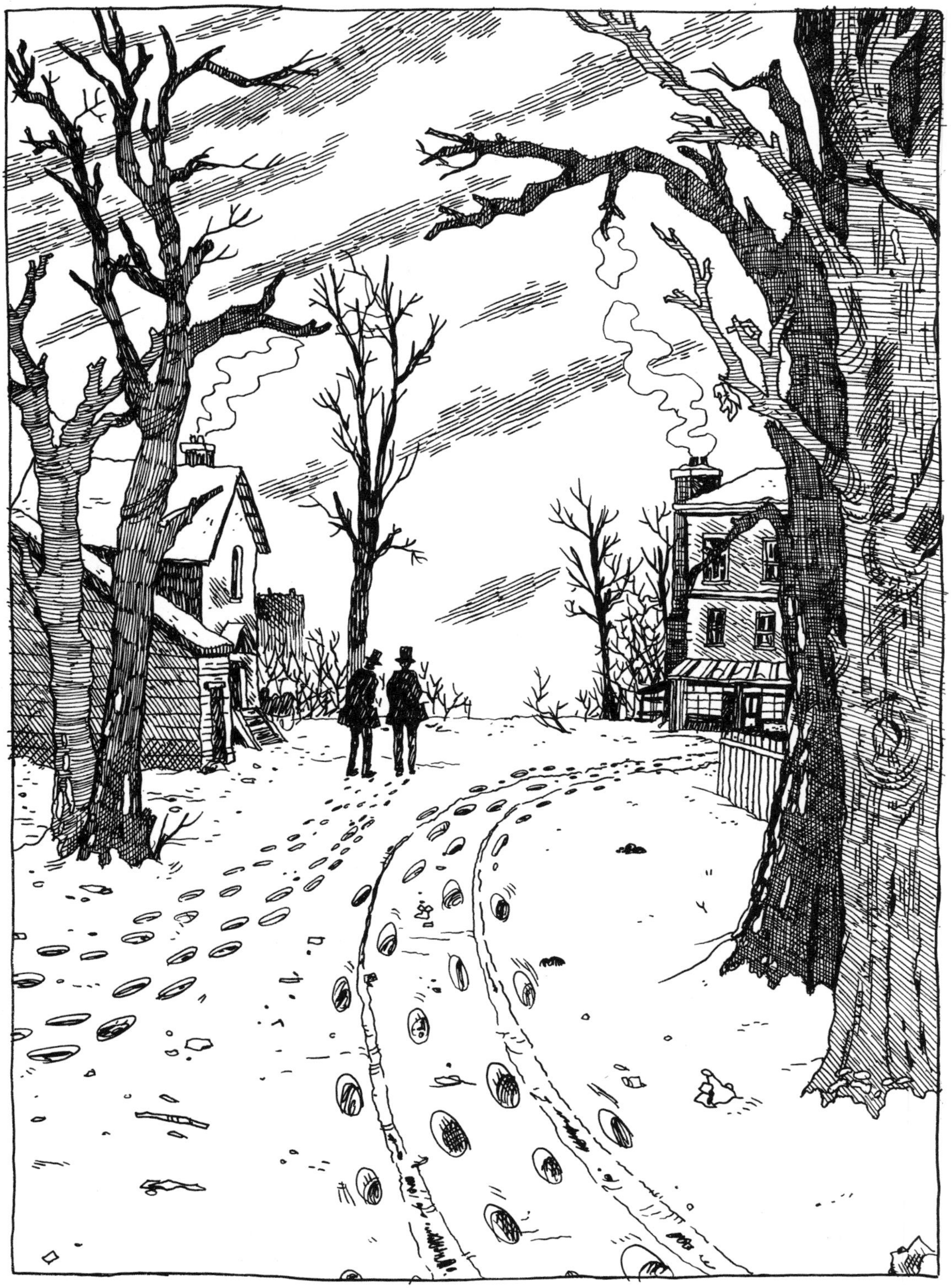

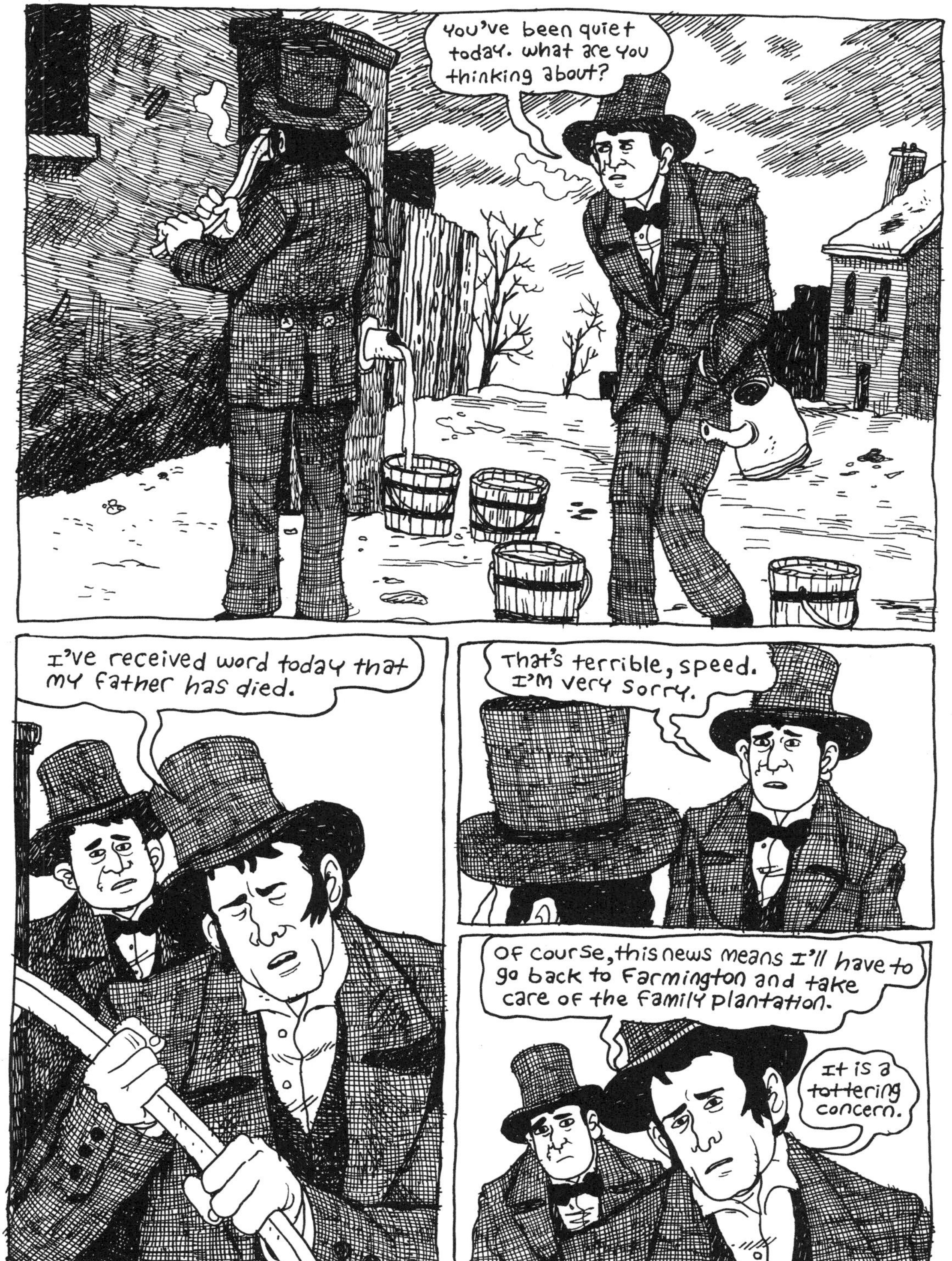
You've been quiet today. What are you thinking about?
I've received word today that my father has died.
That's terrible, Speed. I'm very sorry.
Of course, this news means I'll have to go back to Farmington and take care of the family plantation.
It is a tottering concern.

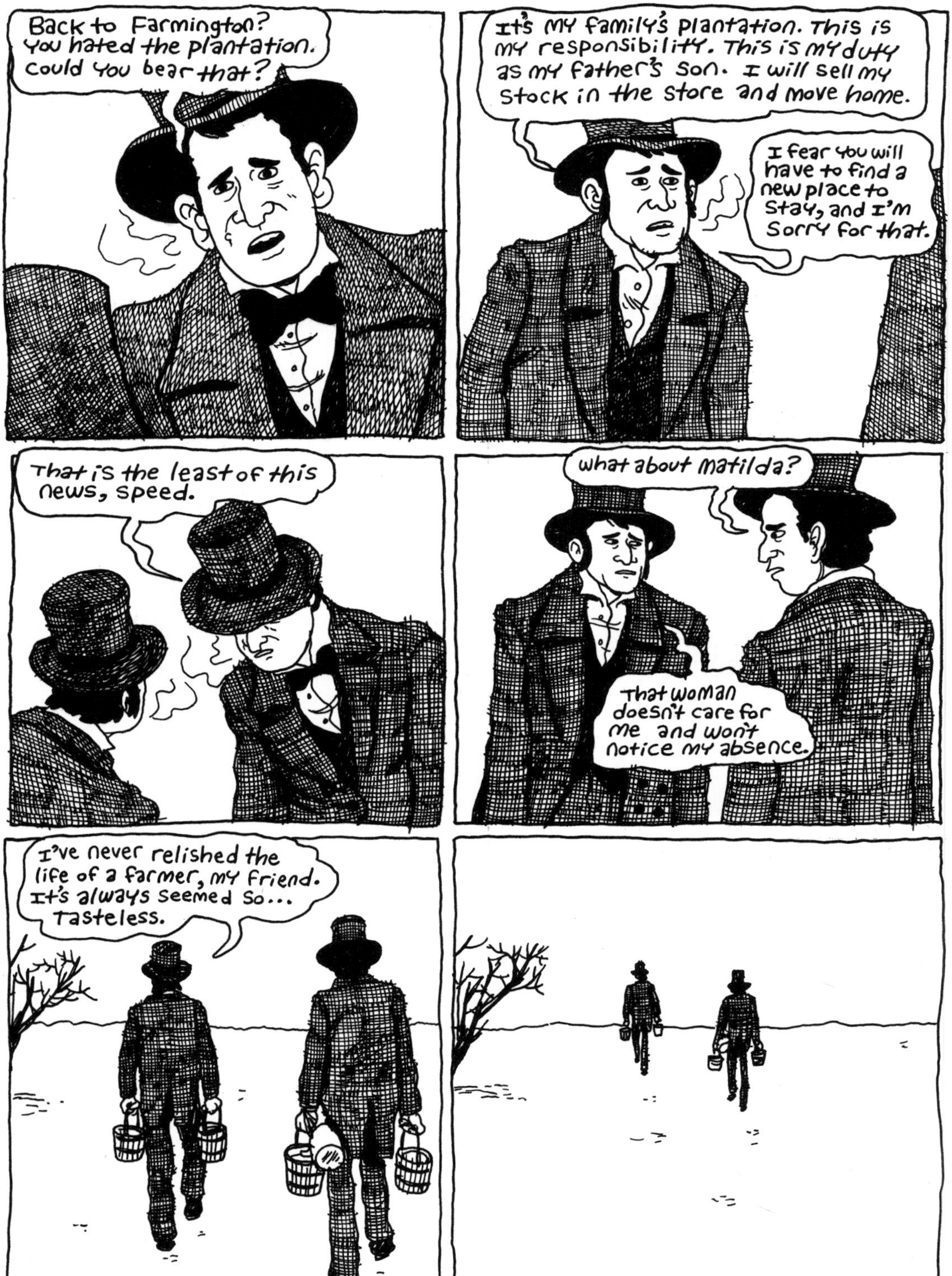
Back to Farmington? You hated the plantation. Could you bear that?
It's my family's plantation. This is my responsibility. This is my duty as my father's son. I will sell my stock in the store and move home.
I fear you will have to find a new place to stay, and I'm sorry for that.
That is the least of this news, Speed.
What about Matilda?
That woman doesn't care for me and won't notice my absence.
I've never relished the life of a farmer, my friend. It's always seemed so... tasteless.

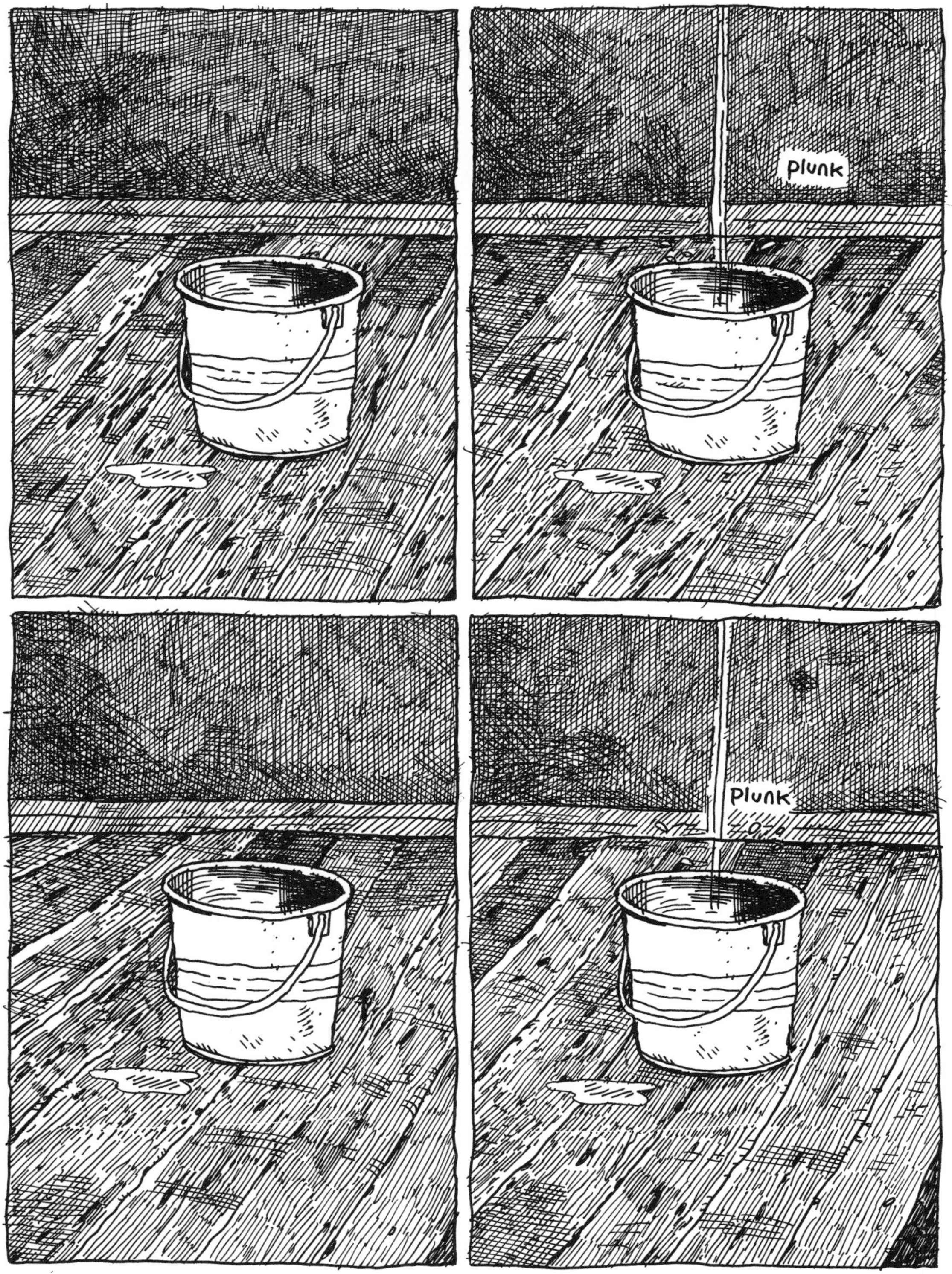
plunk
plunk

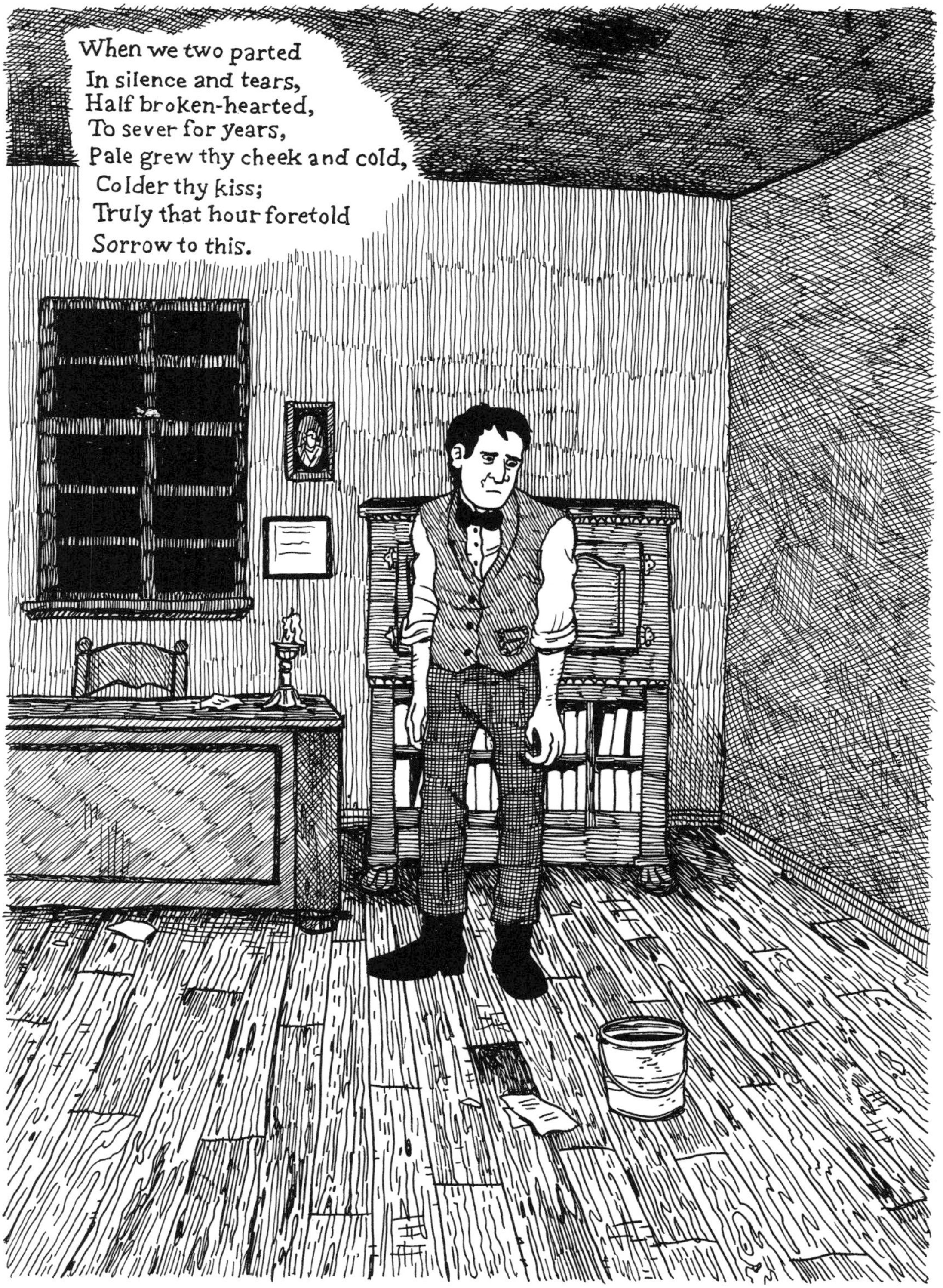
When we two parted
In silence and tears,
Half broken-hearted,
To sever for years,
Pale grew thy cheek and cold,
Colder thy kiss;
Truly that hour foretold
Sorrow to this.

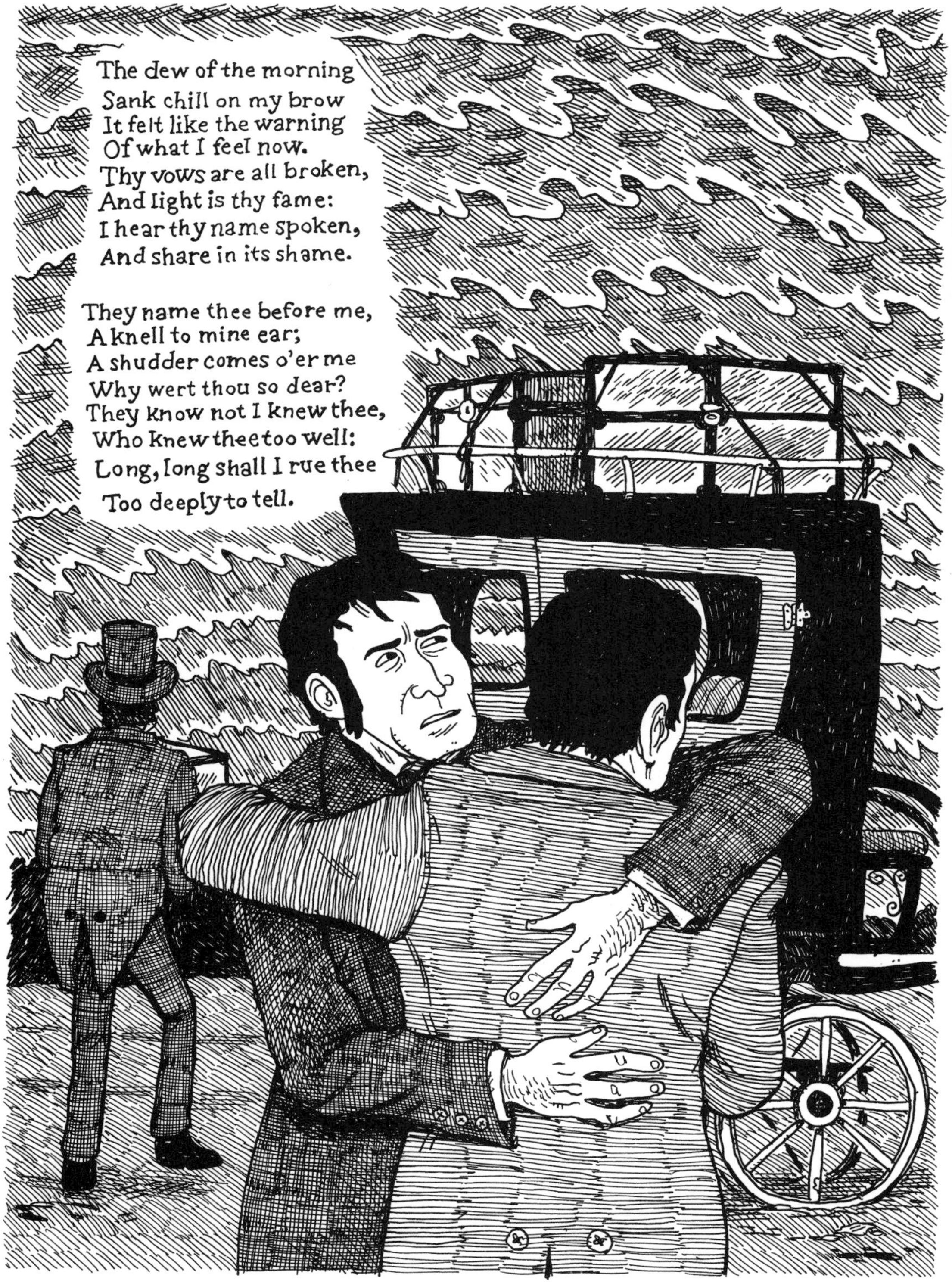
The dew of the morning
Sank chill on my brow
It felt like the warning
Of what I feel now.
Thy vows are all broken,
And light is thy fame:
I hear thy name spoken,
And share in its shame.

They name thee before me,
A knell to mine ear;
A shudder comes o'er me
Why wert thou so dear?
They know not I knew thee,
Who knew thee too well:
Long, long shall I rue thee
Too deeply to tell.

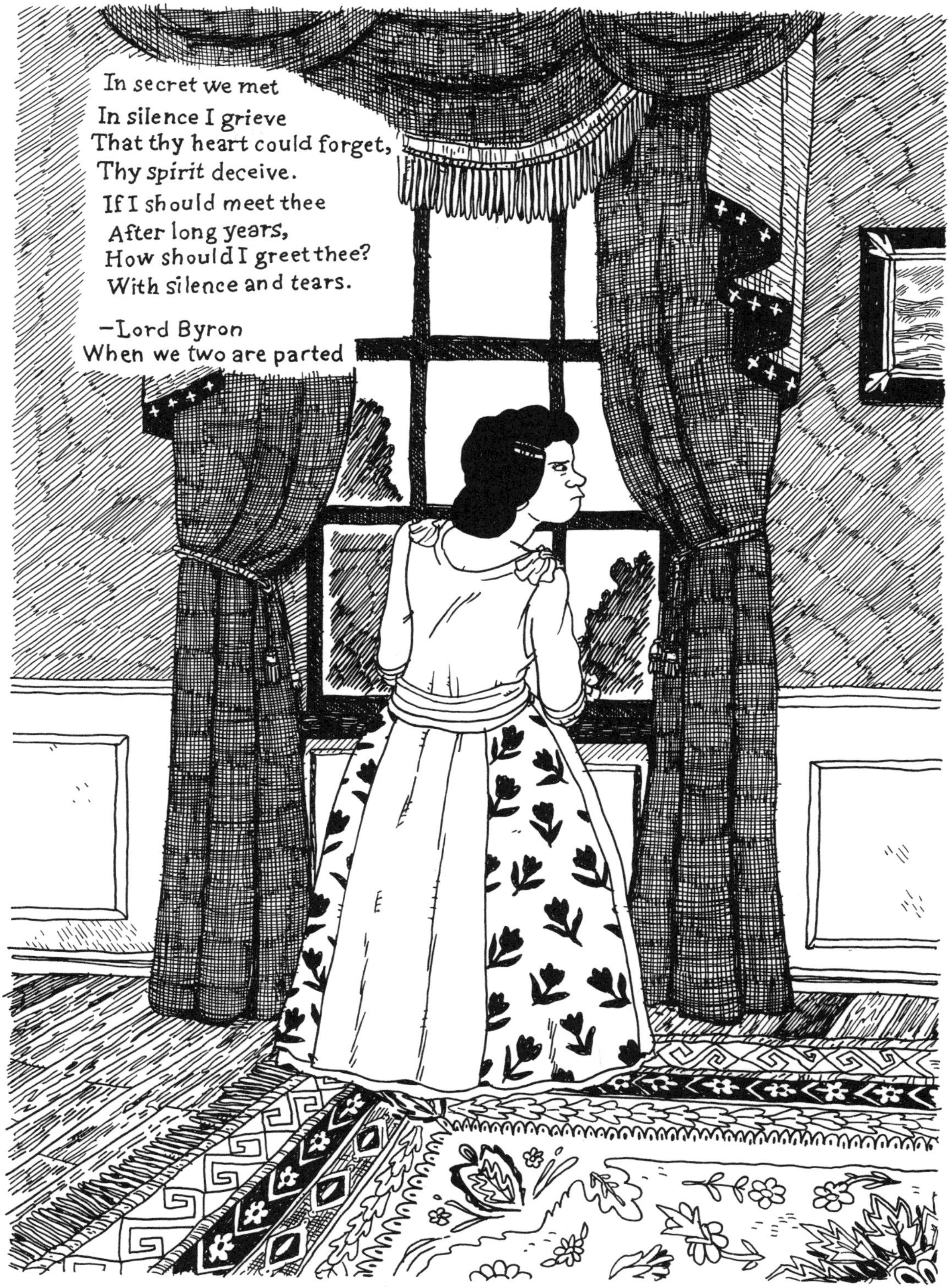
In secret we met
In silence I grieve
That thy heart could forget,
Thy spirit deceive.
If I should meet thee
After long years,
How should I greet thee?
With silence and tears.
—Lord Byron
When we two are parted

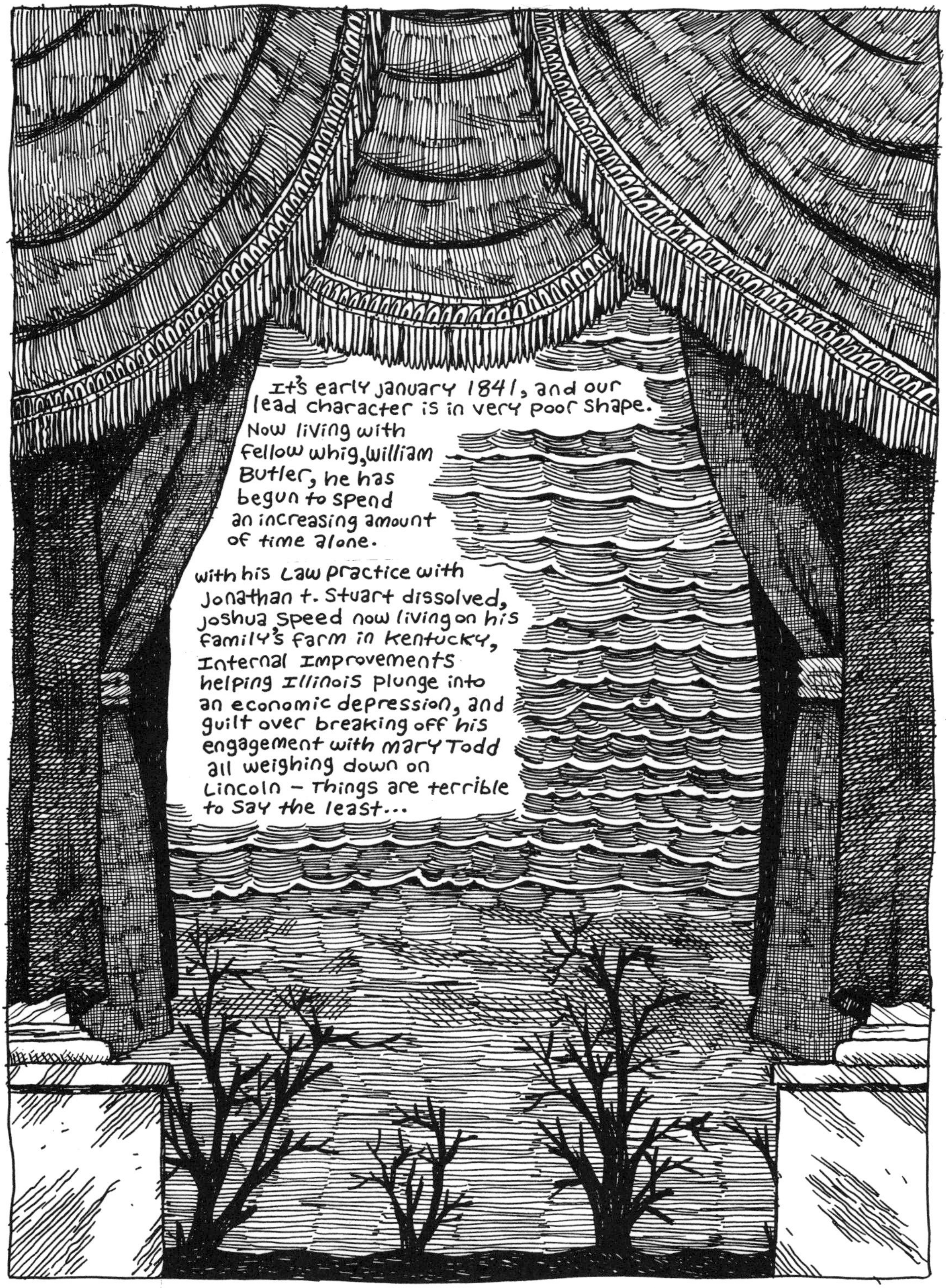
It's early January 1841, and our lead character is in very poor shape.
Now living with fellow whig, William Butler, he has begun to spend an increasing amount of time alone.
With his law practice with Jonathan T. Stuart dissolved, Joshua Speed now living on his family's farm in Kentucky, Internal Improvements helping Illinois plunge into an economic depression, and guilt over breaking off his engagement with Mary Todd all weighing down on Lincoln – Things are terrible to say the least...

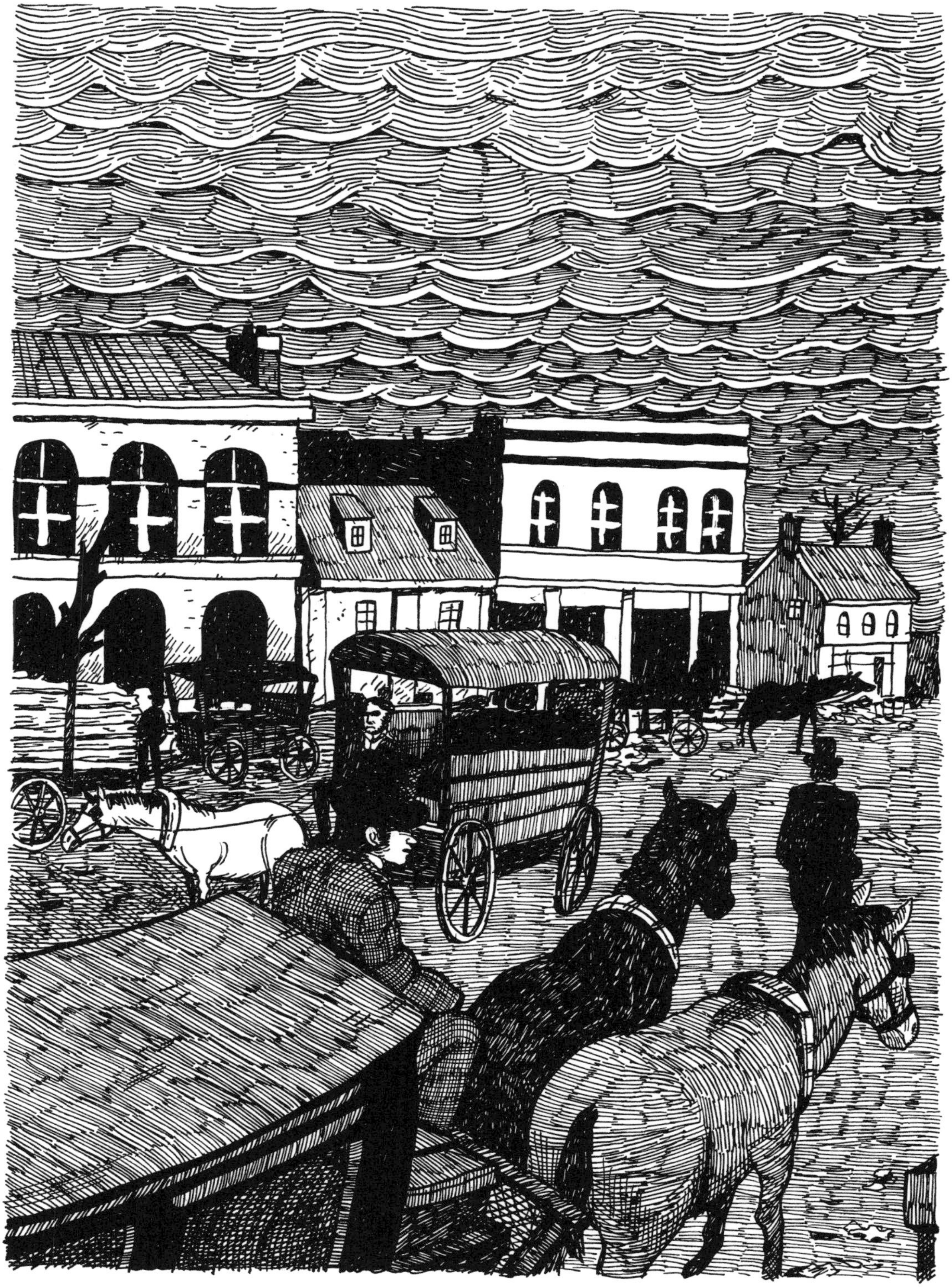

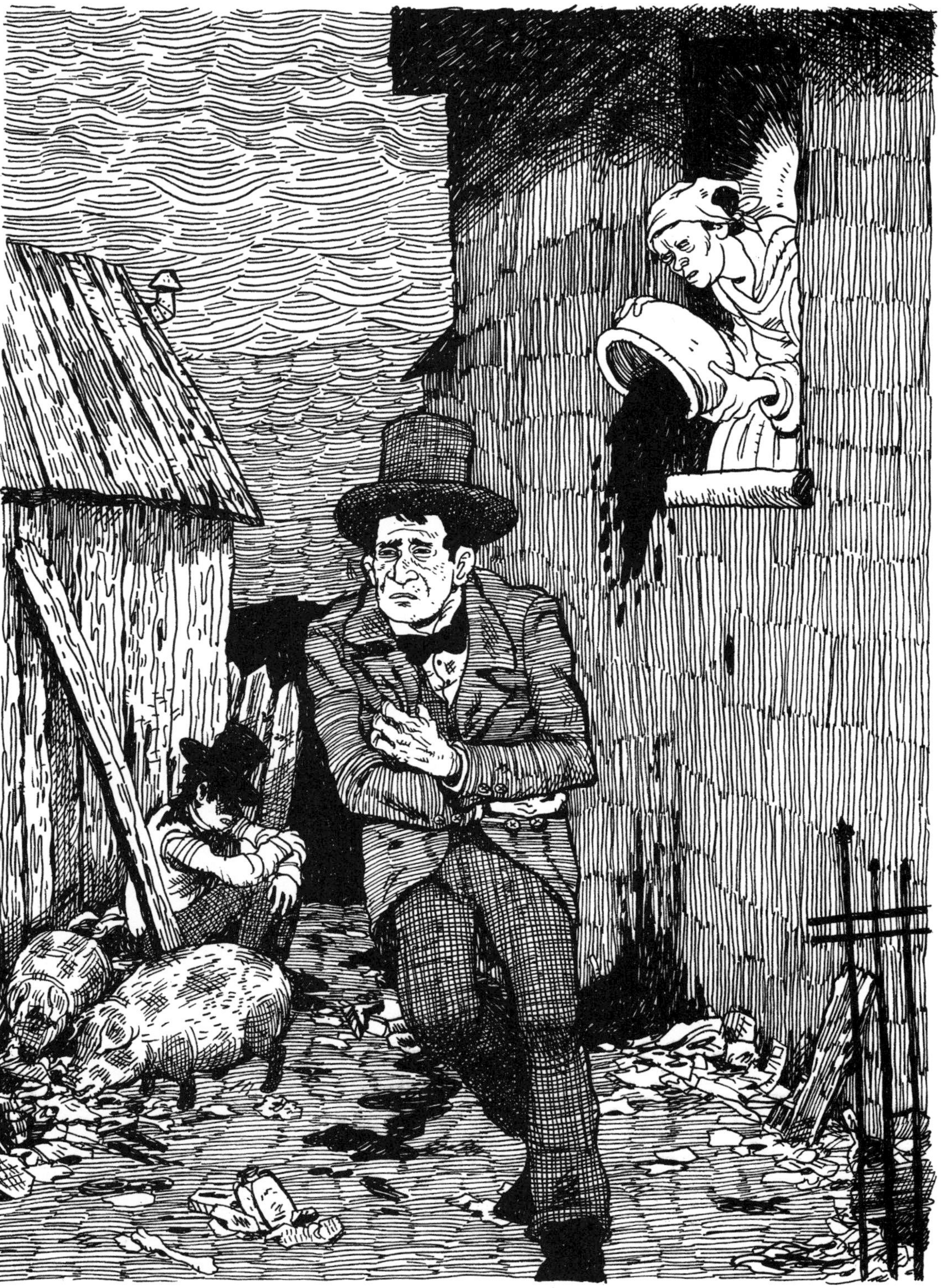

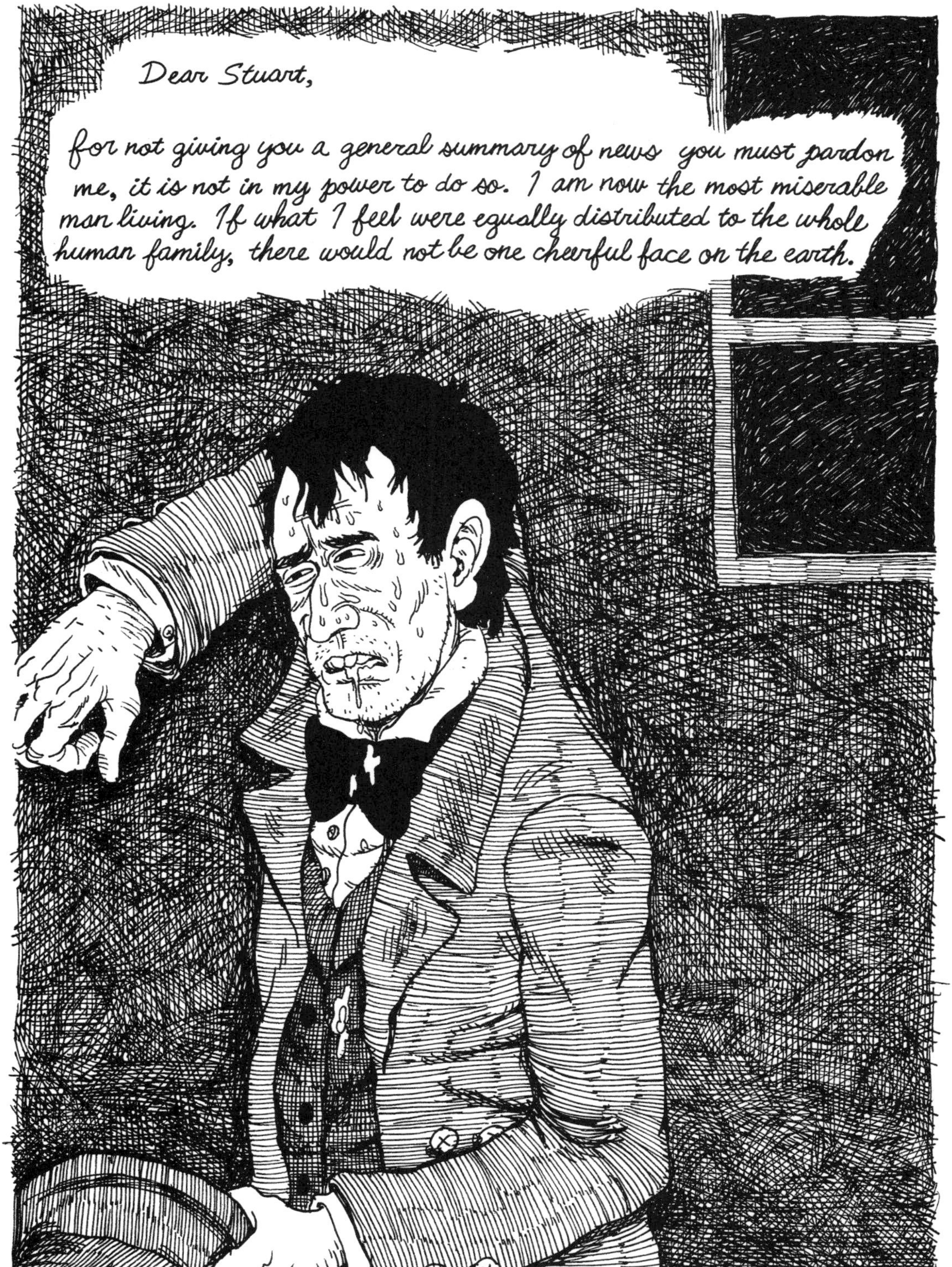
Dear Stuart,
for not giving you a general summary of news you must pardon me, it is not in my power to do so. I am now the most miserable man living. If what I feel were equally distributed to the whole human family, there would not be one cheerful face on the earth.

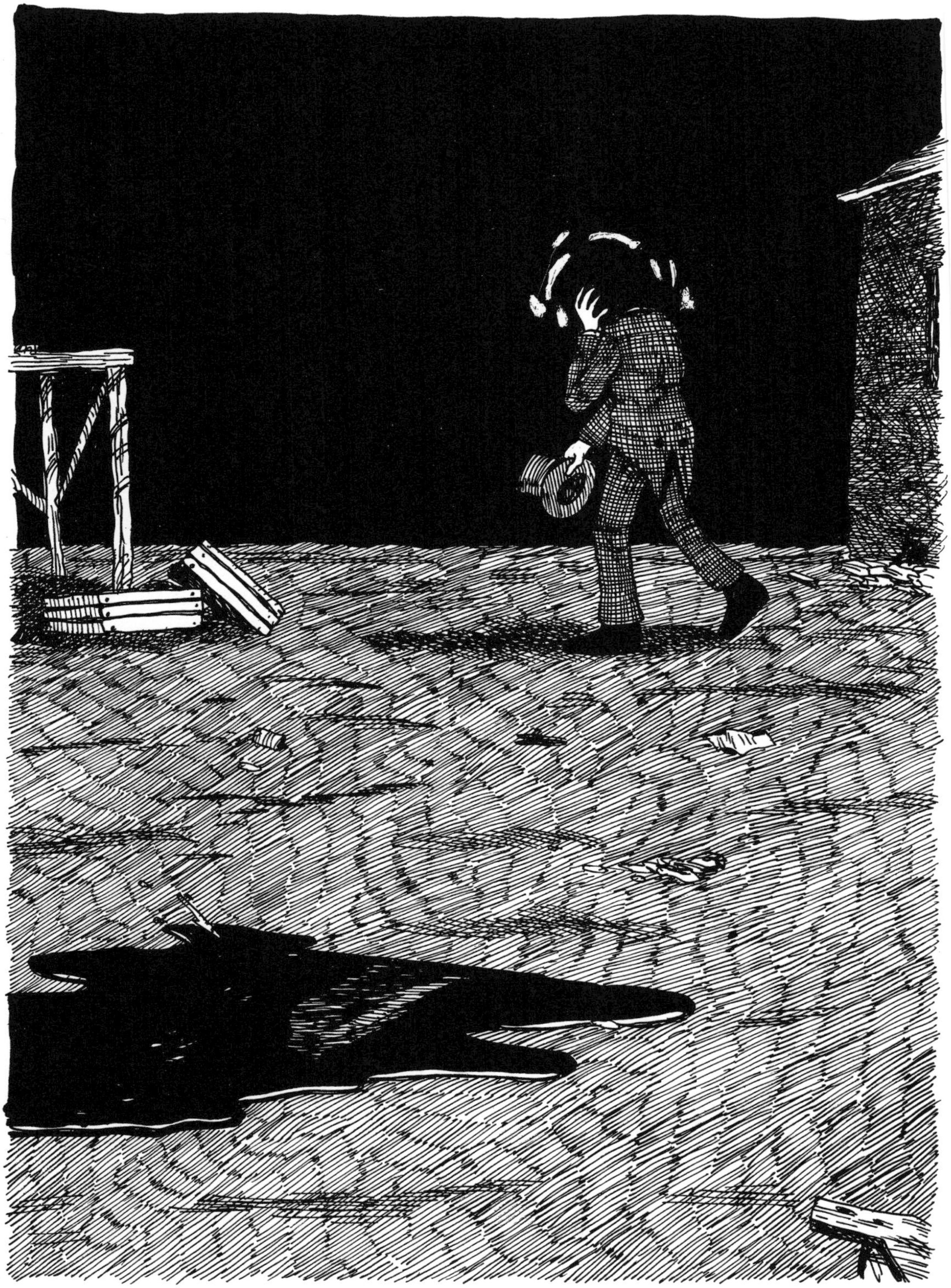

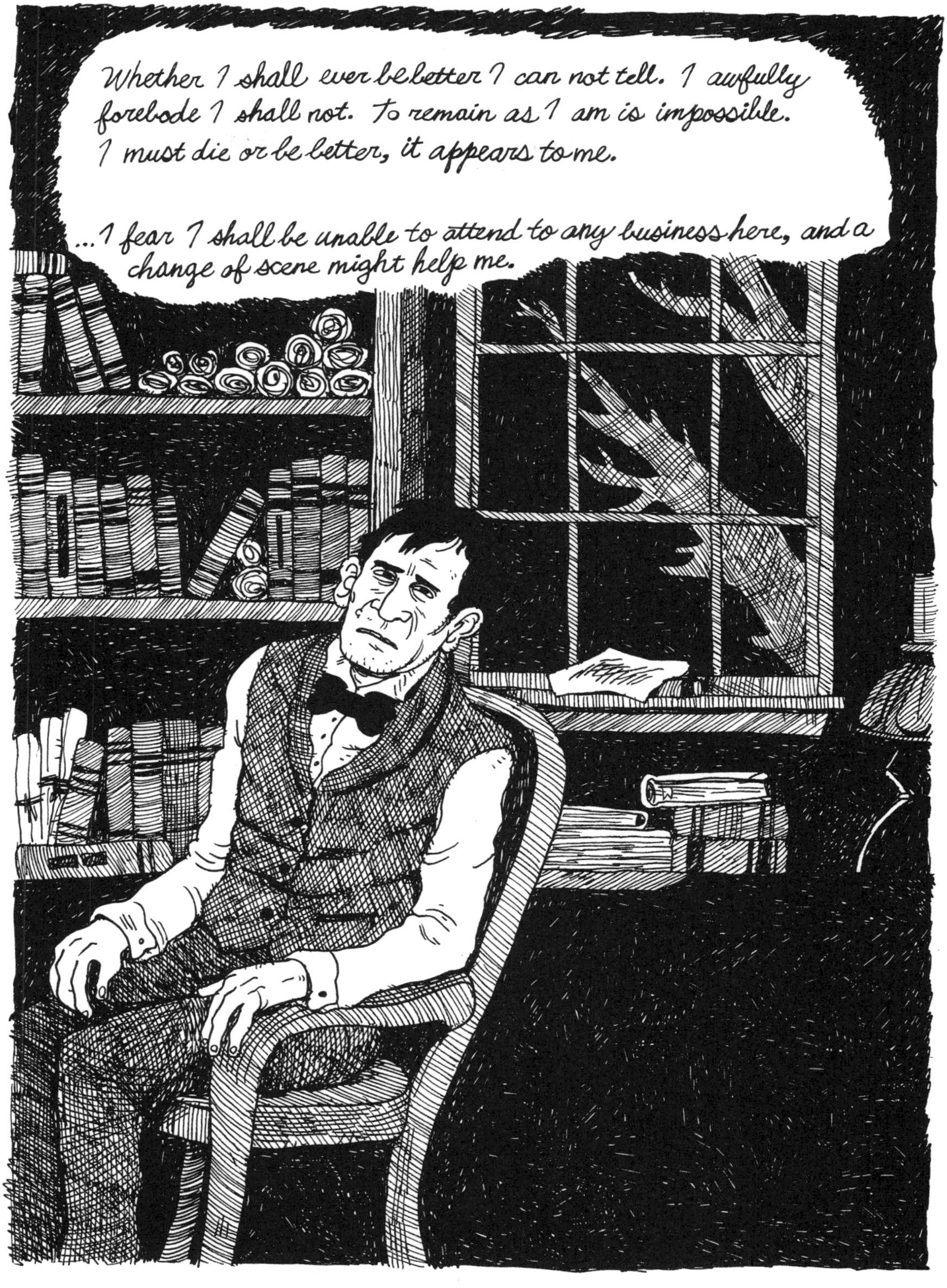
Whether I shall ever be better I can not tell. I awfully forebode I shall not. To remain as I am is impossible. I must die or be better, it appears to me.
...I fear I shall be unable to attend to any business here, and a change of scene might help me.

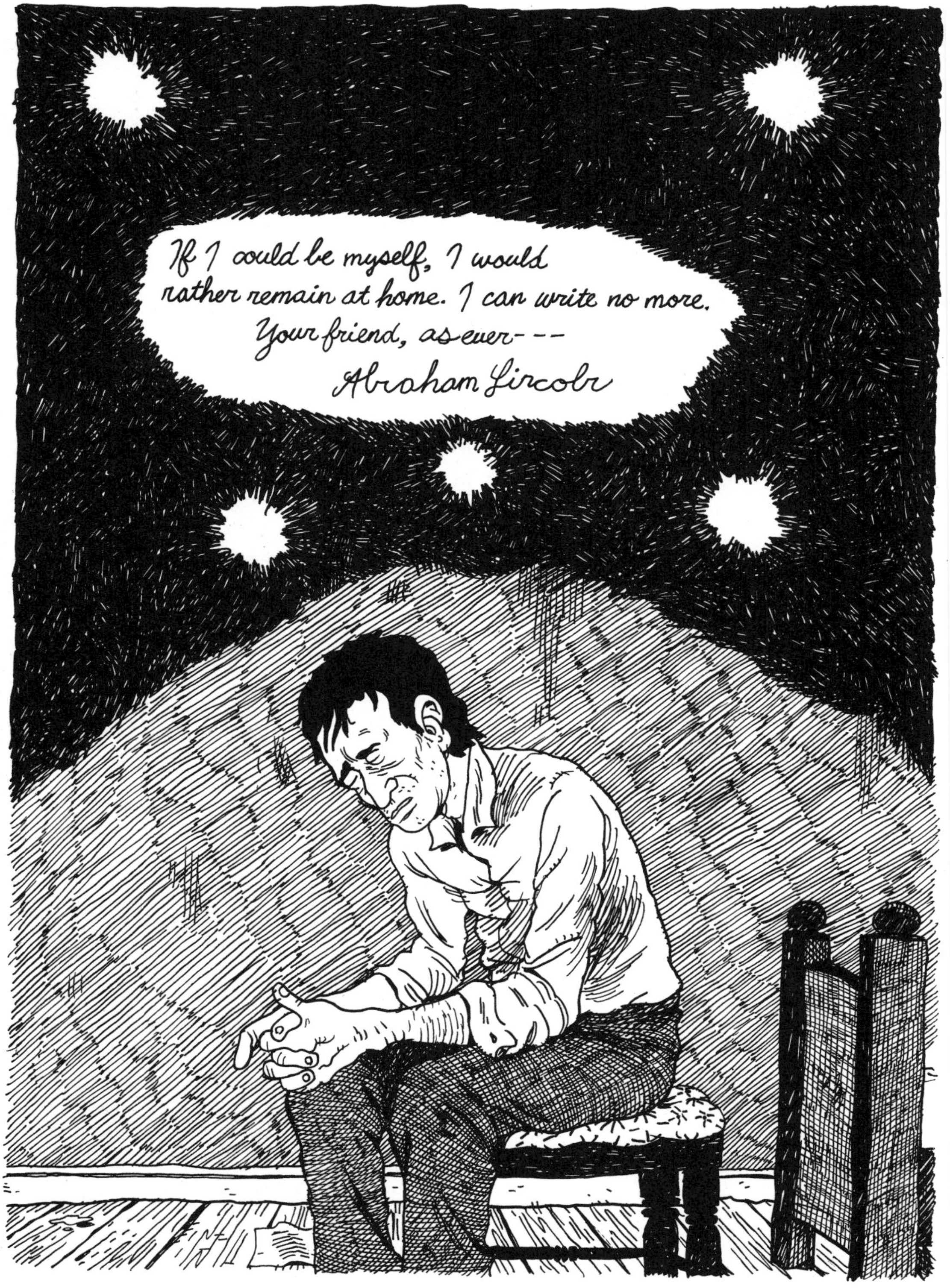
If I could be myself, I would
rather remain at home. I can write no more.
Your friend, as ever---
Abraham Lincoln

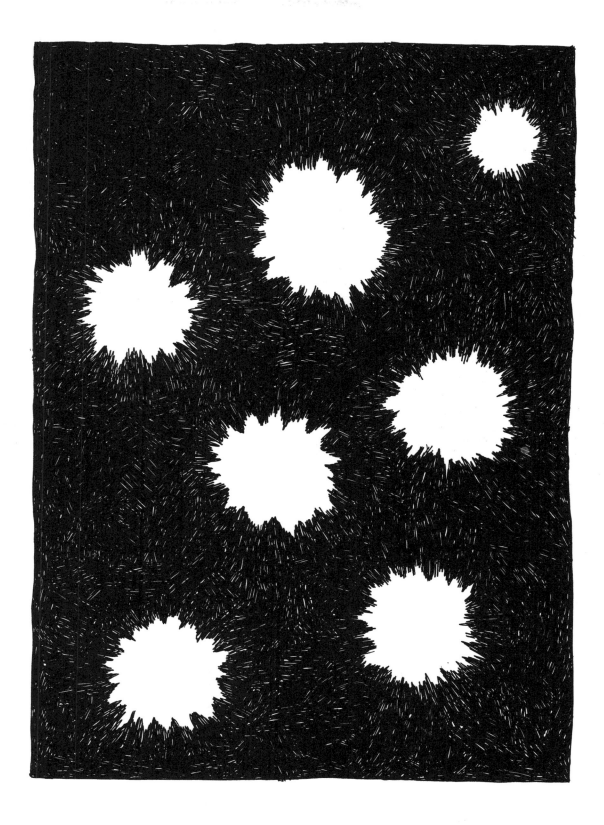

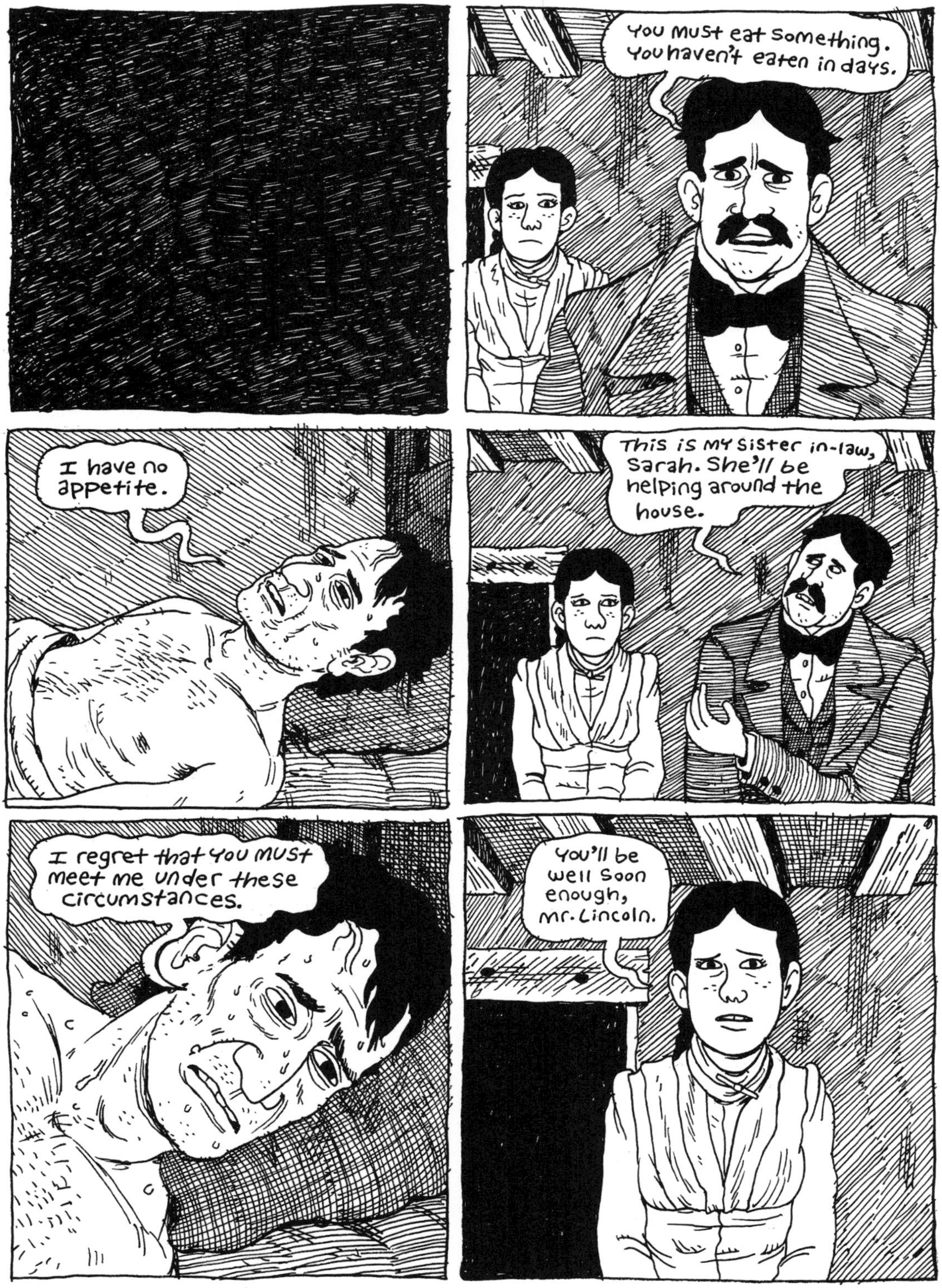
You must eat something. You haven't eaten in days.
I have no appetite.
This is my sister in-law, Sarah. She'll be helping around the house.
I regret that you must meet me under these circumstances.
You'll be well soon enough, Mr. Lincoln.

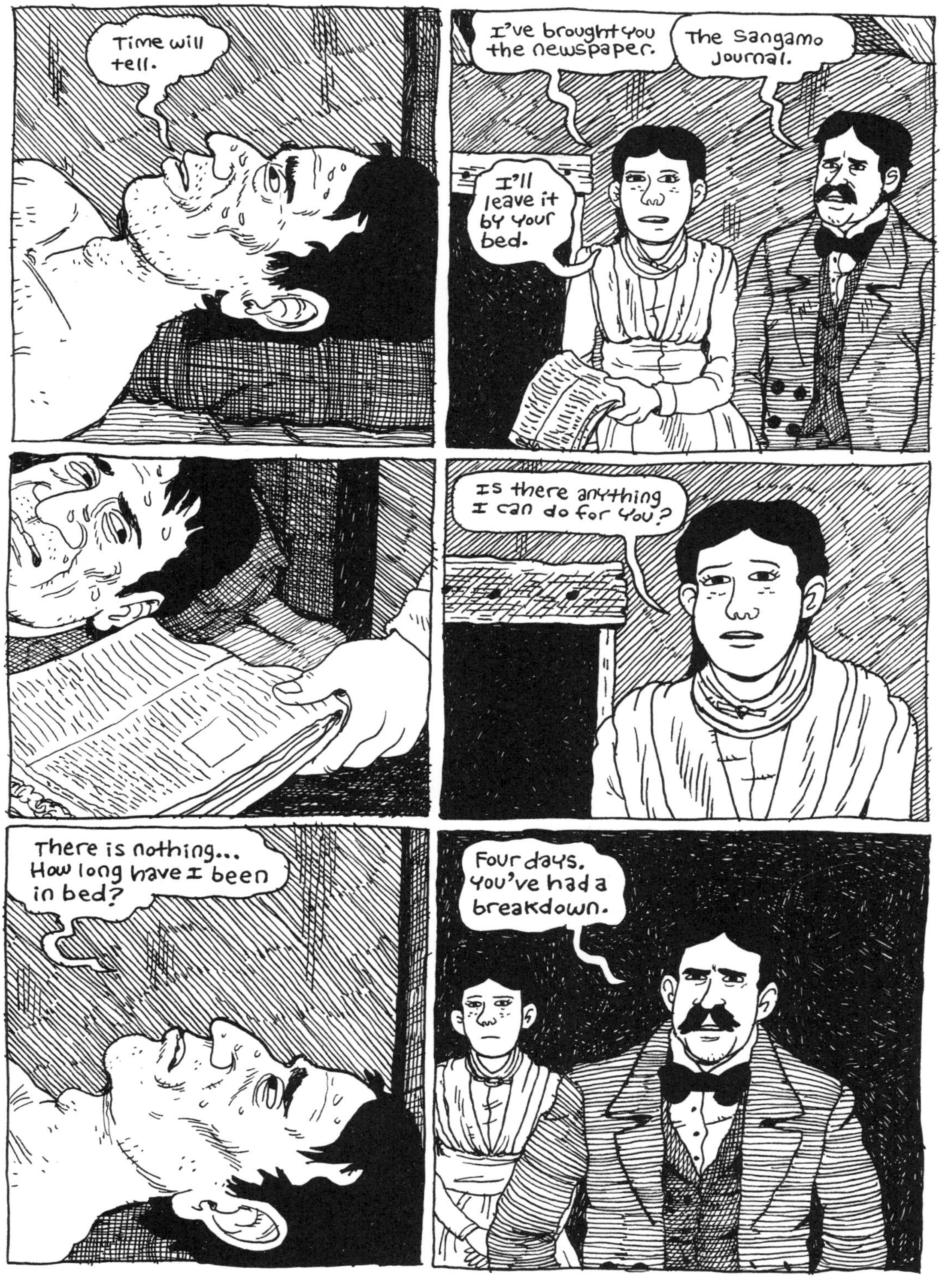
Time will tell.
I've brought you the newspaper.
The Sangamo Journal.
I'll leave it by your bed.
Is there anything I can do for you?
There is nothing... How long have I been in bed?
Four days. You've had a breakdown.

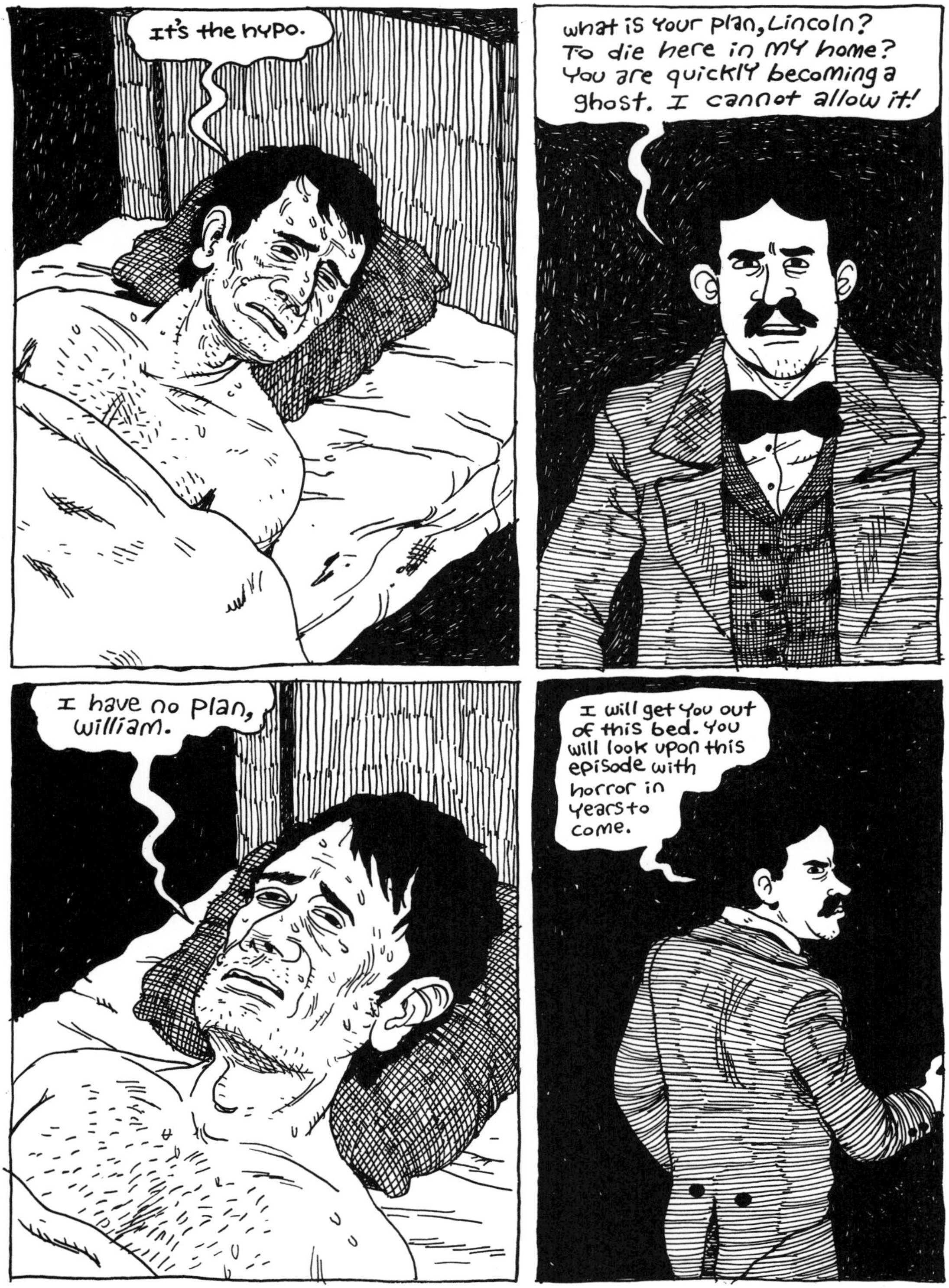
It's the hypo.
what is your plan, Lincoln? To die here in MY home? You are quickly becoming a ghost. I cannot allow it!
I have no plan, william.
I will get you out of this bed. You will look upon this episode with horror in years to come.

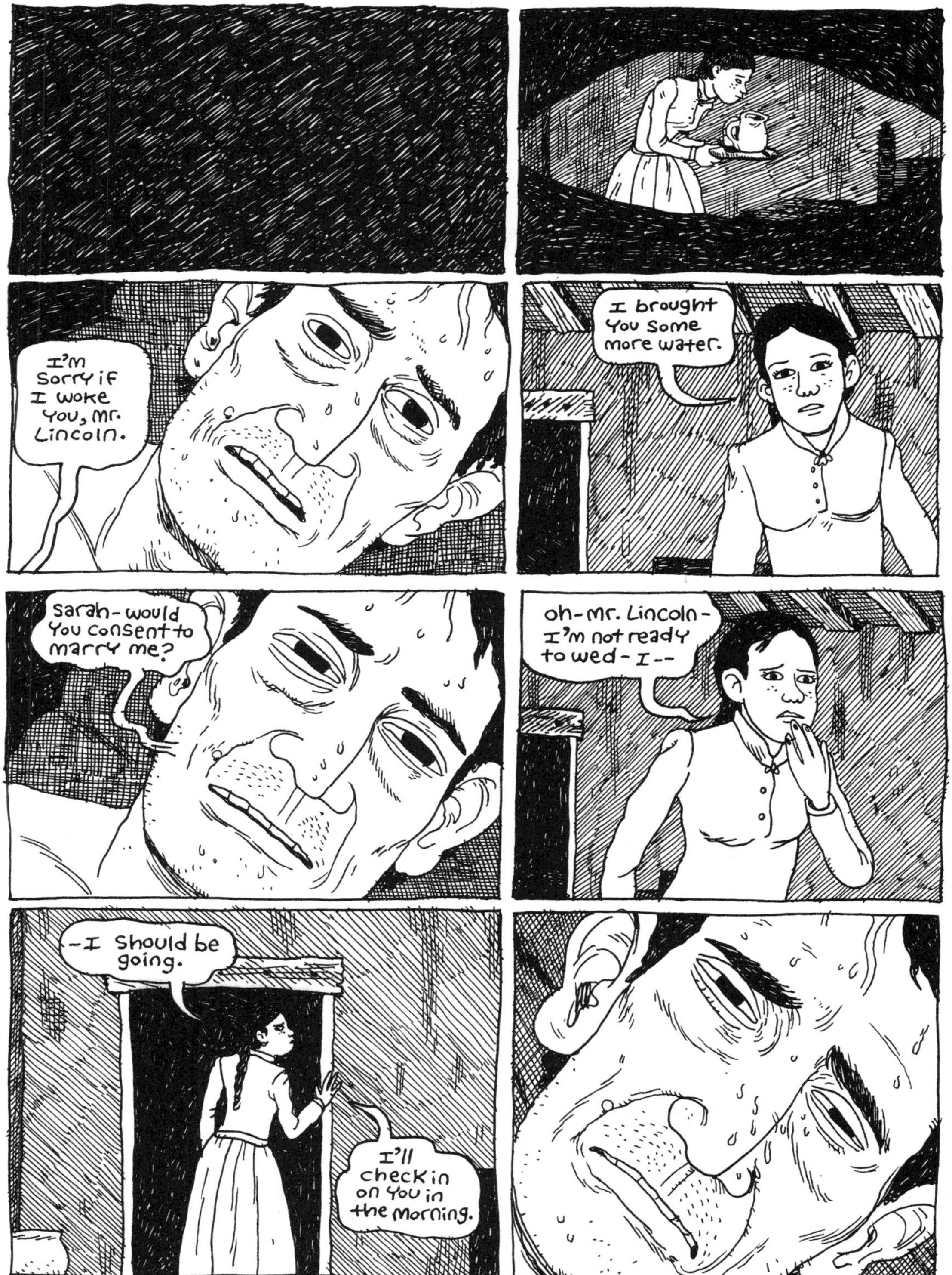
I'm sorry if I woke you, Mr. Lincoln.
I brought you some more water.
Sarah- would you consent to marry me?
Oh- Mr. Lincoln- I'm not ready to wed - I--
-I should be going.
I'll check in on you in the morning.

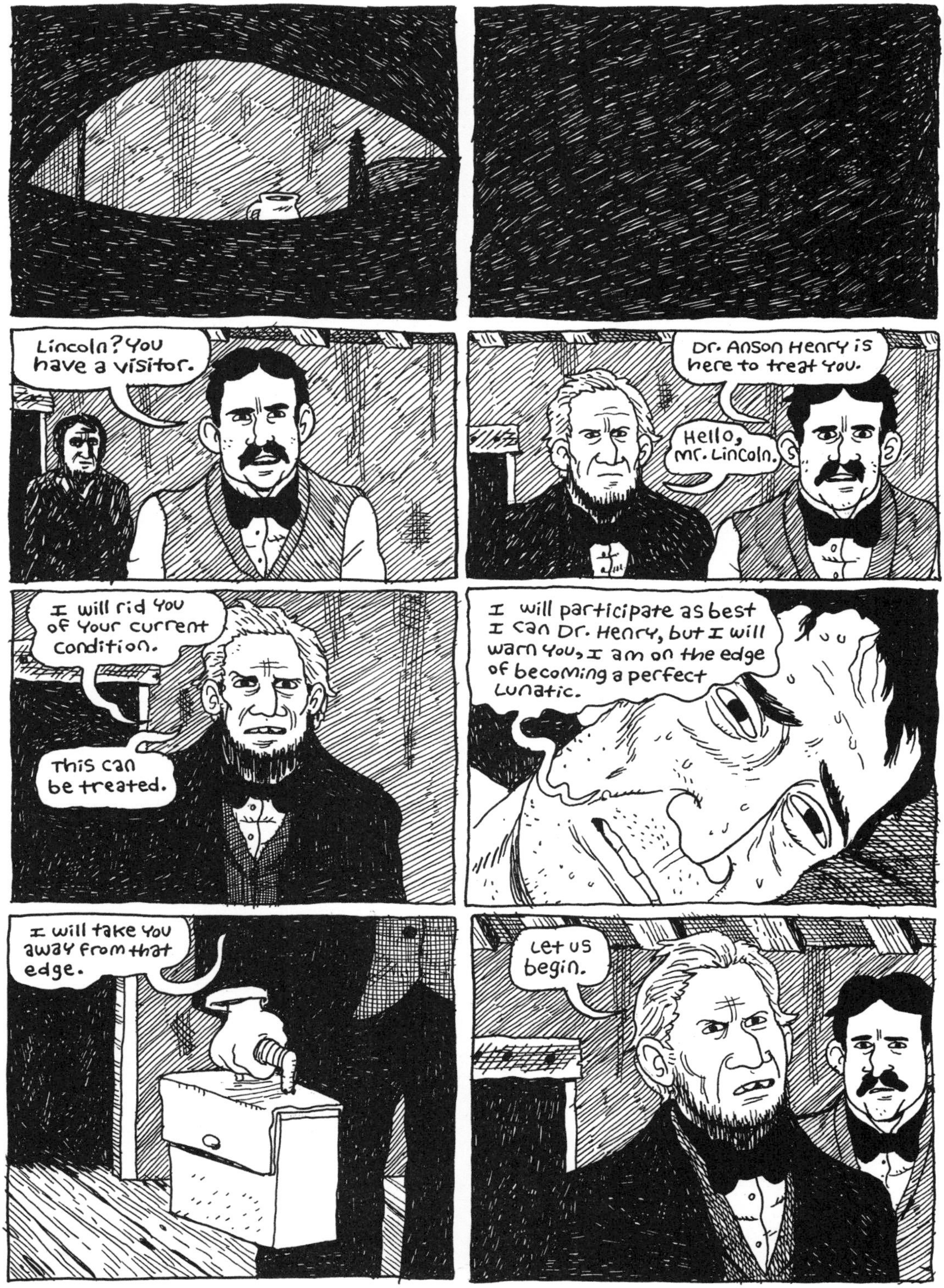
Lincoln? You have a visitor.
Dr. Anson Henry is here to treat you.
Hello, Mr. Lincoln.
I will rid you of your current condition.
This can be treated.
I will participate as best I can Dr. Henry, but I will warn you, I am on the edge of becoming a perfect Lunatic.
I will take you away from that edge.
Let us begin.

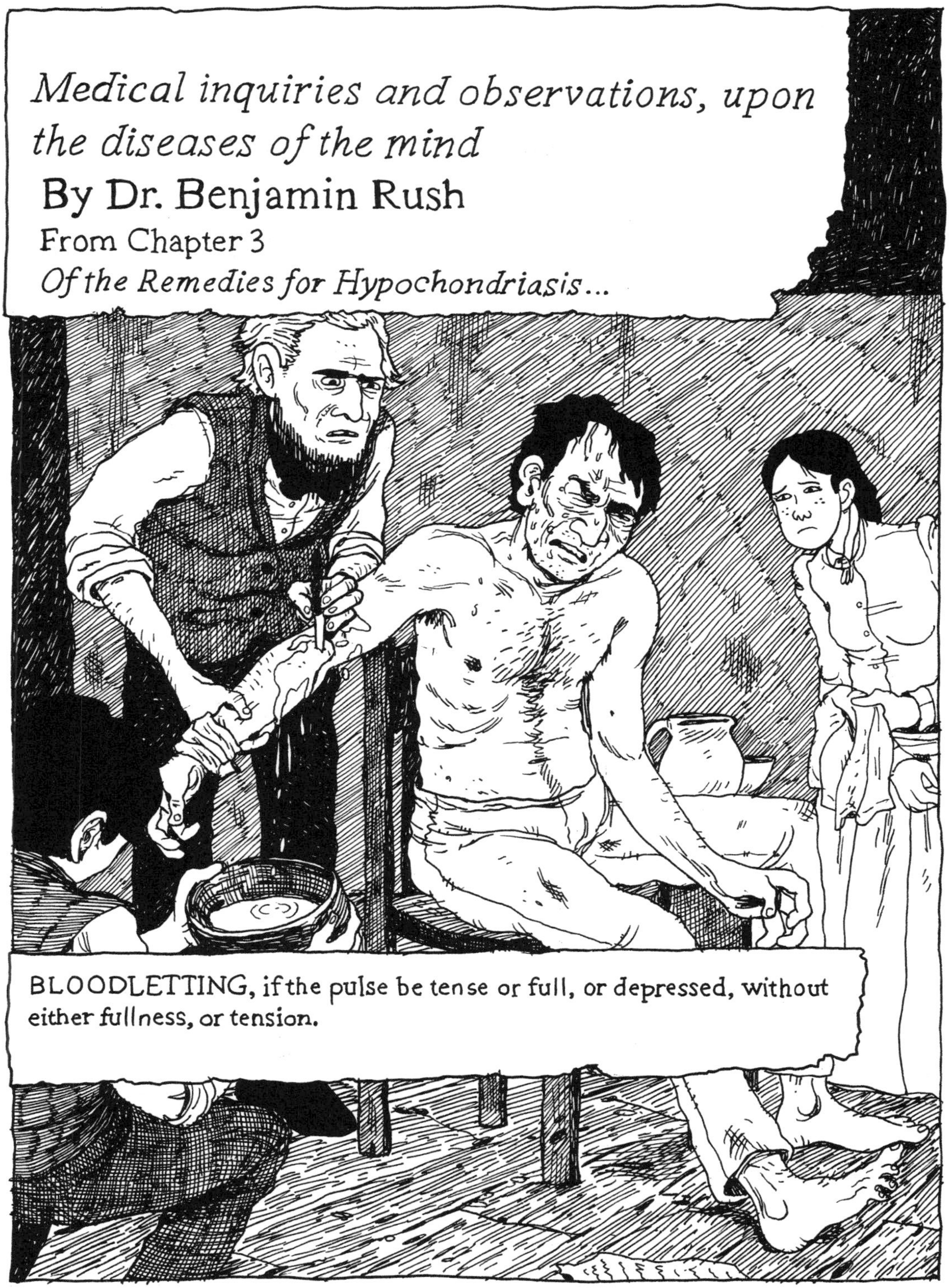
Medical inquiries and observations, upon the diseases of the mind
By Dr. Benjamin Rush
From Chapter 3
Of the Remedies for Hypochondriasis...
BLOODLETTING, if the pulse be tense or full, or depressed, without either fullness, or tension.

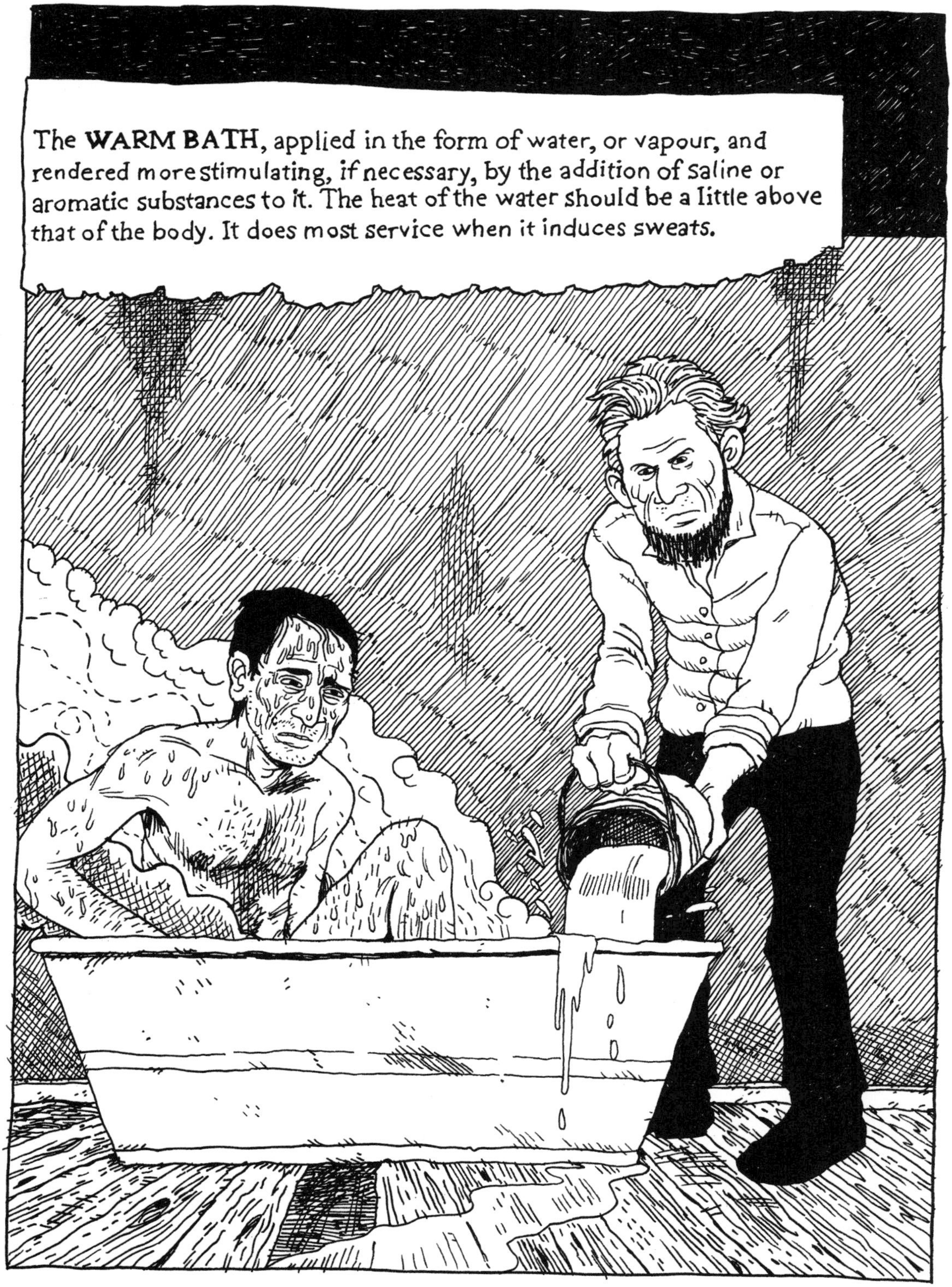
The WARM BATH, applied in the form of water, or vapour, and rendered more stimulating, if necessary, by the addition of saline or aromatic substances to it. The heat of the water should be a little above that of the body. It does most service when it induces sweats.

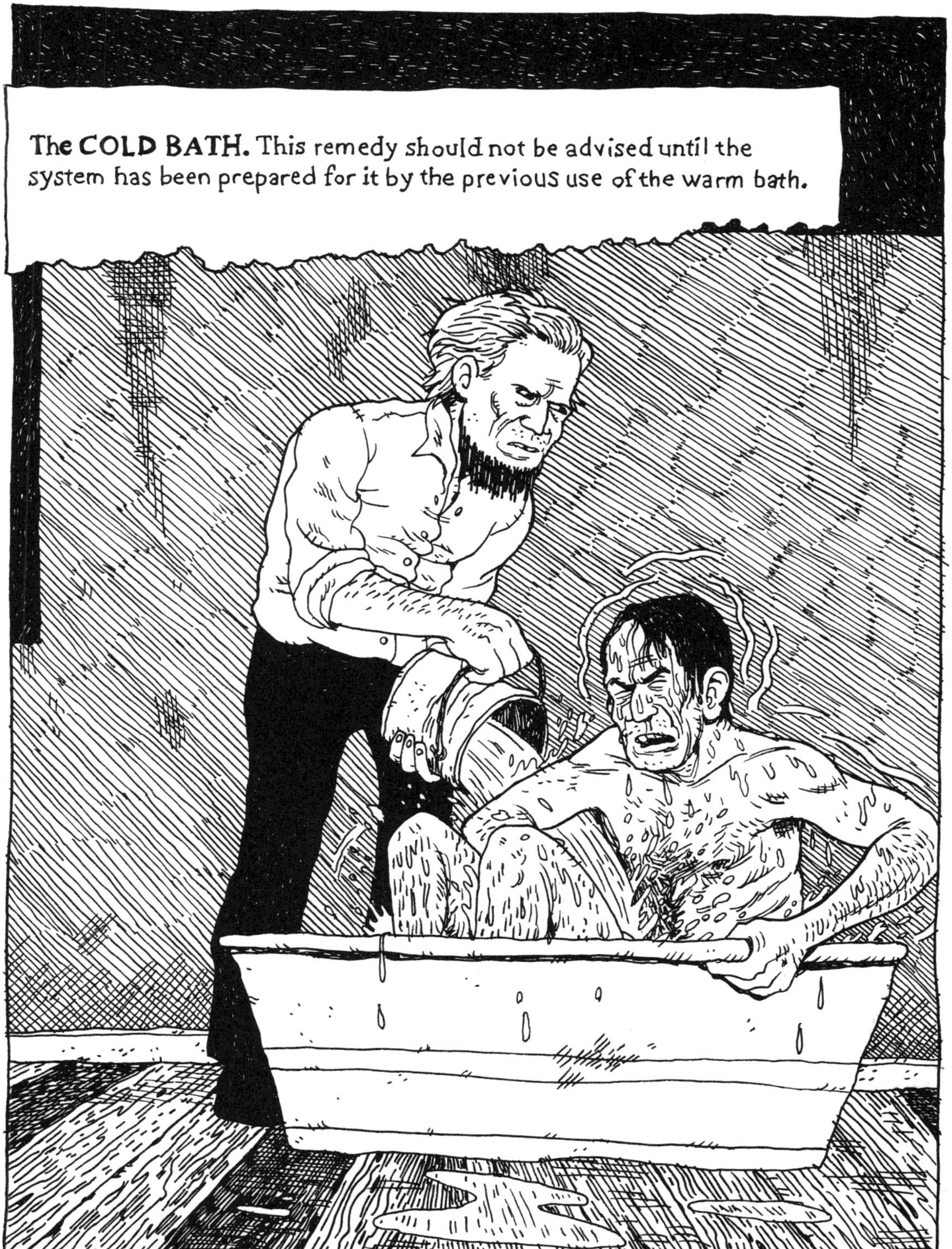
The COLD BATH. This remedy should not be advised until the system has been prepared for it by the previous use of the warm bath.

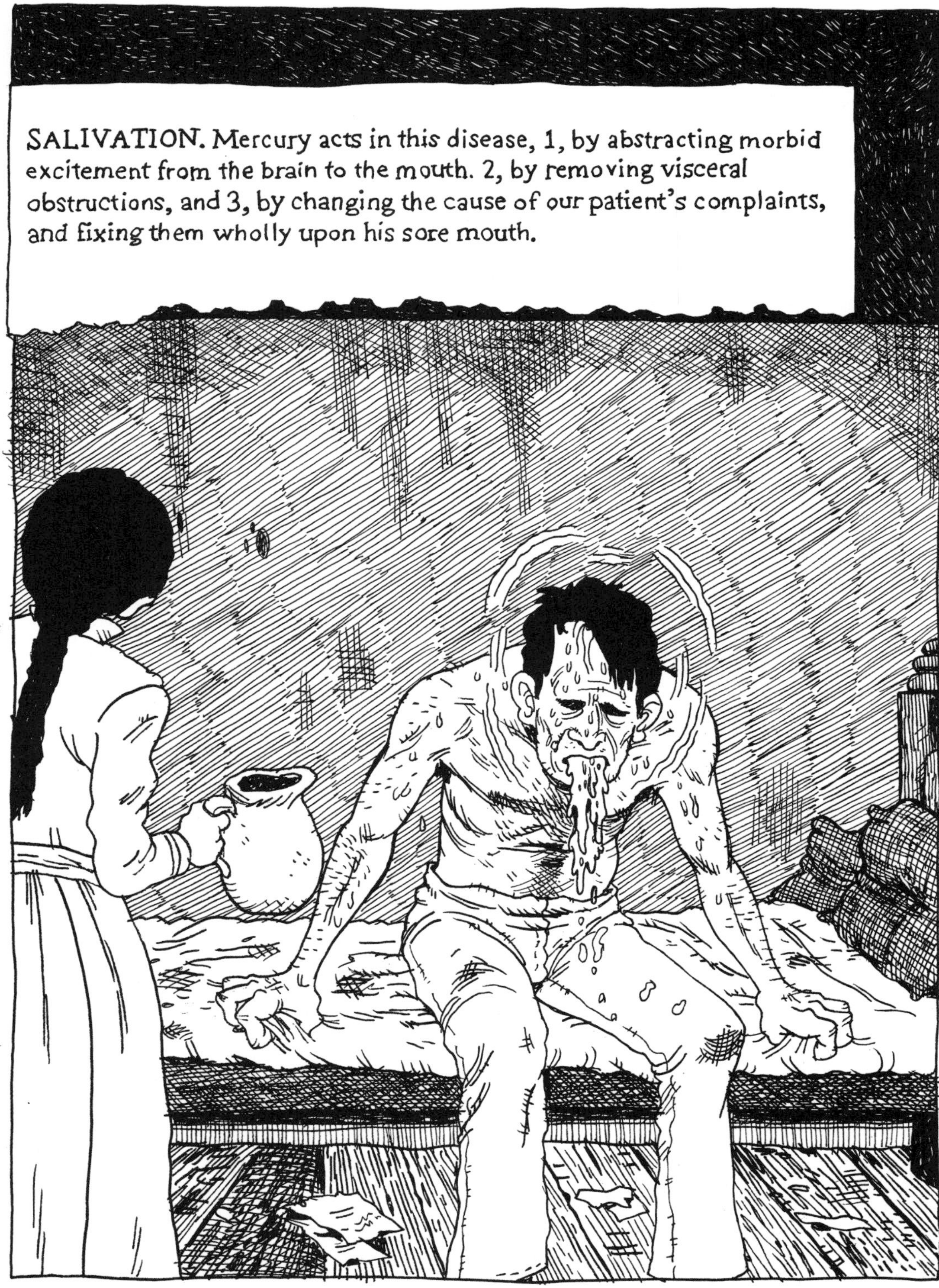
SALIVATION. Mercury acts in this disease, 1, by abstracting morbid excitement from the brain to the mouth. 2, by removing visceral obstructions, and 3, by changing the cause of our patient's complaints, and fixing them wholly upon his sore mouth.

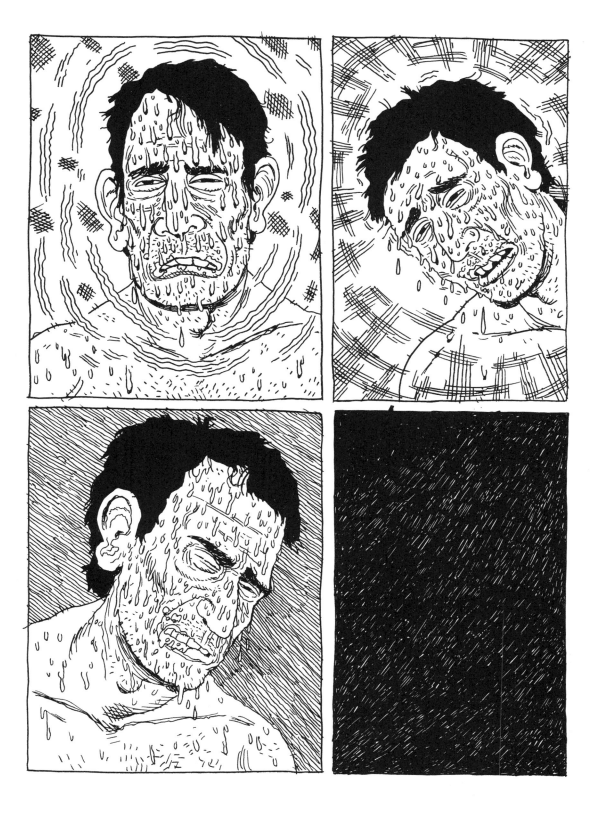

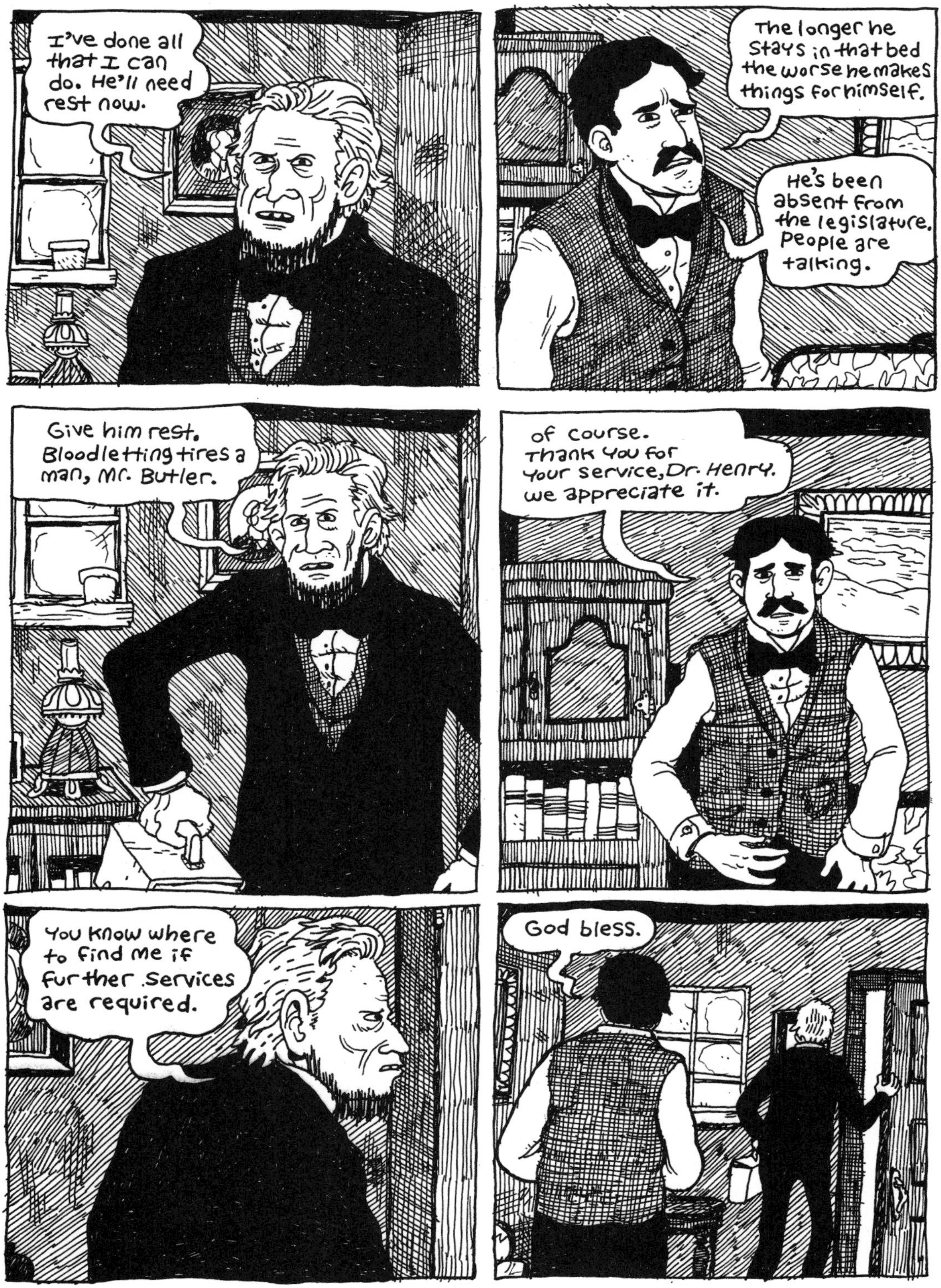
I've done all that I can do. He'll need rest now.
The longer he stays in that bed the worse he makes things for himself.
He's been absent from the legislature. People are talking.
Give him rest. Bloodletting tires a man, Mr. Butler.
of course. Thank you for your service, Dr. Henry. we appreciate it.
You know where to find me if further services are required.
God bless.

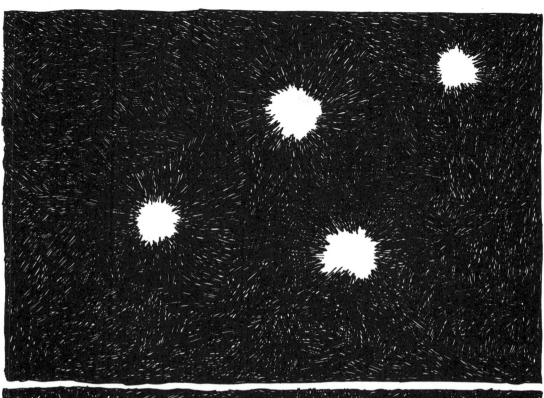
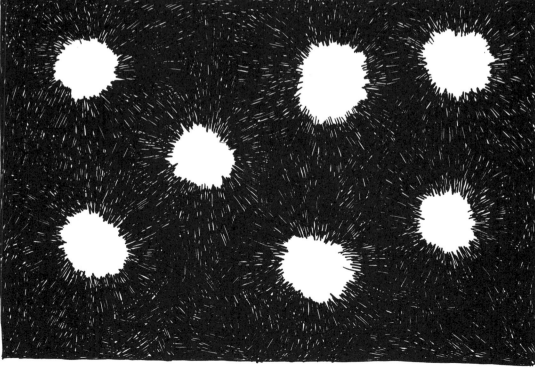

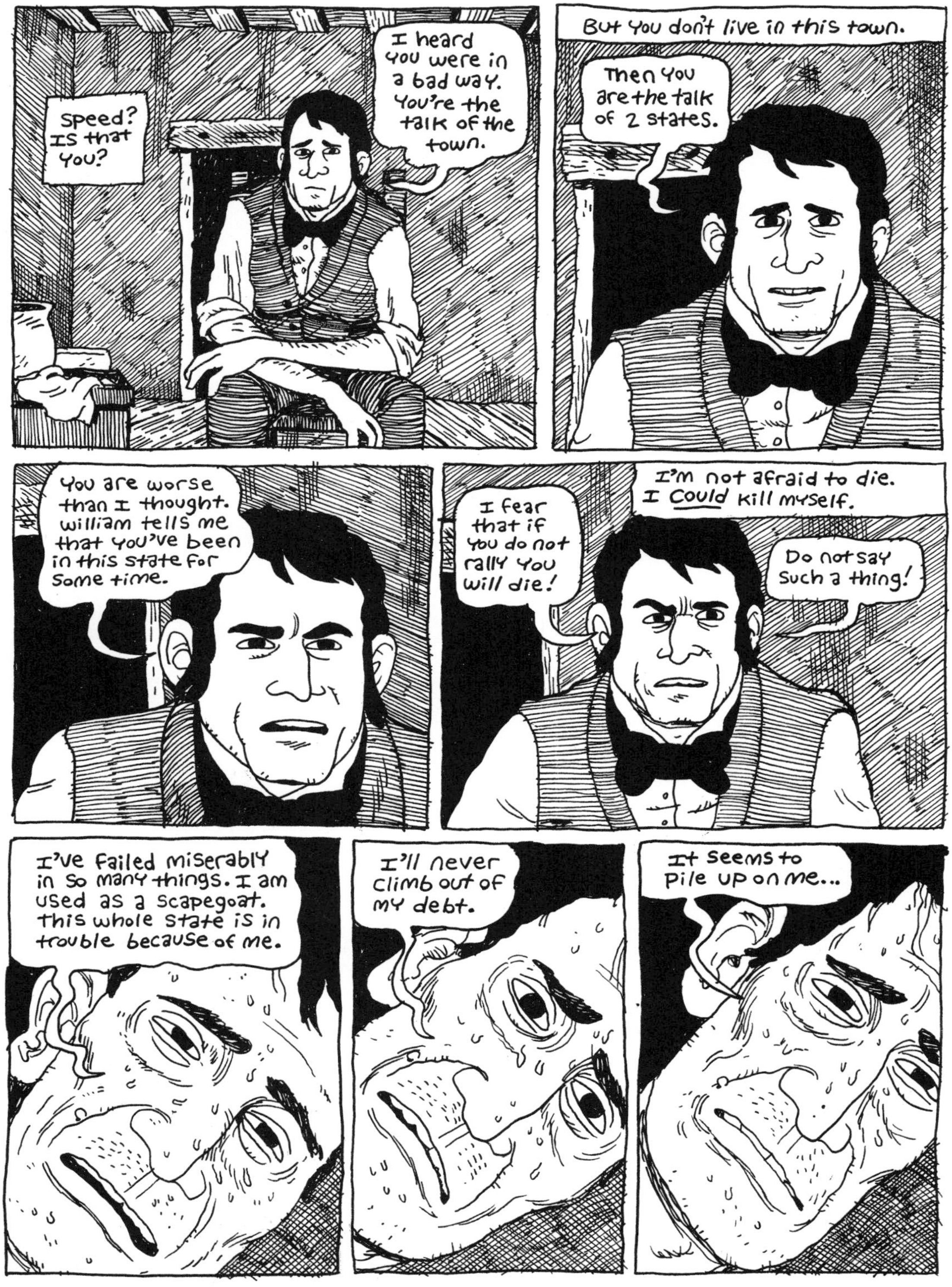
Speed? Is that you?
I heard you were in a bad way. You're the talk of the town.
But you don't live in this town.
Then you are the talk of 2 states.
You are worse than I thought. William tells me that you've been in this state for some time.
I fear that if you do not rally you will die!
I'm not afraid to die. I COULD kill myself.
Do not say such a thing!
I've failed miserably in so many things. I am used as a scapegoat. This whole state is in trouble because of me.
I'll never climb out of my debt.
It seems to pile up on me...

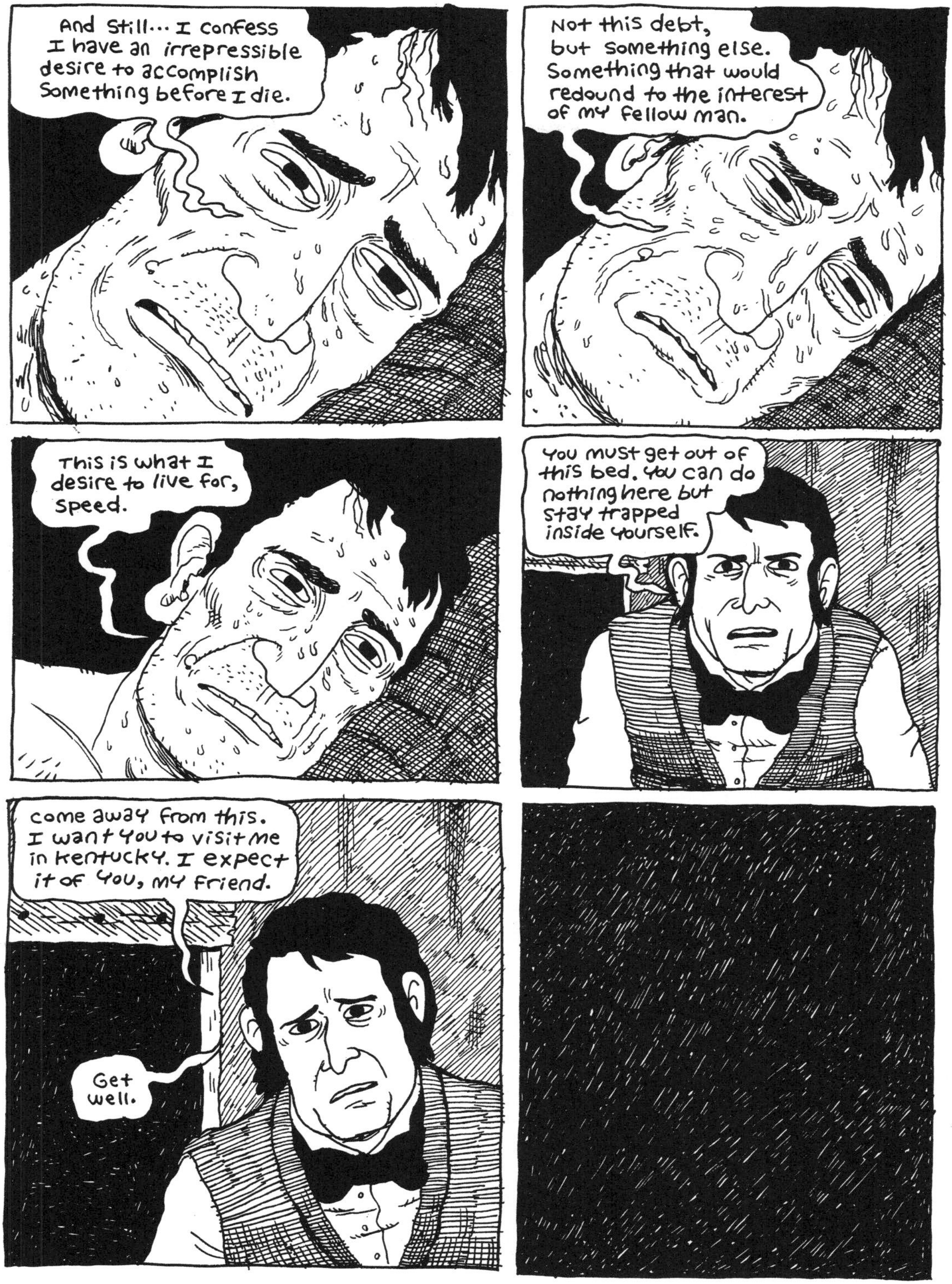
And Still... I confess I have an irrepressible desire to accomplish Something before I die.
Not this debt, but something else. Something that would redound to the interest of my fellow man.
This is what I desire to live for, speed.
You must get out of this bed. You can do nothing here but stay trapped inside yourself.
come away from this. I want you to visit me in Kentucky. I expect it of you, my friend.
Get well.

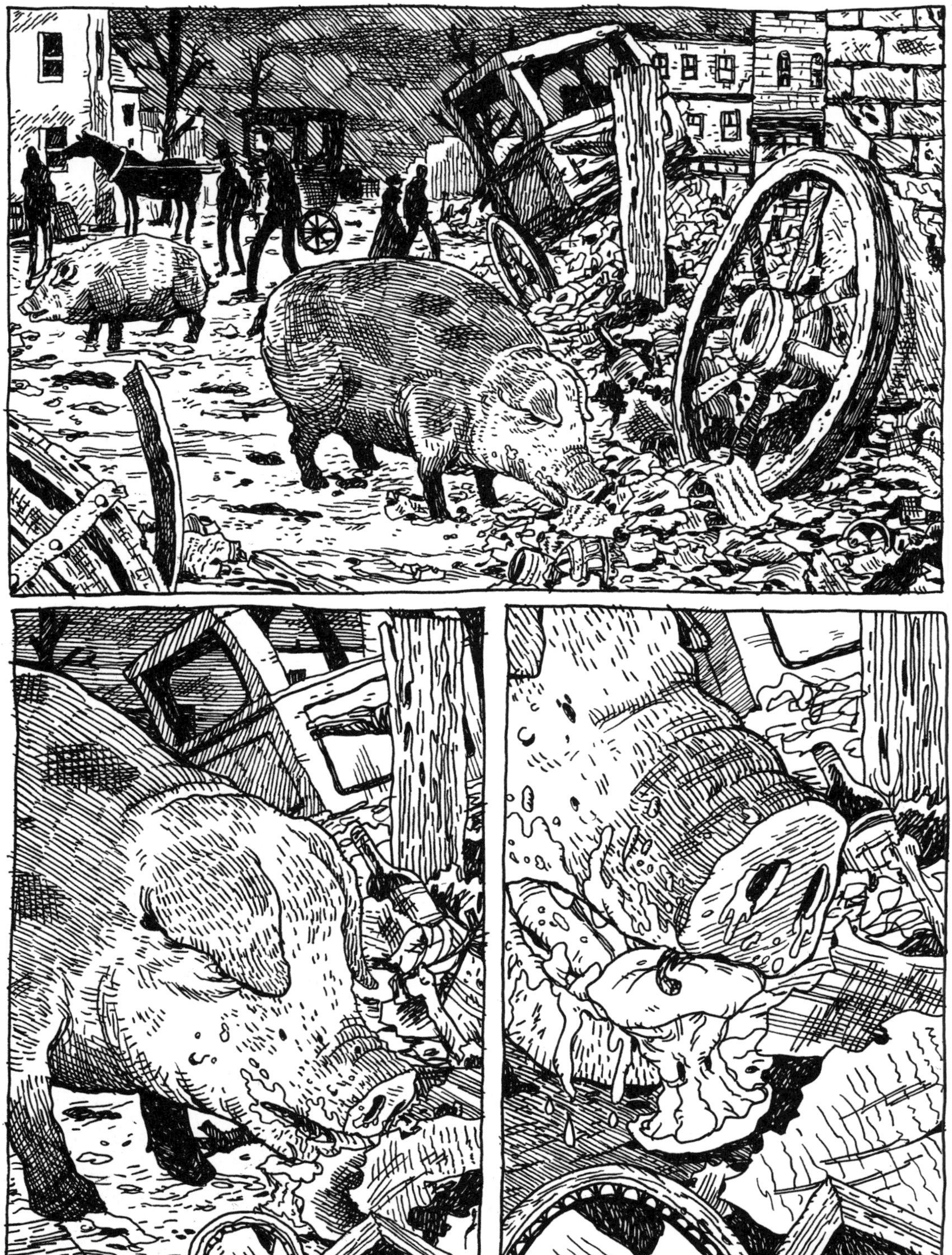

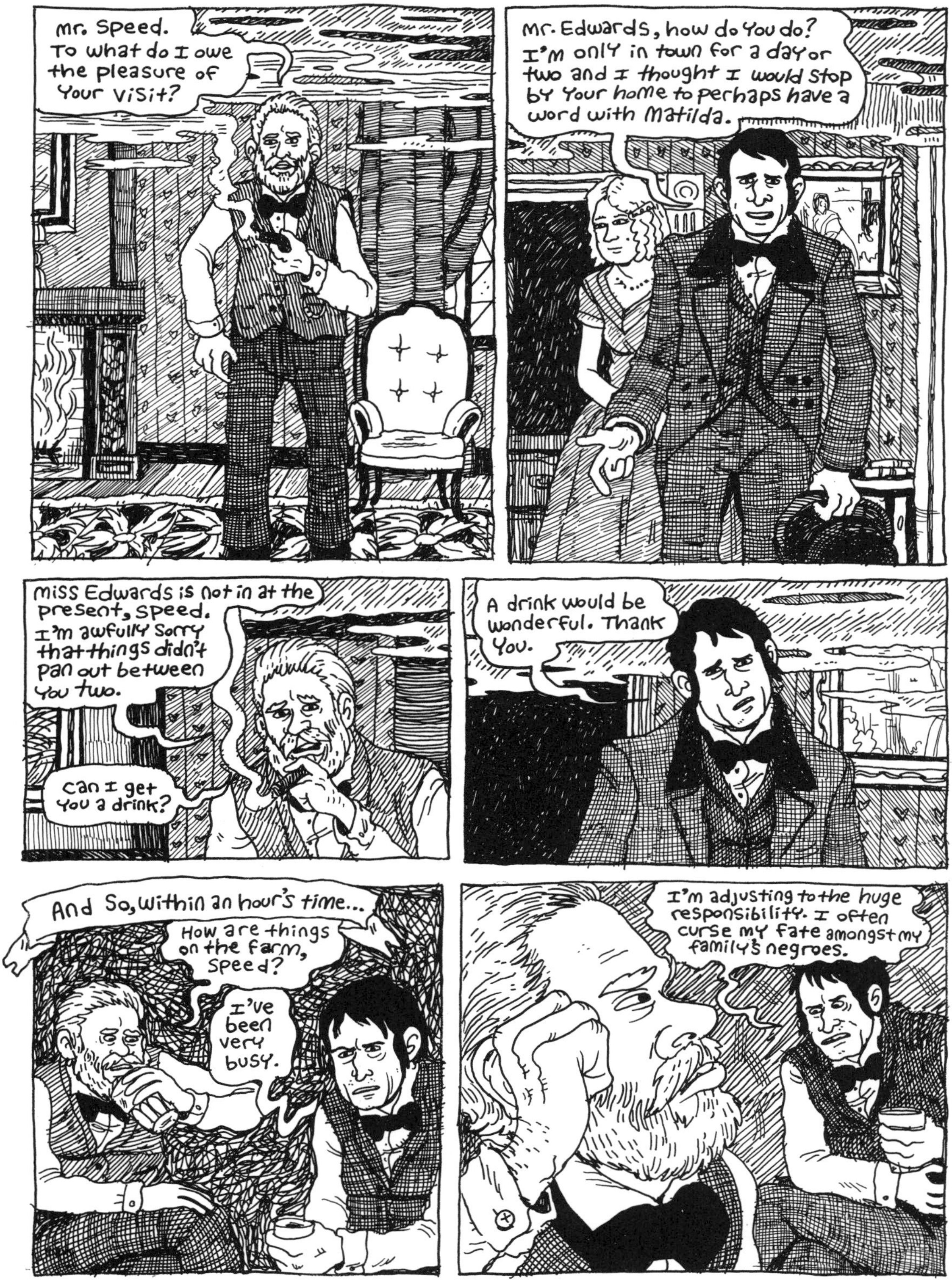
Mr. Speed. To what do I owe the pleasure of your visit?
Mr. Edwards, how do you do? I'm only in town for a day or two and I thought I would stop by your home to perhaps have a word with Matilda.
Miss Edwards is not in at the present, Speed. I'm awfully sorry that things didn't pan out between you two.
Can I get you a drink?
A drink would be wonderful. Thank you.
And so, within an hour's time...
How are things on the farm, Speed?
I've been very busy.
I'm adjusting to the huge responsibility. I often curse my fate amongst my family's negroes.

And how about Lincoln? Have you been over to Mr. Butler's to see him?

I have.

He's taken more knocks than one man should in a short amount of time. He was out for a bit, but he's under the care of Dr. Henry and he's on the mend.

He acted stubbornly and with little foresight while pushing the Internal Improvements Act.

But things will work themselves out. He should learn that.

Let every man learn the hard way if he must. —Uh, how is Miss Todd?

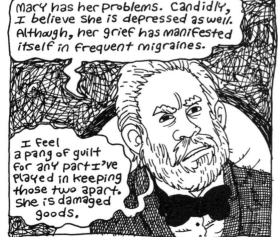

Mary has her problems. Candidly, I believe she is depressed as well. Although, her grief has manifested itself in frequent migraines.

I feel a pang of guilt for any part I've played in keeping those two apart. She is damaged goods.

Is she in?

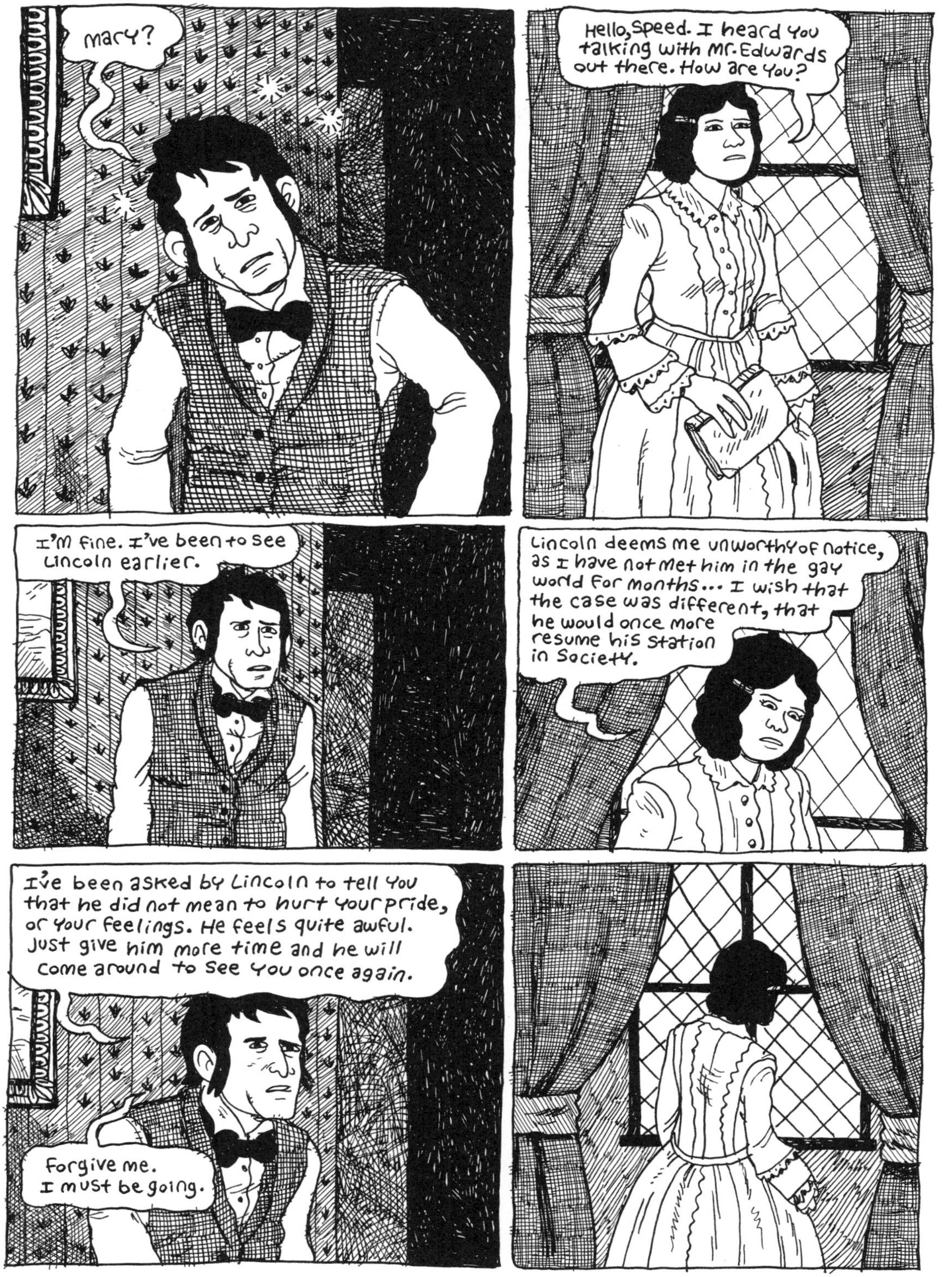
Mary?
Hello, Speed. I heard you talking with Mr. Edwards out there. How are you?
I'm fine. I've been to see Lincoln earlier.
Lincoln deems me unworthy of notice, as I have not met him in the gay world for months... I wish that the case was different, that he would once more resume his station in Society.
I've been asked by Lincoln to tell you that he did not mean to hurt your pride, or your feelings. He feels quite awful. Just give him more time and he will come around to see you once again.
Forgive me. I must be going.

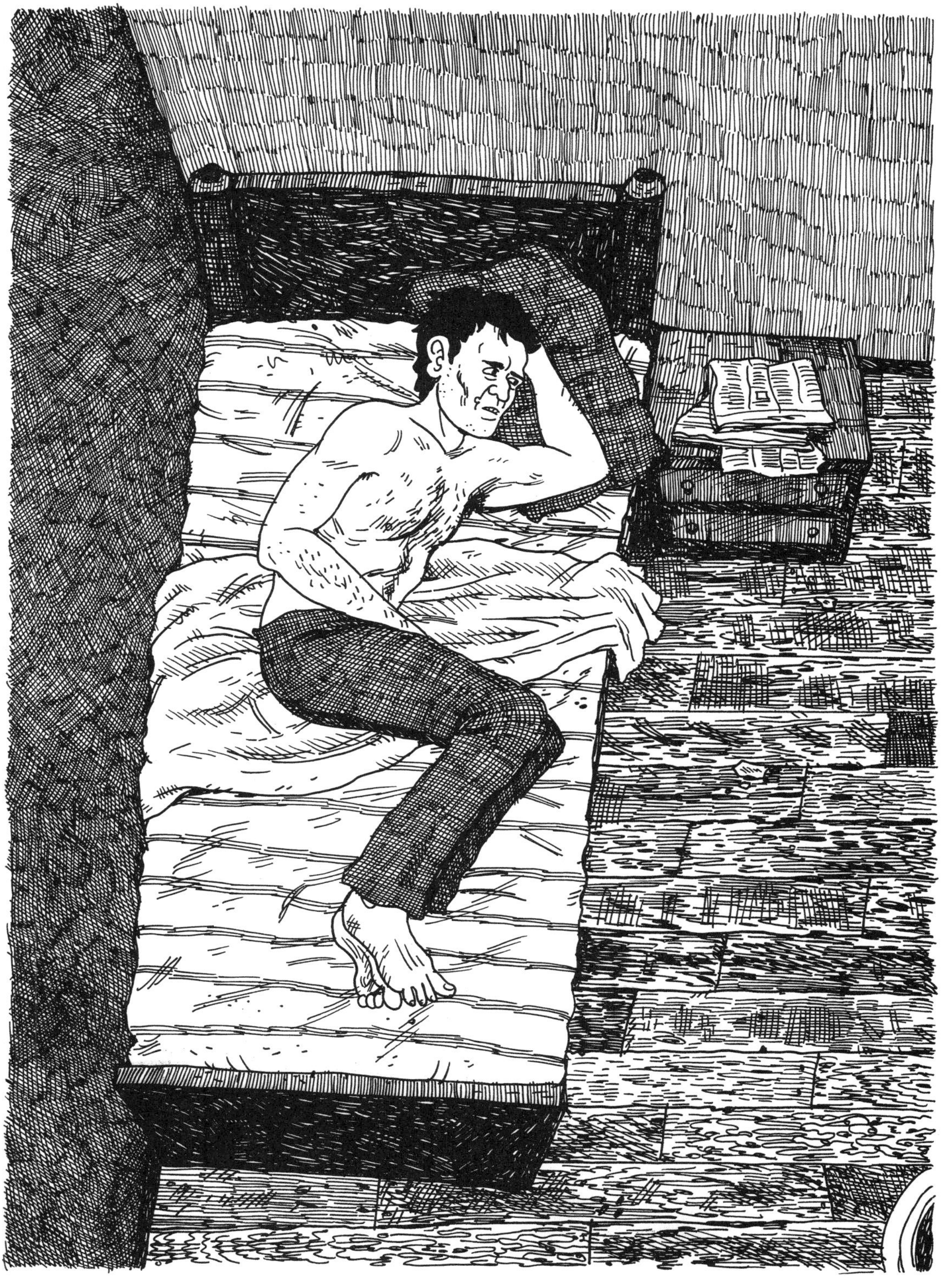

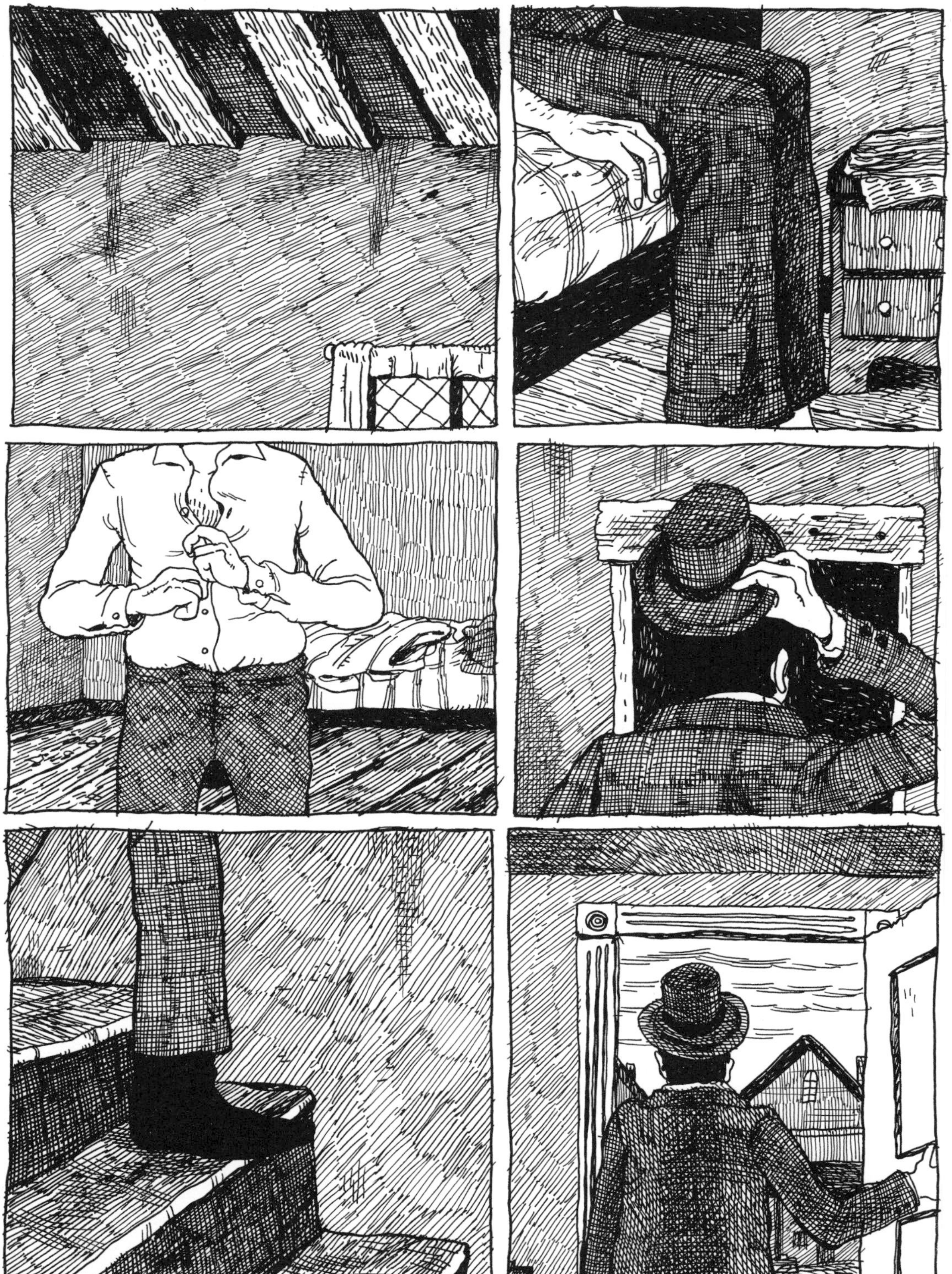

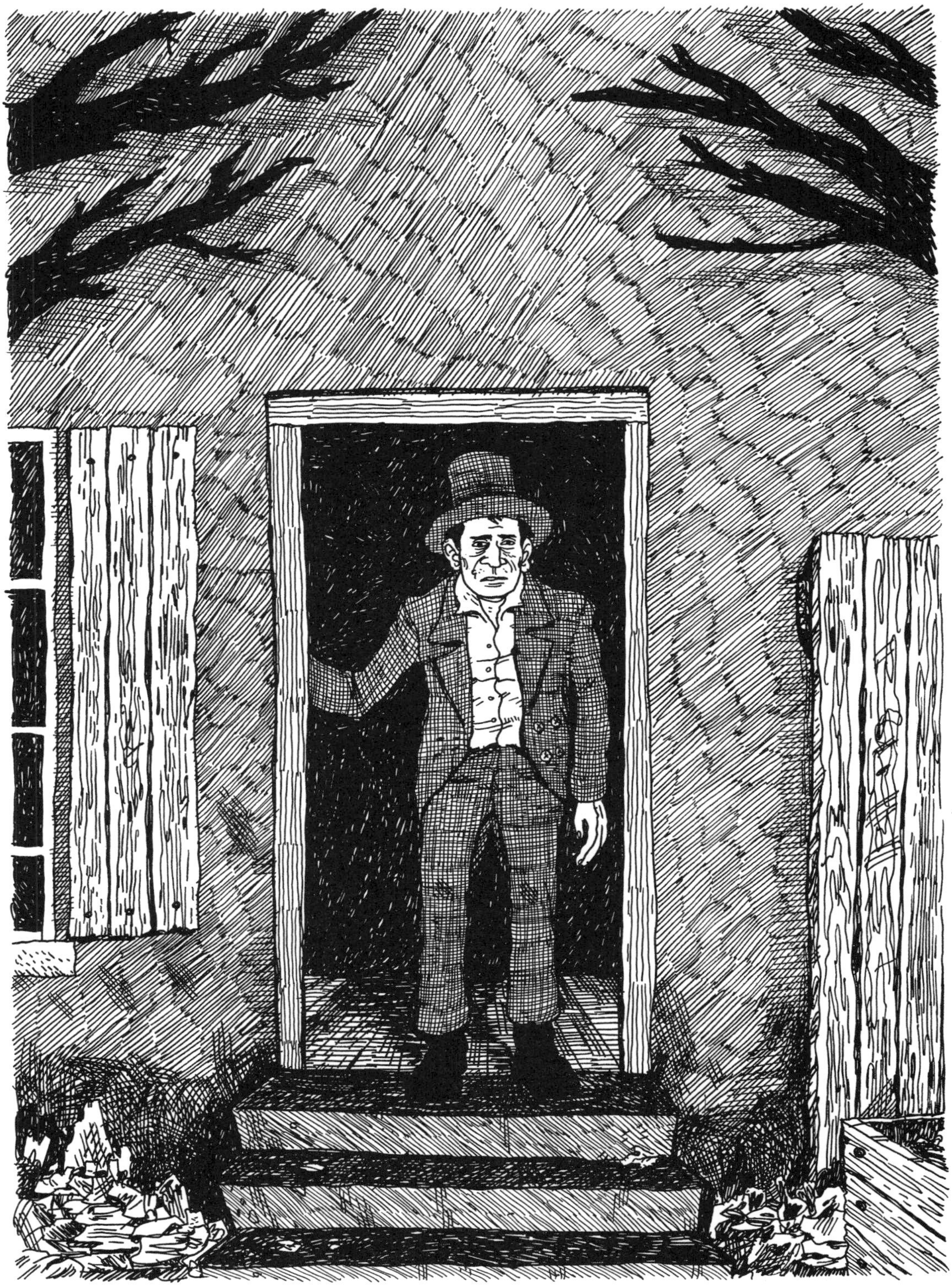

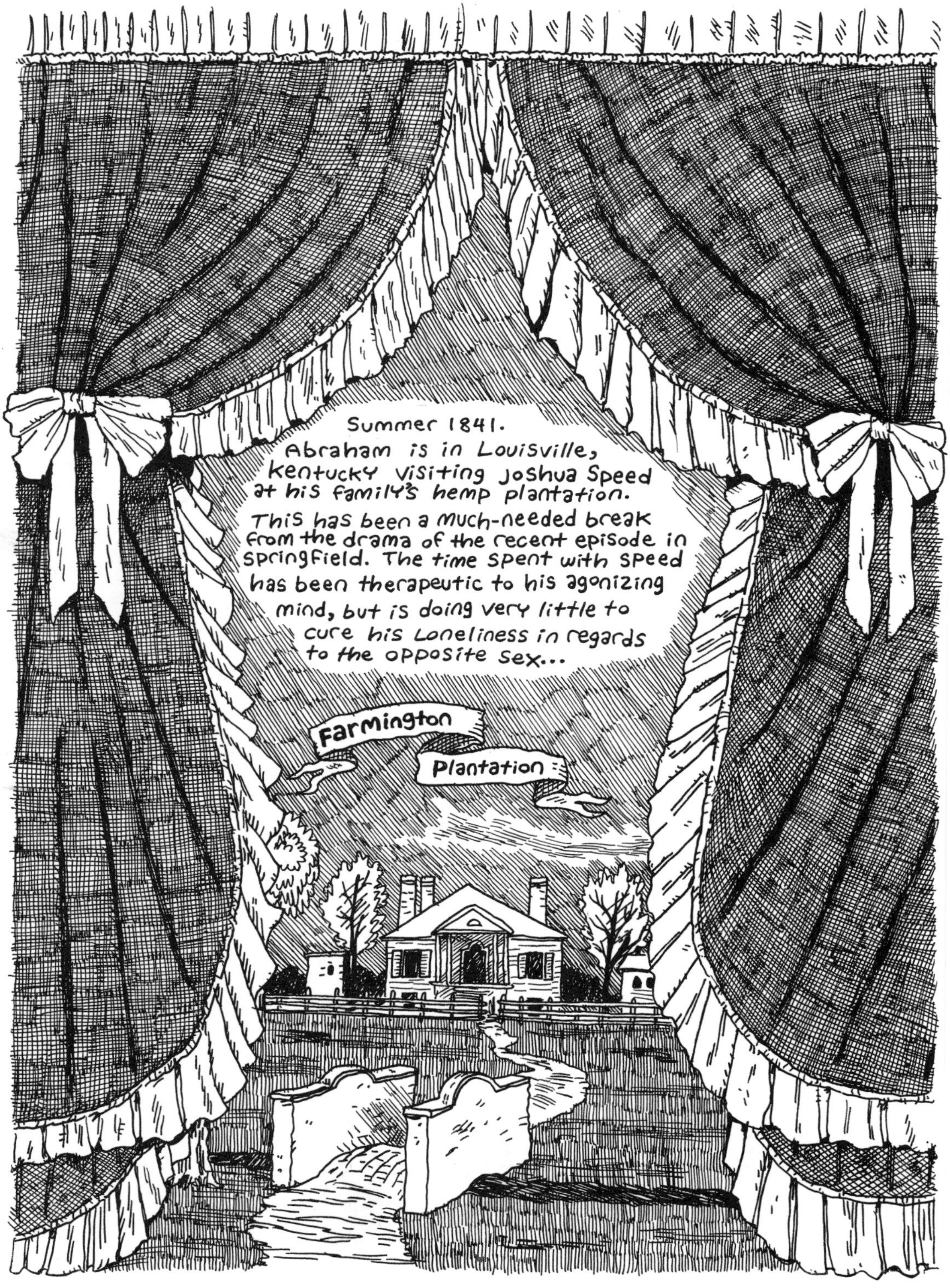
Summer 1841.
Abraham is in Louisville, Kentucky visiting Joshua Speed at his family's hemp plantation.
This has been a much-needed break from the drama of the recent episode in Springfield. The time spent with Speed has been therapeutic to his agonizing mind, but is doing very little to cure his loneliness in regards to the opposite sex...
Farmington
Plantation

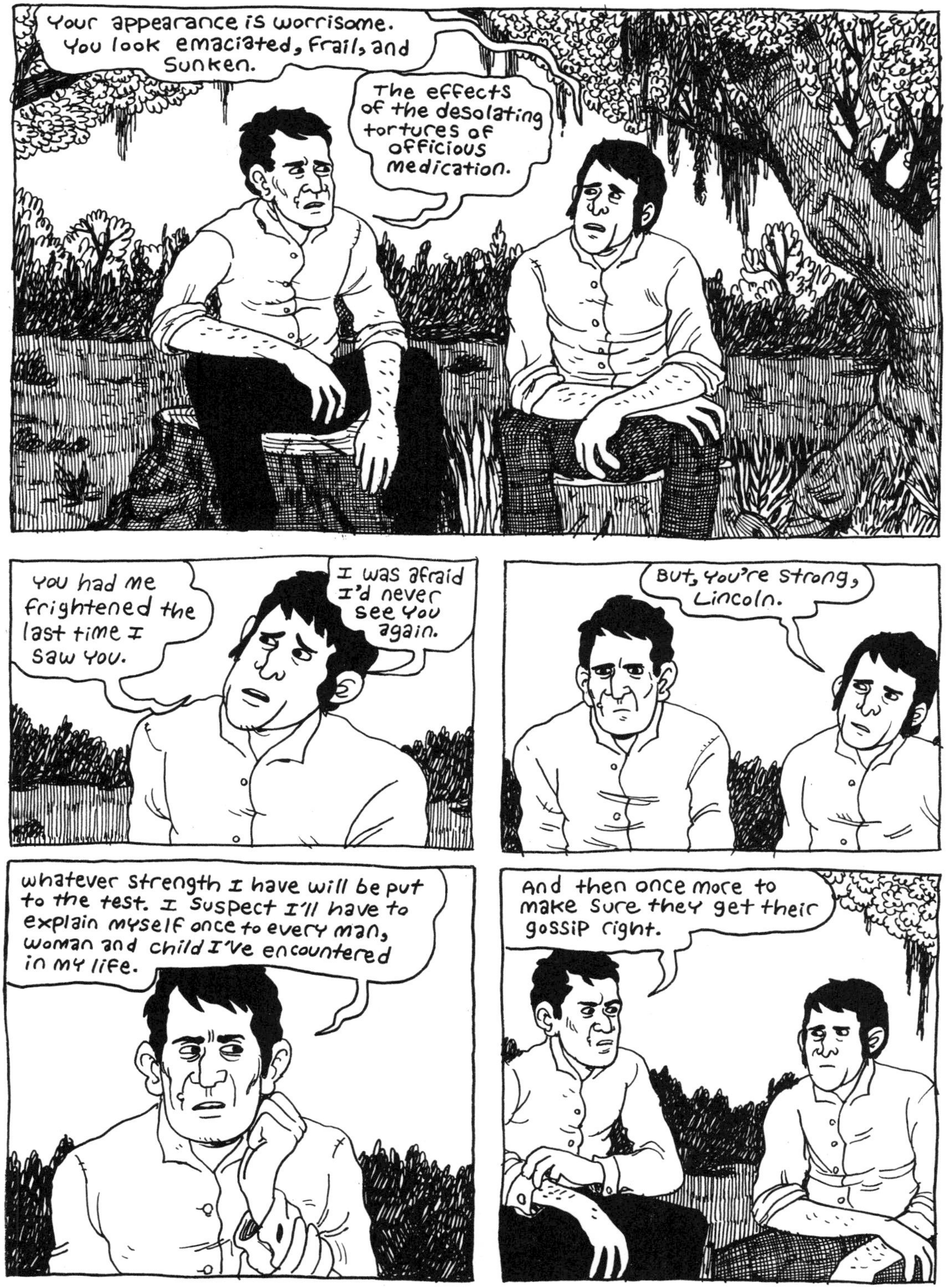
Your appearance is worrisome. You look emaciated, frail, and sunken.
The effects of the desolating tortures of officious medication.
You had me frightened the last time I saw you.
I was afraid I'd never see you again.
But, you're strong, Lincoln.
Whatever strength I have will be put to the test. I suspect I'll have to explain myself once to every man, woman and child I've encountered in my life.
And then once more to make sure they get their gossip right.

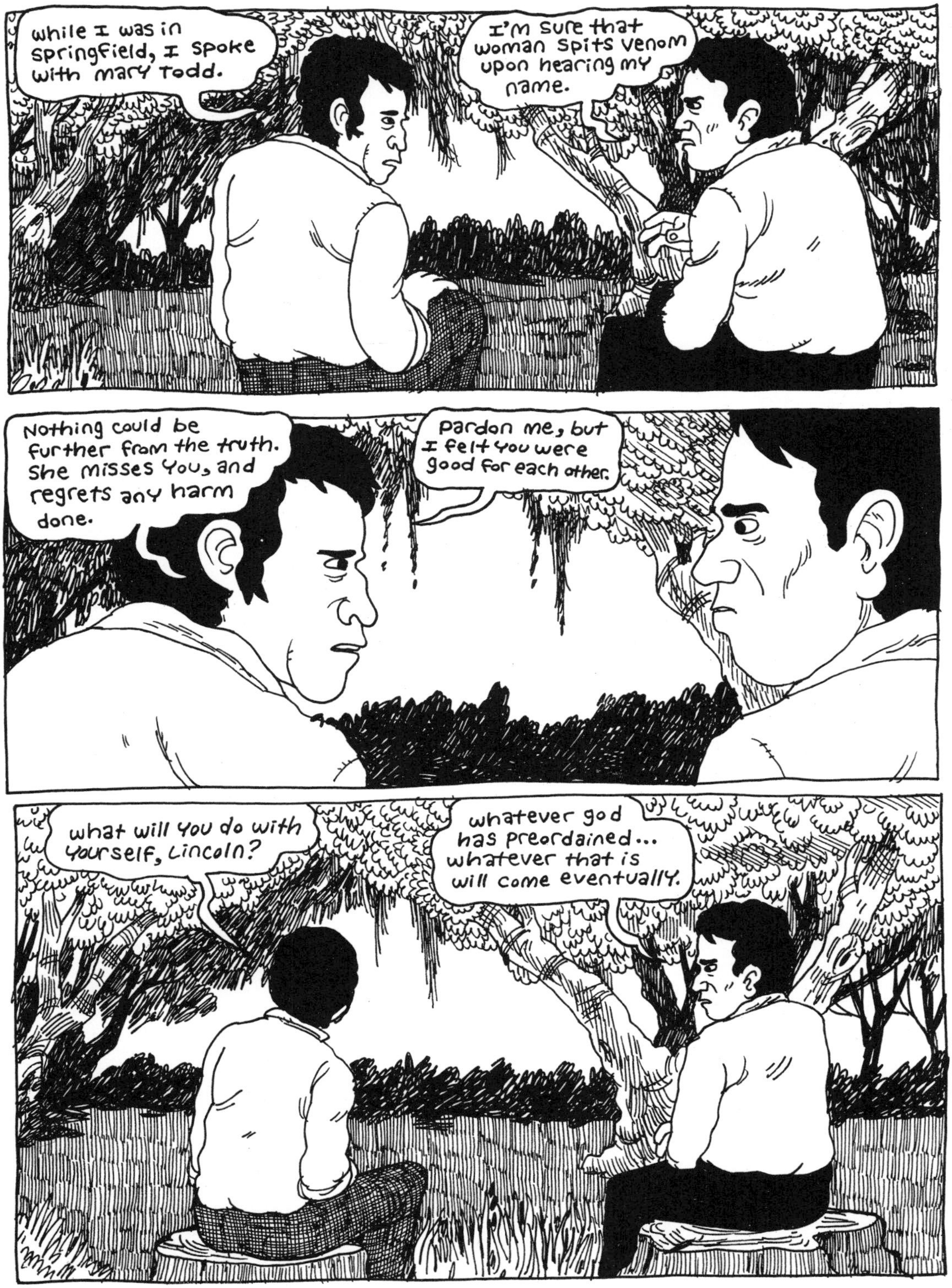
while I was in springfield, I spoke with mary todd.
I'm sure that woman spits venom upon hearing my name.
Nothing could be further from the truth. She misses you, and regrets any harm done.
pardon me, but I felt you were good for each other.
what will you do with yourself, Lincoln?
whatever god has preordained... whatever that is will come eventually.

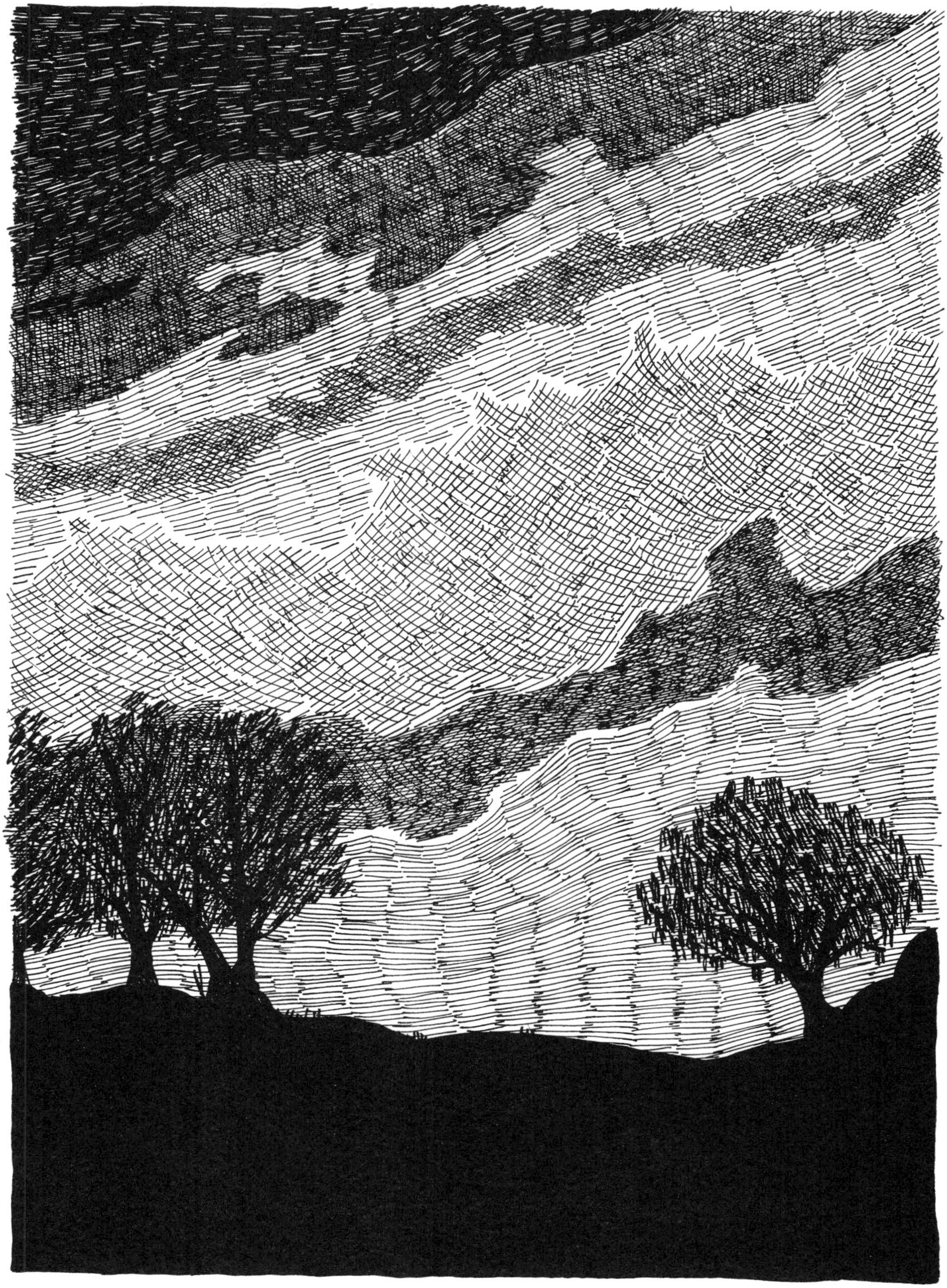

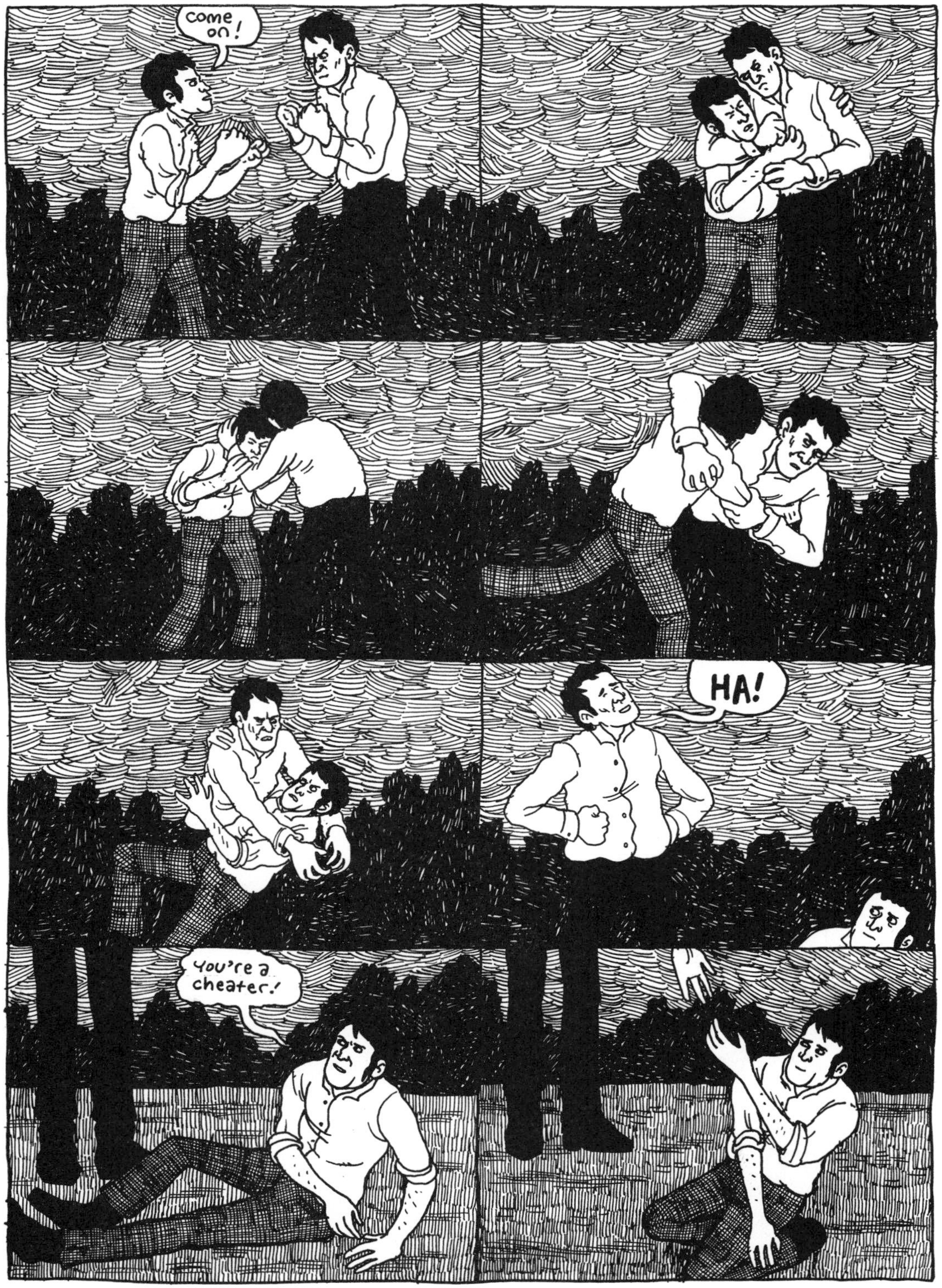
come on!
HA!
You're a cheater!

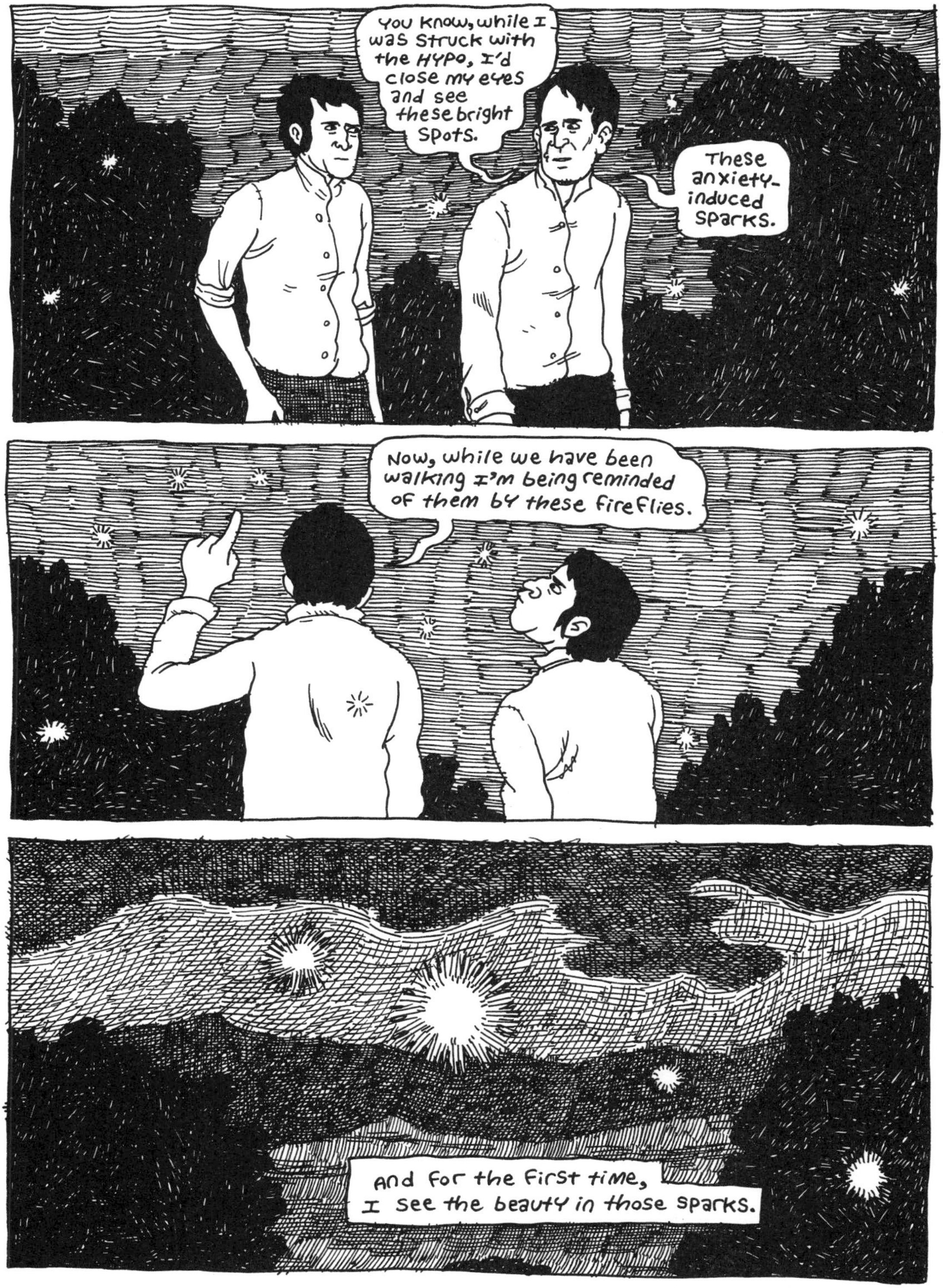
You know, while I was struck with the HYPO, I'd close my eyes and see these bright spots.
These anxiety-induced sparks.
Now, while we have been walking I'm being reminded of them by these fireflies.
and for the first time, I see the beauty in those sparks.

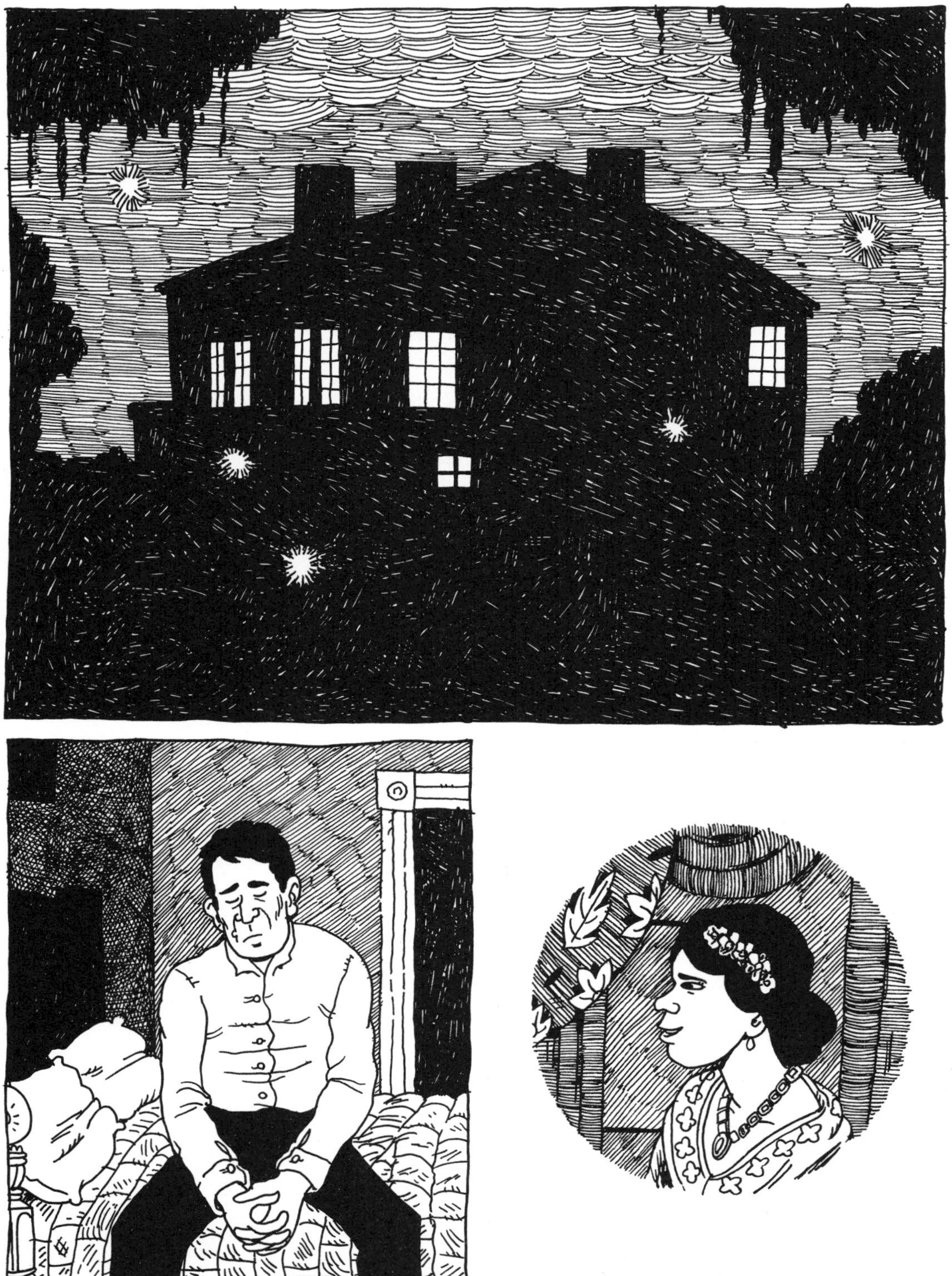

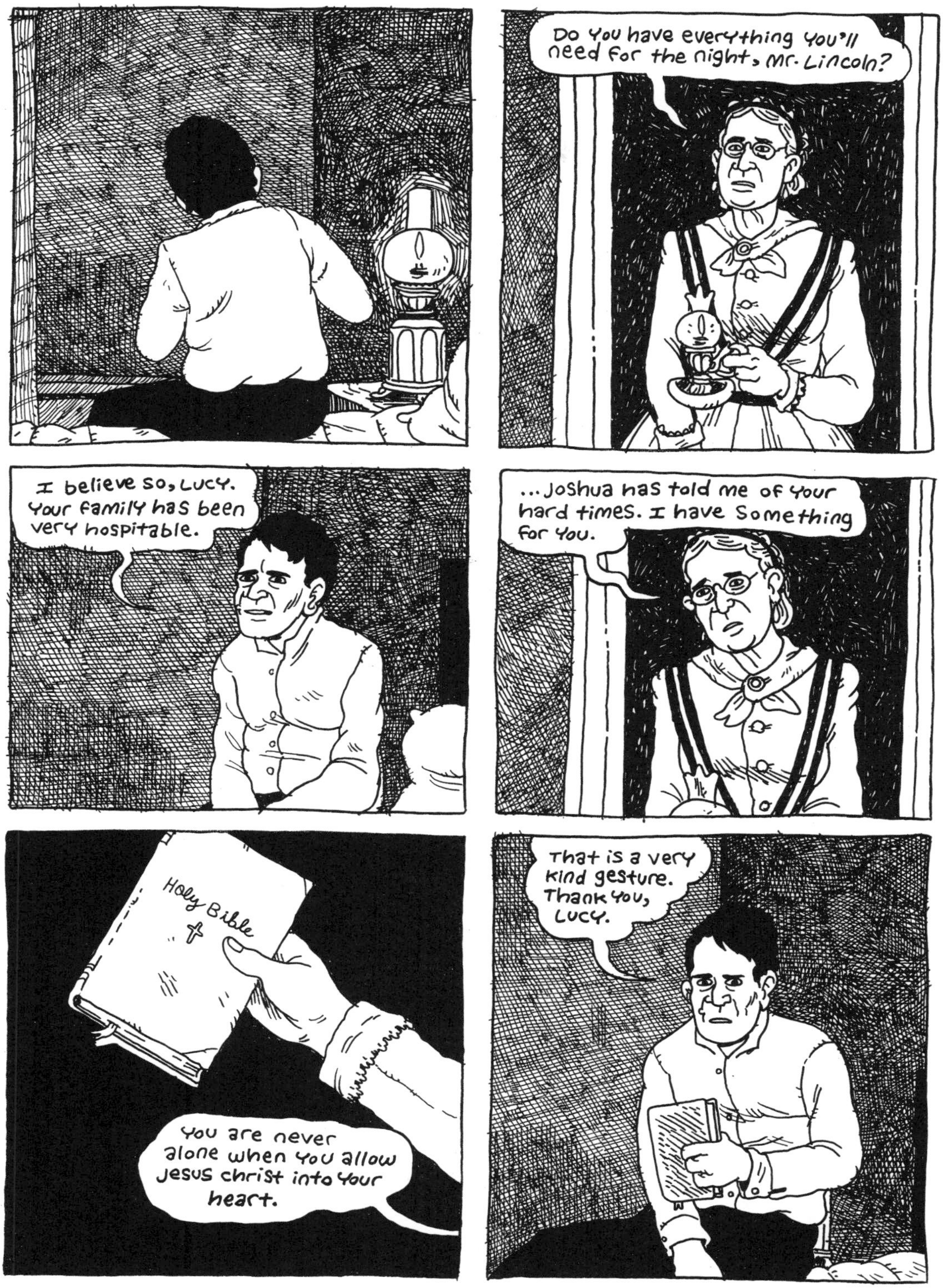
Do you have everything you'll need for the night, Mr. Lincoln?
I believe so, Lucy. Your family has been very hospitable.
...Joshua has told me of your hard times. I have Something for you.
Holy Bible
You are never alone when you allow Jesus christ into your heart.
That is a very kind gesture. Thank you, Lucy.

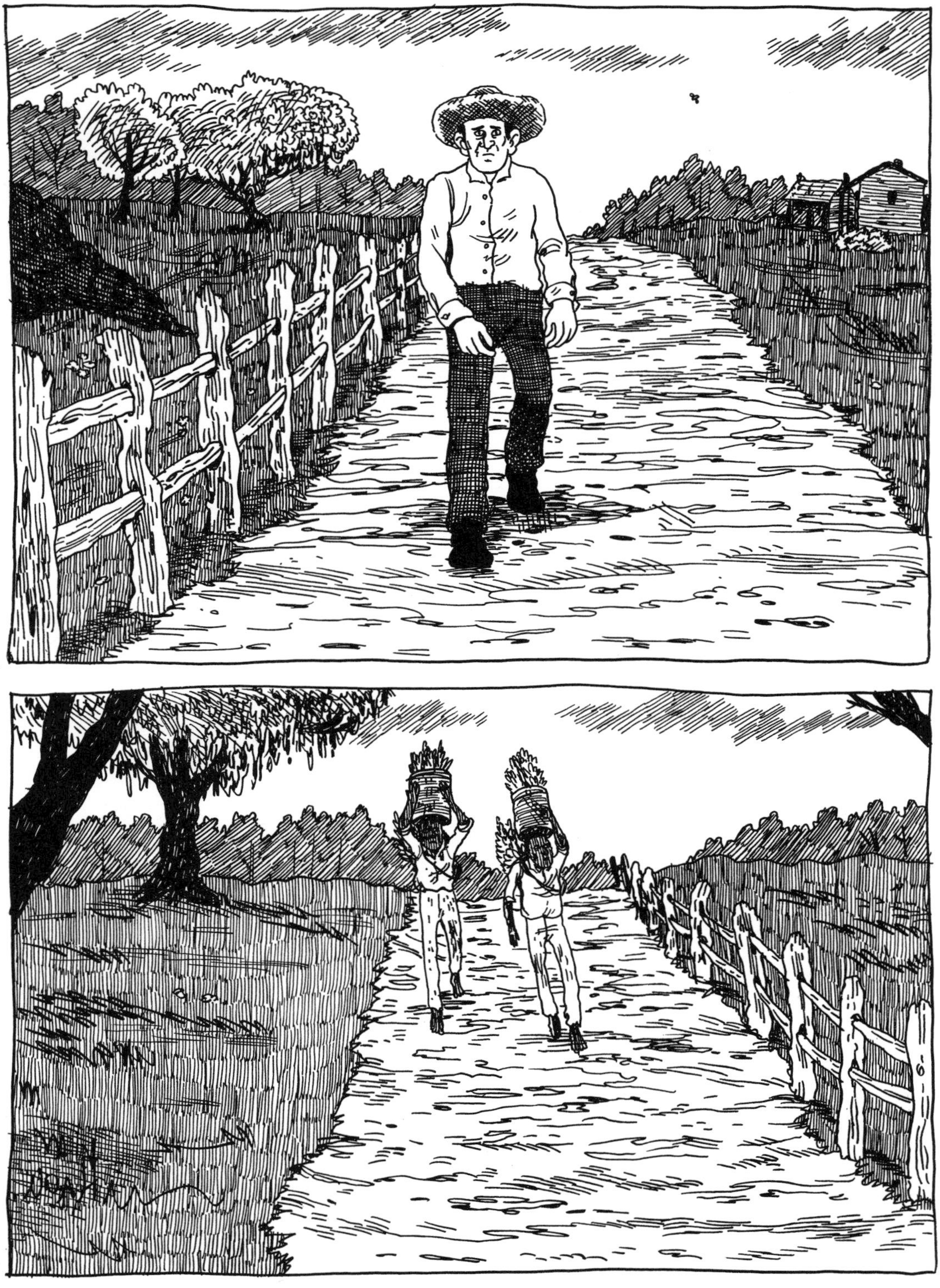

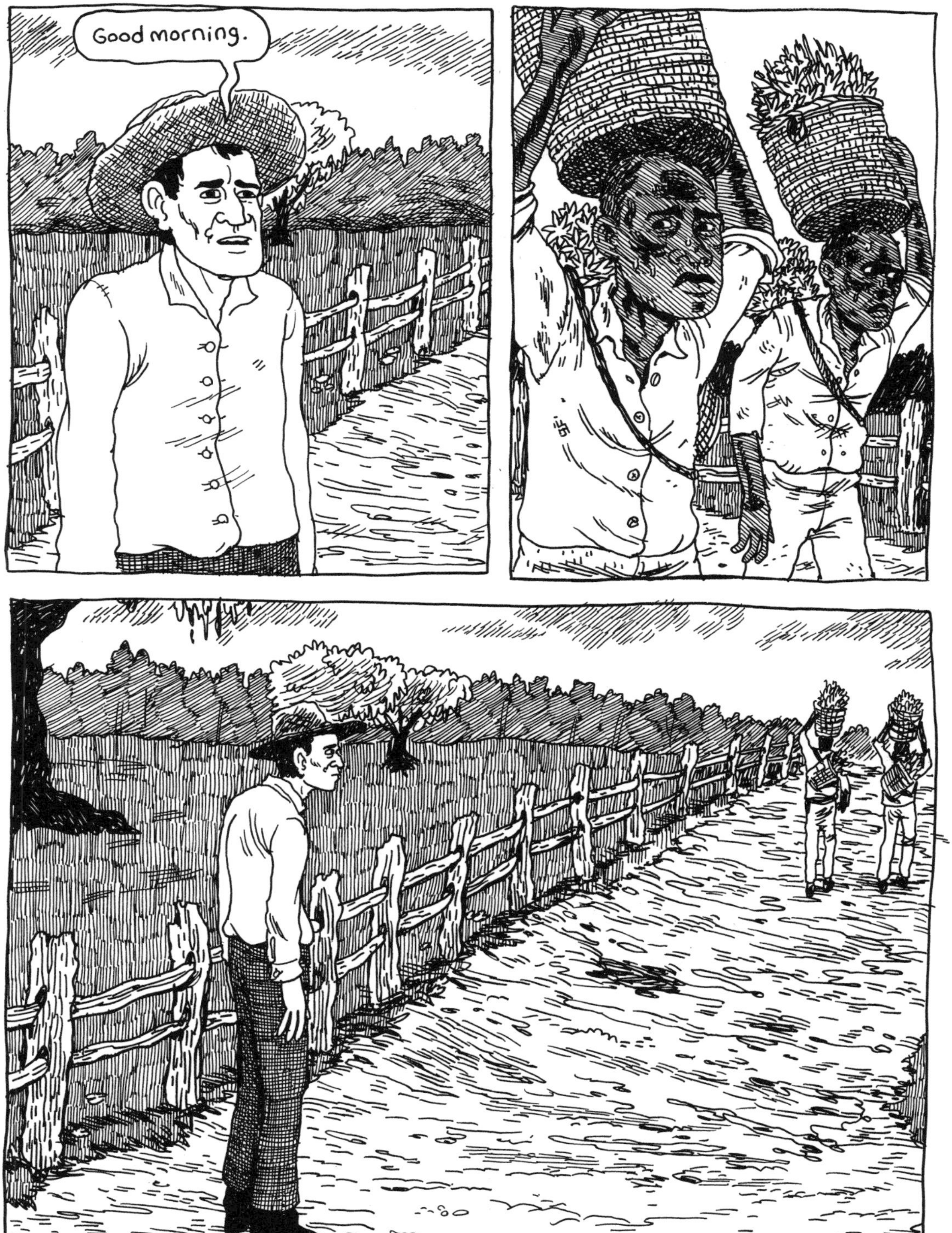
Good morning.

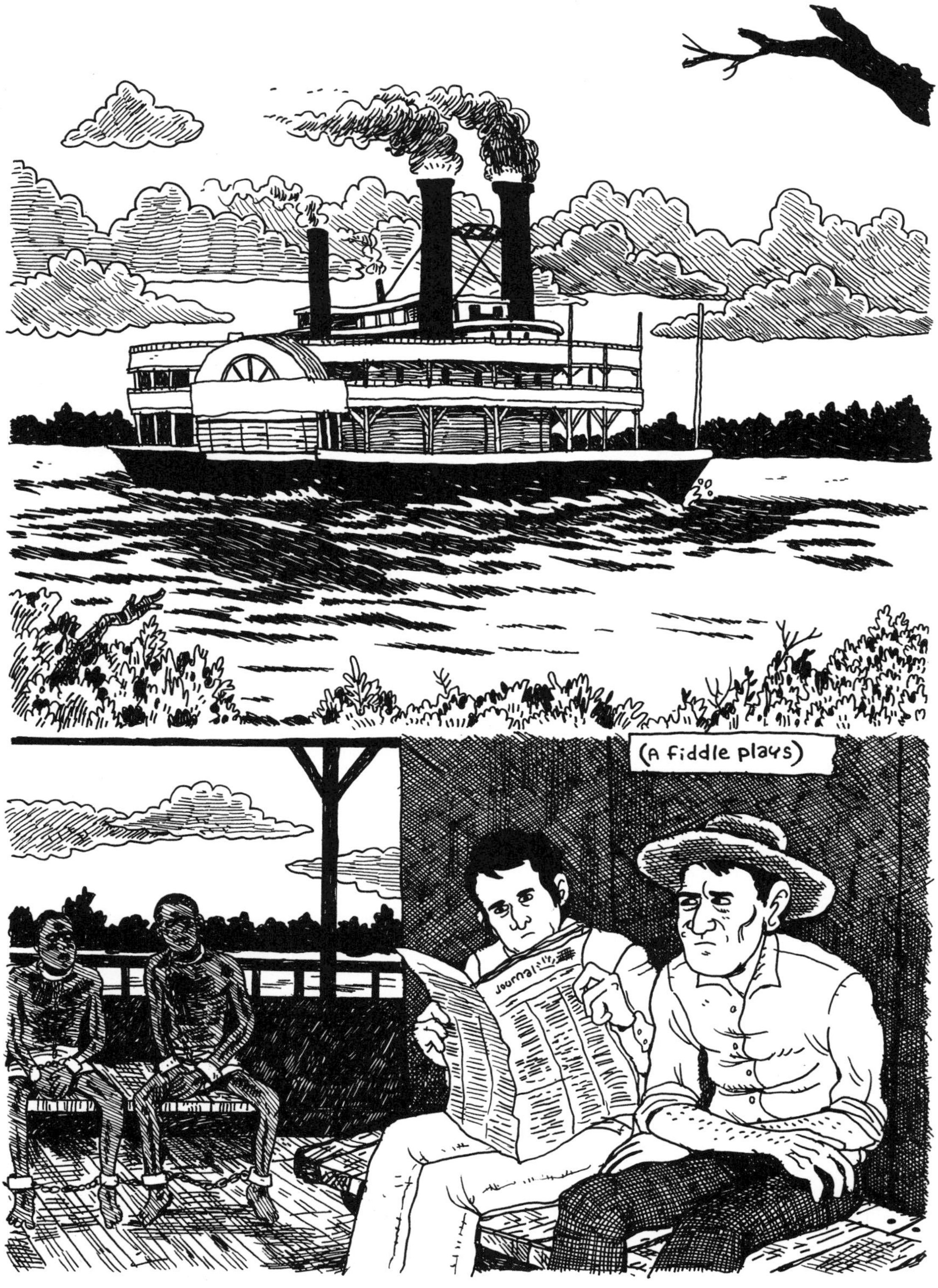
(A fiddle plays)
Journal

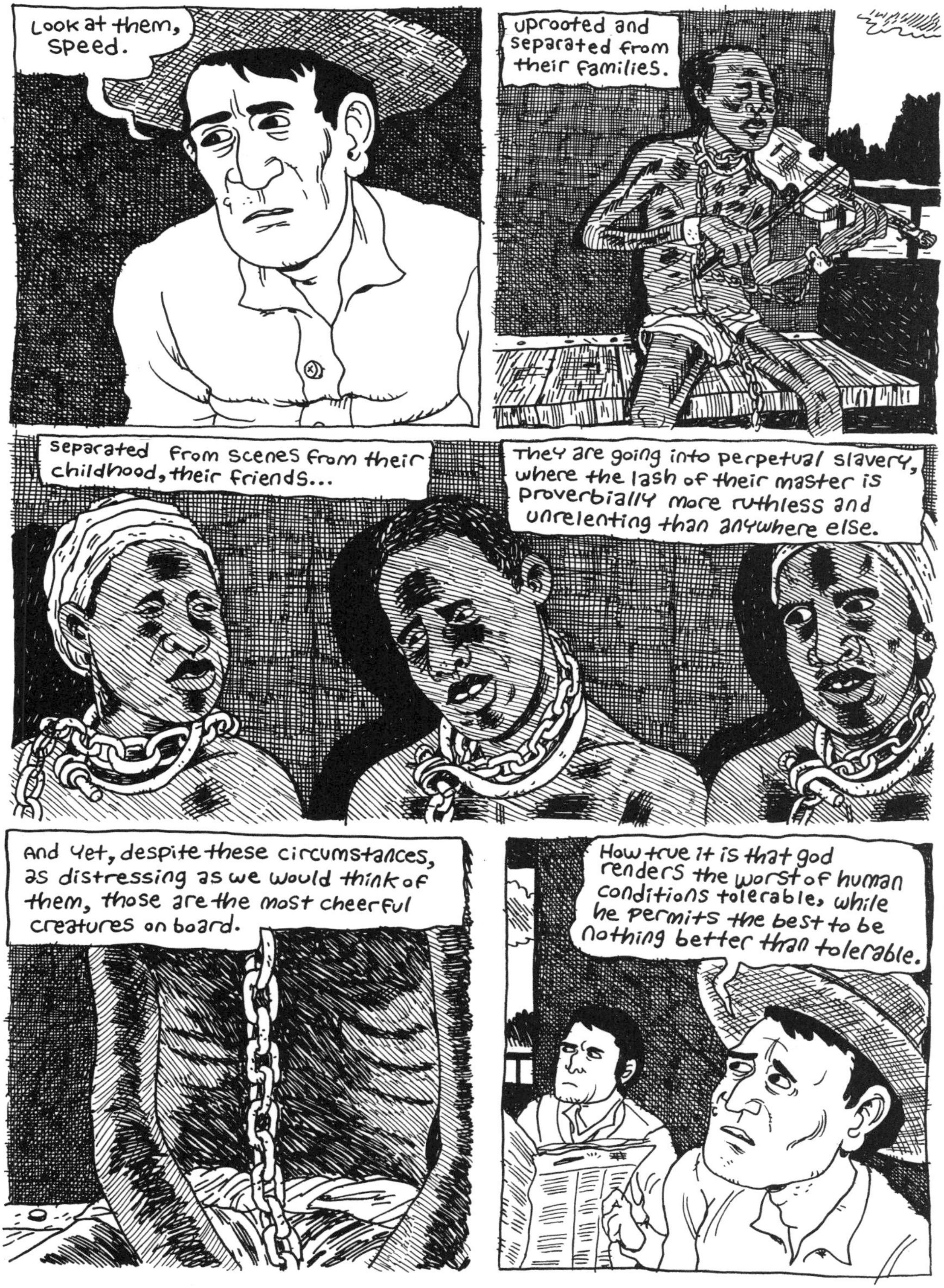

Look at them, speed.
uprooted and separated from their families.
separated from scenes from their childhood, their friends...
They are going into perpetual slavery, where the lash of their master is proverbially more ruthless and unrelenting than anywhere else.
And yet, despite these circumstances, as distressing as we would think of them, those are the most cheerful creatures on board.
How true it is that god renders the worst of human conditions tolerable, while he permits the best to be nothing better than tolerable.

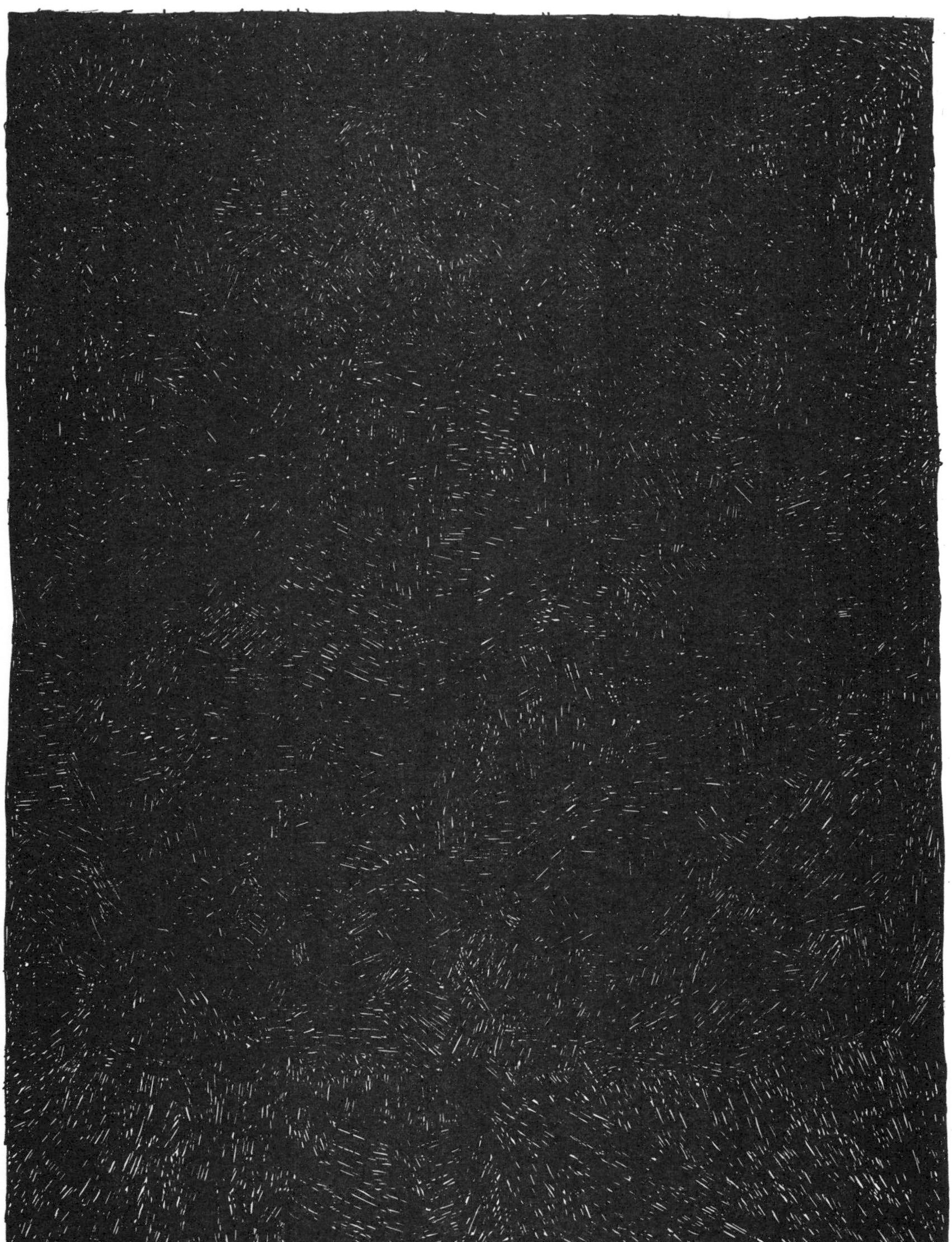

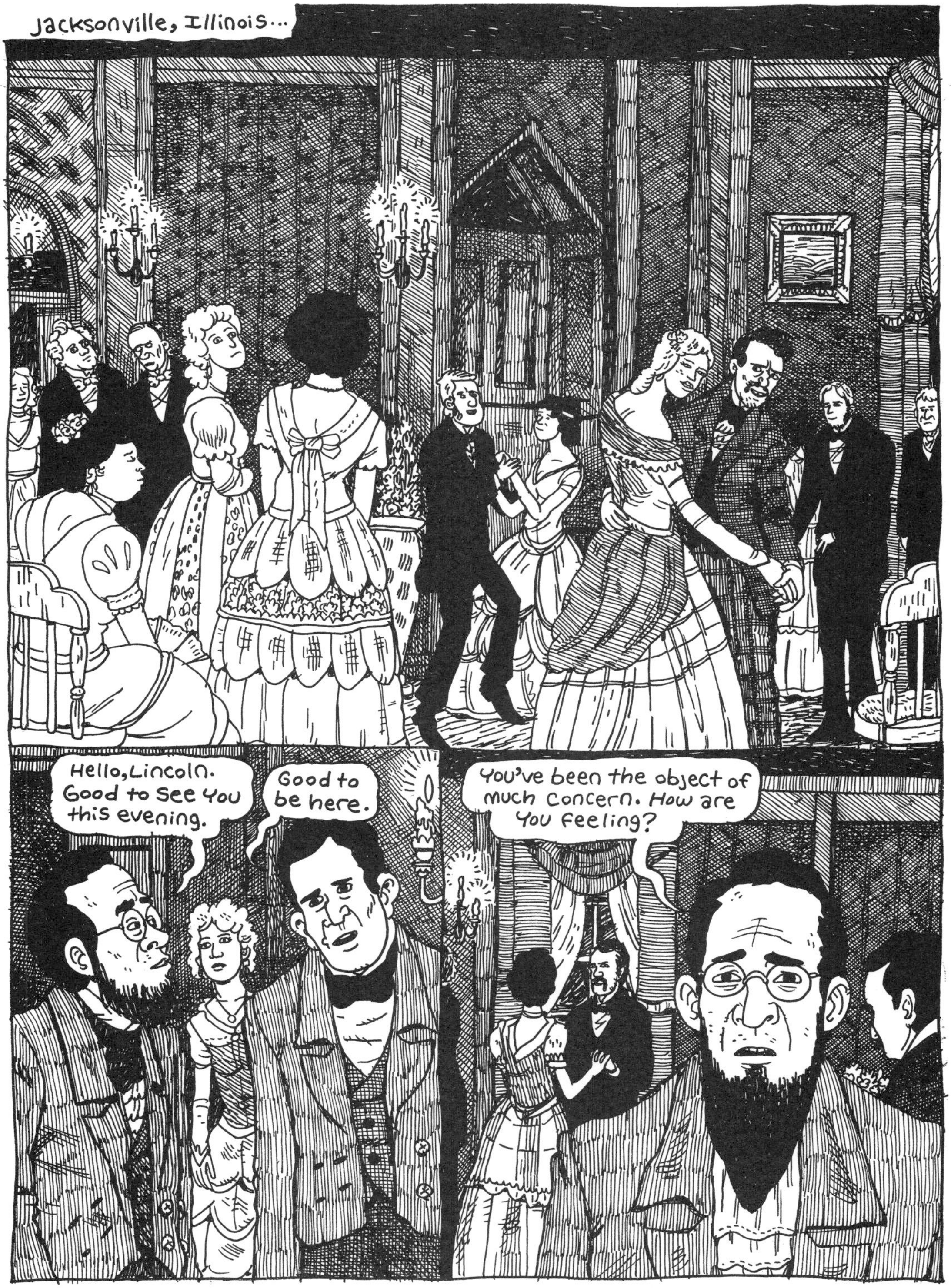
Jacksonville, Illinois...
Hello, Lincoln. Good to see you this evening.
Good to be here.
You've been the object of much concern. How are you feeling?

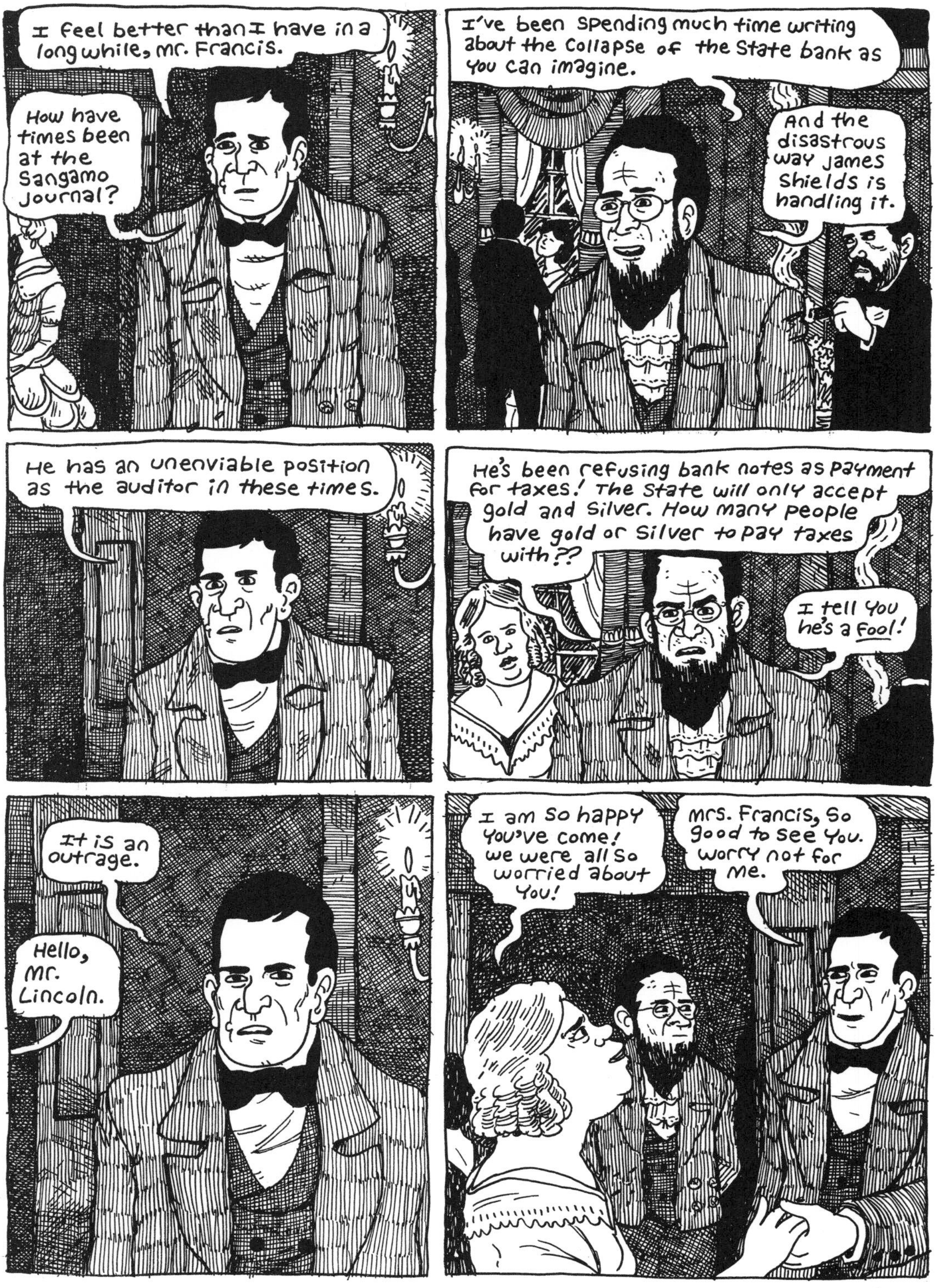
I feel better than I have in a long while, Mr. Francis.
How have times been at the Sangamo Journal?
I've been spending much time writing about the collapse of the State bank as you can imagine.
And the disastrous way James Shields is handling it.
He has an unenviable position as the auditor in these times.
He's been refusing bank notes as payment for taxes! The State will only accept gold and Silver. How many people have gold or Silver to pay taxes with??
I tell you he's a fool!
It is an outrage.
Hello, Mr. Lincoln.
I am so happy you've come! we were all so worried about you!
Mrs. Francis, so good to see you. Worry not for me.

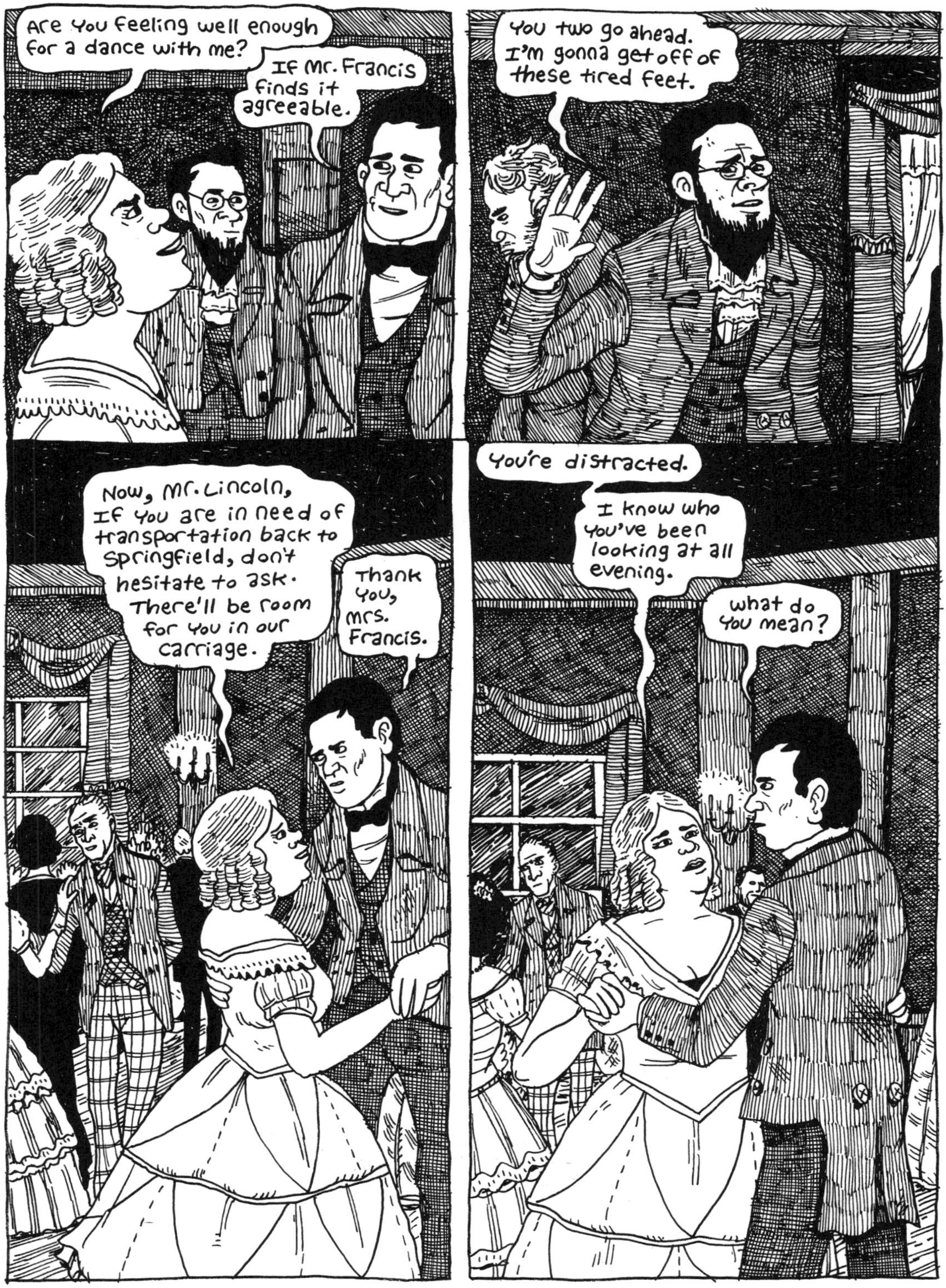
Are you feeling well enough for a dance with me?
If Mr. Francis finds it agreeable.
You two go ahead. I'm gonna get off of these tired feet.
Now, Mr. Lincoln, If you are in need of transportation back to Springfield, don't hesitate to ask. There'll be room for you in our carriage.
Thank you, Mrs. Francis.
You're distracted.
I know who you've been looking at all evening.
What do you mean?

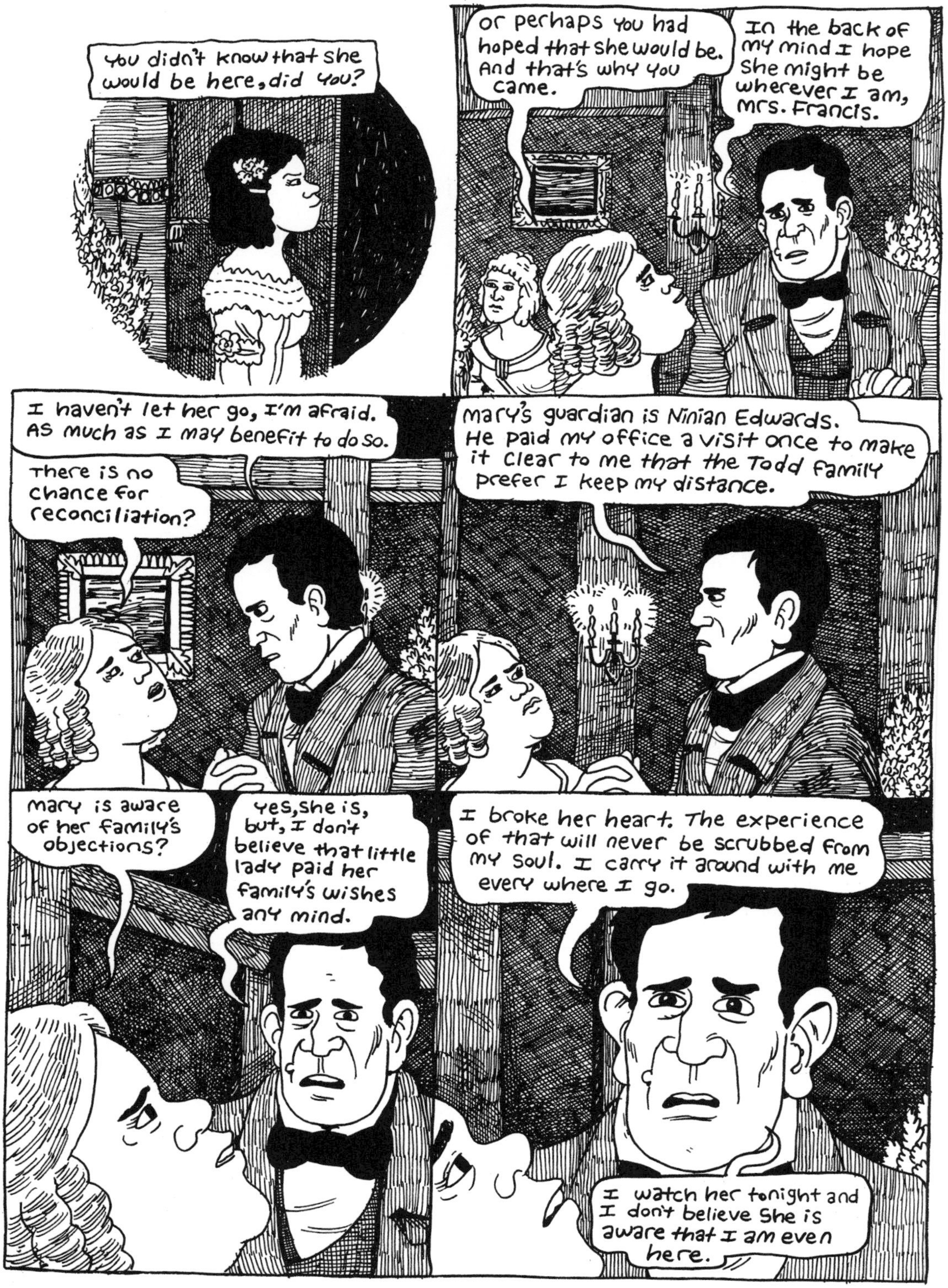
you didn't know that she would be here, did you?
Or perhaps you had hoped that she would be. And that's why you came.
In the back of my mind I hope she might be wherever I am, Mrs. Francis.
I haven't let her go, I'm afraid. As much as I may benefit to do so.
There is no chance for reconciliation?
Mary's guardian is Ninian Edwards. He paid my office a visit once to make it clear to me that the Todd family prefer I keep my distance.
Mary is aware of her family's objections?
Yes, she is, but, I don't believe that little lady paid her family's wishes any mind.
I broke her heart. The experience of that will never be scrubbed from my soul. I carry it around with me every where I go.
I watch her tonight and I don't believe she is aware that I am even here.

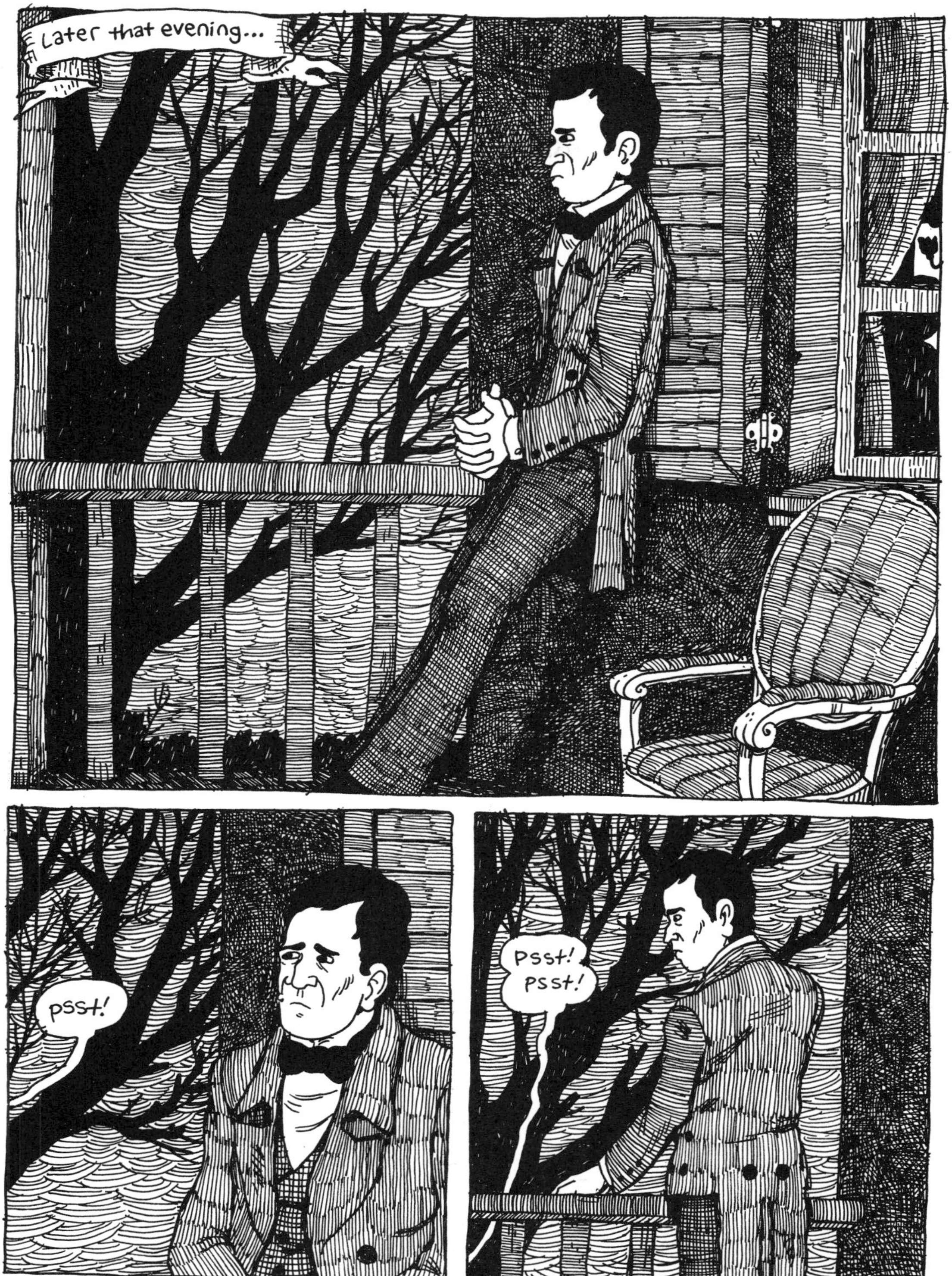
Later that evening...
psst!
Psst! Psst!

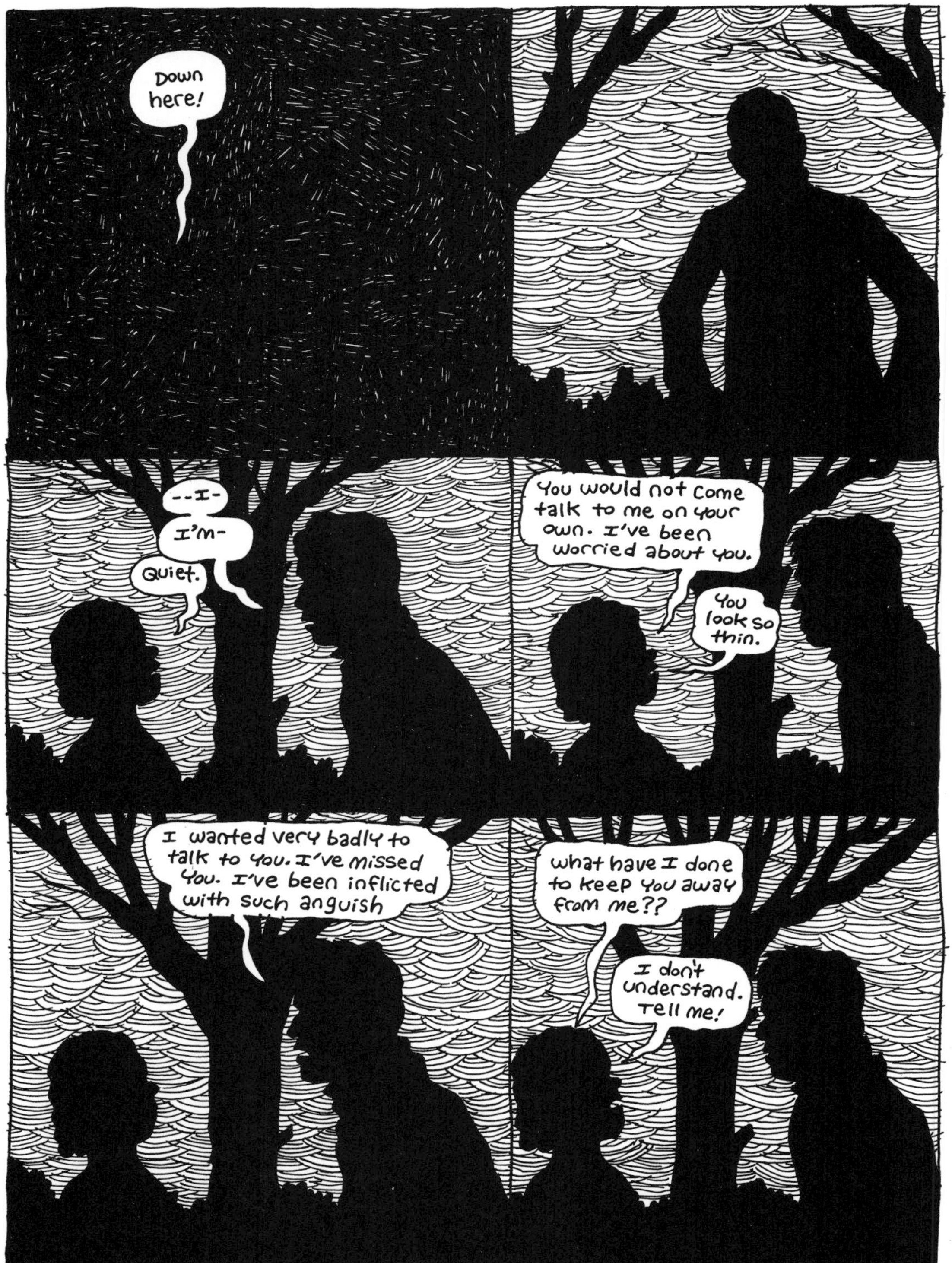
Down here!
--I-
I'm-
Quiet.
You would not come talk to me on your own. I've been worried about you.
You look so thin.
I wanted very badly to talk to you. I've missed you. I've been inflicted with such anguish
What have I done to keep you away from me??
I don't understand. Tell me!

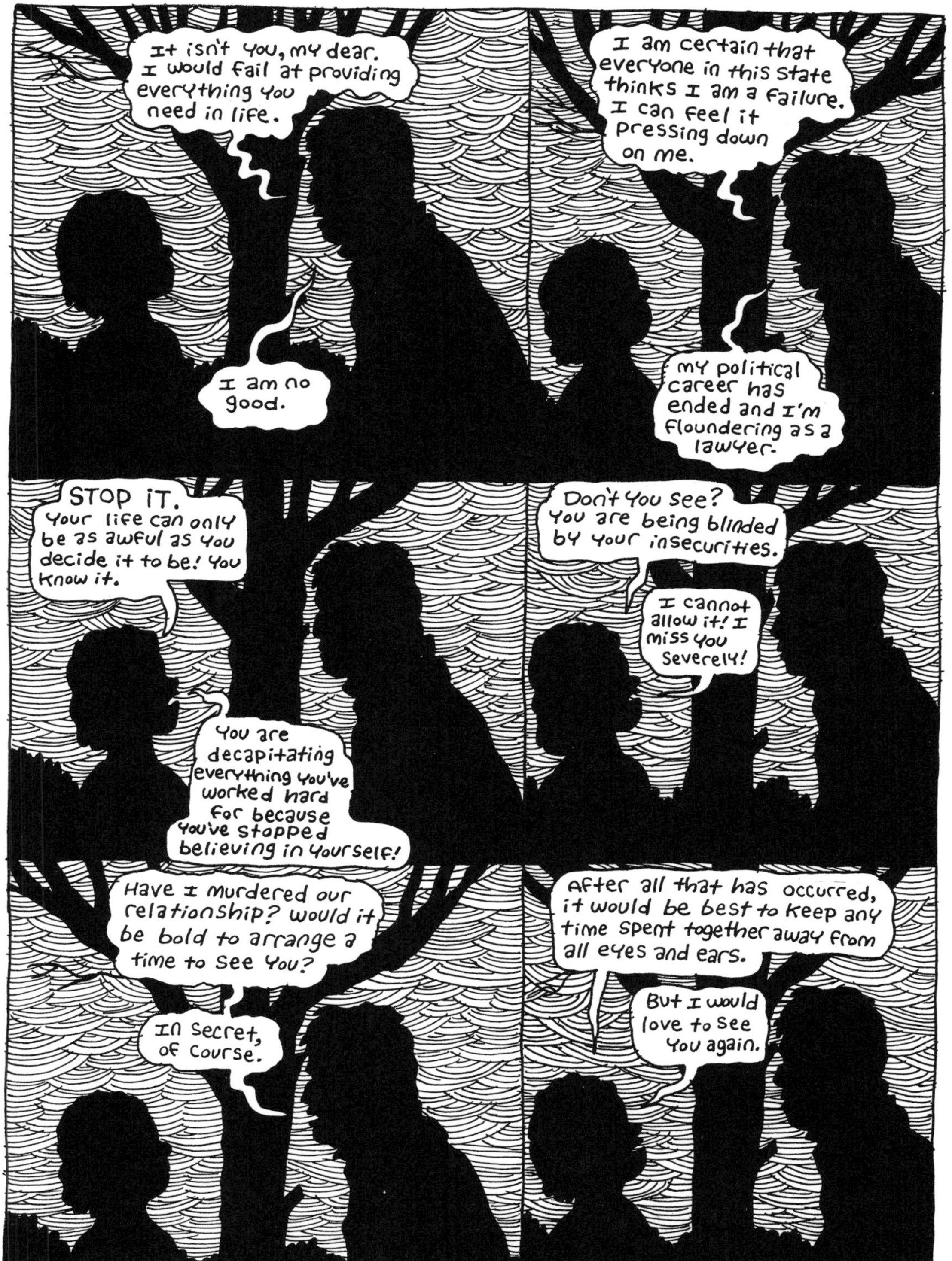
It isn't you, my dear. I would fail at providing everything you need in life.
I am no good.
I am certain that everyone in this state thinks I am a failure. I can feel it pressing down on me.
My political career has ended and I'm floundering as a lawyer.
STOP IT. Your life can only be as awful as you decide it to be! You know it.
You are decapitating everything you've worked hard for because you've stopped believing in yourself!
Don't you see? You are being blinded by your insecurities.
I cannot allow it! I miss you severely!
Have I murdered our relationship? Would it be bold to arrange a time to see you?
In secret, of course.
After all that has occurred, it would be best to keep any time spent together away from all eyes and ears.
But I would love to see you again.

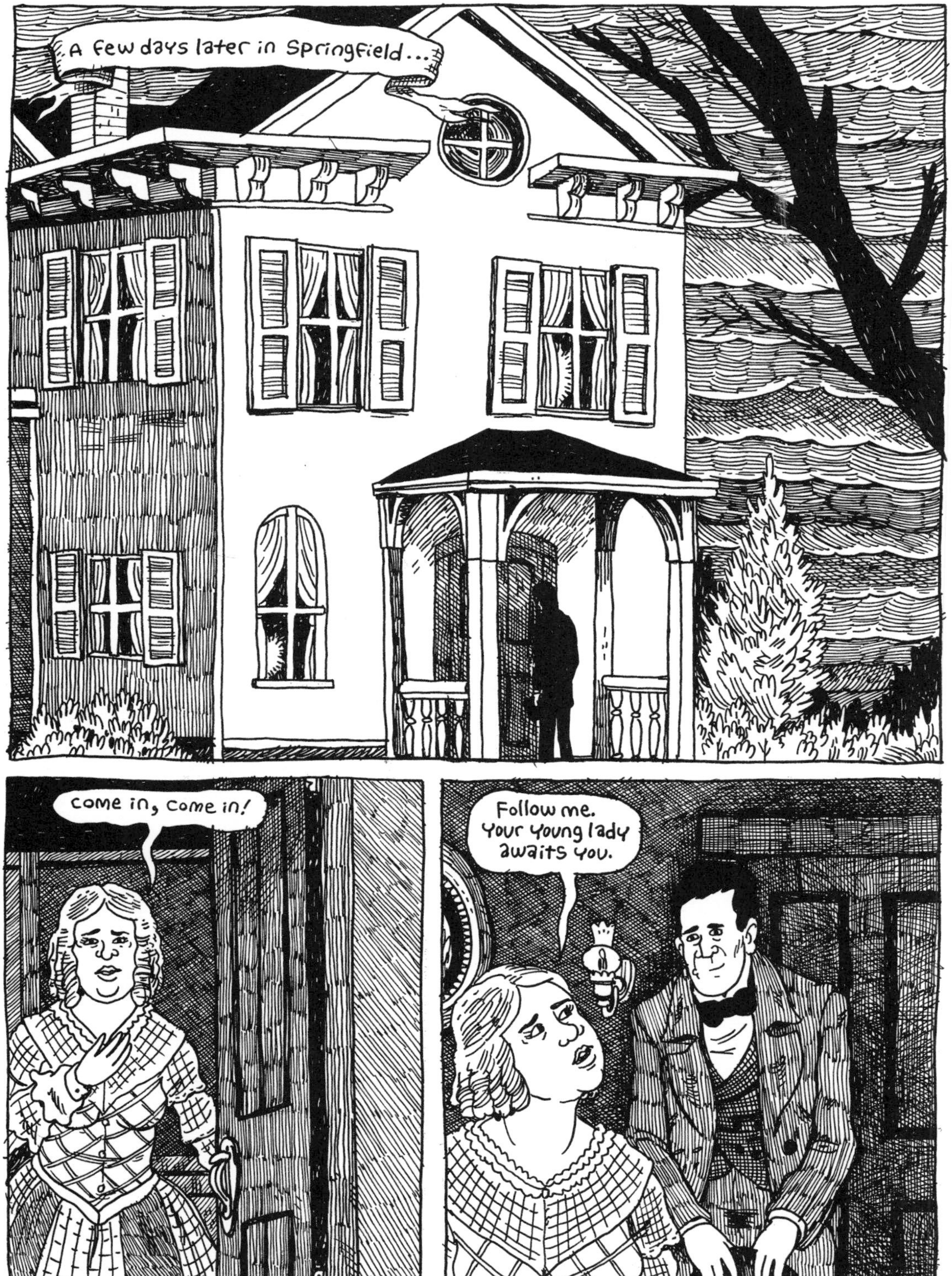
A few days later in Springfield...
Come in, come in!
Follow me. Your young lady awaits you.

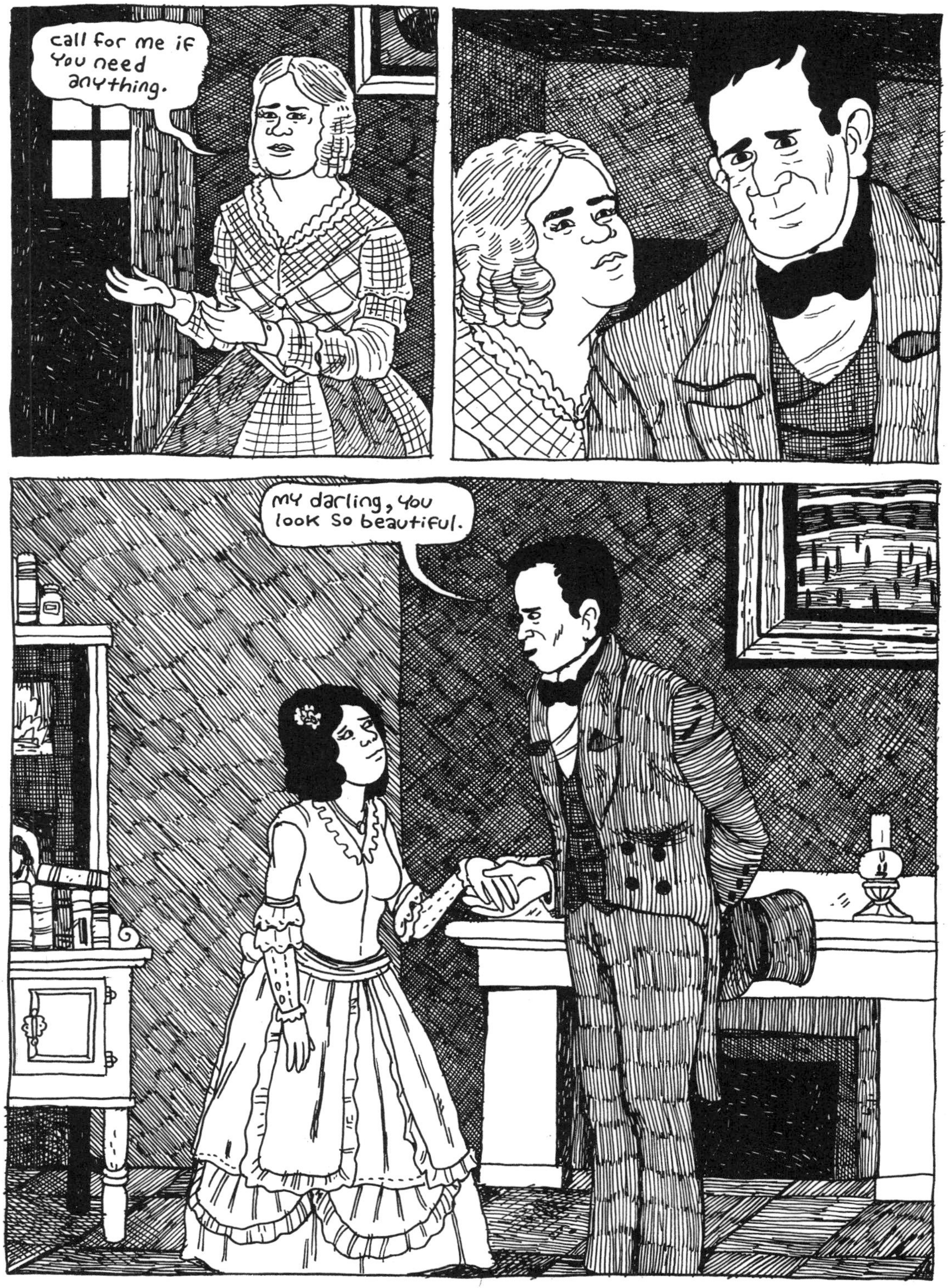
call for me if you need anything.
my darling, you look so beautiful.

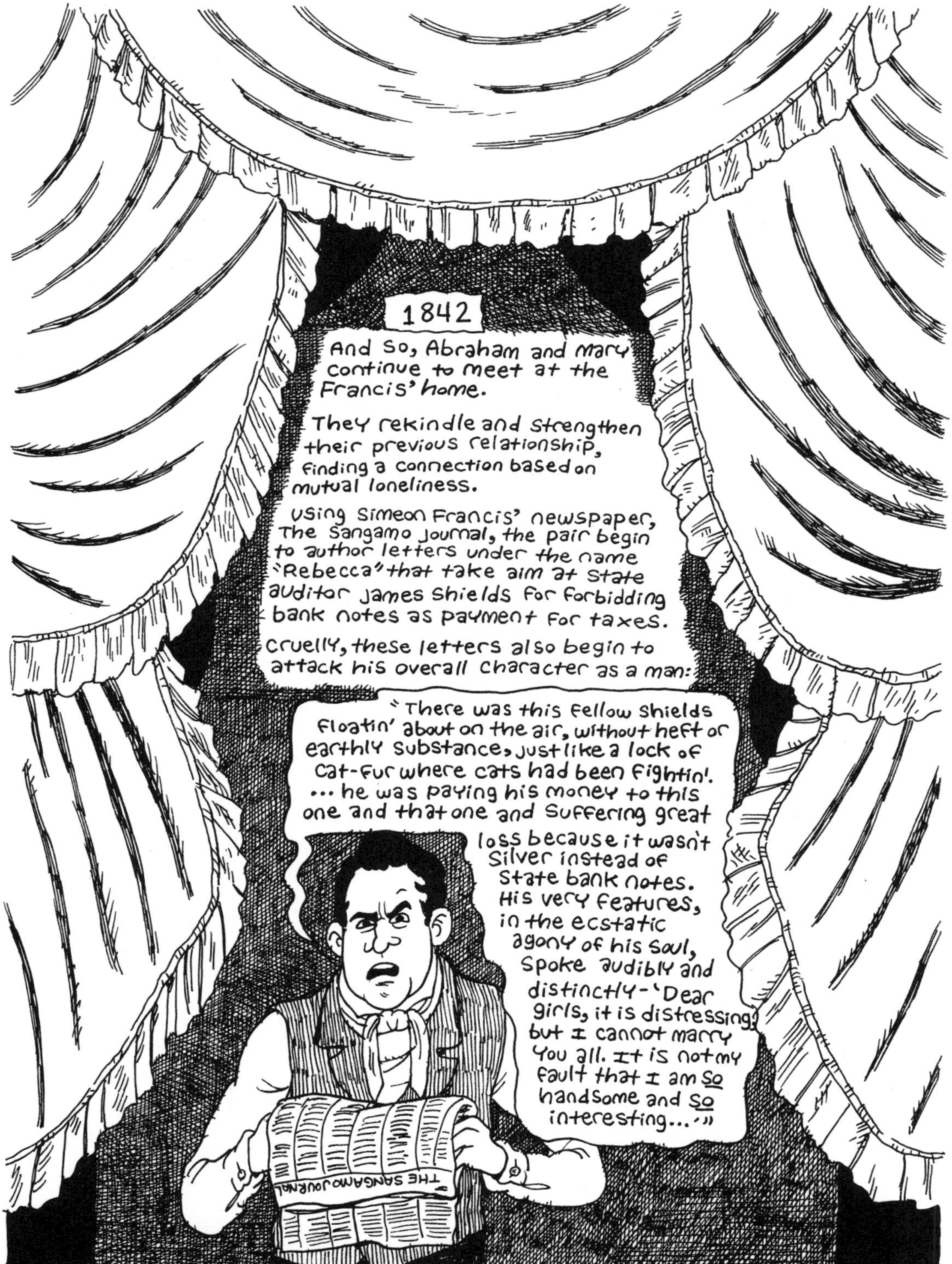
1842
And so, Abraham and Mary continue to meet at the Francis' home.
They rekindle and strengthen their previous relationship, finding a connection based on mutual loneliness.
Using Simeon Francis' newspaper, The Sangamo Journal, the pair begin to author letters under the name "Rebecca" that take aim at state auditor James Shields for forbidding bank notes as payment for taxes.
Cruelly, these letters also begin to attack his overall character as a man:
"There was this fellow Shields floatin' about on the air, without heft or earthly substance, just like a lock of cat-fur where cats had been fightin'. ... he was paying his money to this one and that one and suffering great loss because it wasn't silver instead of state bank notes. His very features, in the ecstatic agony of his soul, spoke audibly and distinctly-'Dear girls, it is distressing, but I cannot marry you all. It is not my fault that I am so handsome and so interesting...'"
THE SANGAMO JOURNAL

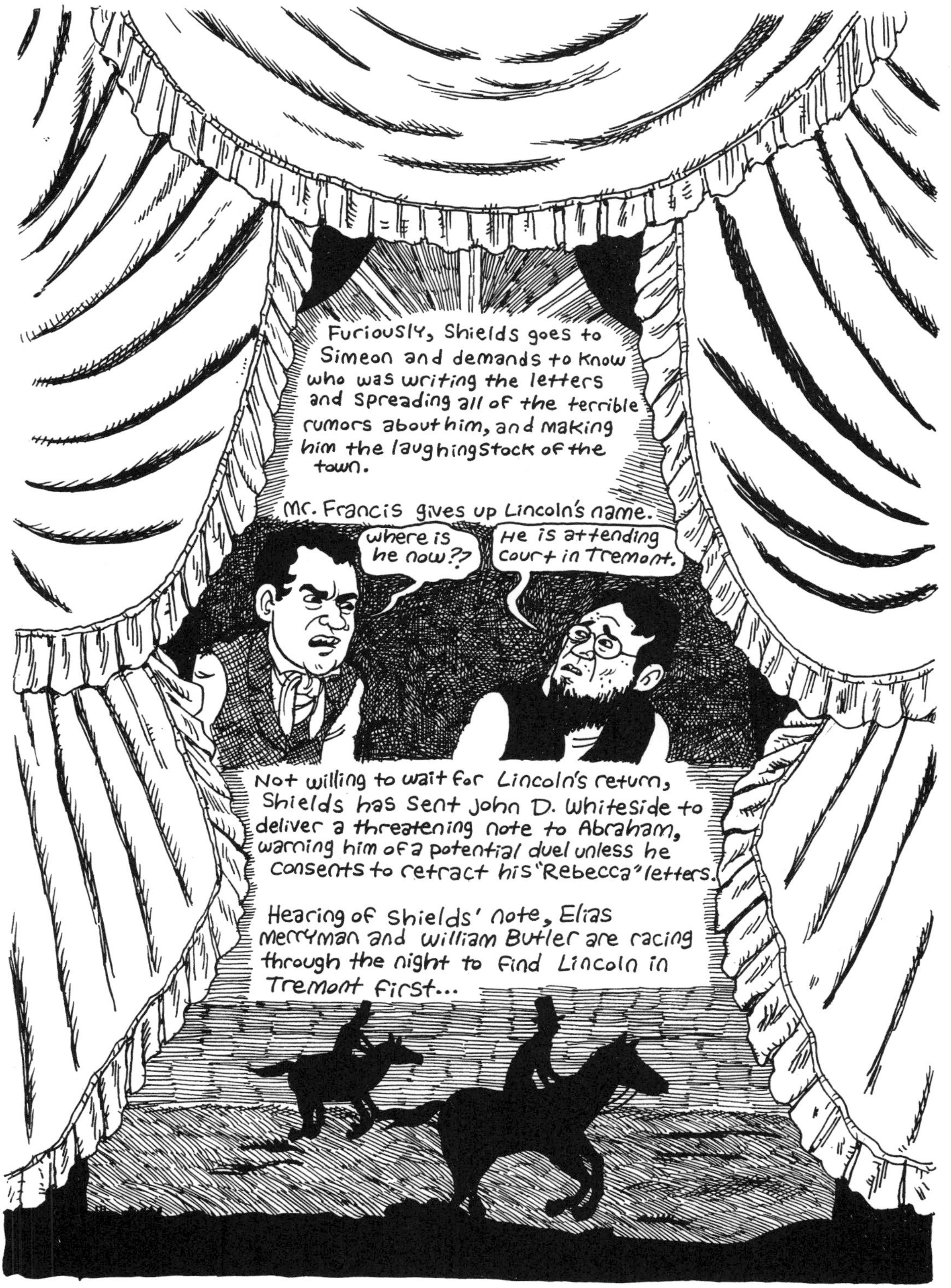
Furiously, Shields goes to Simeon and demands to know who was writing the letters and spreading all of the terrible rumors about him, and making him the laughingstock of the town.
Mr. Francis gives up Lincoln's name.
Where is he now??
He is attending court in Tremont.
Not willing to wait for Lincoln's return, Shields has sent John D. Whiteside to deliver a threatening note to Abraham, warning him of a potential duel unless he consents to retract his "Rebecca" letters.
Hearing of Shields' note, Elias Merryman and William Butler are racing through the night to find Lincoln in Tremont first...

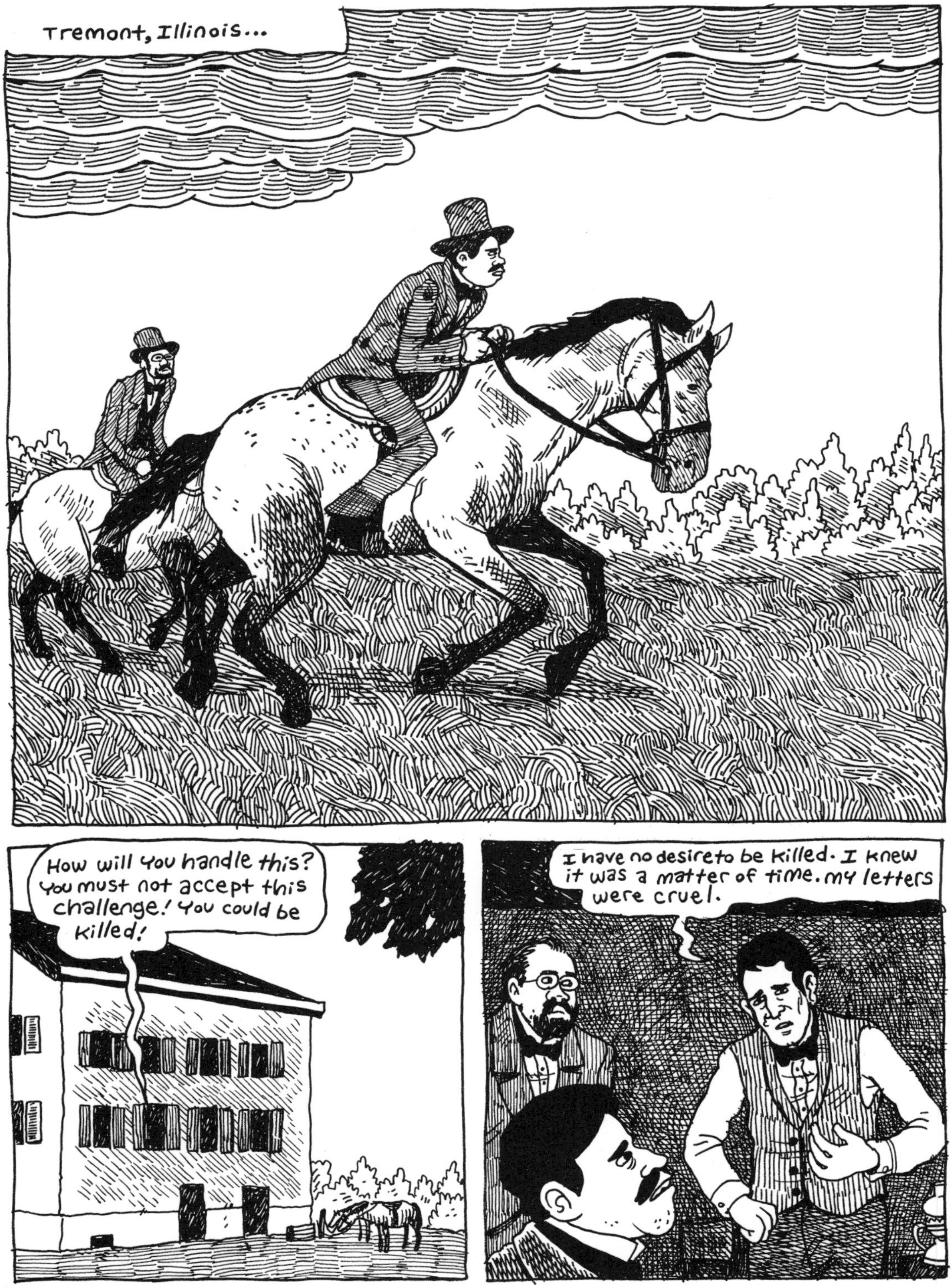
Tremont, Illinois...
How will you handle this? You must not accept this challenge! You could be killed!
I have no desire to be killed. I knew it was a matter of time. My letters were cruel.

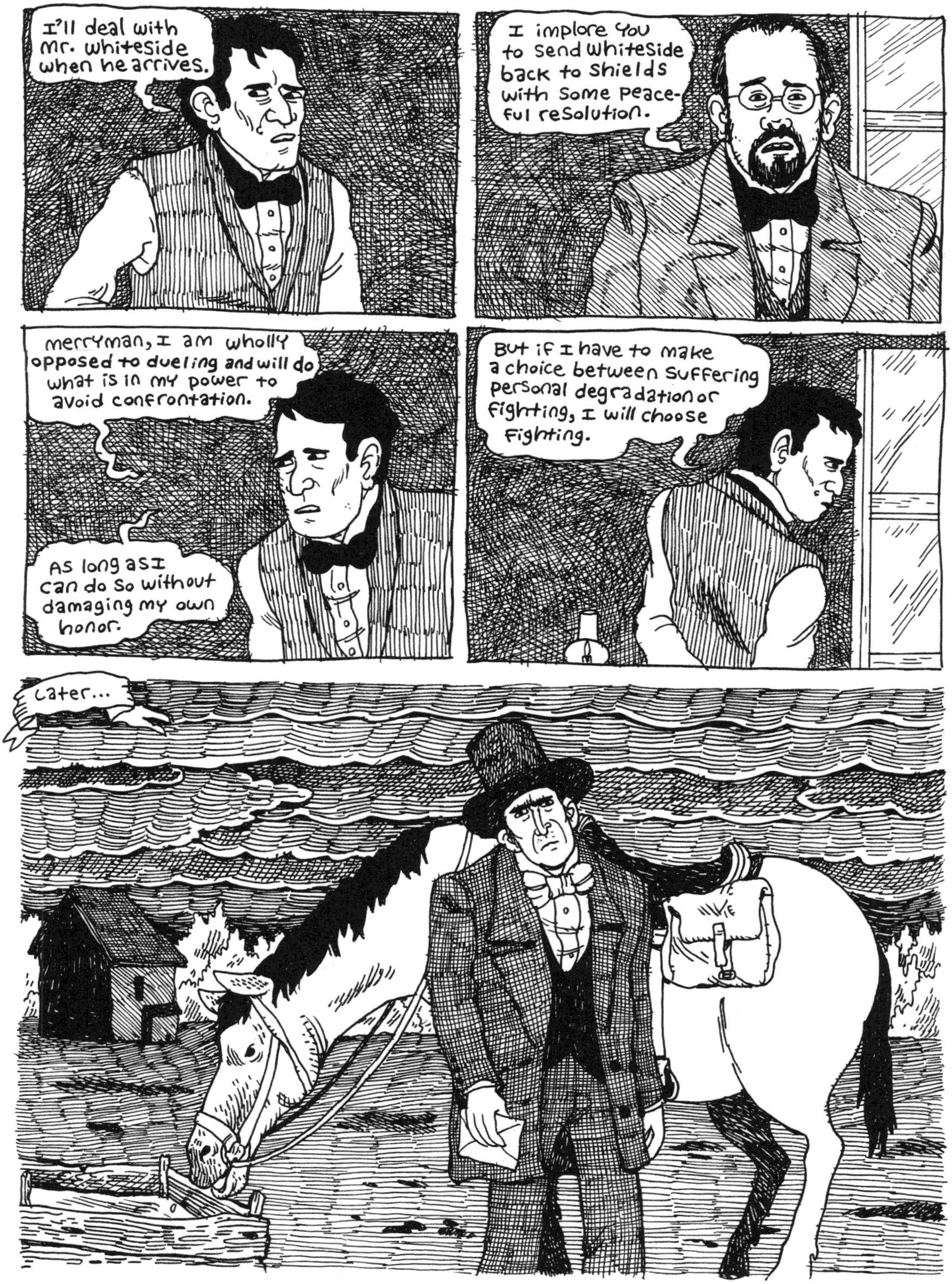
I'll deal with Mr. Whiteside when he arrives.
I implore you to send Whiteside back to Shields with some peaceful resolution.
Merryman, I am wholly opposed to dueling and will do what is in my power to avoid confrontation.
As long as I can do so without damaging my own honor.
But if I have to make a choice between suffering personal degradation or fighting, I will choose fighting.
Later...

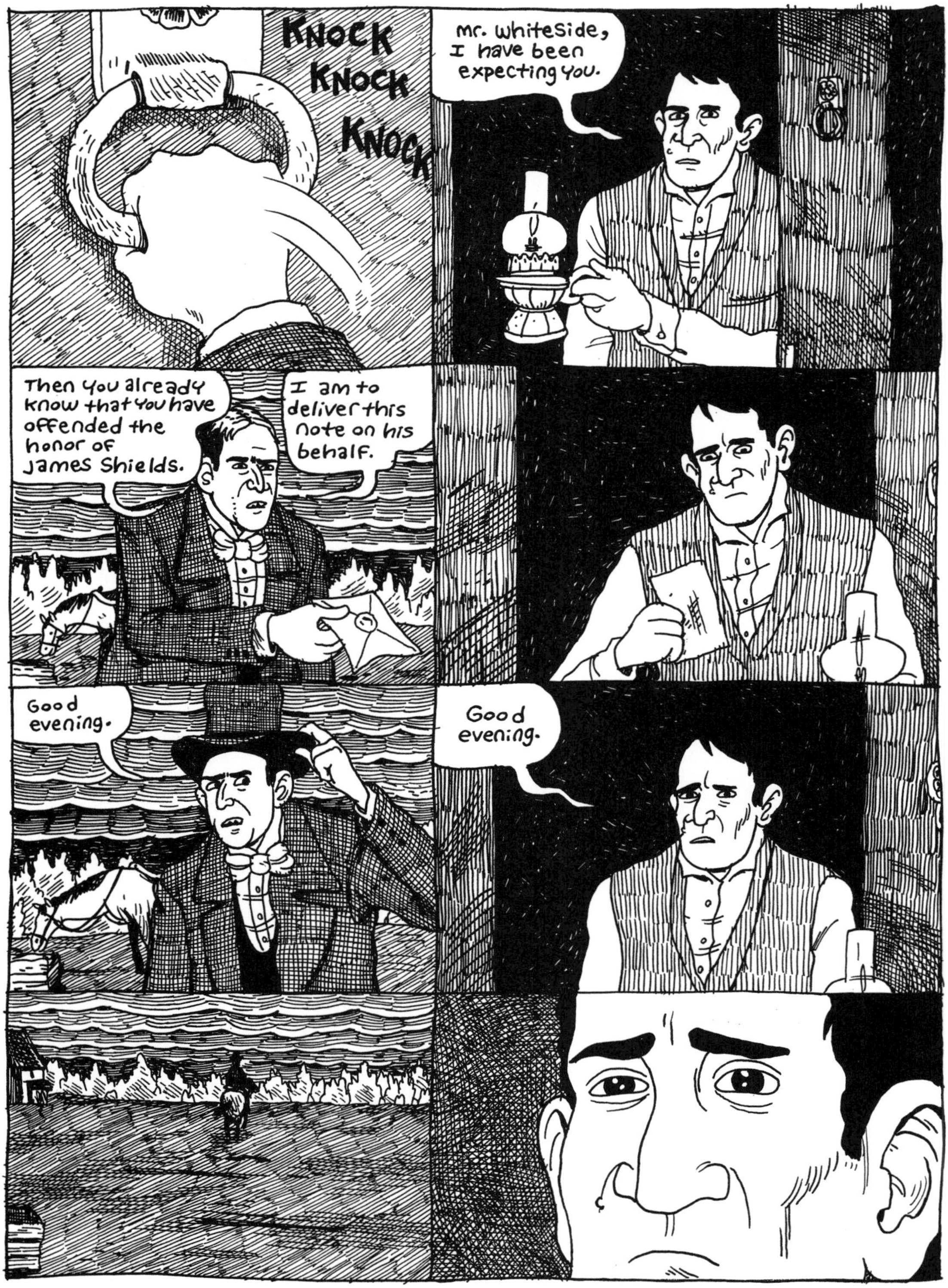
KNOCK
KNOCK
KNOCK
Mr. Whiteside, I have been expecting you.
Then you already know that you have offended the honor of James Shields.
I am to deliver this note on his behalf.
Good evening.
Good evening.

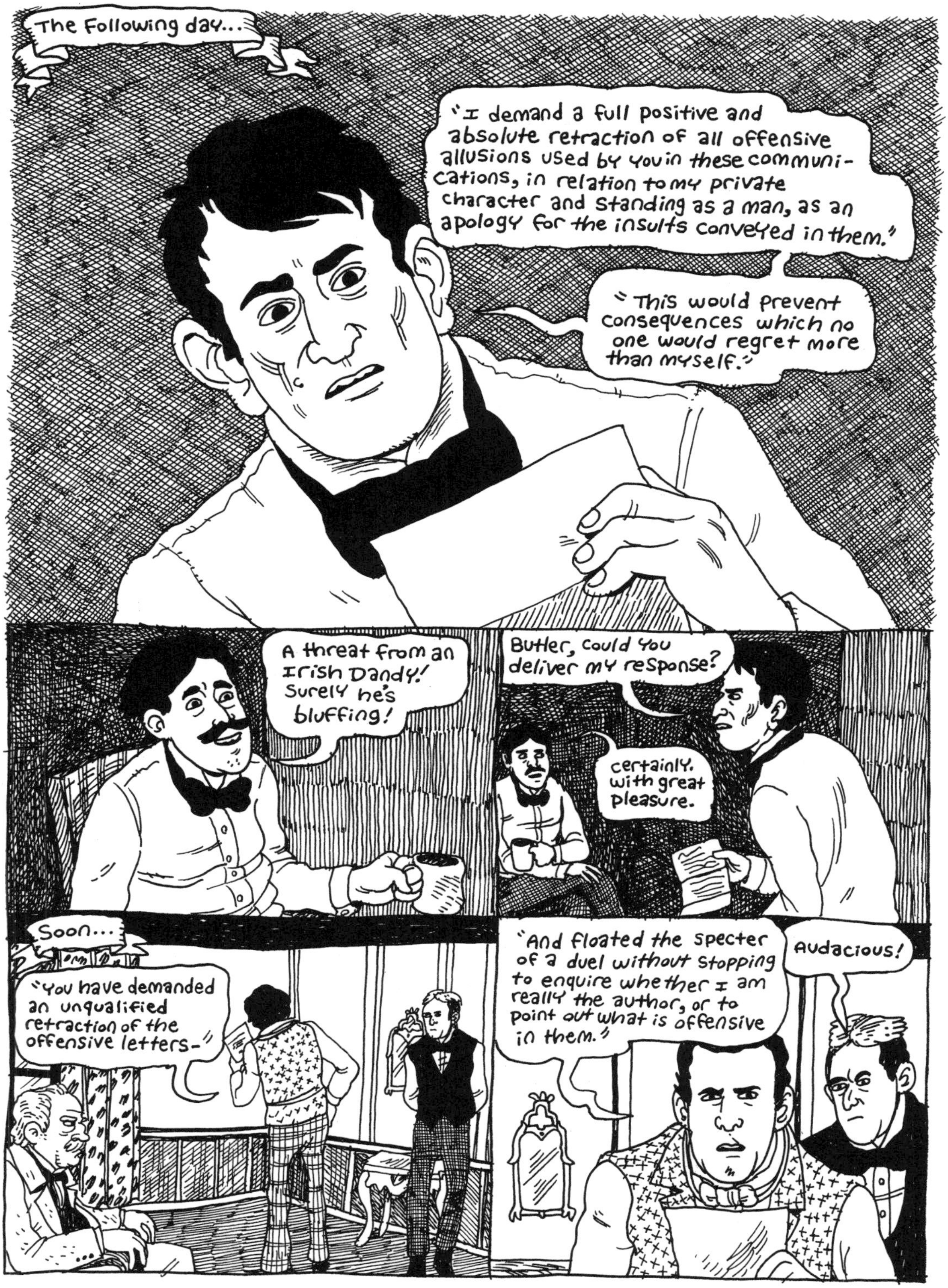
The Following day...
"I demand a full positive and absolute retraction of all offensive allusions used by you in these communi-cations, in relation to my private character and standing as a man, as an apology for the insults conveyed in them."
"This would prevent consequences which no one would regret more than myself."
A threat from an Irish Dandy! Surely he's bluffing!
Butler, could you deliver my response?
Certainly. With great pleasure.
Soon...
"You have demanded an unqualified retraction of the offensive letters-
"And floated the specter of a duel without stopping to enquire whether I am really the author, or to point out what is offensive in them."
Audacious!

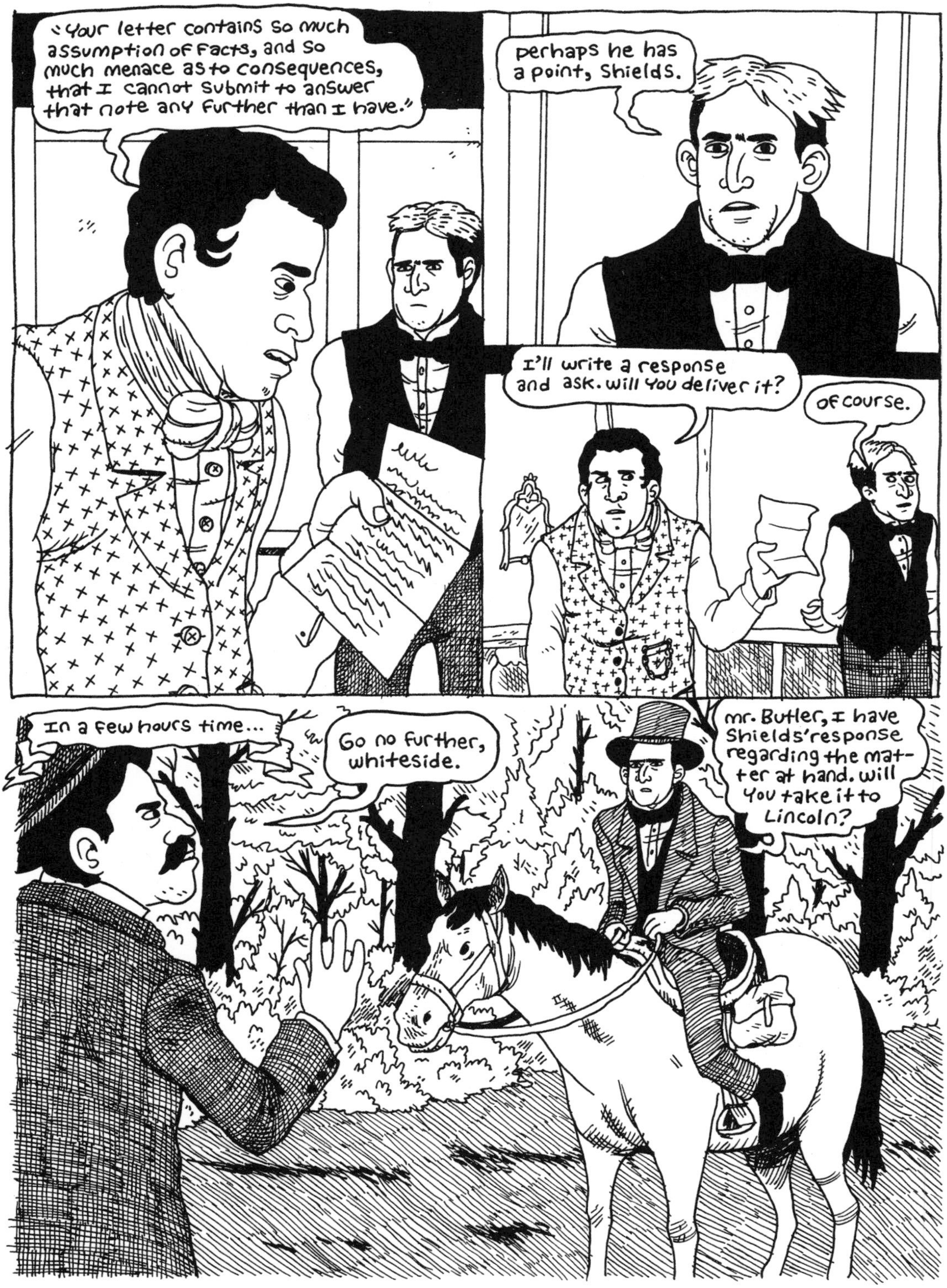
"Your letter contains so much assumption of facts, and so much menace as to consequences, that I cannot submit to answer that note any further than I have."
Perhaps he has a point, Shields.
I'll write a response and ask. Will you deliver it?
Of course.
In a few hours time...
Mr. Butler, I have Shields' response regarding the matter at hand. Will you take it to Lincoln?
Go no further, Whiteside.

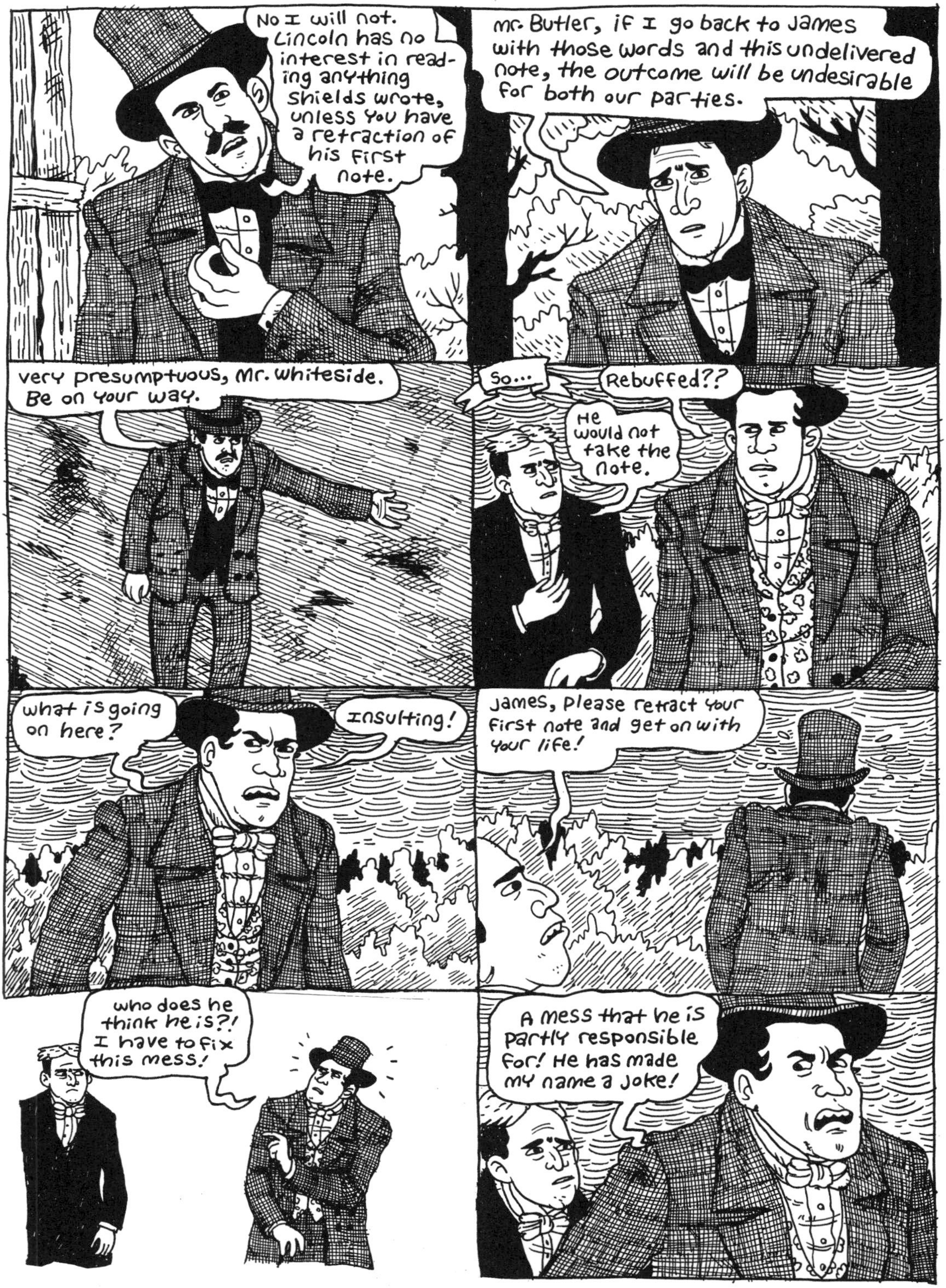
No I will not. Lincoln has no interest in reading anything Shields wrote, unless you have a retraction of his first note.
Mr. Butler, if I go back to James with those words and this undelivered note, the outcome will be undesirable for both our parties.
Very presumptuous, Mr. Whiteside. Be on your way.
So...
Rebuffed??
He would not take the note.
What is going on here?
Insulting!
James, please retract your first note and get on with your life!
Who does he think he is?! I have to fix this mess!
A mess that he is partly responsible for! He has made my name a joke!

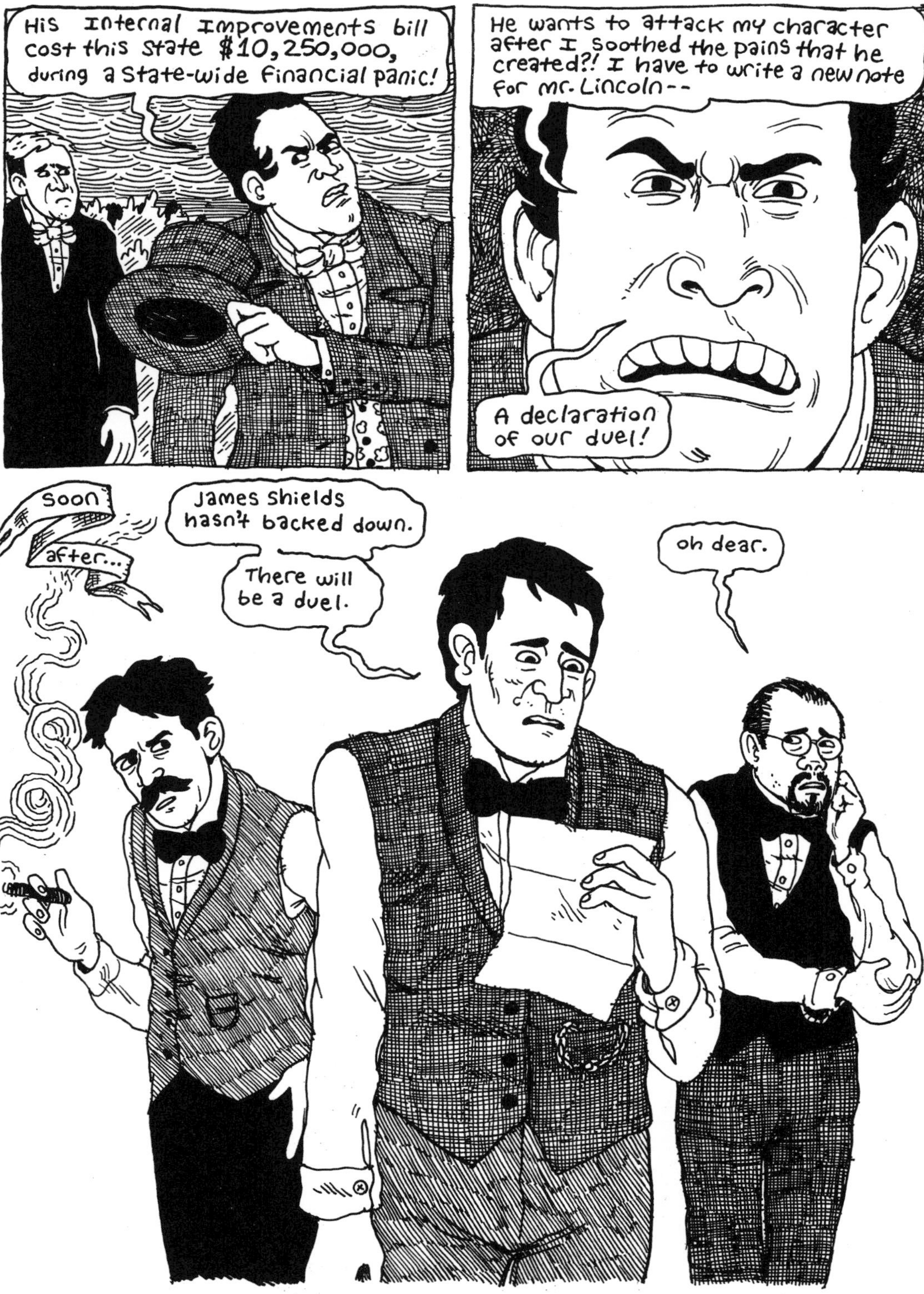
His Internal Improvements bill cost this state $10,250,000, during a State-wide financial panic!
He wants to attack my character after I soothed the pains that he created?! I have to write a new note for Mr. Lincoln--
A declaration of our duel!
Soon after...
James Shields hasn't backed down.
There will be a duel.
oh dear.

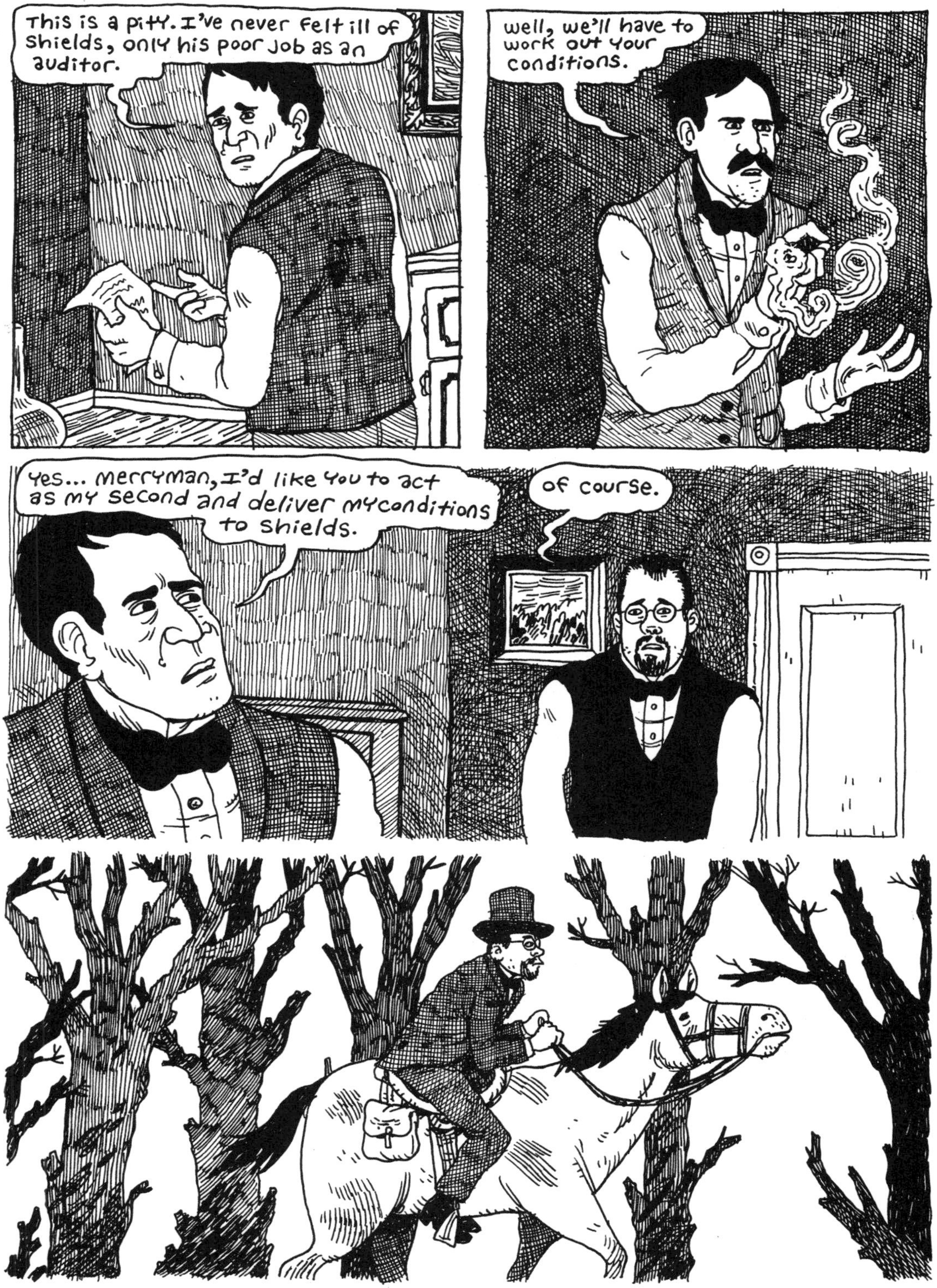
This is a pity. I've never felt ill of Shields, only his poor job as an auditor.
Well, we'll have to work out your conditions.
Yes... Merryman, I'd like you to act as my second and deliver my conditions to Shields.
Of course.

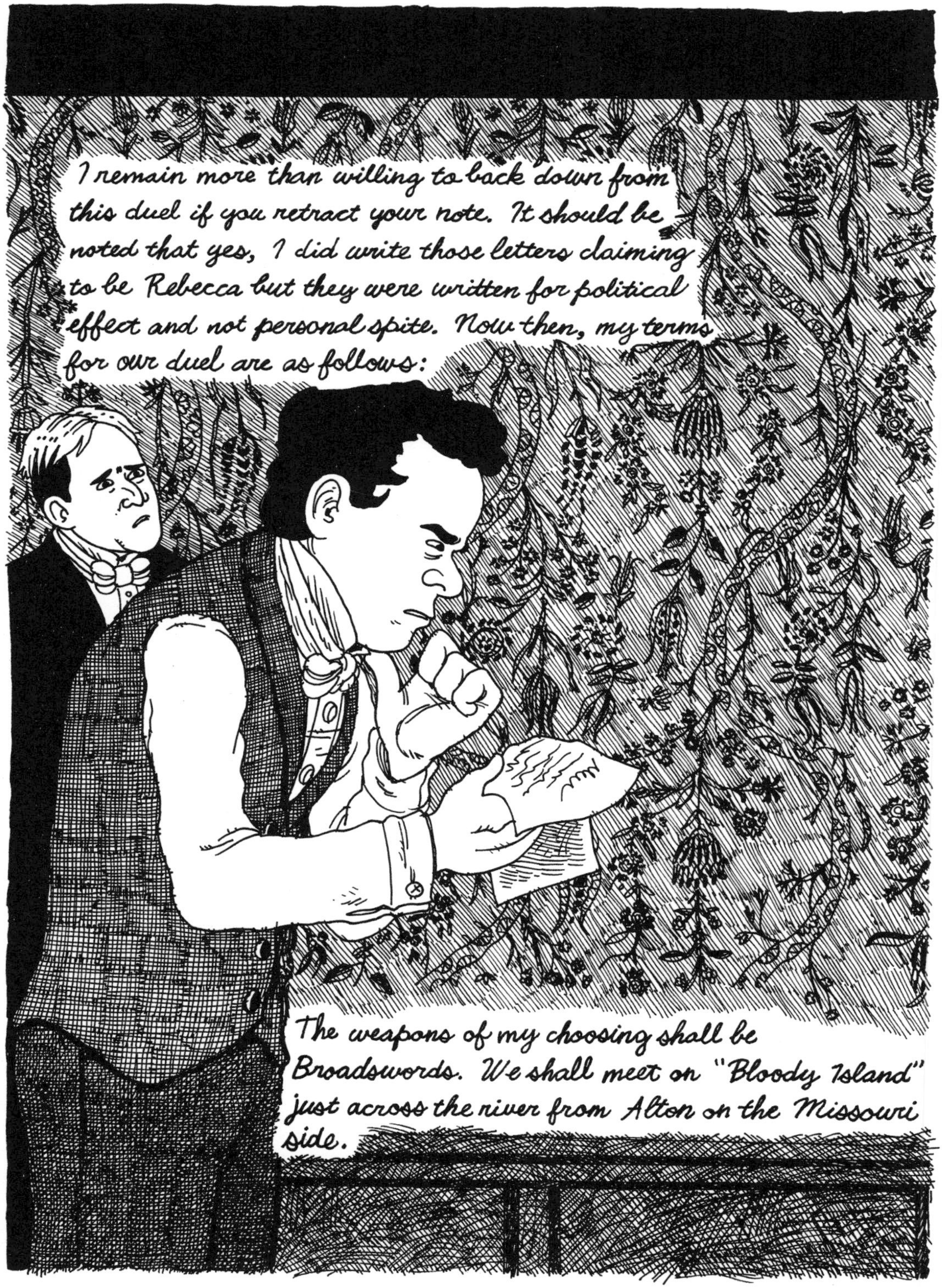
I remain more than willing to back down from this duel if you retract your note. It should be noted that yes, I did write those letters claiming to be Rebecca but they were written for political effect and not personal spite. Now then, my terms for our duel are as follows:
The weapons of my choosing shall be Broadswords. We shall meet on "Bloody Island" just across the river from Alton on the Missouri side.

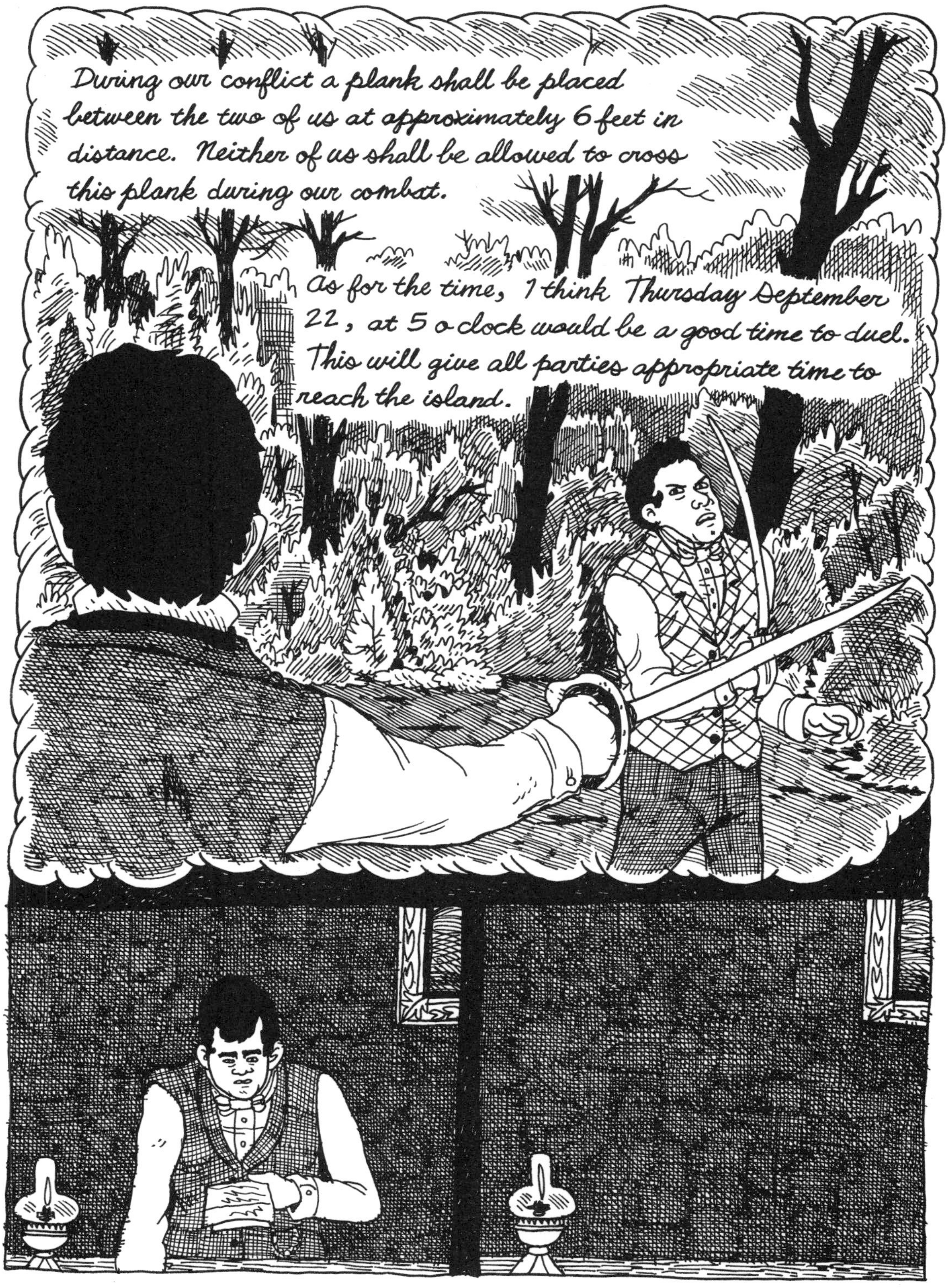
During our conflict a plank shall be placed between the two of us at approximately 6 feet in distance. Neither of us shall be allowed to cross this plank during our combat.
As for the time, I think Thursday September 22, at 5 o clock would be a good time to duel. This will give all parties appropriate time to reach the island.

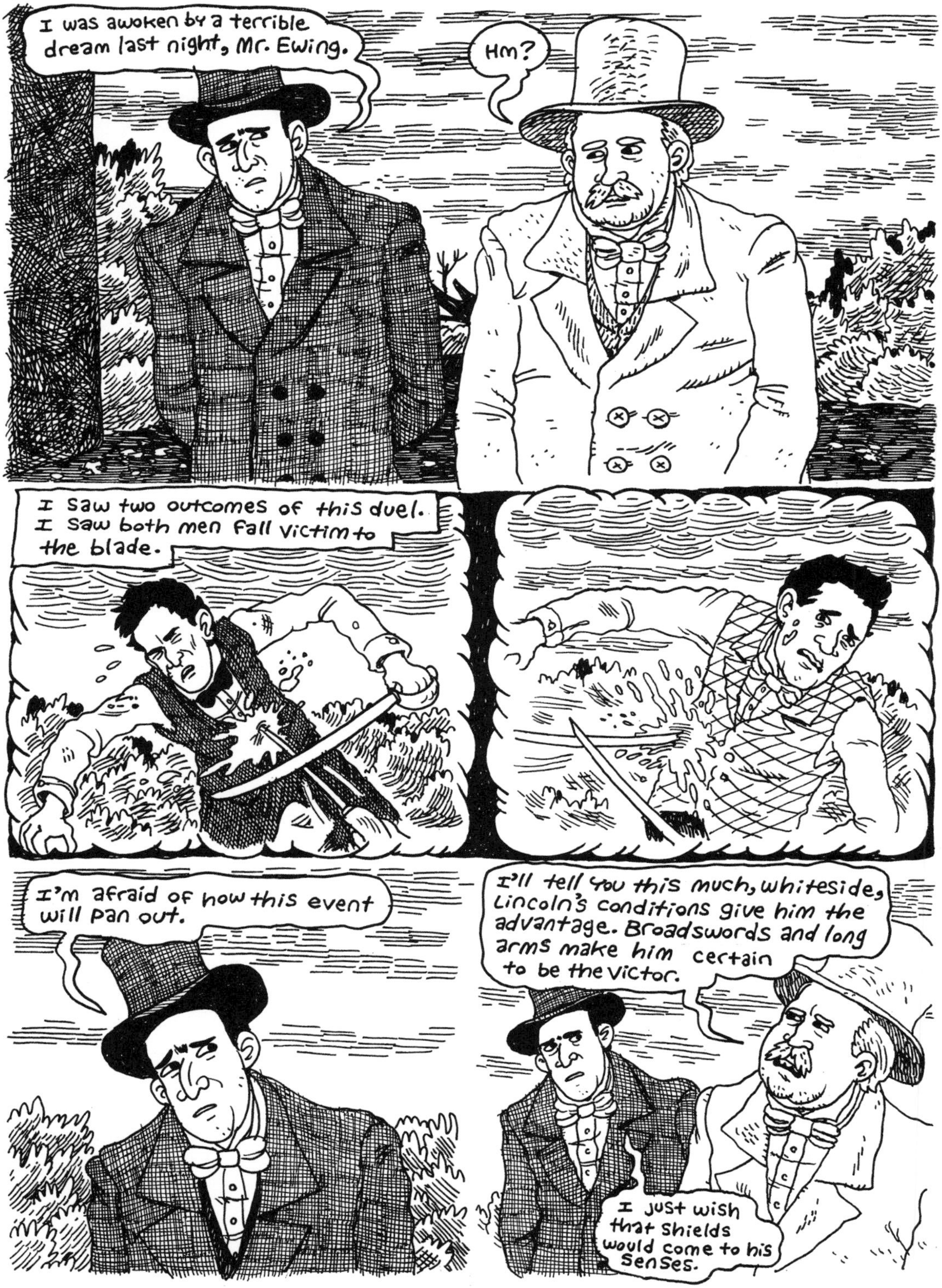
I was awoken by a terrible dream last night, Mr. Ewing.
Hm?
I saw two outcomes of this duel. I saw both men fall victim to the blade.
I'm afraid of how this event will pan out.
I'll tell you this much, Whiteside, Lincoln's conditions give him the advantage. Broadswords and long arms make him certain to be the victor.
I just wish that Shields would come to his senses.

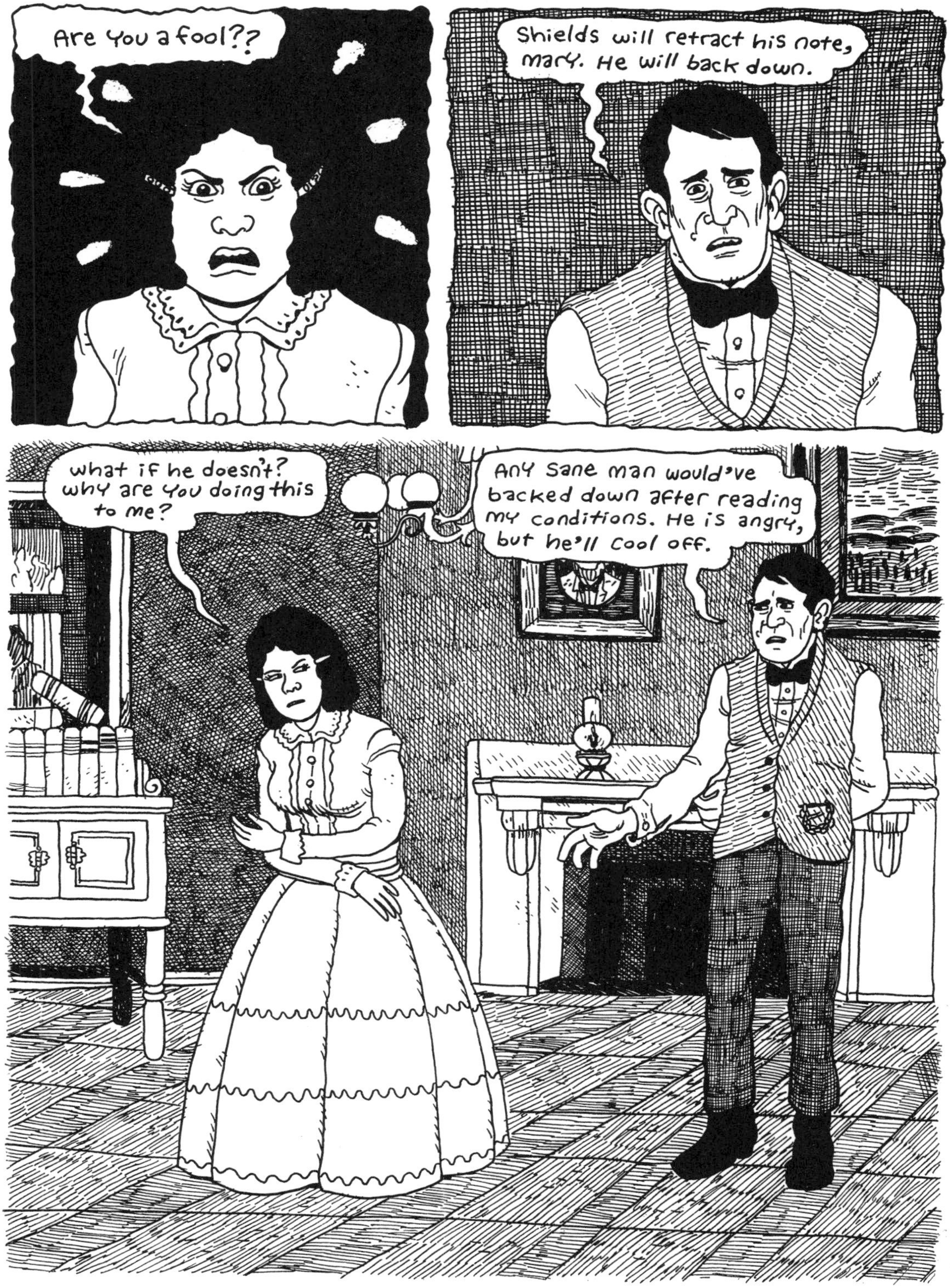
Are you a fool??
Shields will retract his note, mary. He will back down.
what if he doesn't? why are you doing this to me?
Any sane man would've backed down after reading my conditions. He is angry, but he'll cool off.

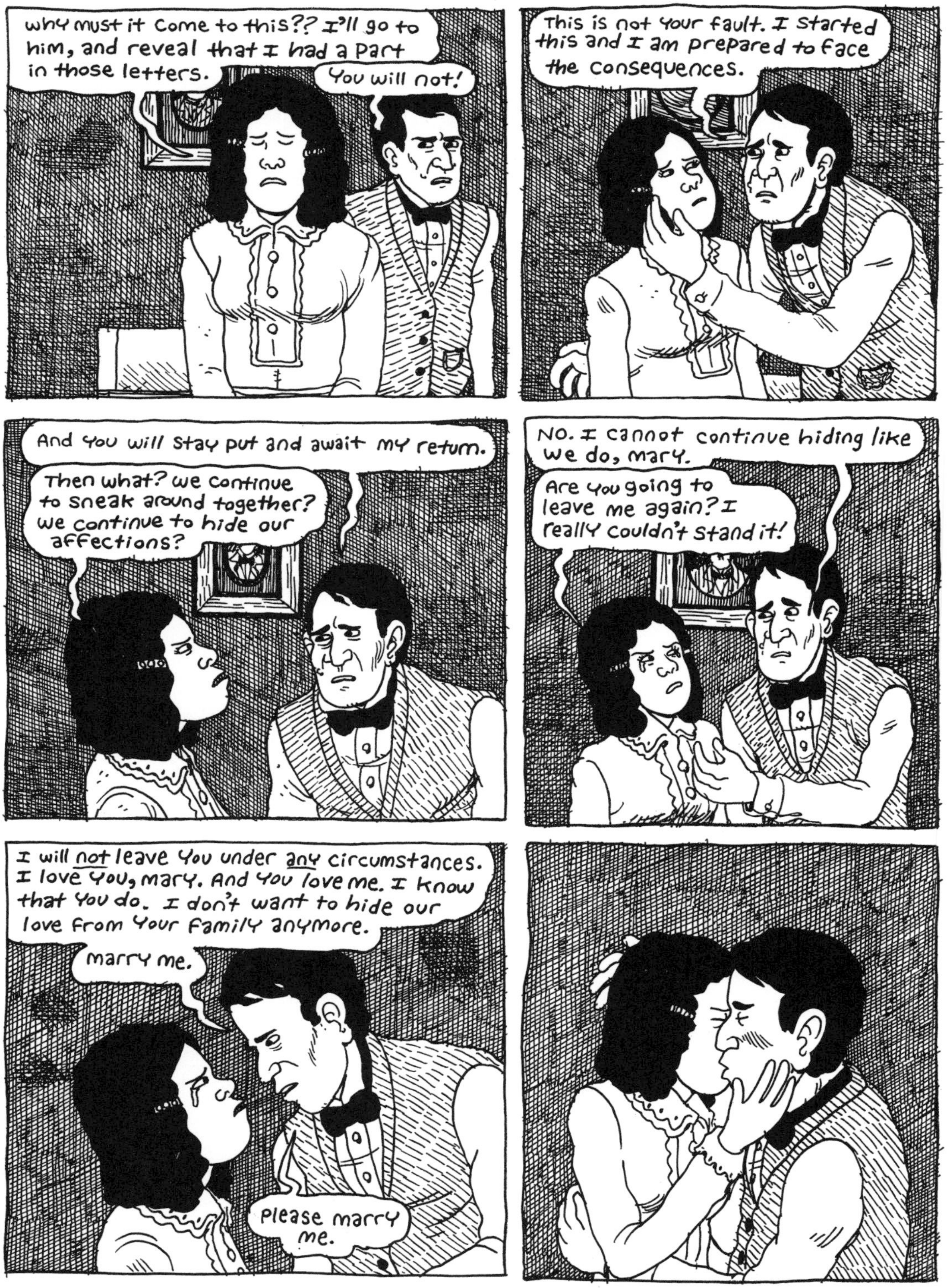
why must it come to this?? I'll go to him, and reveal that I had a part in those letters.
You will not!
This is not your fault. I started this and I am prepared to face the consequences.
And you will stay put and await my return.
Then what? we continue to sneak around together? we continue to hide our affections?
No. I cannot continue hiding like we do, mary.
Are you going to leave me again? I really couldn't stand it!
I will not leave you under any circumstances. I love you, mary. And you love me. I know that you do. I don't want to hide our love from your family anymore.
marry me.
Please marry me.

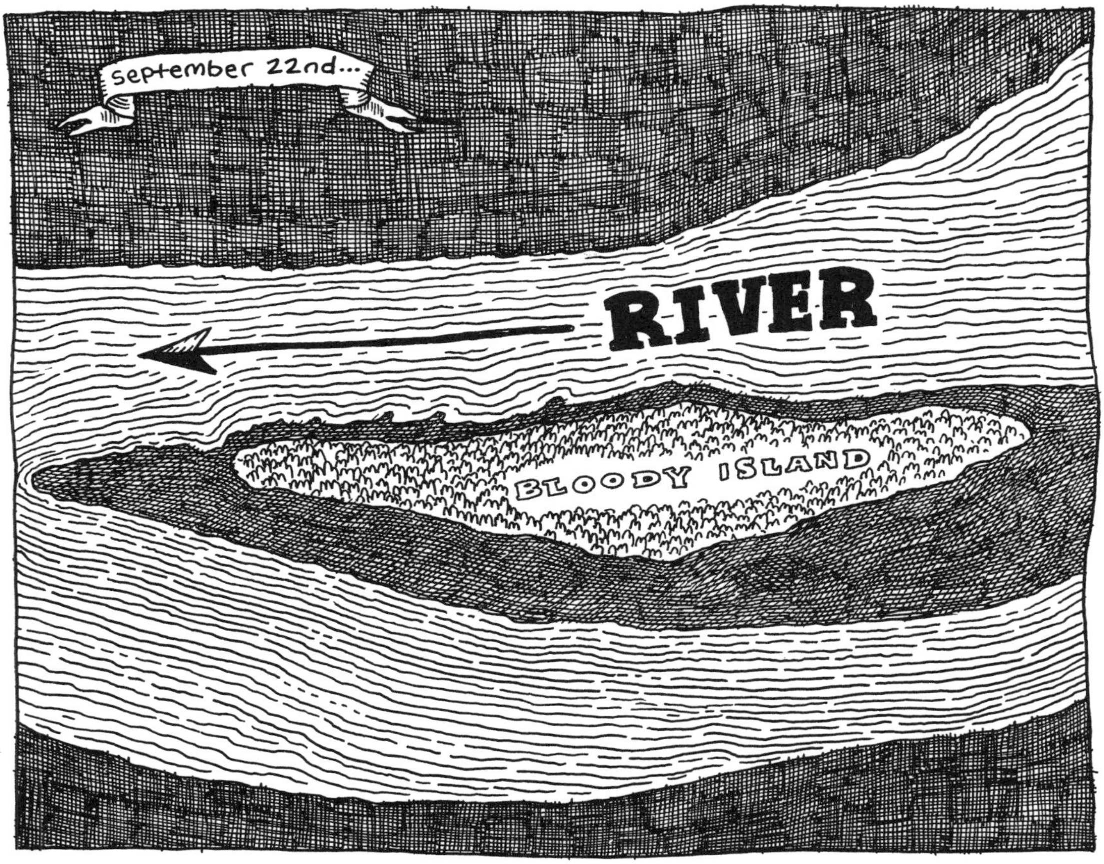
september 22nd...
RIVER
BLOODY ISLAND

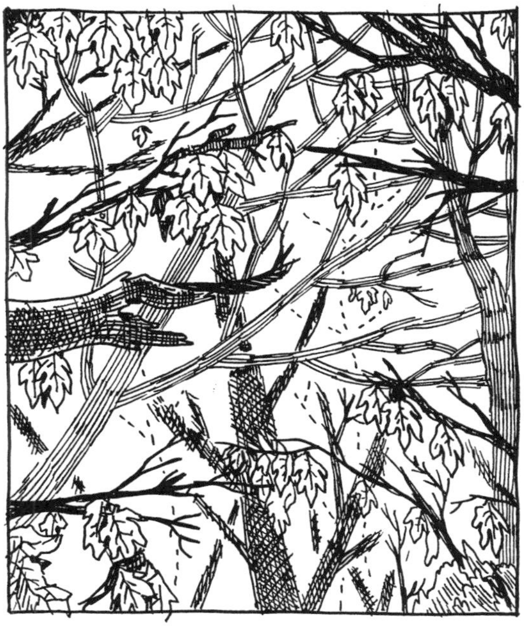

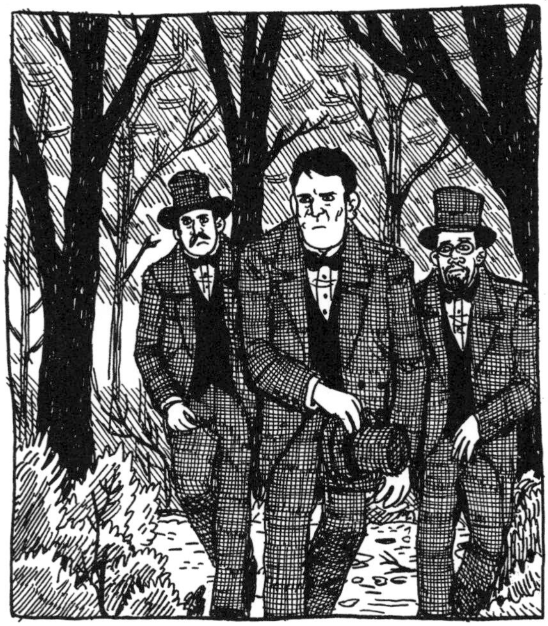

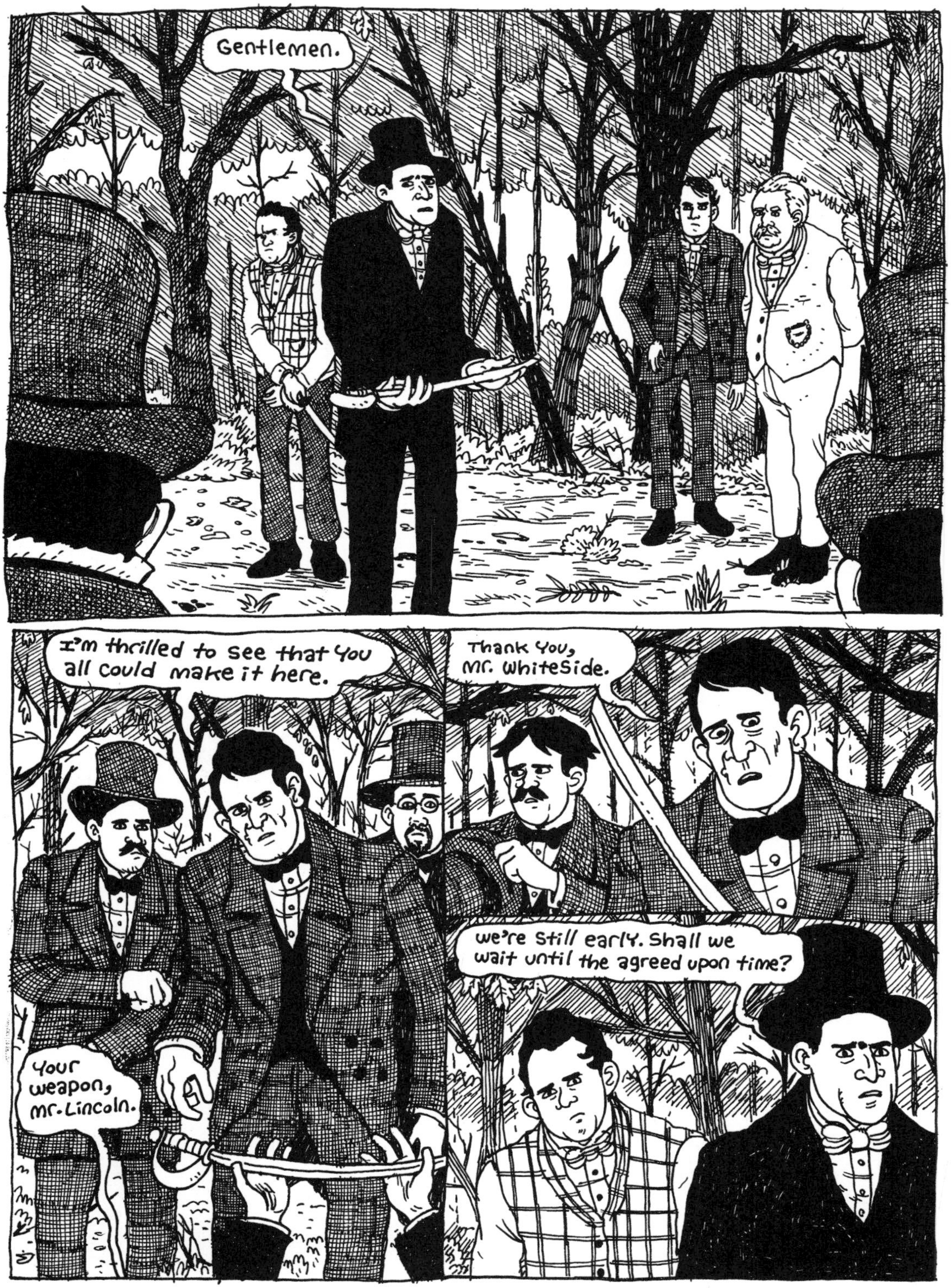
Gentlemen.
I'm thrilled to see that you all could make it here.
Your weapon, Mr. Lincoln.
Thank you, Mr. Whiteside.
We're still early. Shall we wait until the agreed upon time?

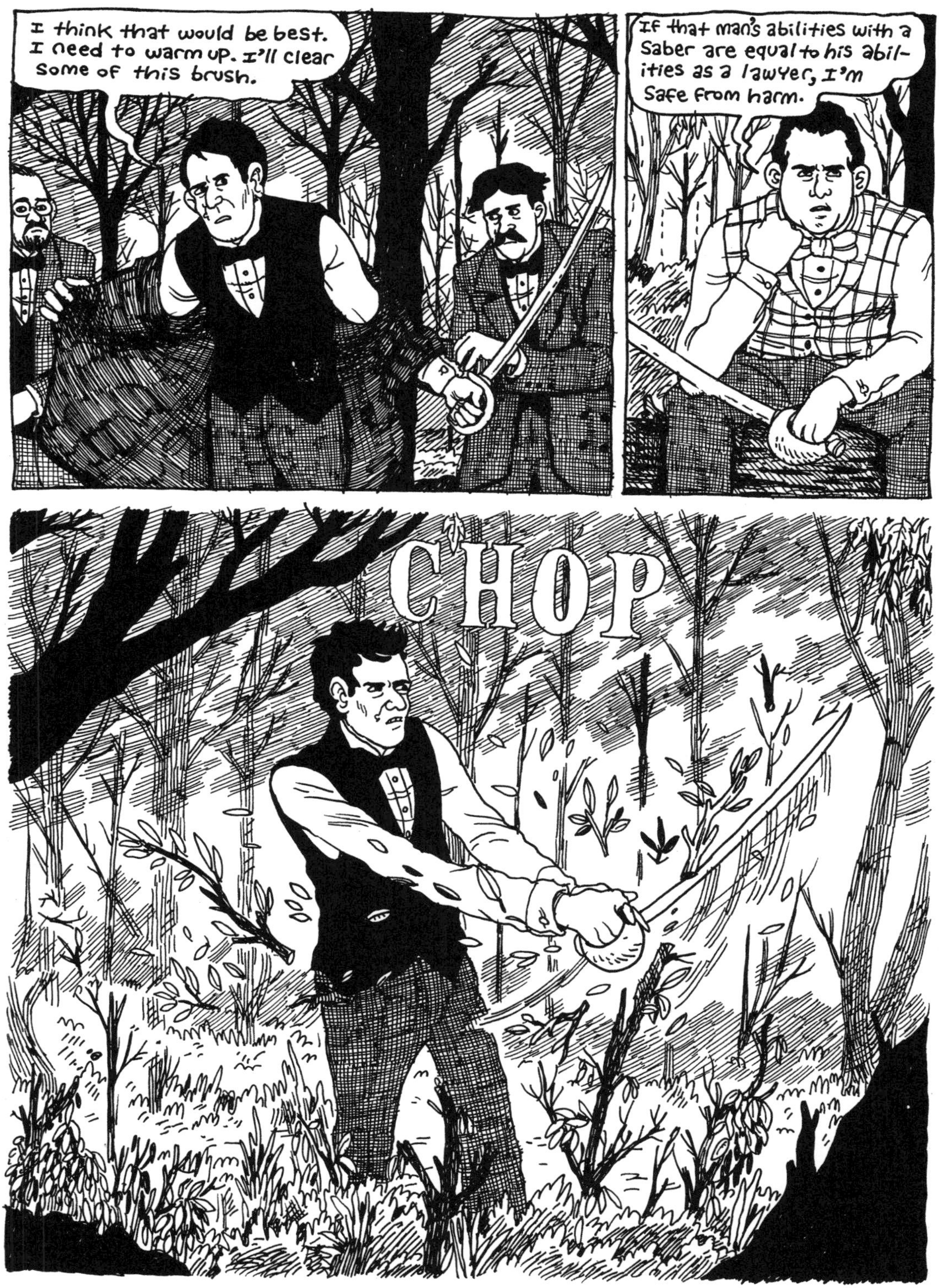
I think that would be best. I need to warm up. I'll clear some of this brush.
If that man's abilities with a saber are equal to his abilities as a lawyer, I'm safe from harm.
CHOP

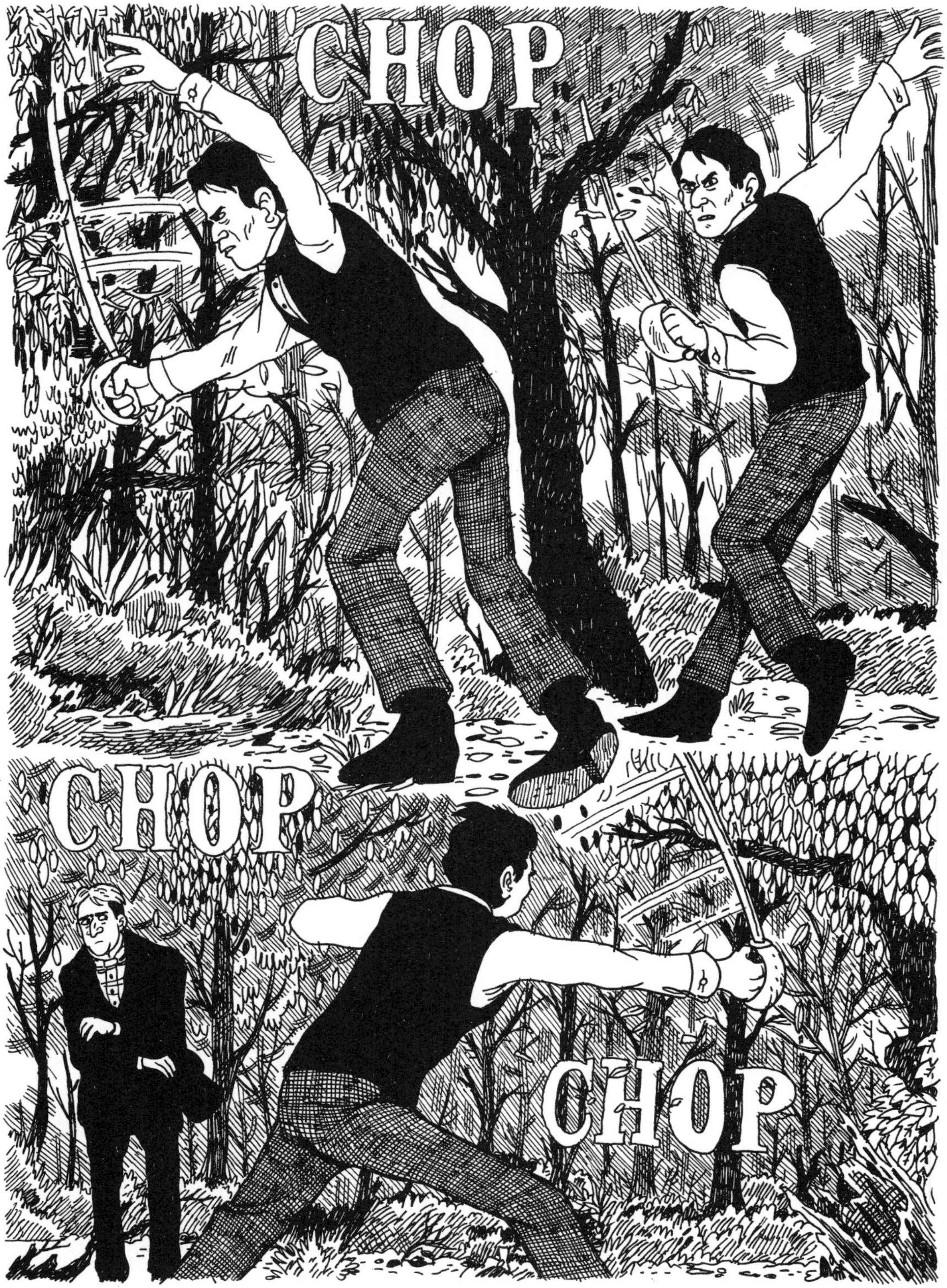
CHOP
CHOP
CHOP

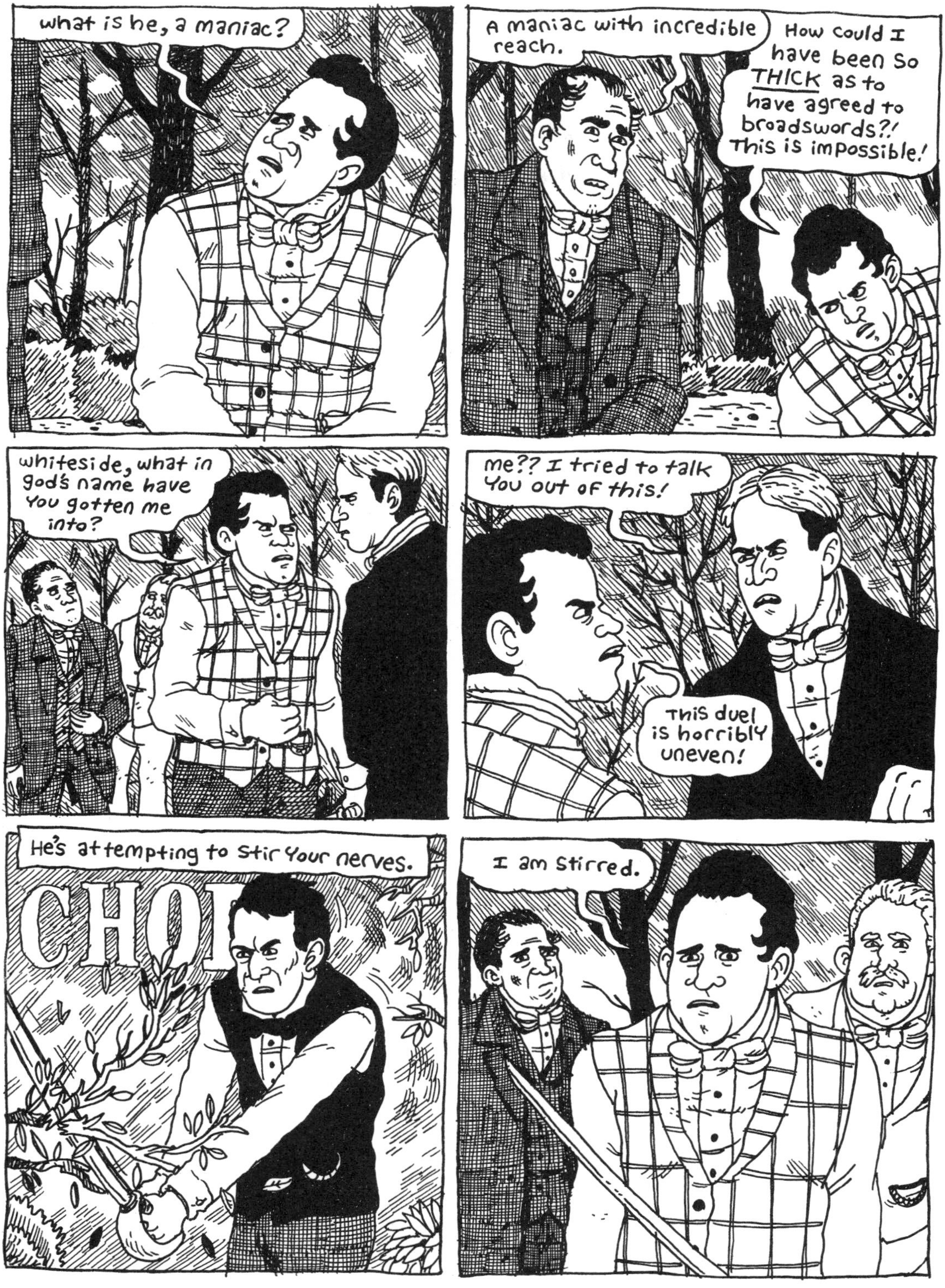

what is he, a maniac?
A maniac with incredible reach.
How could I have been so THICK as to have agreed to broadswords?! This is impossible!
whiteside, what in god's name have you gotten me into?
me?? I tried to talk you out of this!
This duel is horribly uneven!
He's attempting to stir your nerves.
CHO
I am stirred.

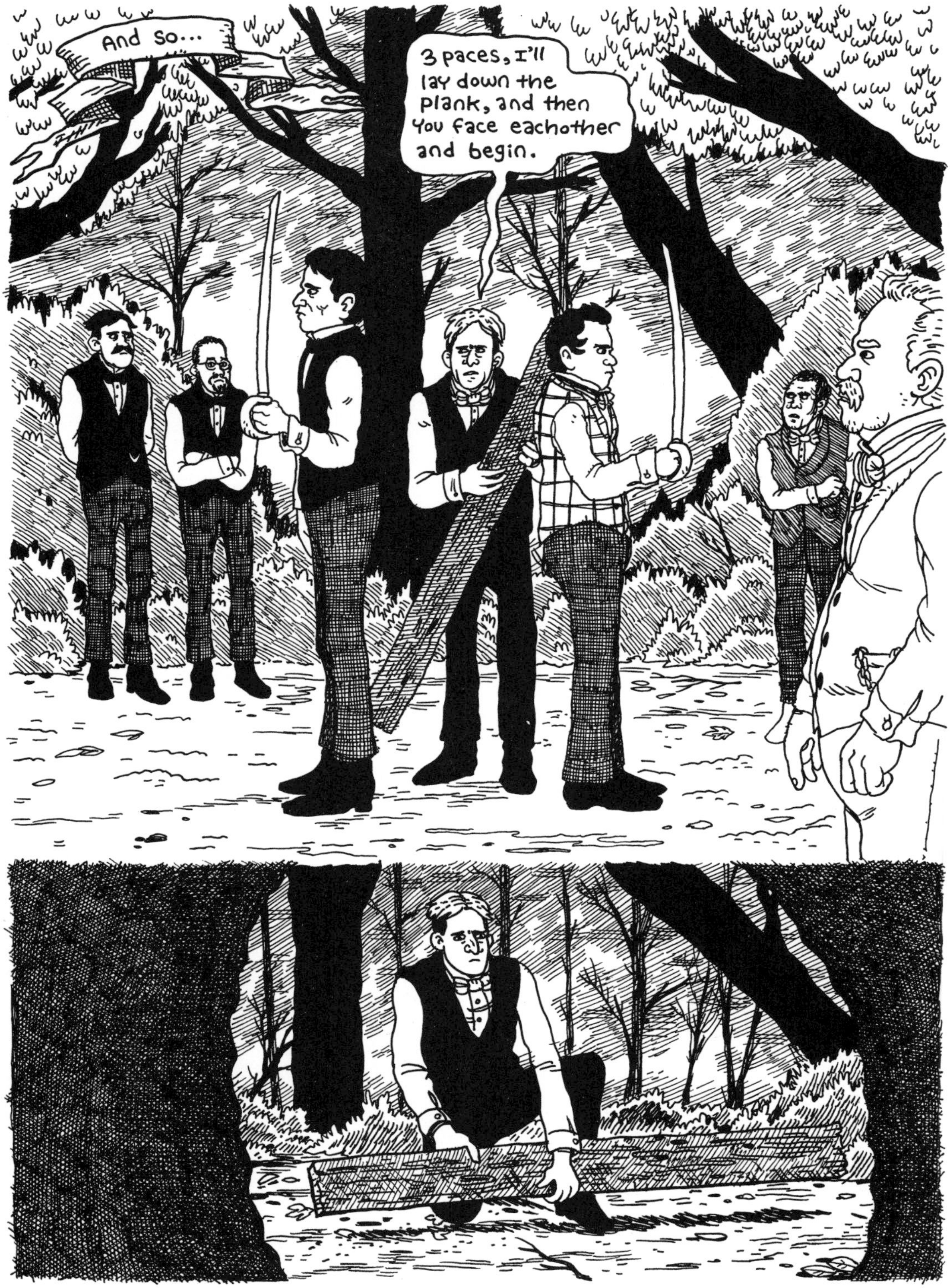
And so...
3 paces, I'll lay down the plank, and then you face eachother and begin.

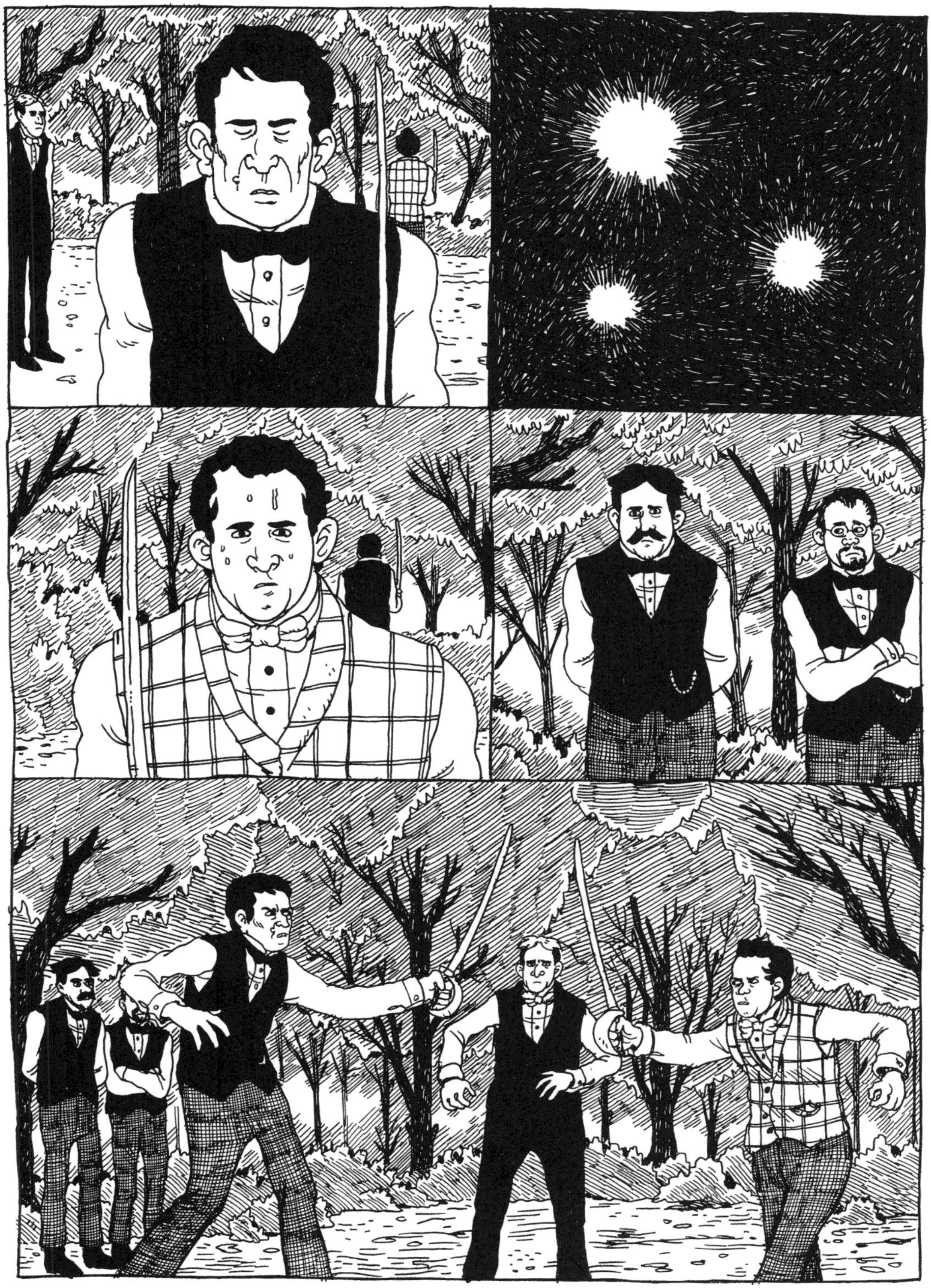

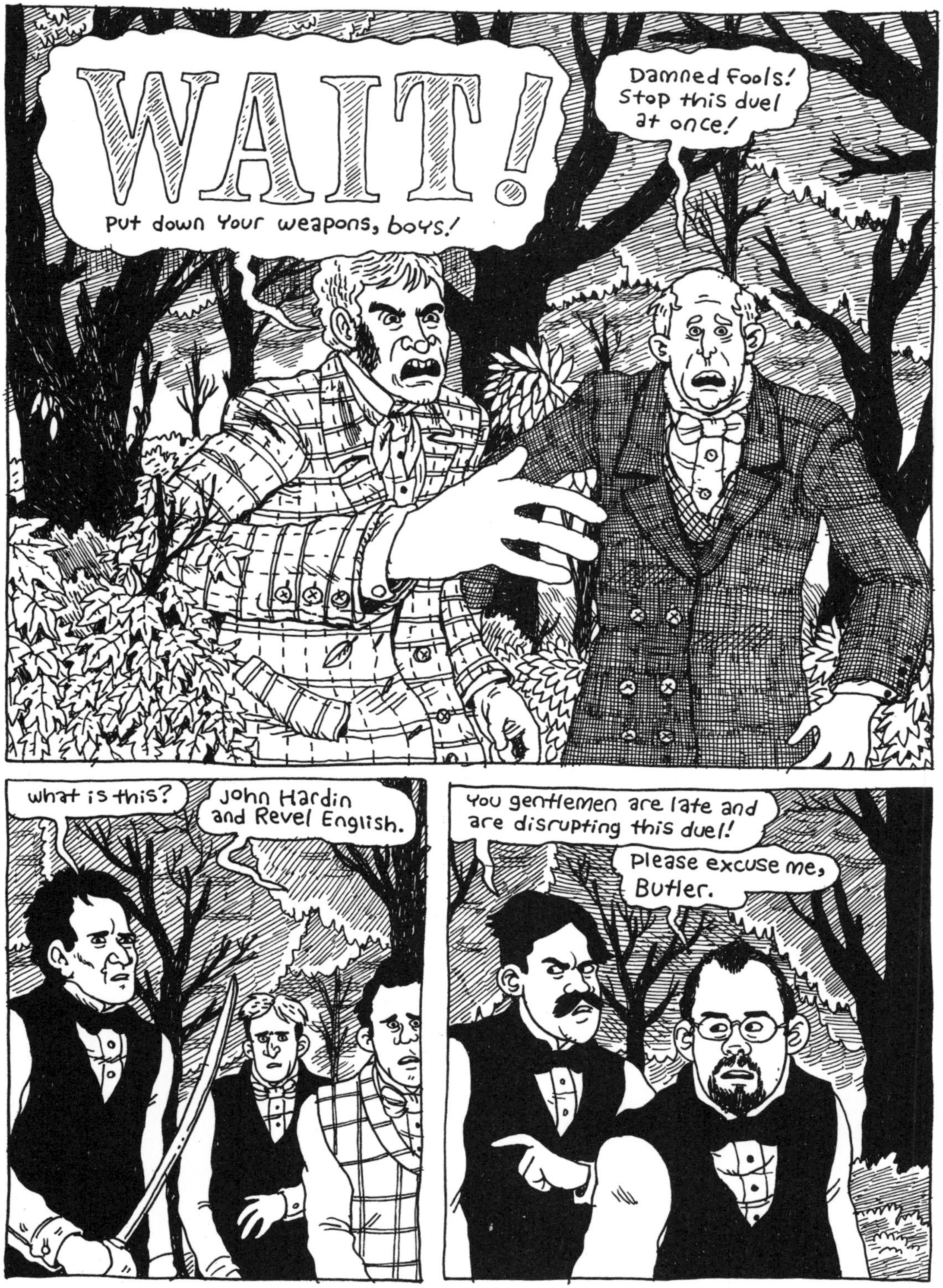
WAIT!
Put down your weapons, boys!
Damned fools! Stop this duel at once!
what is this?
John Hardin and Revel English.
You gentlemen are late and are disrupting this duel!
Please excuse me, Butler.

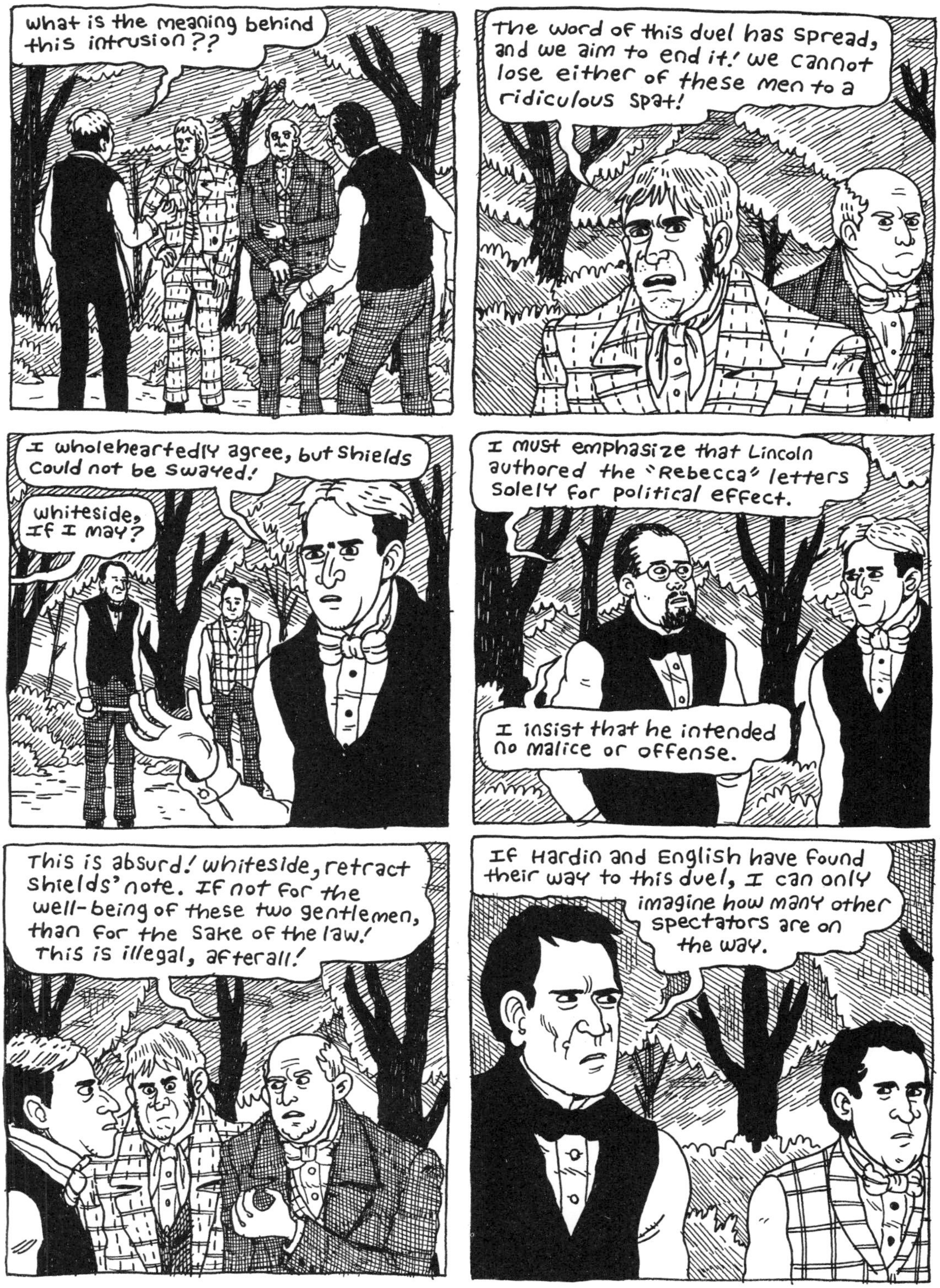
what is the meaning behind this intrusion??
The word of this duel has spread, and we aim to end it! we cannot lose either of these men to a ridiculous spat!
I wholeheartedly agree, but Shields could not be swayed!
whiteside, If I may?
I must emphasize that Lincoln authored the "Rebecca" letters solely for political effect.
I insist that he intended no malice or offense.
This is absurd! whiteside, retract Shields' note. If not for the well-being of these two gentlemen, than for the sake of the law! This is illegal, afterall!
If Hardin and English have found their way to this duel, I can only imagine how many other spectators are on the way.

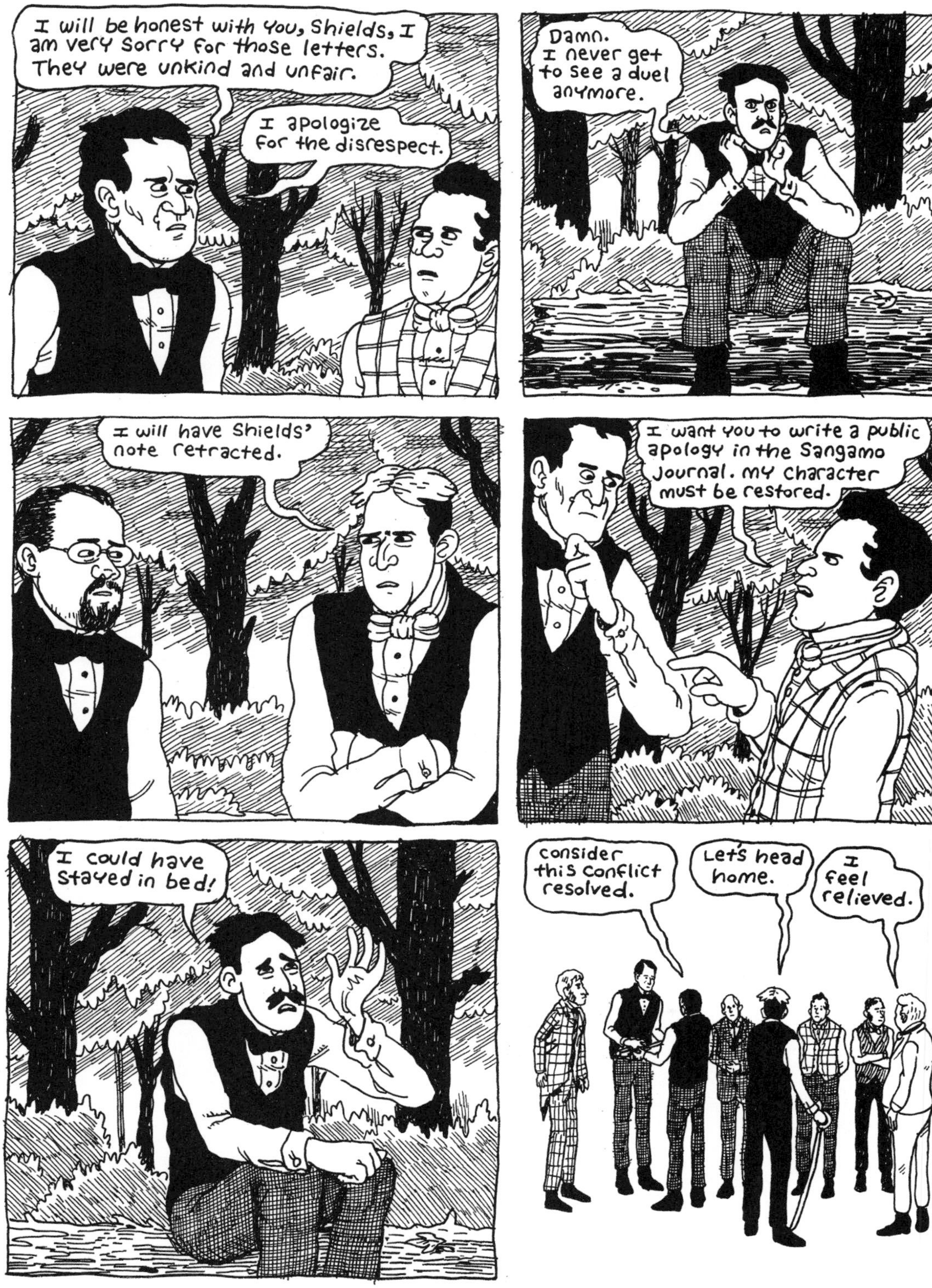

I will be honest with you, Shields, I am very sorry for those letters. They were unkind and unfair.
I apologize for the disrespect.
Damn. I never get to see a duel anymore.
I will have Shields' note retracted.
I want you to write a public apology in the Sangamo Journal. My character must be restored.
I could have stayed in bed!
Consider this conflict resolved.
Let's head home.
I feel relieved.

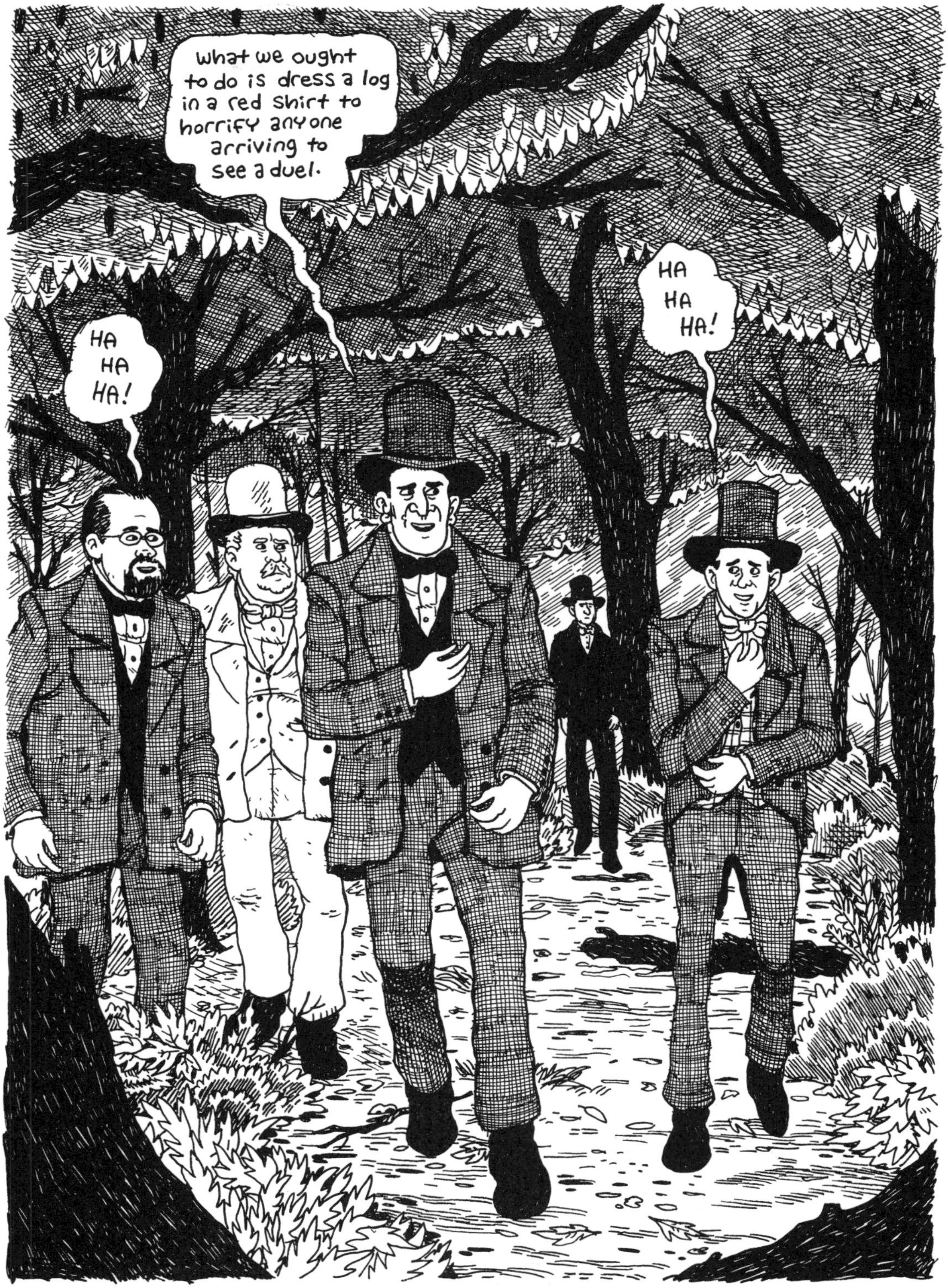
what we ought to do is dress a log in a red shirt to horrify anyone arriving to see a duel.
HA HA HA!
HA HA HA!

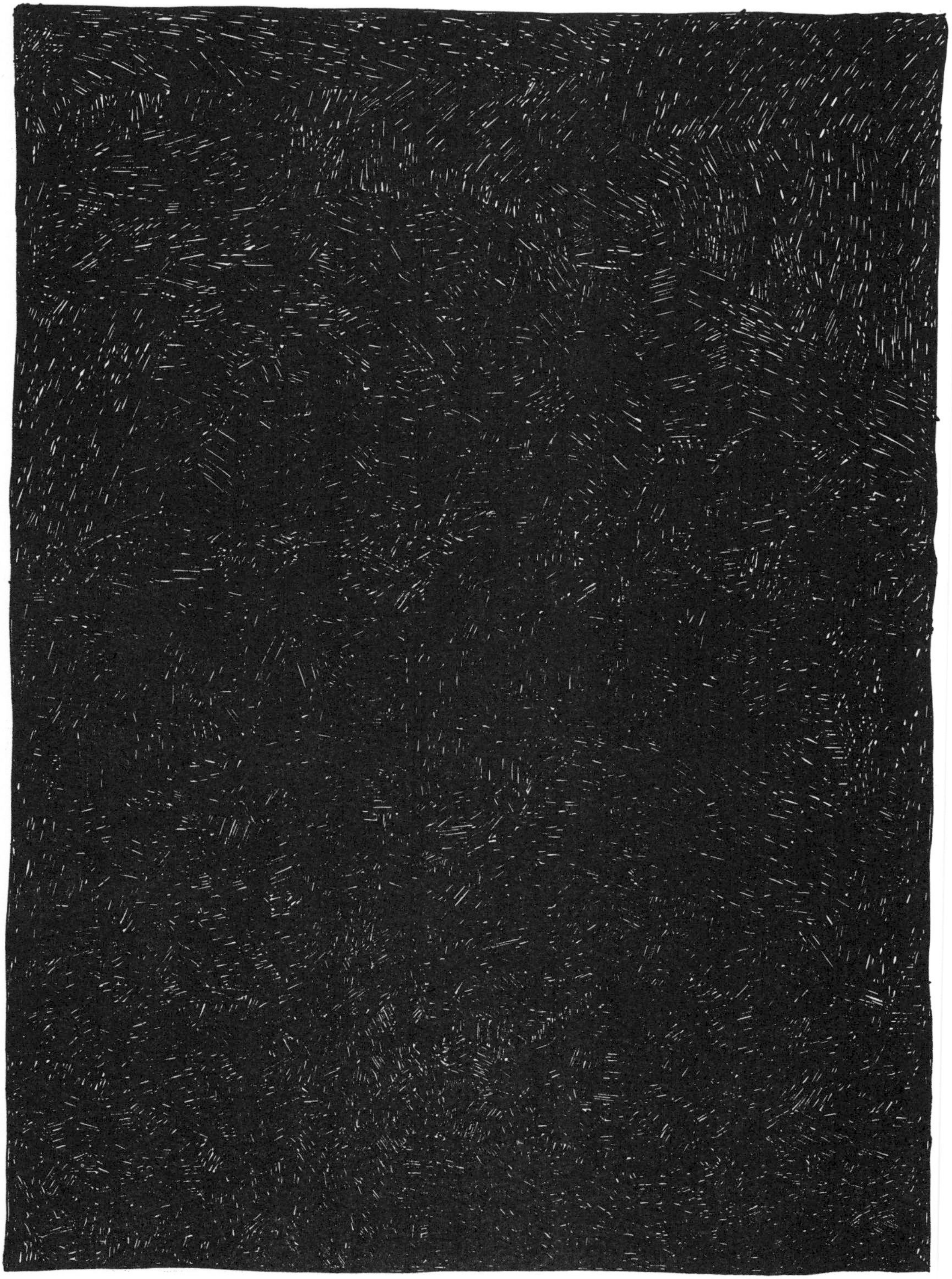

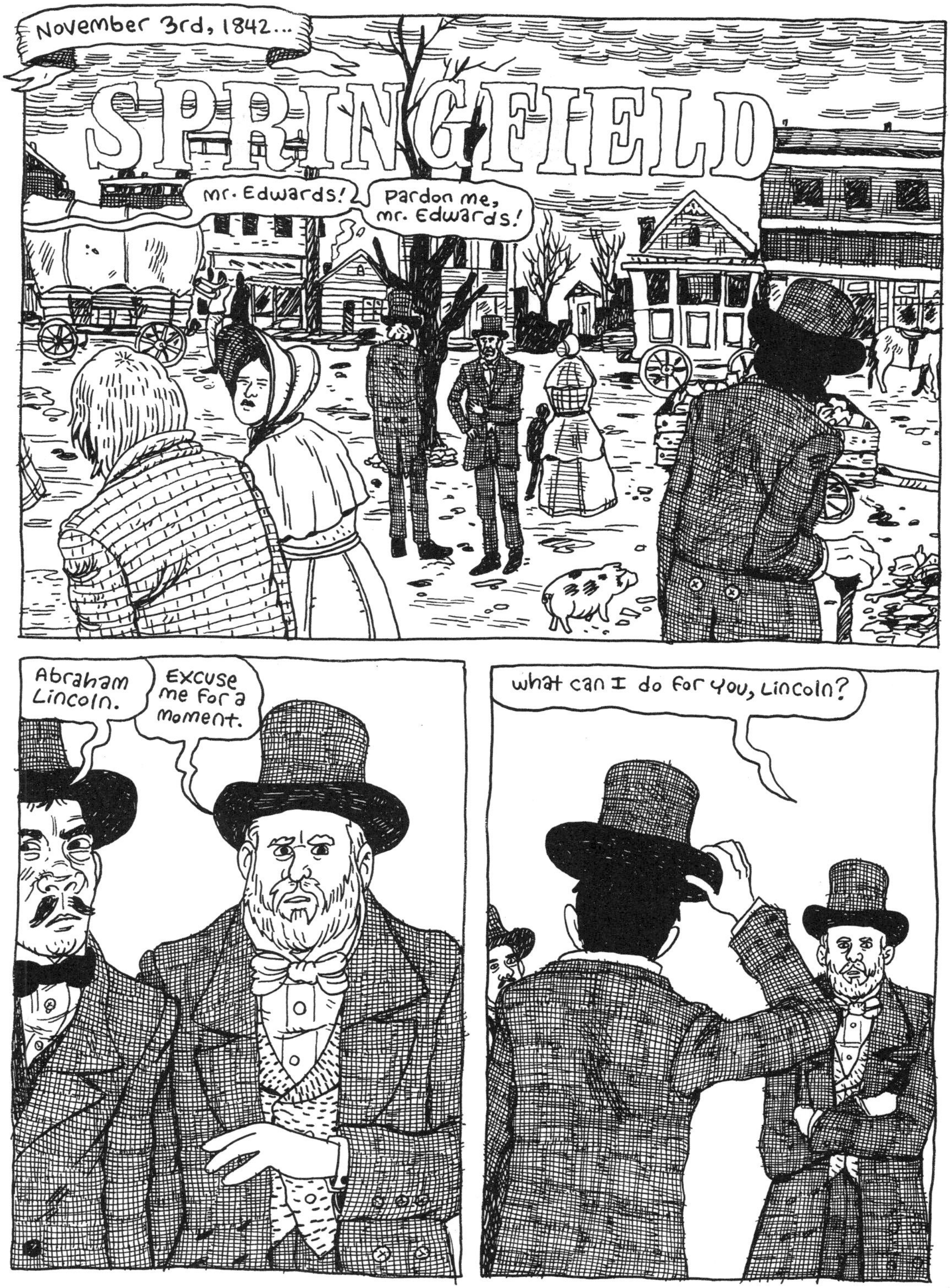
November 3rd, 1842...
SPRINGFIELD
Mr. Edwards!
Pardon me, Mr. Edwards!
Abraham Lincoln.
Excuse me for a moment.
What can I do for you, Lincoln?

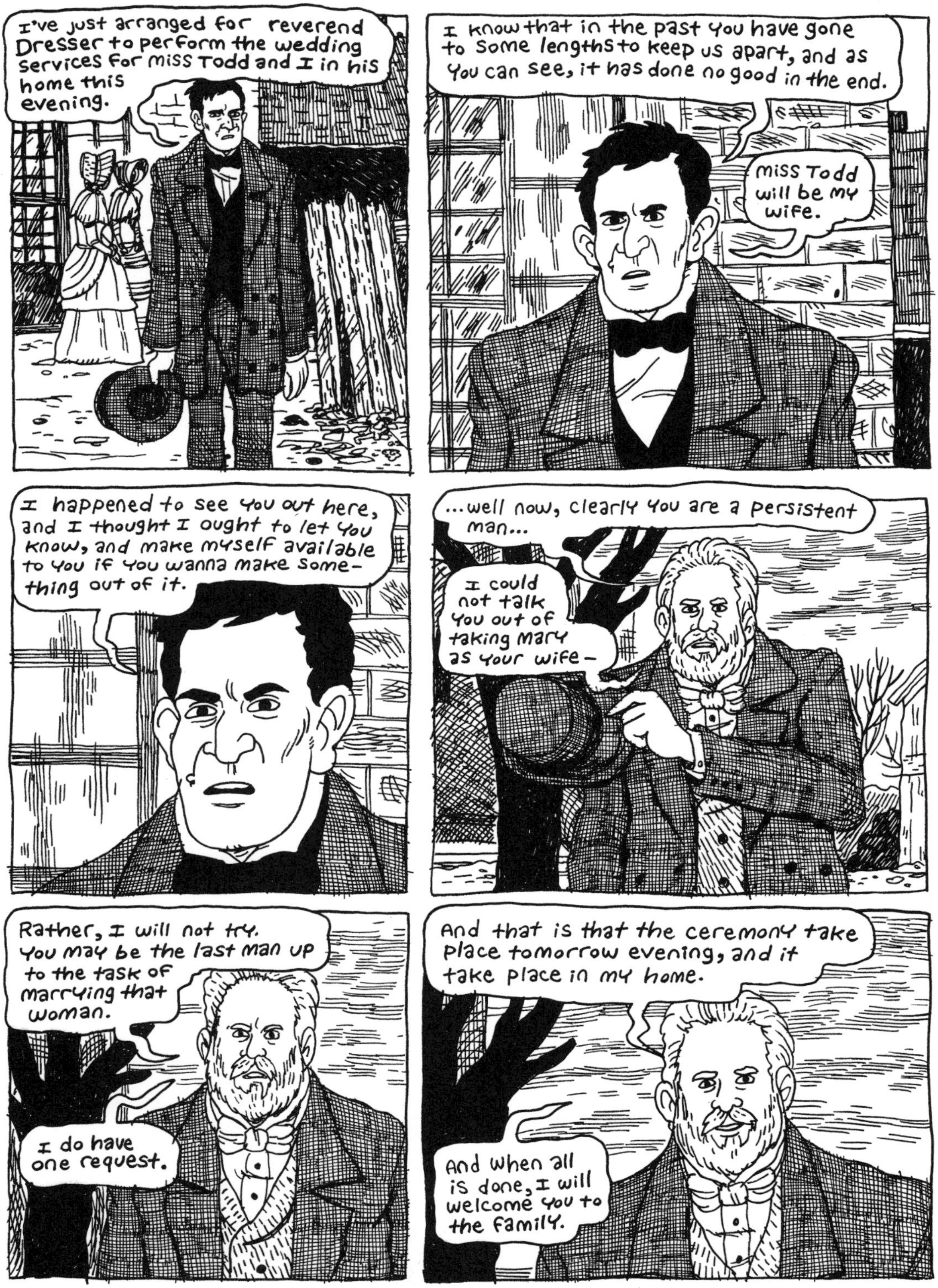
I've just arranged for reverend Dresser to perform the wedding services for miss Todd and I in his home this evening.
I know that in the past you have gone to some lengths to keep us apart, and as you can see, it has done no good in the end.
miss Todd will be my wife.
I happened to see you out here, and I thought I ought to let you know, and make myself available to you if you wanna make some-thing out of it.
...well now, clearly you are a persistent man...
I could not talk you out of taking Mary as your wife–
Rather, I will not try. You may be the last man up to the task of marrying that woman.
I do have one request.
And that is that the ceremony take place tomorrow evening, and it take place in my home.
And when all is done, I will welcome you to the family.

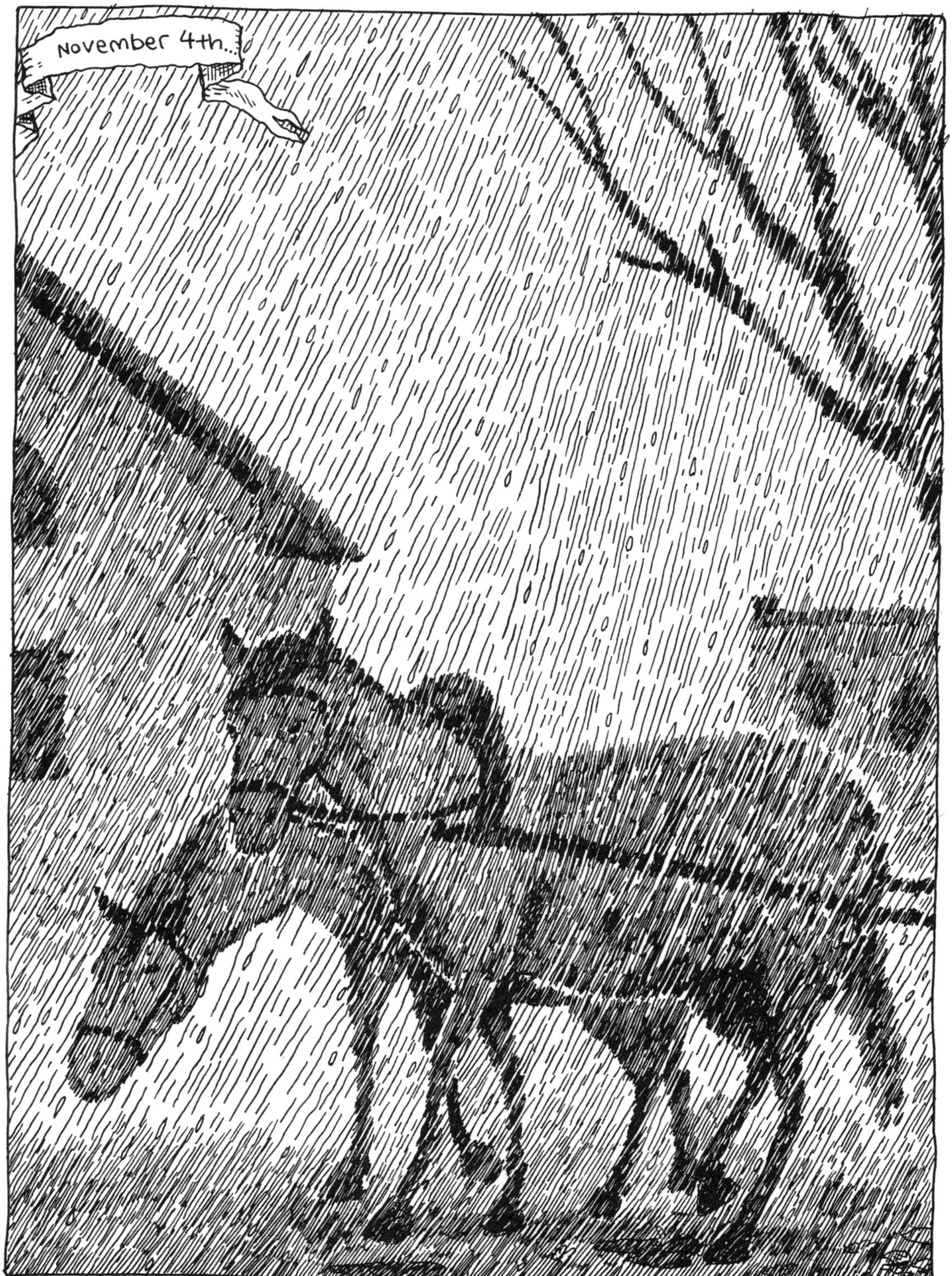
November 4th...

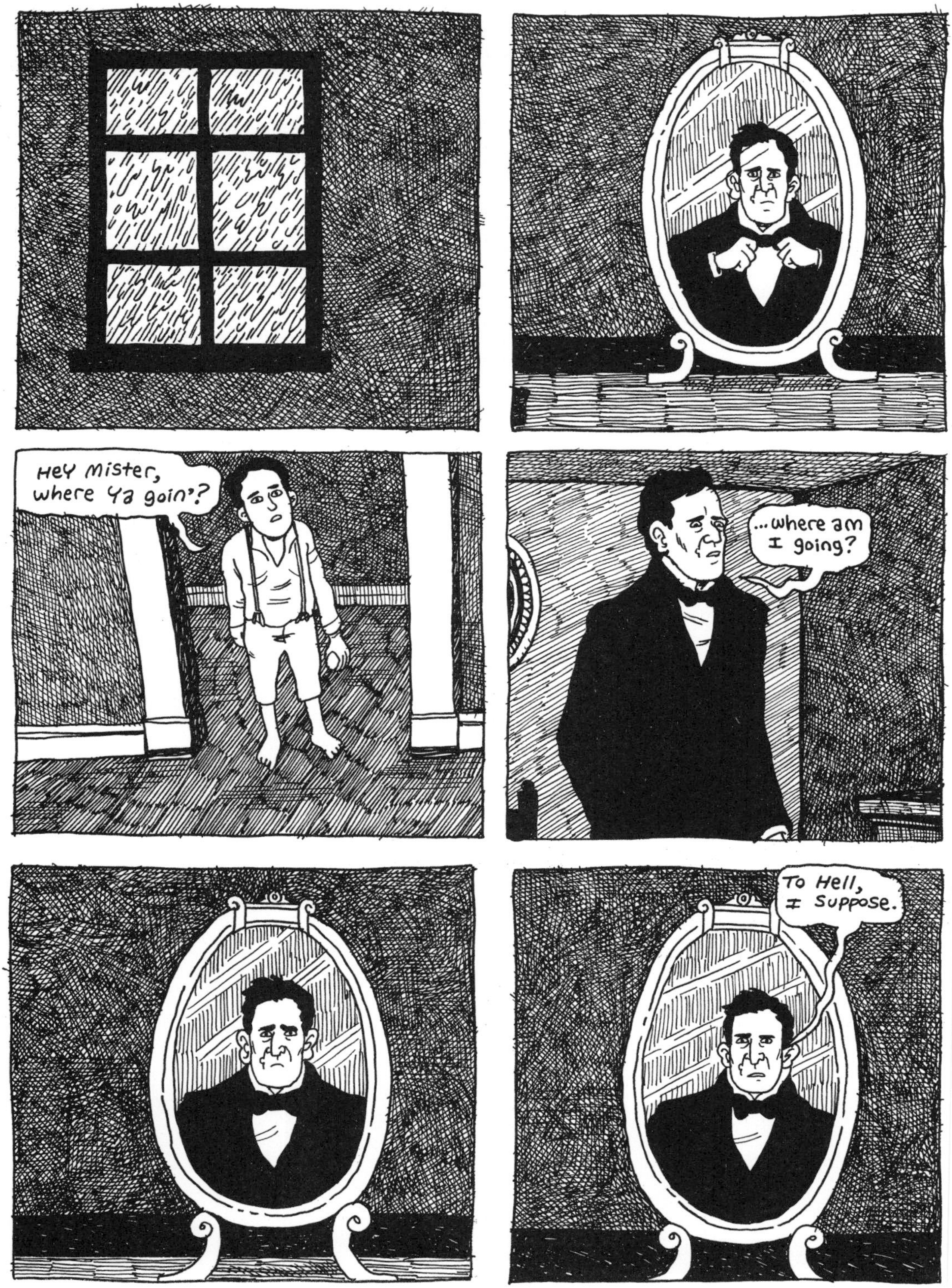
Hey mister, where ya goin'?
...where am I going?
To Hell, I suppose.

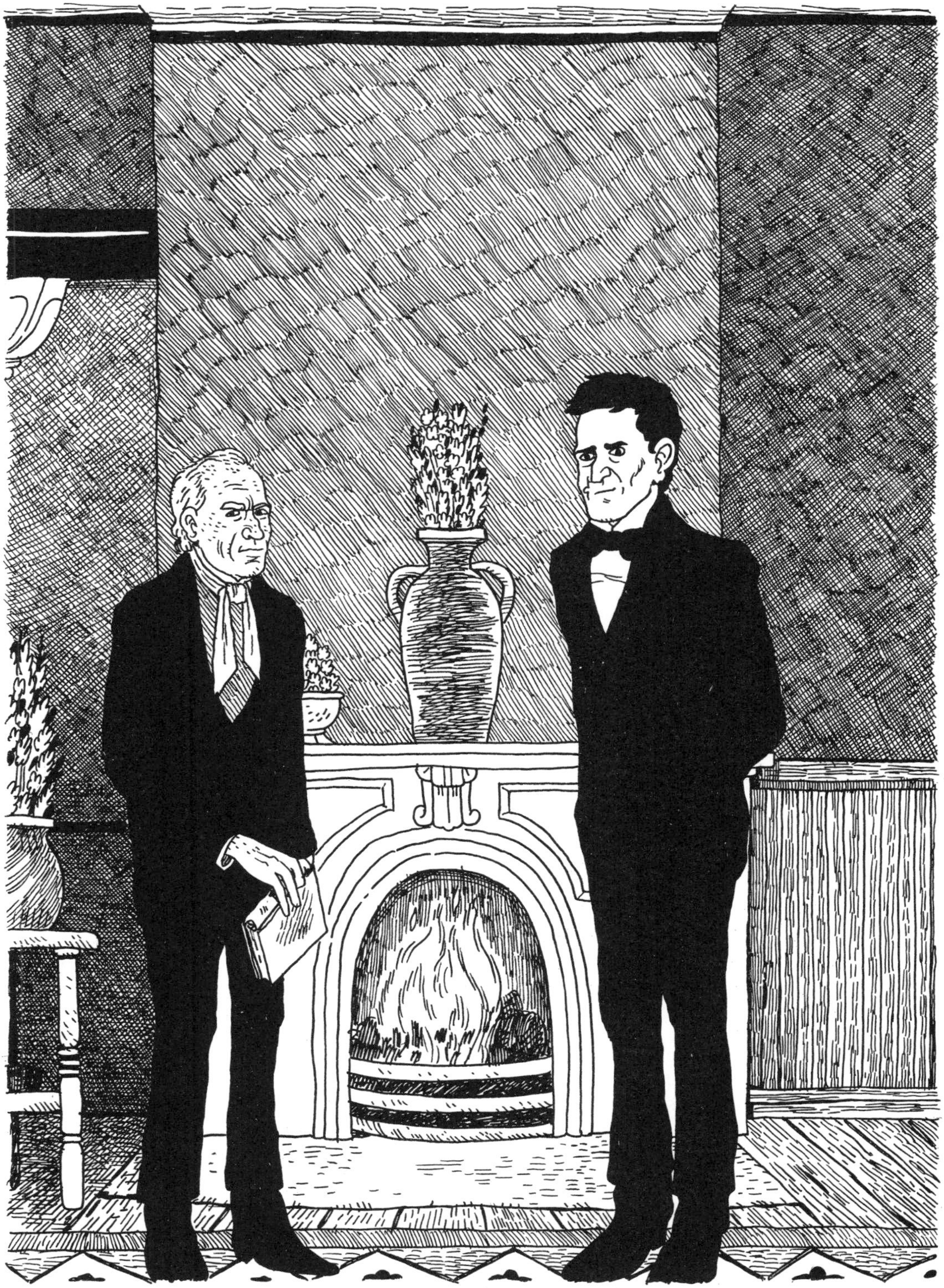

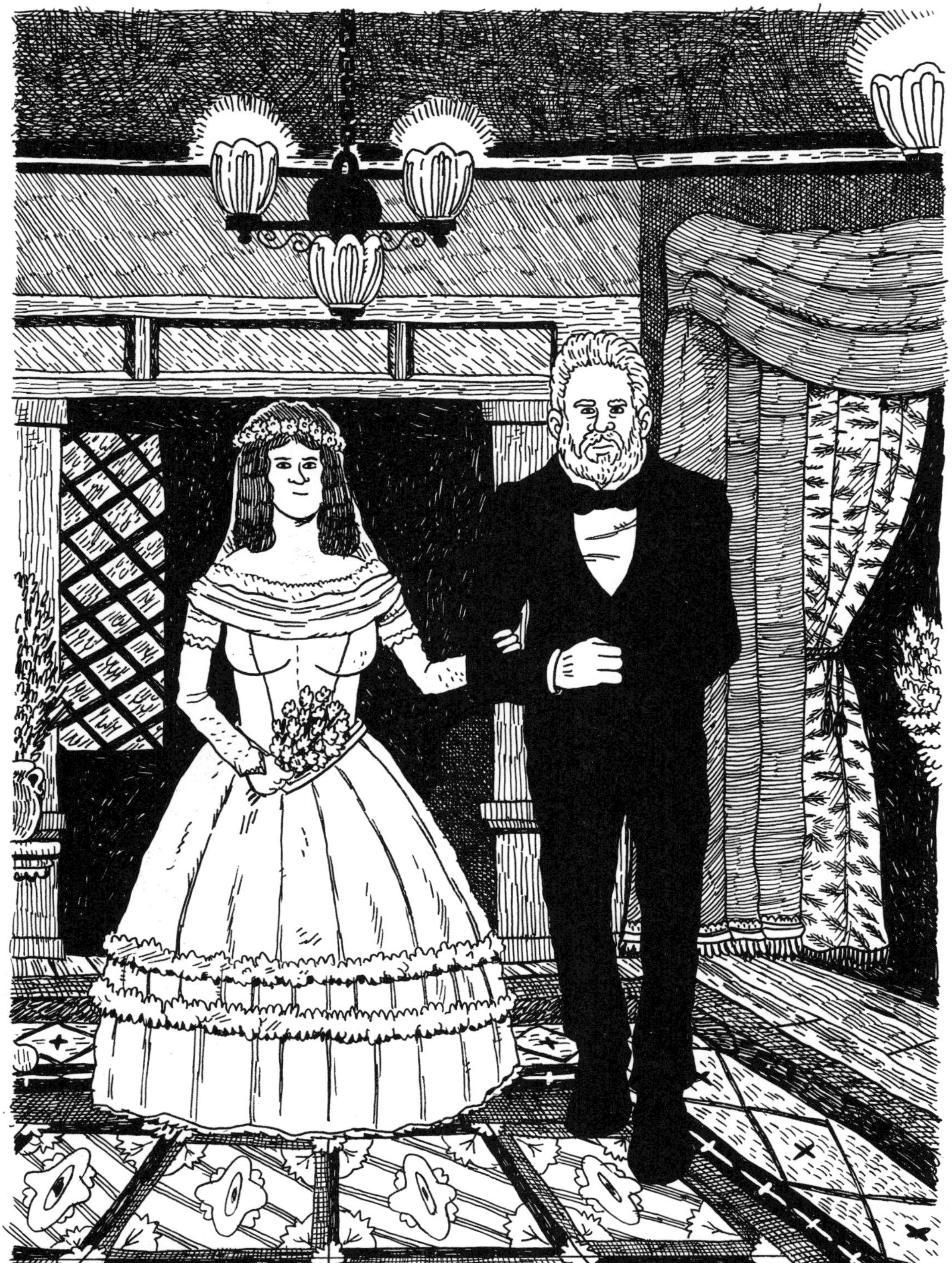

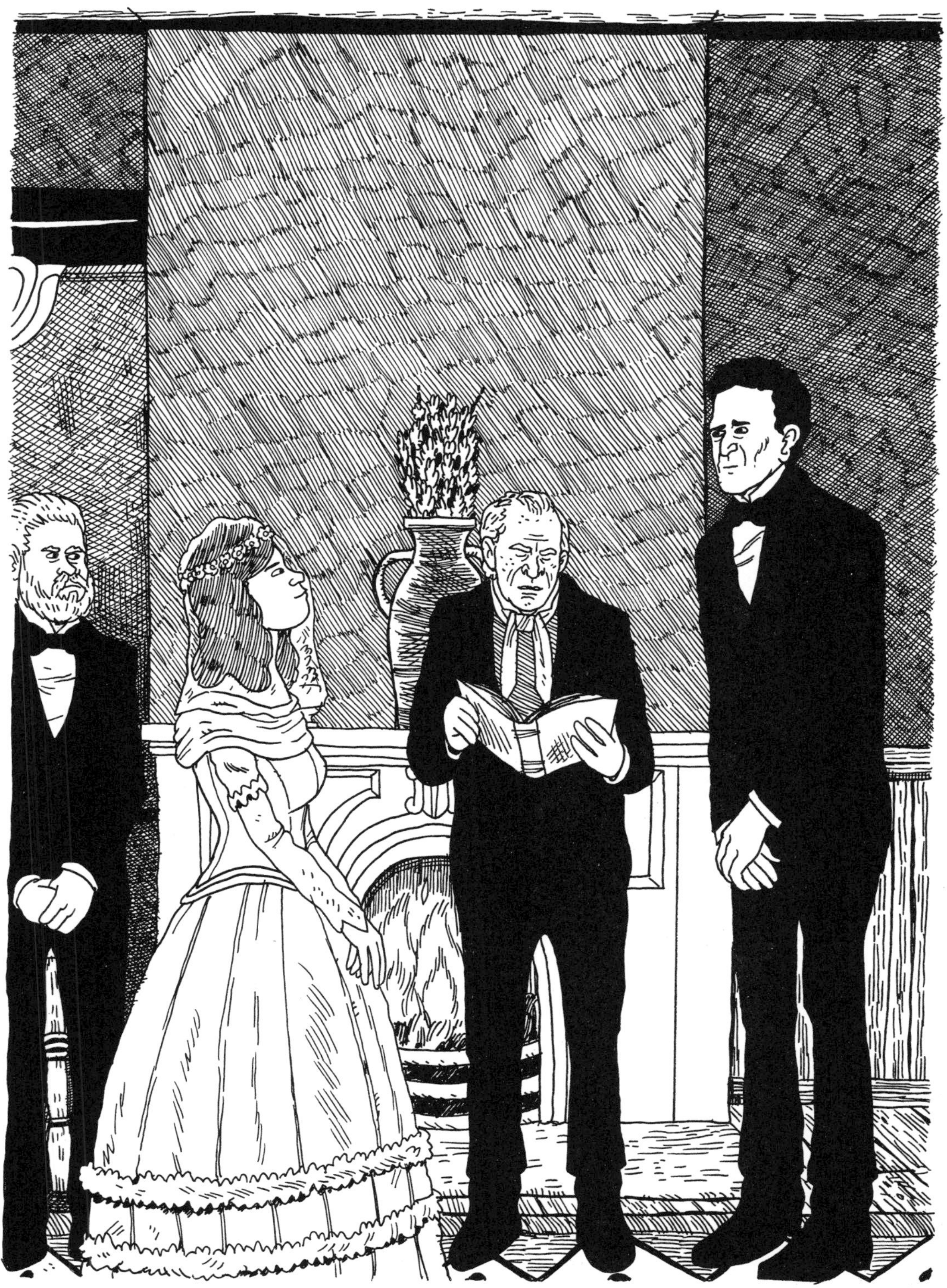

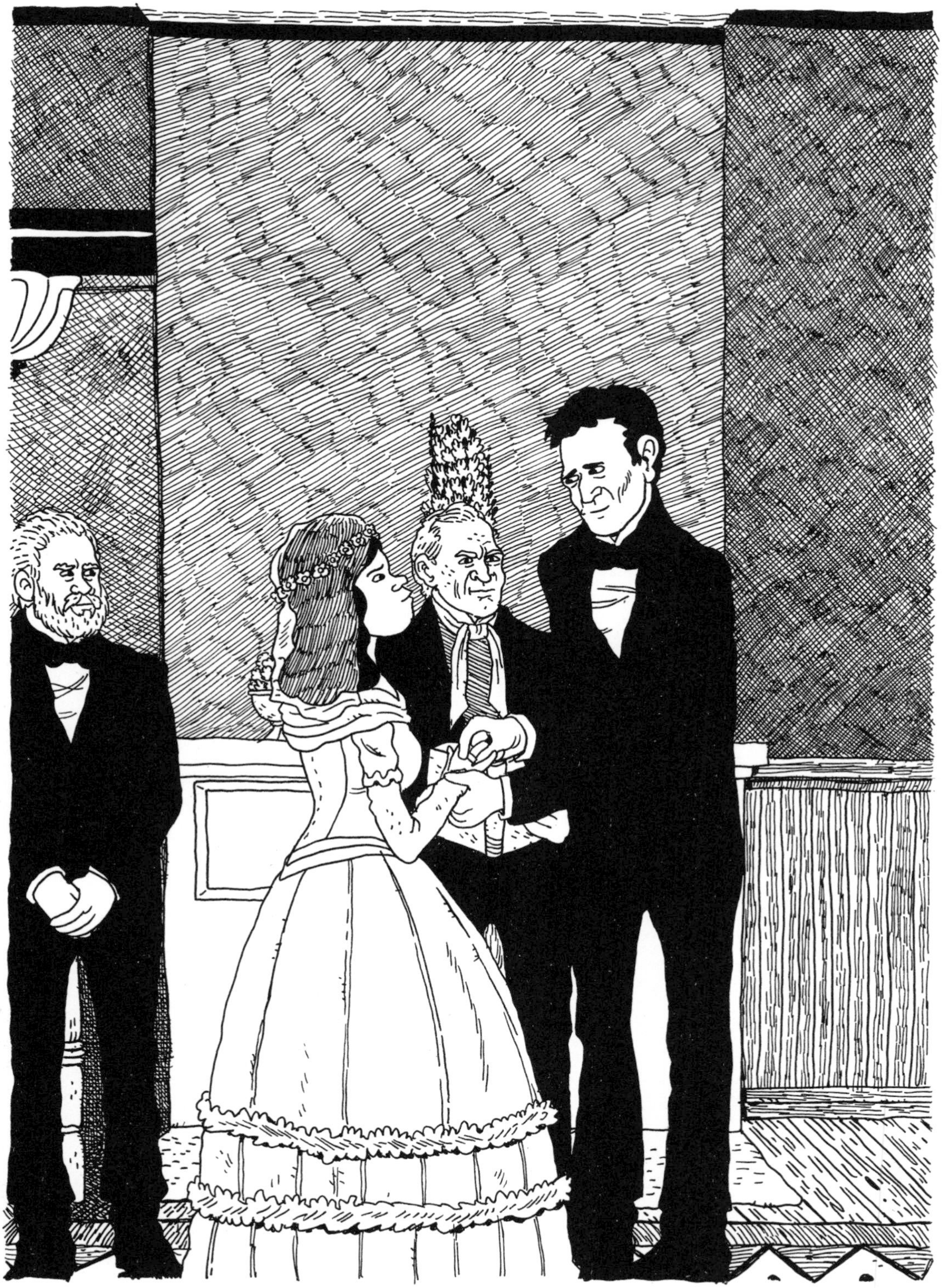

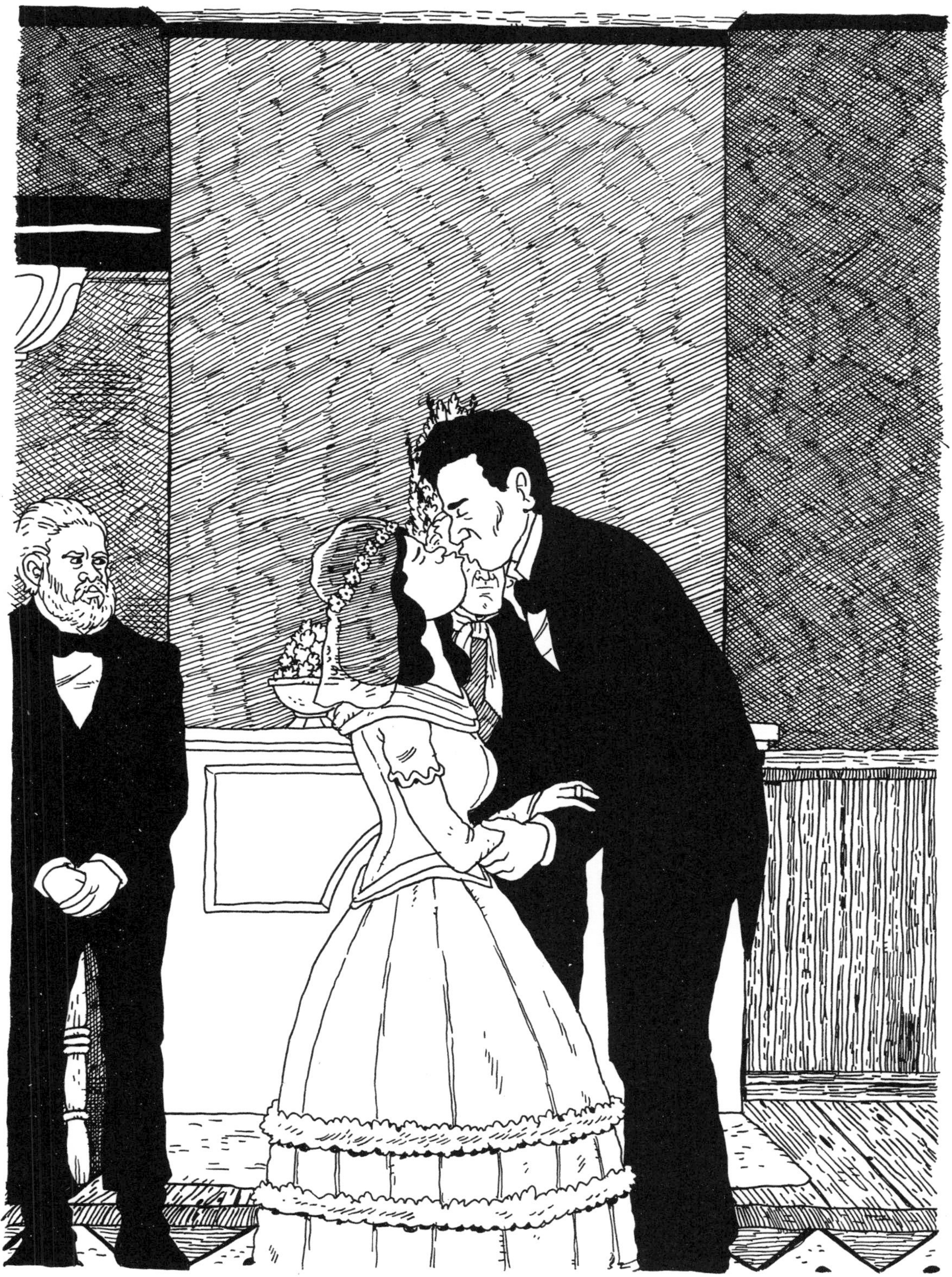

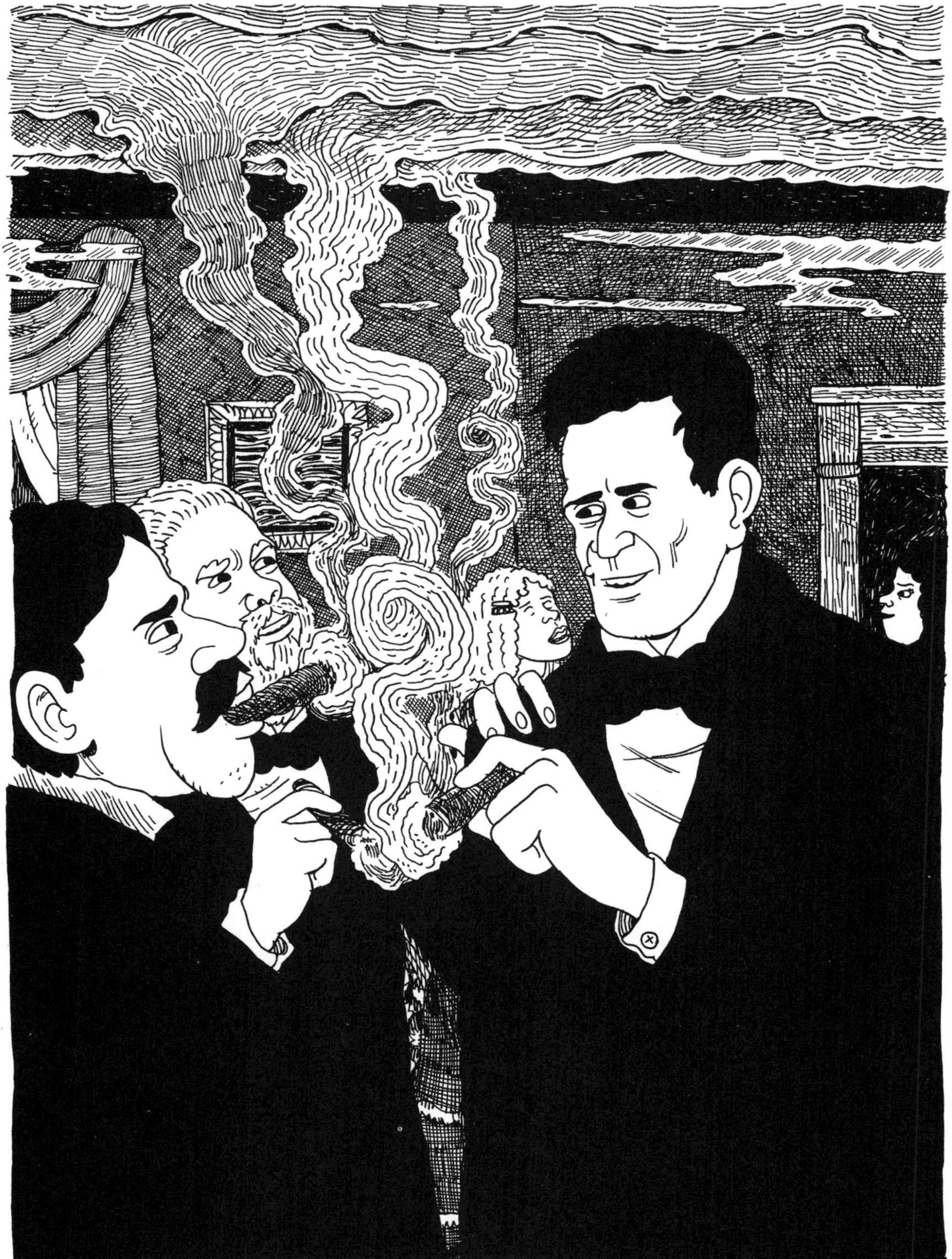

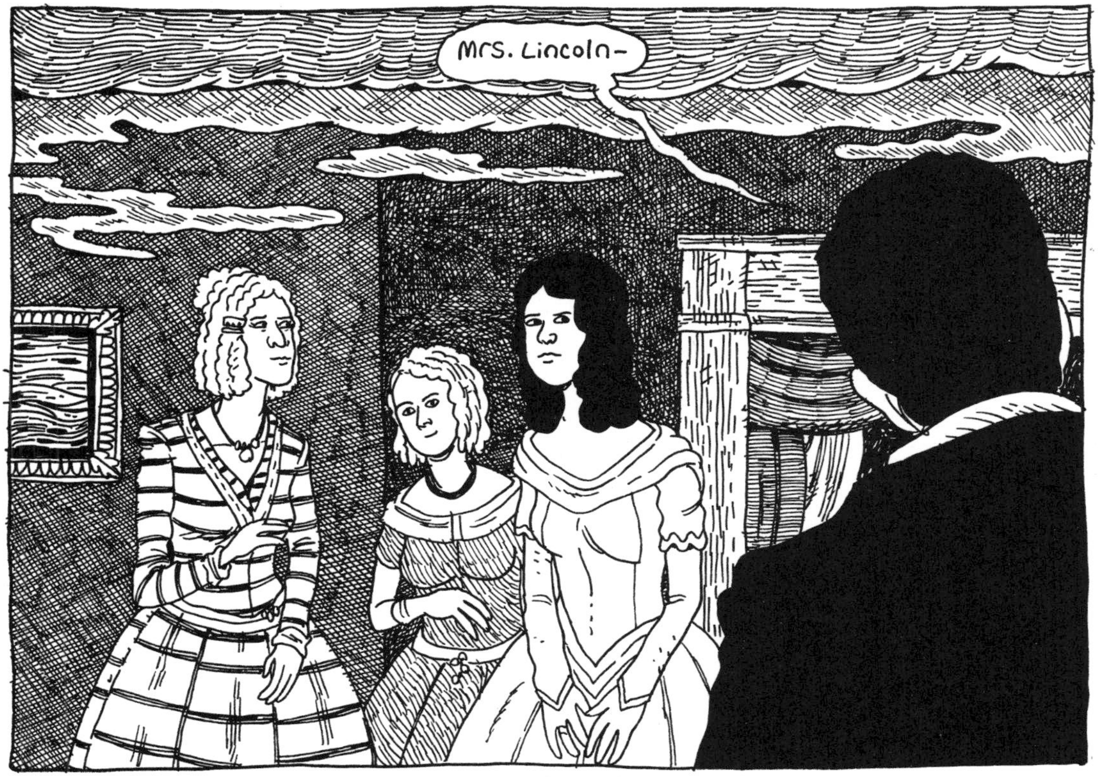
Mrs. Lincoln-

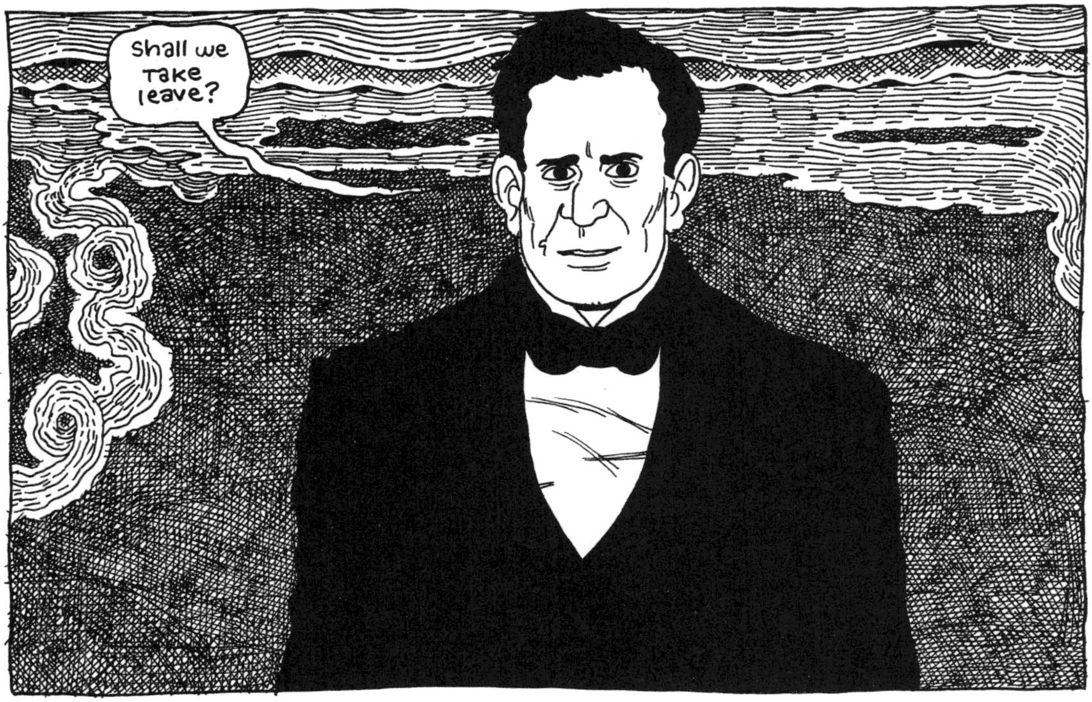
Shall we Take leave?

THE
END

THE SUICIDE'S SOLILOQUY.

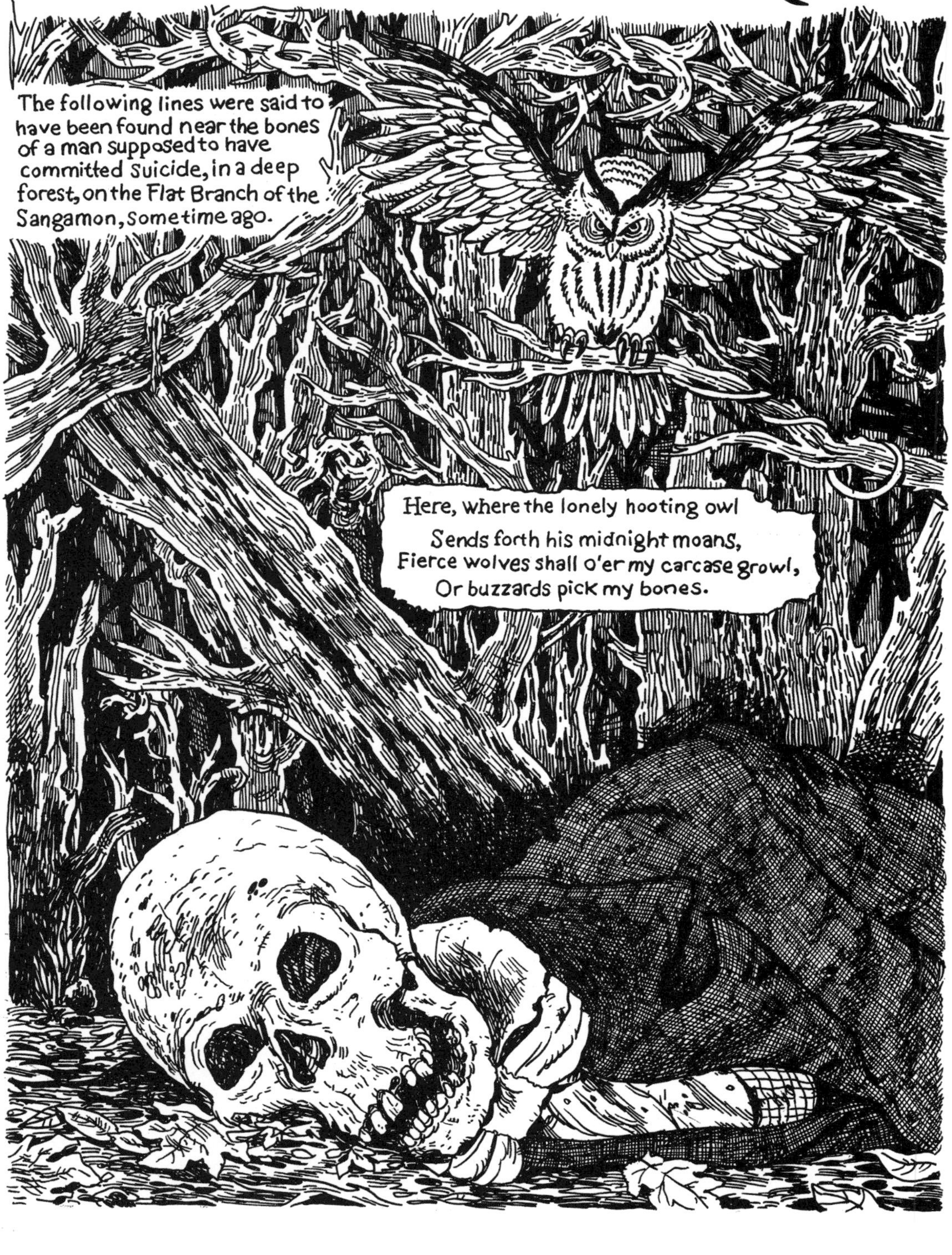
The following lines were said to have been found near the bones of a man supposed to have committed suicide, in a deep forest, on the Flat Branch of the Sangamon, some time ago.
Here, where the lonely hooting owl
Sends forth his midnight moans,
Fierce wolves shall o'er my carcase growl,
Or buzzards pick my bones.

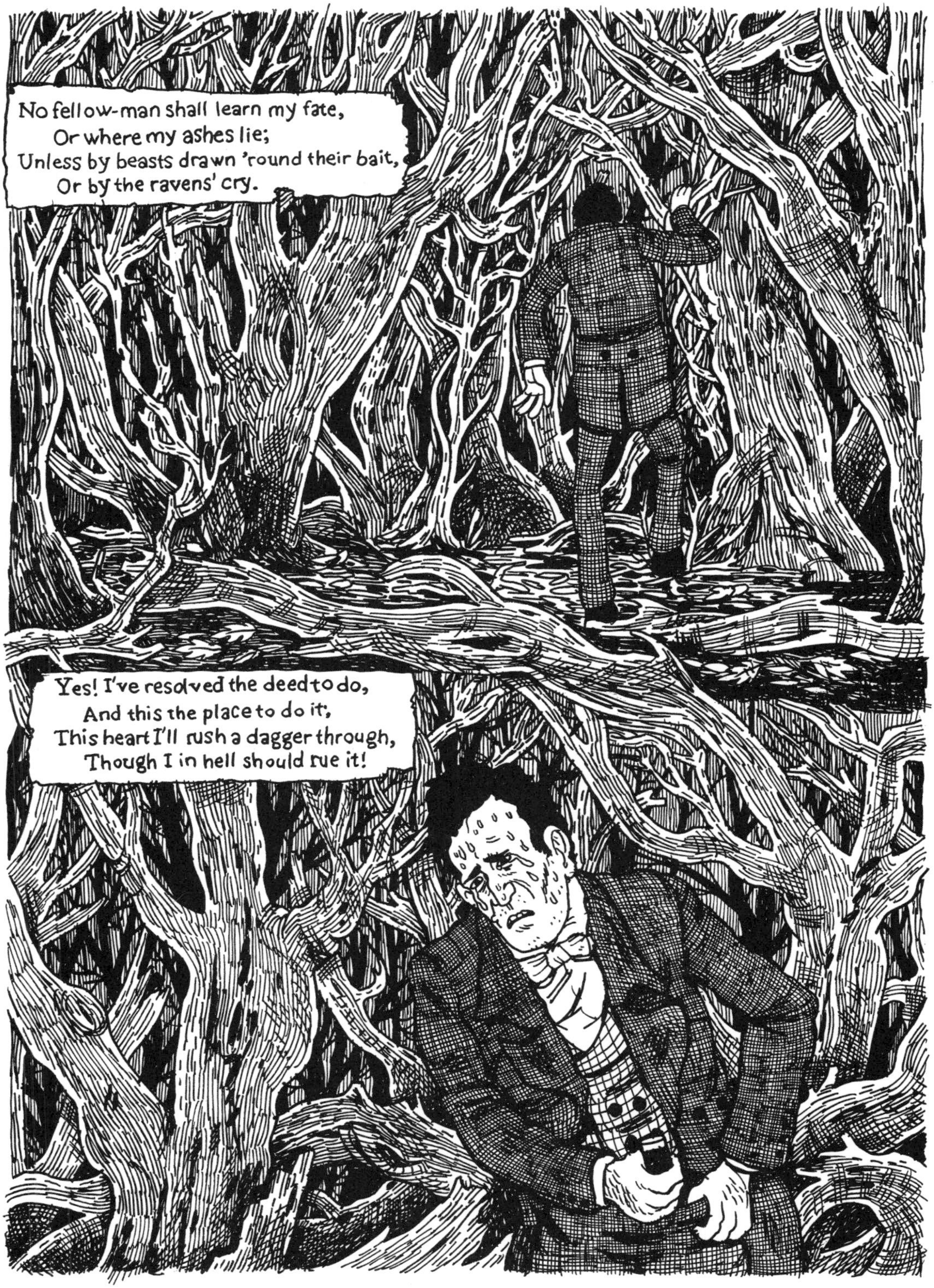
No fellow-man shall learn my fate,
Or where my ashes lie;
Unless by beasts drawn 'round their bait,
Or by the ravens' cry.
Yes! I've resolved the deed to do,
And this the place to do it;
This heart I'll rush a dagger through,
Though I in hell should rue it!

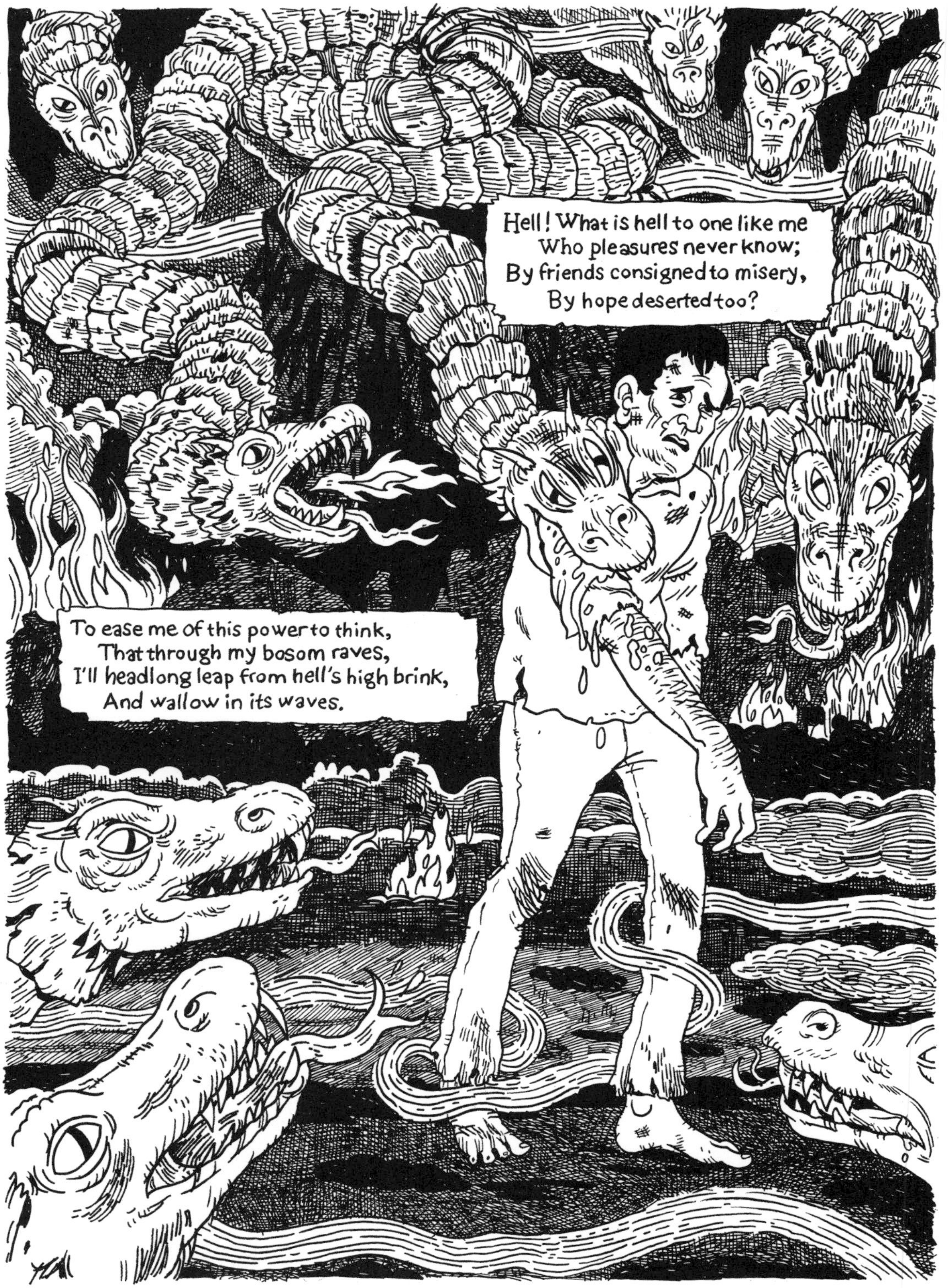
Hell! What is hell to one like me
Who pleasures never know;
By friends consigned to misery,
By hope deserted too?
To ease me of this power to think,
That through my bosom raves,
I'll headlong leap from hell's high brink,
And wallow in its waves.

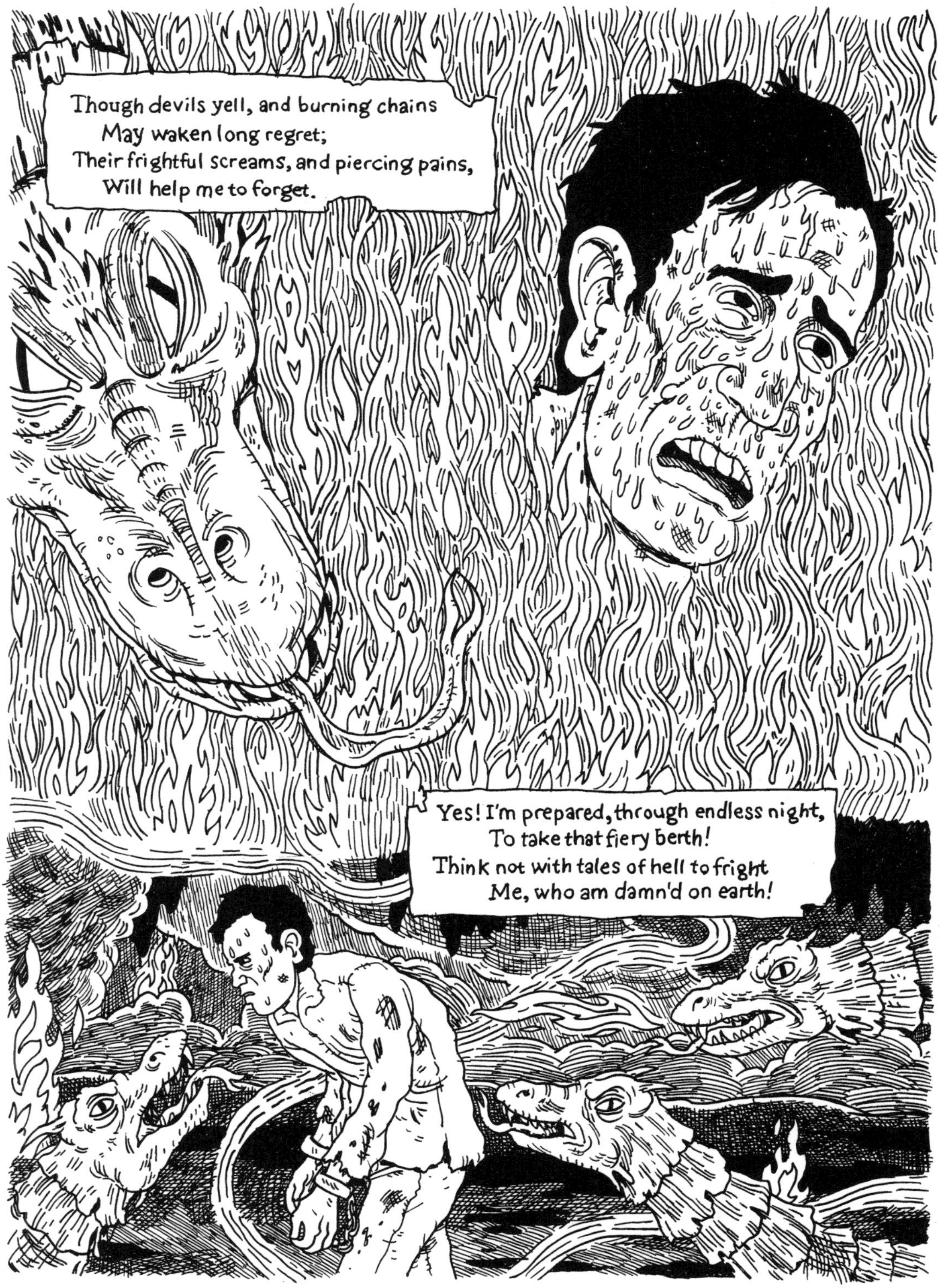
Though devils yell, and burning chains
May waken long regret;
Their frightful screams, and piercing pains,
Will help me to forget.
Yes! I'm prepared, through endless night,
To take that fiery berth!
Think not with tales of hell to fright
Me, who am damn'd on earth!

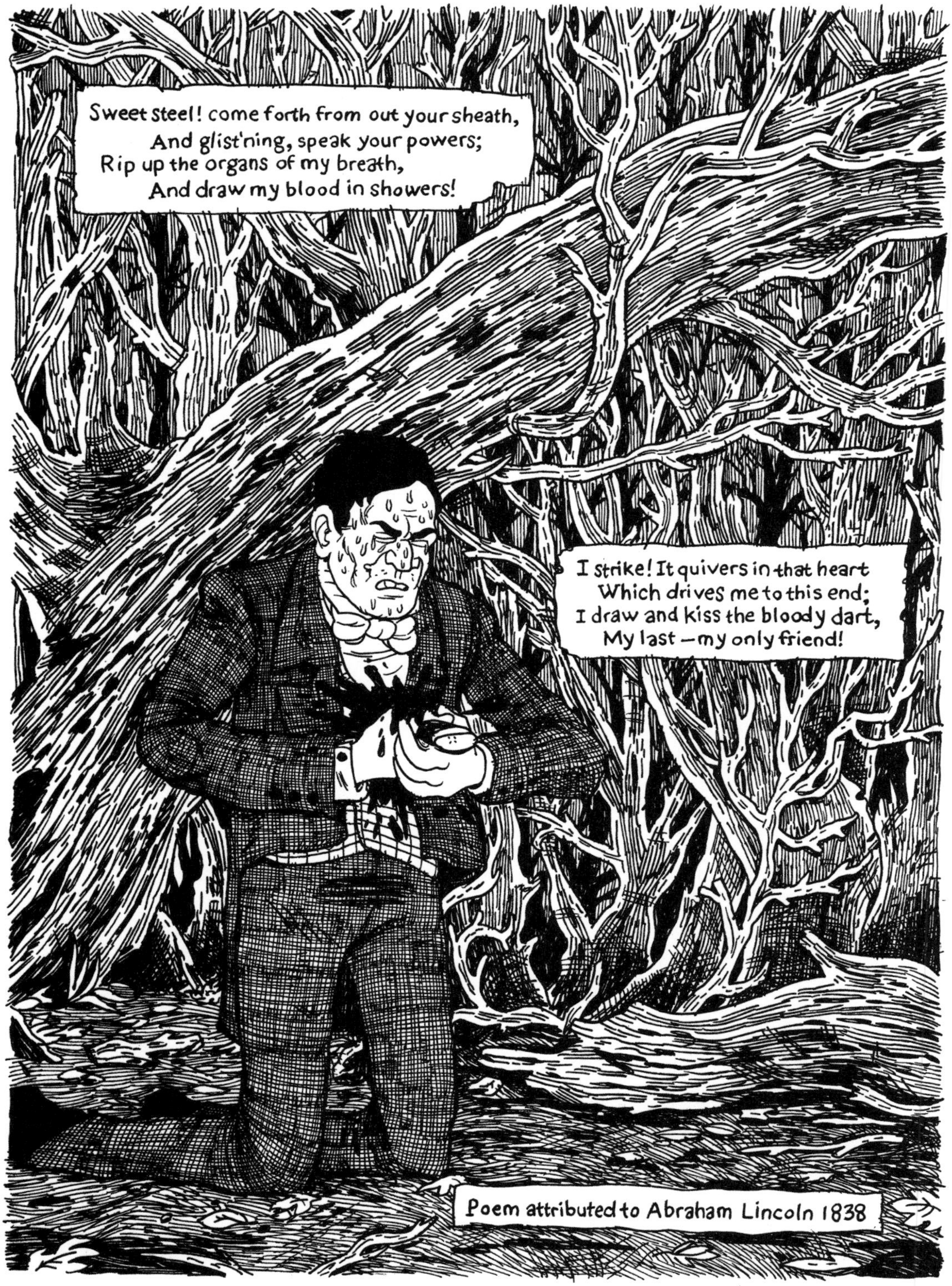
Sweet steel! come forth from out your sheath,
And glist'ning, speak your powers;
Rip up the organs of my breath,
And draw my blood in showers!
I strike! It quivers in that heart
Which drives me to this end;
I draw and kiss the bloody dart,
My last — my only friend!
Poem attributed to Abraham Lincoln 1838

THANKS

John Porcellino, Zak Sally, Jeff Brown, Robin Edwards and her family. Justin Skarhus, Raighne Hogan and 2D cloud. Dan Stafford and Luke Janes at Kilgore books for taking care of me and publishing my amazing comic series, Blammo. My dear mother, Candace Baker Foyt and my new dad David Foyt. Joseph Remnant and his wife Hilary. I wish I lived near you two. Thanks to Gary Groth, Eric Reynolds and Mike Baehr at Fantagraphics books.

Thank you, Dylan Williams. I wish I was half the man you were. R.I.P. seriously. Everyone I know loved you. Tom Neely, Julia Wertz, Sarah Glidden, Hawk Krall, Box Brown, all of my brothers and sisters, including, of course, Ethan.

Thank you, Westword, the alternative weekly that has paid me to do my comic strip since 2008, And most of all, thank you to the city of Denver, colorado, where this entire book was written and drawn. You truly are the "Queen city of the plains." And thank you to you for reading this book.

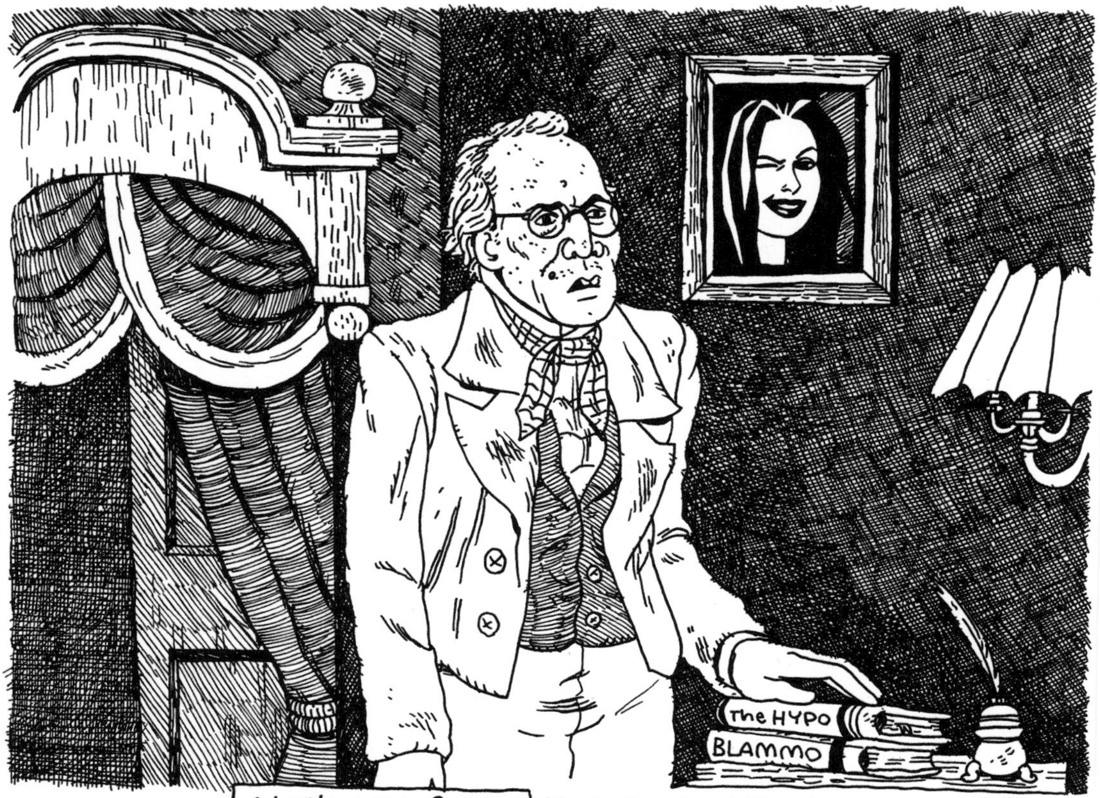
The HYPO
BLAMMO

Noah van Sciver is a cartoonist currently living in Denver, Colorado. For more please visit nvansciver.wordpress.com

MARY DOLL

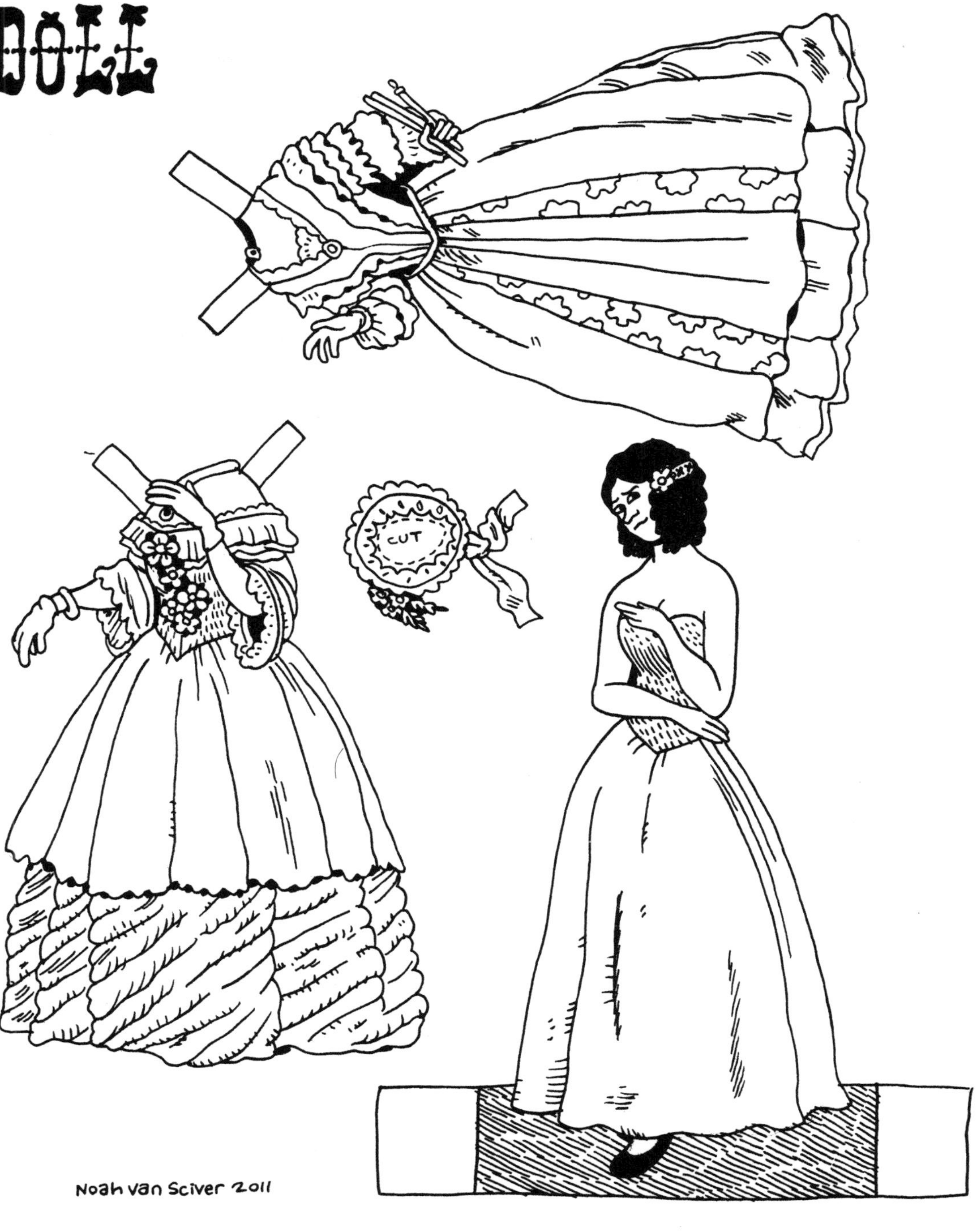
CUT
Noah van Sciver 2011

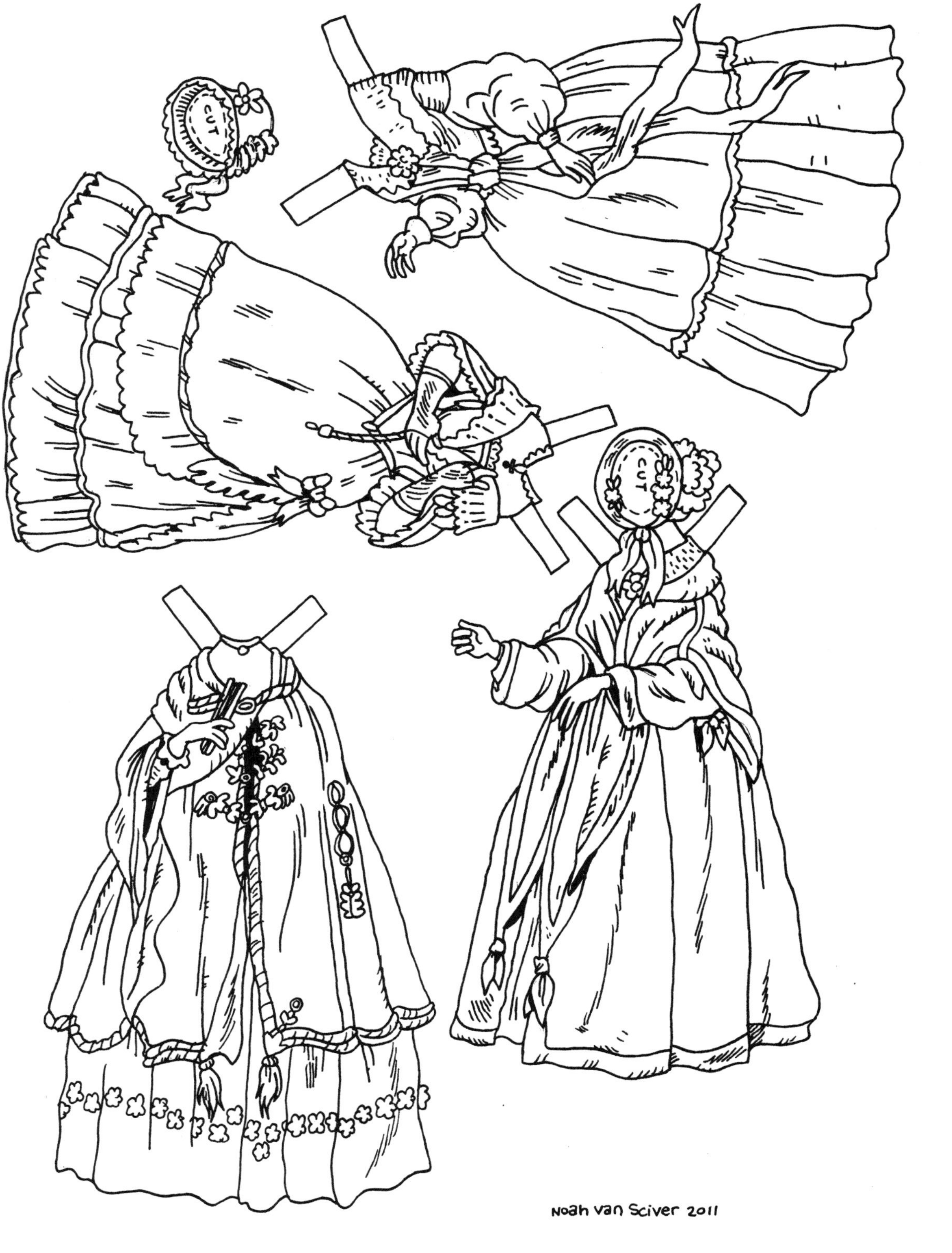
CUT
CUT

Noah van Sciver 2011